Constitutional Adjudication in European Community and National Law

Essays for the Hon. Mr. Justice T. F. O'Higgins

A portrait of The Chief Justice painted in 1975 by the artist James LeJeune (1910–1983) which hangs in the Dining Hall of the King's Inns, Dublin.

Constitutional Adjudication in European Community and National Law

Essays for the
Hon. Mr. Justice T. F. O'Higgins

EDITED BY

Deirdre Curtin BCL (NUI), M. Litt (Dublin), LLD (NUI)

Barrister of the King's Inns
Professor of the Law of International Organisations, University of Utrecht

David O'Keeffe BCL, LLM (NUI), LLM (Yale), Doctorandos (Leyden)

Solicitor
Allen & Overy Professor of European Law, University of Durham

Butterworth (Ireland) Ltd 1992

Ireland	Butterworth (Ireland) Ltd, 16 Upper Ormond Quay, DUBLIN 7
Australia	Butterworths Pty Ltd, SYDNEY, MELBOURNE, BRISBANE, ADELAIDE, PERTH, CANBERRA and HOBART
Belgium	Butterworths, 48 Rue de Namur/Naamestraat, 1000 BRUXELLES/BRUSSELS.
Canada	Butterworths Canada Ltd, TORONTO and VANCOUVER
Malaysia	Malaysian Law Journal Sdn Bhd, KUALA LUMPUR
New Zealand	Butterworths of New Zealand Ltd, WELLINGTON and AUCKLAND
Singapore	Butterworth & Co (Asia) Pte Ltd, SINGAPORE
United Kingdom	Butterworth & Co (Publishers) Ltd, 88 Kingsway, LONDON WC2B 6AB and 4 Hill Street, EDINBURGH EH2 3JZ
USA	Butterworths Legal Publishers, St Paul, Minnesota, SEATTLE, Washington, BOSTON, Massachusetts, AUSTIN, TEXAS and D & S Publishers, CLEARWATER, FLORIDA

Published 1992

A CIP Catalogue record for this book is available from the British Library

ISBN 1 85475 001

© Butterworth (Ireland) Ltd
Typeset by Phoenix Photosetting, Chatham, Kent
Printed and bound in Great Britain by Mackays of Chatham PLC, Chatham, Kent

Preface

Tom O'Higgins and I came to know each other in the best possible way: we were neighbours. It was 1968 and we sat two seats away from one another in the Law Library. And, though – like all neighbours – we have differed at times, I have never ceased to value his wonderful mixture of legal acumen and humanity.

A few years later we got to know each other better when we were part of a small band who went to various European capitals as members of the Irish Council of the European Movement. I think we saw ourselves as early evangelists for the European cause. I can still see Tom, at the end of a day in Paris or Brussels, his coat off, in his shirt sleeves, thumbs in his braces. Not exactly an image of missionary zeal perhaps, but the soul of conviviality and good conversation for all that.

If I put an emphasis on these qualities it is because I think they have a real bearing on the achievements and distinction of Thomas F. O'Higgins, public representative, lawyer and judge. His presence on the Court of Justice of the European Communities was, of course, a deserved honour. It is worth pointing out that the contribution he made there is closely linked to his enormous legal knowledge and understanding. As a working barrister, as a judge of the High Court and then Chief Justice, he brought a treasury of insight and practical experience of the common law and Irish constitutional law to a forum of European law where academic training and legal specialisation are more often the norm. In inviting him to become chairman of the Irish Centre for European Law on its establishment in 1988 I was delighted to bring these qualities back to Irish legal circles.

Tom O'Higgins and I were not likely to agree on every subject, but I never found his views predictable nor was his conservatism ever inhumane. Quite the contrary in fact. His warmth, his obvious interest in people always seemed to me to have their source in a compassionate openness to what was happening around him. As the pace of social change quickened I could see that he took a real interest and responded in surprising ways to new situations.

We stand at the edge of a new Europe. Perhaps the best tribute I can pay to Tom O'Higgins is to record that he – and indeed the generation he comes from – represent for me so much of what Ireland can offer to a continent. He and his generation were shapers and builders of our society. They worked for little gain. They put up the structures and institutions which shelter us, while keeping all those wonderful and nurturing values of family and friendship

v

without which such institutions and structures could quickly become cold and oppressive. They had a sense of humour and a zest for social occasions. And in all of this, I think Tom O'Higgins is one of their finest representatives. I wish him a retirement blessed and enriched by all those qualities he brought to a lifetime of work and achievement.

MARY ROBINSON
Uachtarán na hÉireann
December 1991

Introduction

The idea for this book came from the desire to pay tribute to a remarkable person who has held office in the highest Irish and European Community judicial forums, on the occasion of his retirement from the Bench in October 1991. Given Judge O'Higgins' active involvement in shaping via interpretation both the Irish Constitution and the Constitutional Charter of the European Communities, the Treaty of Rome, the theme of constitutional adjudication seemed an appropriate and unifying axis around which to construct a *liber amicorum* of friends and former colleagues drawn from the different legal systems of the European Communities.

This book thus deliberately focuses on the judicial function and the various areas of Judge O'Higgins involvement (Irish law, European Community law and the interaction between the two) as well as certain aspects of judicial review in the legal systems of other Member States. This is not however to ignore the truly remarkable breadth of his activities outside of the law. A brief scan of the detailed biography included at the back of this book reveals the extent of his political involvement from Member of Parliament (for 25 years), Deputy Chairman of his Party, Fine Gael to Minister of Health and candidate (twice) for President of Ireland. His interest in matters European dates from his days as a Parliamentarian in Strasbourg and his veteran involvement in the European Movement in the days before Ireland's accession to the European Communities. In tandem with all of this he steadily made his mark on the law as a practising barrister and later Senior Counsel, leading in time to the highest possible judicial offices, Chief Justice of Ireland and Judge of the Court of Justice of the European Communities. We feel that Judge O'Higgins himself would be the first to agree that the credit for enabling him to engage in such wide ranging and demanding activities must go to his wife, Terry.

We were greatly facilitated in our task as editors of this book by the efficient and pleasant cooperation with our publishers, Butterworth (Ireland) Ltd, Thérèse Carrick, Finola O'Sullivan and Professor John Wylie.

When it came to the difficult task of drawing up a (short) list of contributors who would reflect this multi-faceted background and approaching the various potential authors, we were very struck by the warmth and generosity of the response. Very busy people with extremely demanding and full schedules agreed to participate in this project, despite strict deadlines, because of the extent of the personal affection and regard which they have for Judge

O'Higgins. This is perhaps the greatest tribute possible to one who has led such an active and busy public life.

Those who know only the public figure will not be surprised to learn that in the Court of Justice in Luxembourg, where we first came to know him, Judge O'Higgin's personal charm and small kindnesses in daily life as well as his gifted story-telling ability were legend throughout the entire building. It is perhaps this ease with people in general, as well of course as the extent of his polital and judicial involvement, that enabled Judge O'Higgins to achieve that rare feat for a judge: to become a household name in his country.

Together with all the contributors we are delighted to be able to offer him this tribute.

Deirdre Curtin   David O'Keeffe
Brussels   Durham

February 1992

List of Contributors

Mary Robinson:	President of Ireland.
Jean-Yves Art:	Legal Secretary, Court of Justice of the European Communities; former Legal Secretary to Judge O'Higgins.
Karen Banks:	Member of the Legal Service, Commission of the European Communities.
Donal Barrington:	Judge of the Court of First Instance of the European Communities.
James Casey:	Professor of Law, University College, Dublin.
Anthony M. Collins:	Legal Secretary, Court of Justice of the European Communities; former Legal Secretary to Judge O'Higgins.
Declan Costello:	Judge of the High Court, Ireland.
Deirdre Curtin:	Professor of the Law of International Organisations, University of Utrecht; Of Counsel, Freshfields, Brussels; former Legal Secretary to Judge O'Higgins.
Ole Due:	President of the Court of Justice of the European Communities.
David Edward:	Judge of the Court of Justice of the European Communities.
Nial Fennelly:	Senior Counsel, Dublin; Chairman of the General Council of the Bar of Ireland.
Thomas A. Finlay:	Chief Justice of Ireland.
Mary Finlay Geoghegan:	Senior Counsel, Dublin.
Francis G. Jacobs:	Advocate General, Court of Justice of the European Communities.

Thijmen Koopmans: Advocate General at the Hoge Raad (Netherlands Court of Cassation); former Judge of the Court of Justice of the European Communities 1979–90.

Lord Mackenzie-Stuart: Judge of the Court of Justice of the European Communities, 1973–84; President, 1984–1988.

G. Federico Mancini: Judge of the Court of Justice of the European Communities.

Niall McCarthy: Judge of the Supreme Court, Ireland.

David O'Keeffe: Allen & Overy Professor of European Law and Chairman of the Board of Studies in Law (Head of Law School), University of Durham; former Legal Secretary to Judge O'Higgins.

James O'Reilly: Senior Counsel, Dublin.

Fergus Randolph: Barrister, Brick Court Chambers, London and Brussels.

Pierre Roseren: Legal Secretary, Court of Justice of the European Communities; former Legal Secretary to Judge O'Higgins.

Peter D. Sutherland   Senior Counsel; Chariman of Allied Irish Banks, plc; former member of the Commission of the European Communities and former Attorney General of Ireland.

John Temple Lang: Director, Directorate General for Competition, Commission of the European Communities.

David Vaughan: Queen's Counsel, Brick Court Chambers, London and Brussels; Visiting Professor of Law, University of Durham.

Brian Walsh: Judge of the European Court of Human Rights; former Judge of the Supreme Court, Ireland.

Philippa Watson: Barrister, Four Raymond Buildings, Brussels and London; Visiting Fellow, Durham European Law Institute; former Legal Secretary to Judge O'Higgins.

Contents

Preface   v
Introduction   vii
List of Contributors   ix
Table of Cases   xiii
Table of Statutes   xxv

Part 1: European Community Law

1   A Constitutional Court for the European Communities   3
     by Ole Due

2   Joining the Threads: the Influences Creating a European Union   11
     by Peter D. Sutherland

3   Subsidiarity – A Busted Flush?   19
     by Lord Mackenzie-Stuart

4   Is the Court of Justice of the European Communities a Constitutional
       Court?   25
     by F. G. Jacobs

5   The Decentralised Enforcement of Community Law Rights. Judicial
       Snakes and Ladders   33
     by Deirdre Curtin

6   Judicial Review and the Common Fisheries Policy in Community
       Law   51
     by James O'Reilly

7   The Free Movement of Workers in the Case-Law of the European
       Court of Justice   67
     by G. Federico Mancini

8   Wandering Students: Their Rights under Community Law   79
     by Philippa Watson

9   Judicial Interpretation of the Public Service Exception to the Free
       Movement of Workers   89
     by David O'Keeffe

10   Constitutional Implications of Community Sex Equality Law   107
     by Karen Banks

11 Legislative Lacunae, the Court of Justice and Freedom to Provide
    Services   121
    by Jean-Yves Art

Part 2: Irish Law

12 The Constitution of Ireland in a Changing Society   137
    by Thomas A. Finlay

13 The Judicial Power, Justice and the Constitution of Ireland   145
    by Brian Walsh

14 The Irish Judge as Law-Maker   159
    by Declan Costello

15 Some Problems of Constitutional Interpretation   169
    by Donal Barrington

16 Observations on the Protection of Fundamental Rights in the Irish
    Constitution   179
    by Niall McCarthy

17 The Irish Constitution and Freedom of Expression   183
    by Nial Fennelly

18 Criminal Justice and the Constitution in Ireland   193
    by James Casey

19 Administrative Law Remedies under Chief Justice O'Higgins   203
    by Anthony M. Collins

Part 3: The Impact of European Community Law on National Law

20 The Interface between Community Law and National Law: the United
    Kingdom Experience   219
    by David Vaughan and Fergus Randolph

21 The Widening Scope of Constitutional Law   229
    by John Temple Lang

22 The Status of Non Implemented Directives before Irish Courts: Post
    Marleasing   247
    by Mary Finlay Geoghegan

23 Review by French Courts of the Conformity of National Provisions
    with Community Law   257
    by Pierre Roseren

Part 4: Judicial Review in Other European Jurisdictions

24 Judicial Review of Legislation in the Netherlands   273
    by T. Koopmans

25 Administrative Law in Scotland: The Public Law/Private Law
    Distinction Revisited   283
    by David Edward

Bibliographical Note   295
Index   297

Table of Cases

Ireland   *page*

Ambiorix Ltd v Minister for the Environment (unreported judgment, Supreme Court, 23
   July 1991) 239
Article 26 and the Electoral (Amendment) Bill [1984] IR 268 152
Article 26 and the Housing (Private Rented Dwellings) Bill 1981 [1983] IR 181 .... 147, 171
Attorney General v Ryan's Car Hire [1965] IR 642; 101 ILTR 57 154
Attorney General v Paperlink [1984] ILRM 373 186
Attorney General v X (unreported judgment, High Court, 17 February 1992) 214
Blake and Madigan v Attorney General [1982] IR 117; [1981] ILRM 34 .... 147, 231
Brady V Donegal County Council [1989] ILRM 282 209
Brennan v Attorney General [1984] ILRM 94 147
Burke v Minister for Labour [1979] IR 354 238
Byrne v Ireland [1972] IR 241 152
Cahill v Sutton [1980] IR 269 172
Central Dublin Development Association & Ors v Attorney General [1975] 109 ILTR 69
   .... 148, 176
Connors v Delpa [1989] ILRM 93 214
Costello v DPP and Attorney General [1984] IR 436; [1984] ILRM 413 201
Cox v Ireland and Attorney General (unreported judgment, Supreme Court, (no 361/
   1990) 11 July 1990) 202
Crotty v An Taoiseach [1987] ILRM, 400; [1987] ILRM 400 235
Cullen v Tobin [1984] ILRM 577 185
Dawson v Hamill [1990] ILRM 257 .... 205, 211
DPP v Healy [1990] ILRM 313 .... 153, 195, 197
DPP v Ryan [1989] IR 399; [1989] ILRM 333 .... 195, 197
Dreher v Land Commission [1984] ILRM 94 148
Dunne v Clinton 1 Frewen 563 194
East Donegal Co-Operative v Attorney General [1970] IR 317; 104 ILTR 81 .... 173, 190,
                                                          238, 239
Eccles v Ireland [1985] IR 545; [1986] ILRM 343 199
Ellis v Assistant Commissioner O'Dea [1990] ILRM 87; [1989] IR 534 238
Educational Co of Ireland v Fitzpatrick [1961] IR 345 97 ILTR 16 .... 150, 175, 176
Employers' Mutual Insurance Association, Re [1965] IR 176 242
Flynn v Ruane [1989] ILRM 690 205
Garvey v Ireland [1981] IR 75; 113 ILTR 61 .... 214, 238, 239, 240
Gill v Connellan [1988] ILRM 448; [1988] 448 204
Glavin v Governor, Training Unit, Mountjoy Prison [991] ILRM 478 .... 199, 212,
                                                          216, 239
Glover v BLN [1973] IR 388 .... 238, 241
Gunn v Bord an Cholaiste Naisunta ealaine is Deartha (unreported judgment, Supreme
   Court, 12 May 1988) 238, 240
Hand v Dublin Corporation and Attorney General [1991] ILRM 556 231
Haughey, Re [1971] IR 217 238
Hibernia National Review Ltd [1976] IR 388 185

page

International Fishing Vessels Ltd v Minister for the Marine (unreported Supreme
  Court, 22 February 1991)   239
Irish Family Planning Association Ltd v Ryan [1979] IR 295   191
KM v the Minister for Foreign Affairs (unreported judgment, High Court, 29 May
  1978)   141
Kearney v Minister for Justice [1986] IR 116; [1987] ILRM 52   186
Kennedy v McCann, Re [1976] IR 386   185
Kiely v Minister for Social Welfare (no 2) [1977] IR 267 .... 238, 239
King v Attorney General [1981] IR 233 .... 193, 194
Leary v National Union of Vehicle Builders [1976] IR 400   238
Loftus v Attorney General [1979] IR 221 .... 187, 238
M v M (unreported judgment, Supreme Court, 8 October 1979)   238
McDonald v Bord na gCon [1965] IR 217; 100 ILTR 89 .... 173, 238
McGee v The Attorney General [1974] IR 284; 109 ILTR 29 .... 141, 142, 153, 163
McGlinchey v Governor Portlaoise Prison [1988] IR 671   199
McMahon v Attorney General [1972] IR 111; 106 ILTR 89   181
Macauley v The Minister for Posts and Telegraphs [1966] IR 345   141
Meskill v CIE [1973] IR 121 .... 150, 238
Moore v Attorney General [1934] IR 44; 68 ILTR 55   180
Murphy v Attorney General [1982] IR 241 .... 155, 215, 231
Murphy v DPP [1989] ILRM 71   205
Murphy v Dublin Corporation [1972] IR 215; 107 ILTR 65   239
Murphy v Stewart [1973] IR 97; 107 ILTA 117   141
Murphy v Turf Club [1989] IR 171   208
Murtagh Properties v Cleary [1972] IR 330 .... 141, 238
Mythen v Employment Appeals Tribunal [1990] IR 98; [1989] ILRM 844   214
N v K [1986] ILRM 75   238
National Union of Railwaymen v Sullivan [1947] IR 77; 81 ILTR 55   187
Norris v Attorney General [1984] IR 36 .... 172, 179
O'Brien v Bord na Mona [1983] IR 255; [1983] ILRM 314   238
O'Brien v Manufacturing Engineering Co Ltd [1973] IR 334; 108 ILTR 105   177
O'Donoghue v Vetinary Council [1975] IR 398   238
O'Donovan v Attorney General [1961] IR 114; 96 ILTR 137   152
O'Donnell v Corporation of Dun Laoghaire [1991] ILRM 301 .... 207, 213
O'Keeffe v An Bord Pleanala (unreported judgment, Supreme Court, February 1991) ..   189
O'Leary v Attorney General [1991] ILRM 454 .... 197, 200
O'Neill v Beaumont Hospital Board [1990] ILRM 419   208
O'Neill v Iarnrod Eireann [1991] ILRM 129   208
O'Shea v DPP and Attorney General [1989] ILRM 309; [1988] IR 664   202
Pesca Valentia Limited v Ministry for Fisheries and Forestry, Ireland and the Attorney
  General [1986] ILRM 68; [1985] IR 193 .... 55, 56, 61
People v Madden [1977] IR 336   153
People v O'Brien [1965] IR 142   153
People v Quilligan [1986] IR 495; [1987] ILRM 606 .... 153, 201
People v State (Williams) v Army Pensions Board [1983] IR 308   238
People (Attorney General) v Conmey [1975] IR 341 .... 177, 201
People (Attorney General) v Edge [1943] IR 115; 78 ILTR 125   194
People (Attorney General) v Gilliland [1986] ILRM 357; [1985] IR 643   195
People (Attorney General) v O'Callaghan [1966] IR 501; 102 ILTR 45   195
People (DPP) v Conroy [1988] ILRM 4; [1986] IR 460   238
People (DPP) v Higgins (unreported, Supreme Court, 22 November 1985)   195
People (DPP) v Kenny [1990] ILRM 569 .... 195, 196
People (DPP) v Lynch [1982] IR 64; [1981] ILRM 389   238
People (DPP) v Quilligan (no 2) [1989] IR 46; [1989] ILRM 245   201
People (DPP) v O'Shea [1982] IR 384   201
People (DPP) v Shaw [1982] IR 1   195
Pigs Marketing Board v Donnelly [1939] IR 413   176
Quirke v Bord Luthchleas na hEireann [1988] IR 83   208
R, In re [1989] IR 126   146
R v McHugh [1901] 2 IR 569   184
R (Miller) v Monaghan JJ (1906) 40 ILTR 51   212
Royal Fishery of the Banne Davies Reports 147   51

Ryan v Attorney General [1965] IR 294 .... 140, 150, 182, 193, 232
Ryan v VIP Taxi Co-Operative Ltd ILTR 10 April 1989 .... 208, 240
S v S [1983] IR 68 238
Sharpe (P & F) v Dublin City and County Manager [1989] IR 712; [1989] ILRM 565 .. 214
Shelley v District Justice Mahon [1990] IR 36 198
Singh v Ruane [1990] ILRM 62 211
Sloan v Culligan and Windle [1991] ILRM 641 199
Society for the Protection of Unborn Children (Ireland) Limited v Grogan & Ors [1990]
    ILRM 350; [1990] CMLR 96-7; [1989] IR 760 .... 150, 214
State (Abenglen Properties v Dublin Corporation [1984] IR 381 ....207, 208,
                                                209, 210, 211, 213, 214, 216
State (Byrne) v Frawley [1978] IR 326 .... 214, 215, 216
State (Burke) v Lennon [1940] IR 567 206
State (Butler) v Ruane (unreported judgment, High Court, 5 May 1986) 212
State (C) v Frawley [1976] IR 365 141
State (Cork County Council) v Fawcitt (unreported judgment, High Court, 13 March
    1981) 205
State (Creedon) v Criminal Injuries Compensation Tribunal (unreported judgment,
    Supreme Court, 14 March 1988) 239
State (Cunningham) v O Floinn [1960] IR 198; 95 ILTR 24 212
State (Daly) v Ruane [1988] ILRM 117 213
State (Furey) v Minister for Defence [1988] ILRM 88 .... 213, 214, 216
State (Gleeson) v Minister for Defence [1976] IR 280 238
State (Glover) v McCarthy [1981] ILRM 47 213
State (Healy) v Donoghue [1976] IR 325; 110 ILTR 9; 112 ILTR 37 ....141, 142,
                                                197, 198, 203, 204, 205, 238
State (Holland) v Kennedy [1977] IR 193 205
State (Hunt) v O'Donovan [1975] IR 90 155
State (Irish Pharmaceutical Union) v Employment Appeals Tribunal [1987] ILRM 36 . 238
State (Keegan) v Stardust Victims Compensation Tribunal [1986] IR 642 189
State (Lynch) v Cooney [1982] IR 337 .... 151, 187, 188, 190, 191,
                                                205, 206, 207
State (McFadden) v Governor of Mountjoy [1981] ILRM 113 238
State (McKeown) v Scully [1986] ILRM 133 238
State (Nicolaou) v An Bord Uchtala [1966] IR 567 .... 206, 207, 213, 214
State (O'Connell) v Fawsitt [1986] IR 362 .... 196, 197, 212
State (Quinn) v Ryan [1965] IR 70 .... 176, 238
State (Roche) v Delap [1980] IR 170 .... 212, 213
State (Royle) v Kelly [1974] IR 259 203
State (Sheerin) v Kennedy [1966] IR 379 .... 155, 169
State (Toft) v Galway Corporation [1981] ILRM 439 .... 211, 212
State (Vossa) v O'Floinn [1957] IR 227 .... 210, 213, 214
State (Wilson) v Neilan [1985] IR 89 213
Tierney v Amalgamated Society of Woodworkers [1959] IR 254 241
Walsh President of the Circuit Court [1989] ILRM 325 202
Webb v Ireland [1988] ILRM 565 241
White v Hussey [1989] ILRM 109 214

England
Ambard v Attorney General for Trinidad and Tobago [1936] AC 322 184
Anismic Ltd v Foreign Compensation Commission [1969] AC 147; [1969] WLR 163;
    [1969] 1 All ER 208 205
Associated Provincial Picture Houses Ltd v Wednesbury Corporation [1948] 1 KB 223 . 189
Attorney General v Times Newspapers Ltd [1974] AC 273, [1973] 3 All ER 54 183
Birmingham Six, see R v McIlkenny 153
Bonham, Dr 77 Enr Rep 646; Coke 114a (CP 1610) 149
Bourgoin v Minister of Agriculture, Fisheries and Food [1986] QB 716 .... 45, 225
Bulk Oil (Zug) AG v Sun International Ltd [1984] 1 WLR 147 225
Bulmer v Bollinger [1974] Ch 401 226
Campbell v Spottiswoode (1863) 3 B & S 769 184
Cocks v Thanet District Council [1983] 2 AC 286 .... 283, 292, 293, 294
Davy v Spelthorne Borough Council [1984] 1 AC 262 283

page

De Falco v Crawley Borough Council [1980] QB 460 .... 286, 293
Doughty v Rolls Royce plc (unreported judgment, Court of Appeal, 19 December 1991) . 37, 38
Duke v Greater Reliance Systems Ltd [1988] AC 618; [1988] WLR 2 359; [1988] ICR
   339; [1988] 1 All ER 626; [1988] QB 108 .... 40, 222
Garden Cottage Foods Ltd v Milk Marketing Board [1983] 2 All ER 770 225
Guildford Four, see R v Armstrong, R v Conlon, R v Hill 153
Hinds v The Queen [1977] AC 195 194
Hoani Te Tukino v Aotea District Maori Land Board [1941] AC (PC) 322 274
Litster v Forth Dry Dock & Engineering Co Ltd [1989] 1 All ER 1134; [1989] 2 CMLR
   194 222
Liversidge v Anderson [1942] AC 206 179
Livingstone v Hepworth Refractories Limited, EAT 1643/90 5 December 1991 (tran-
   script); Times 23 December 1991 49
Maguire Family 153
Merivale v Carson (1887) 20 QBD 275 184
Mortesen v Peters (1906) 8 F (Just Cas) 93 274
O'Reilly v Mackman [1983] AC 237; [1983] WLR 1096; [1982] 3 All ER 1124 .... .207, 283,
                                                            292, 294
R v Armstrong, Conlon and Hill, Times 20 October 1989 (transcript) 153
R v Cobbett [1804] 29 state trials 1 183
R v East Berkshire Health Authority ex parte Walsh [1985] QB 15 286
R v Henn and Darby [1981] AC 850 227
R v London Boroughs Transport Committee, ex parte Freight Transport Association
   Ltd [1991] 3 All ER 915; [1991] 1 WLR 828 227
R v McIlkenny 93 Cr App Rep 287 153
R v Secretary of State for Transport, ex parte Factortame Limited (HL no 1) [1991] 1 All
   ER 70; [1990] 2 AC 85; [1990] 3 WLR 818 .... 220, 223, 224
R v Stafford JJ [1940] 2 KB 33 209
Ridge v Baldwin [1964] AC 40 284
Stoke-on-Trent City Council v B & Q plc [1991] 4 All ER 221; [1991] 2 WLR 42 224
Swain v The Law Society [1983] 1 AC 598 .... 292, 293
Thornton v Kirkless Metropolitan Borough Council [1979] QB 626 286
Town Investments Ltd v Department of Environment [1978] AC 359 283
Wednesbury Corporation v Ministry of Housing and Local Government [1965] 1 WLR
   261 225

Scotland

Brown v Hamilton Council 1983 SC (HL) 1 .... 283, 284, 287, 289, 291, 292, 293, 294
Forbes v Underwood (1886) 13 R 465 288
Gordon (Sir John) of Invergordon v Sir John Gordon of Embo (1751) M 7345, Elchies
   no 52 291
Sutherland of Swinzie v Sutherland of Langwell (1751) M 2436, Elchies no 52 290

Netherlands

Cruise Missile case (Ned Jurispr 1991 no 248) 278
Harmonisatiewet (Ned Jurispr 1989 no 469) 278

United States of America

Maybury v Madison (1803) 5 US (1 Cranch) 137 155
Miranda v Arizona (1966) 384 US 436 197
Myers v United States 272 US 52, 293 (1926) 149
Papachristou v City of Jacksonville (1972) 405 US 156 194
US v Leon (1984) 468 US 897 196
US v Salerno (1987) 481 US 739 197

European

Administration des Douanes v Societe des Cafes Jacques Vabre [1975] 2 CMLR 336 ... 261
Adoui and Cornuaille v Belgium (joined cases 115, 116/81) [1982] ECR 1665; 3 CMLR
   631 .... 69, 75
Airola v Commission (case 21/74) [1975] ECR 221 109
Aktien- Zuckerfabrik Schoppenstedt, (case 5/71), [1971] ECR 975 7
Al-jubail Fertilizer (case C-49/88) [1991] 3 CMLR 377 240

page

Alaimo v Prefet du Rhone (case 68/74) [1975] ECR 109; [1975] 1 CMLR 262 87
Algerian Semolina, see Syndicat General de Fabricants de Semoules de France 262
Allue and Coonan v Universita delgi Studi di Venezia (case 33/88) [1989] ECR 1591 ... 95, 96,
 100, 101
Alusuisse Italia SpA (case 307/81), [1983] 3 CMLR 388; [1982] ECR 3463 7
Am & S Europe Limited v Commission of the European Communities (case 165/79)
 [1982] ECR 1575 240
Amministrazione delle Finanze dello Stato v Simmenthal SpA (case 106/77) [1978] ECR
 629; [1978] 3 CMLR 263 .... 73, 231, 265, 266, 267
Anglo Irish Meat v Minister for Agriculture (case 196/80) [1981] ECR 2263 230
ASTI (case C-213/90) (judgment of 4 July 1991) 89, 105
Association des Centres Distributeurs Edouard Leclerc [1985] ECR 1; [1985] 2 CMLR
 286 263
Assurances du Credit and Compagnie Belge d'Assurance Credit v EC Council and
 Commission (case C-63/89) [1991] 2 CMLR 737 128
B v Austria (1991) 13 EHRR 20 196
Baggetta v Italy (1988) 10 EHRR 325 196
Barber v Royal Guardian Exchange Assurance Group (case C-262/88) [1990] ECR
 1889, 1912; [1990] 2 CMLR 513 .... 39, 108, 111, 112
Baudin v Commission (case 32/71) [1972] ECR 363; [1972] CMLR 945 108
Becker v Finanzamt Munster Innenstadt (case 8/81) [1982] ECR 53; [1982] CMLR
 499 .... 7, 222, 247, 248, 269
Beet-Proper v Lanschot Bankiers (case 262/84) [1986] ECR 773; 2 [1987] 2 CLMR 616 . 116
Belgian State v Hombel (case 262/86) [1988] ECR 5365; [1989] 1 CMLR 393 .... 84, 86, 87
Benedetti v Munari (case 52/76) [1977] ECR 163 242
Benthem v The Netherlands (series A, no 97) case 8848/80; (1986) 8 EHRR 1 279
Bernini v Minister for Education and Science (case C-3/90 OJ 1990 C 35/13 82
Bettray v Staatssecretaris van Justitie (case 344/87) [1989] ECR 1621; [1991] 1 CMLR
 459 70
Bilka Kaufhaus v Weber (case 170/84) [1986] ECR 1607; [1986] 1 CMLR 701 .... 112, 113
Biologische Producten (case 272/80) [1981] ECR 3277; [1982] 2 CMLR 497 243
Blaizot v University of Liege (case 24/86) [1988] ECR 355; [1989] 1 CMLR 57 .... 85, 86
Bleis (case C-4/91) (judgment, 27 November 1991) 96, 97, 100
Boisdet [1991] 1 CMLR 3 .... 264, 267
Bond van Adverteerders et al v Netherlands State (case 352/85) [1988] ECR 2085;
 [1989] 3 CMLR 113 128
Bonsignore v Oberstadtdirektor der Stadt Koln (case 67/74) [1975] ECR 297; [1975] 1
 CMLR 492 .... 74, 76
Bord Bainne Co-Operative v Milk Marketing Board [1984] 2 CMLR 584 224
Brown v Secretary of State for Scotland (case 197/86) [1988] ECR 3205 ; [1988] 3 CMLR
 403 .... 69, 81, 83
Bulk Oil v Sun Oil (case 174/84) [1986] ECR 559; [1986] 2 CMLR 732 .... 230, 244
Case 30/82 [1983] ECR 2011 262
Casagrande v Landeshaupstadt Munchen (case 9/74) [1974] ECR 773; [1974] 2 CMLR
 423 .... 72, 87
Cassis de Dijon, see Rewe-Zentral AG v Director of the Landwirtschaftstammer Rhein-
 land 132
Castelli v ONPTS (case 261/83) [1984] ECR 3199; [1987] 1 CMLR 465 .... 74, 84
CILFIT Srl et al v Ministry of Health (case 283/81) [1982] ECR 3415; [1983] 1 CMLR
 472 .... 227, 228
Cinetheque SA & Others v Federation Nationale des Cinemas Francais (joined cases 60,
 61/84) [1985] ECR 2605; [1986] CMLR 365 .... 31, 243
Coditel et al v Cine Vog et al (case 62/79) [1980] ECR 881; [1981] 2 CMLR 362 123
Comet BV v Produktschap voor Siergewassen (case 45/76) [1976] ECR 1989, 1997;
 [1977] 1 CMLR 588 .... 35, 38, 39, 48
Commission v Belgium no 1 (case 149/79) [1980] ECR 3881; [1981] 2 CMLR 413 ...... 92, 93,
 95, 96, 97, 98, 99, 100, 102, 103
Commission v Belgium no 2 (case 149/79) [1982] ECR 1845; [1982] 2 CMLR 539 ...... 99, 100
Commission v Belgium (case 52/84) [1986] ECR 89; [1989] 1 CMLR 710 233
Commission v Belgium (pending) (case C-2/90) 10
Commission v Council (case 22/70) [1971] ECR 363; [1971] CMLR 335 53
Commission v Council (case 242/87) [1989] ECR 1425; [1991] 1 CMLR 478 85

page

Commission v Council (case C-301/90) (pending) 28
Commission v France (case 167/73) [1974] ECR 359; [1974] 2 CMLR 216 71
Commission v France (case 68/76) [1977] ECR 515; [1977] 2 CMLR 161 269
Commission v France (case 307/84) [1986] ECR 1725; [1987] 3 CMLR 555 .... 91, 94
                                95, 96, 97, 98, 99, 101, 102, 105
Commission v France (case 318/86) [1988] ECR 3559; [1989] 3 CMLR 663 114
Commission v France (case 169/87) [1988] ECR 4093; [1990] 1 CMLR 49 263
Commission v France (case C-154/89) (unreported judgment, 26 February 1991) 123, 124
Commission v France (case C-294/89) (unreported judgment, 10 July 1991) 123, 132
Commission v Germany (case 427/85) [1988] ECR 1123; [1989] 2 CMLR 677 .... 123, 132
Commission v Germany (case 249/86) [1989] ECR 1263; [1990] 3 CMLR 540 71
Commissioner v Greece (case 305/87) [1989] ECR 1461; [1991] 1 CMLR 611 73
Commission v Greece (case 281/87) [1989] ECR 4015 230
Commission v Greece (case C-287/87) [1990] ECR 125 44
Commission v Greece (case C-198/89) (unreported judgment, 26 February 1991) 123,
                                124, 131
Commission v Hellenic Republic (case 305/87) [1989] ECR 146; [1991] 1 CMLR 611 .. 63
Commission v Ireland (case 61/77) [1978] ECR 417; [1978] 2 CMLR 466 53
Commission v Ireland (case 61/77r) [1977] ECR 1411 231
Commission v Ireland (case C-98/89) [1991] ECR 1 62
Commission v Ireland (case C- 280/89) 65
Commission v Italy (case 39/72) [1973] ECR 101; [1973] CMLR 439 205
Commission v Italy (case 103/84) [1986] ECR 1759; [1987] 2 CMLR 825 44
Commission v Italy (case 309/84) [1986] ECR 599; [1987] 2 CMLR 657 44
Commission v Italy (case 118/85) [1987] ECR 2599; [1988] 2 CMLR 255 90
Commission v Italy (case 154/85) ECR 2717; [1988] 2 CMLR 951 44
Commission v Italy (case 225/85) [1987] ECR 2625; [1988] 3 CMLR 635 .... 95, 96, 101
Commission v Italy (case 104/86) [1988] ECR 1799; [1989] 3 CMLR 25 120
Commission v Italy (case 180/89) (unreported judgment, 5 December 1990) 123, 124,
                                131
Commission v Luxembourg and Belgium (joined cases 90, 91/63) [1964] ECR 625;
   [1965] CMLR 58 266
Commission v United Kingdom (case 32/79) [1980] ECR 2403; [1981] 1 CMLR 219 ... 243
Commission v United Kingdom (case 804/79) [1981] ECR 1045; [1982] CMLR 543 ... 28, 131,
                                230, 244
Commission v United Kingdom (case C-246/89) [1991] ECR 1; [1991] 3 CMLR 706 ... 55, 58,
                                59, 62, 63
Commission v United Kingdom (case C-279/89) (pending) 65
Costa v ENEL (case 6/64) [1964] ECR 585 .... 7, 10, 132, 257, 266, 267
Council v Parliament (case 34/86) [1986] ECR 2155; [1986] 3 CMLR 94 .... 8, 27
Council v Parliament (case C-284/90) (pending) 27
Cowan v Tresor Public (case 186/87) [1989] ECR 195; [1990] 2 CMLR 613 .... 84, 89,
                                243
Cristini v SNCF (case 32/75) [1975] ECR 2681 74
De Compte (case 141/84) [1985] ECR 1951 240
Debauve (case 52/79) [1980] ECR 833; [1981] 2 CMLR 362 242
Defrenne v Sabena (no 1) (case 80/70) [1971] ECR 445; [1974] 1 CMLR 494 112
Defrenne v Sabena (no 2) (case 43/75) [1976] ECR 455; [1976] 2 CMLR 98 ....107, 108,
                                114, 231, 232
Defrenne v Sabena (no 3) (case 149/77) [1978] ECR 1365; [1978] 3 CMLR 312 ....108, 109,
                                110, 111
Dekerand and Hertz (joined cases C-177/88, 179/88) [1990] ECR 1889, 1912 39
Dekker (case C-177/88) [1990] ECR I-3941 .... 42, 116
Demirel (case 12/86) [1987] ECR 3719; [1989] 1 CMLR 421 242
Deutsche Milchkontor (joined cases 205-215/82) [1983] ECR 2633; [1984] 3 CMLR
   586 242
Devred v Commission (case 257/78) [1979] ECR 3767 110
Di Leo v Land Berlin (case C-308/89) (unreported judgment, 13 November 1990) 83, 87
Diatta v Land Berlin (case 267/83) [1985] ECR 567; [1986] 2 CMLR 160 72
Dietz-Matti v Bundesamt fur Ernahrung und Forstwirtschaft (case C-158/89) [1990]
   ECR I-2013; [1991] 3 CMLR 551 131
Dik (case 80/87) [1988] ECR 1601; [1989] 2 CMLR 963 119

page

Donckerwolcke (case 41/76) [1976] ECR 1921; [1977] 2 CMLR 535 230
Dudgeon v United Kingdom (series A, no 45) (1982) 4 ECHR 149, 235
Echternach and Moritz v Netherlands Minister for Education and Science (joined cases
  389, 390/87) [1989] ECR 723; [1990] 2 CMLR 305 . . . . 74, 83, 87
Elliniki Radiophonia Tileorassi (ERT) (case C-260/89) (unreported judgment, 18 June
  1991) 31, 232, 243
Emmott v Minister for Social Welfare (Case C-208/90) (unreported judgment, 25 July
  1991) 37, 46, 47, 48, 120, 253, 254, 268
Engel (June 8 1976, CEDH A vol 22); (1979–80) 1 EHRR 647 277
Eridania (case 230/78) [1979] ECR 2749 242
Express Dairy Food v IBAPI (case 130/79 [1980] ECR 1887; [1981] 1 CMLR 451 48
FNV (case 71/85) see State (Nederlands) v Federatie Nederlandse Vakbeweging 119
Factortame I: Factortame v Secretary of State for Transport (case C-213/89) [1990]
  ECR I-2433, 2455; [1990] 3 CMLR 1; [1982] 2 WLR 15, 42,
                                                                              43, 46, 48, 55, 56, 231
Factortame II: The Queen v Secretary of State for Transport, ex parte Factortame Ltd &
  others (case C-221/89) [1991] ECR 1; [1991] 9 CMLR 589 . . . . 54, 56, 58, 59, 60, 62, 64
Finnegan v Clowney Youth Training Programme Ltd [1990] 2 CMLR 859; [1990] WLR
  1305 40
Forscheri v Belgian State (case 152/82) [1983] ECR 2323; [1984] 1 CMLR 334 . . . . 82, 85
Foster and Others v British Gas plc (case C-188/89) [1990] 2 CMLR 833; [1990] 3 All
  ER 897 . . . . 37, 38, 49, 91, 117, 222, 248
Foto-Frost (case 314/85) [1987] ECR 4199; [1988] 3 CMLR 57 30
France v Commission (case C-202/88) (unreported judgment, 19 March 1991) 15
France v Commission (case C-303/90) (unreported judgment, 13 November 1991) 9
Francovich and Bonifaci v Italy (joined cases C-6/90, C-9/90) (unreported judgment, 19
  November 1991) 36, 43, 46, 49, 120, 222,
                                                                          223, 224, 234, 254, 269
Frascogna v Caisse des Depots et Consignations (case 157/84) [1985] ECR 1739 84
Garland v British Rail (case 12/81) [1982] ECR 359; [1982] 1 CMLR 696 112
Germany v Commission (case 24/62) [1963] ECR 63; [1963] CMLR 347 240
Germany v Commission (case C-342/89) (unreported judgment, 17 October 1991) 9
Gmurzynska-Bscher (case C-231/89) [1990] ECR 1–4003 9
Golder (21 February 1975) CADH A vol 17; [1979–80] 1 EHRR 524 279
Grad (case 9/70) [1970] ECR 825; [1971] CMLR 1 36
Gravier v City of Liege (case 293/83) [1985] ECR 595; [1985] 3 CMLR 1 . . . . 80, 85
Grimaldi (case C-322/88) [1989] ECR 4407; [1991] 2 CMLR 265 39
Groener v Minister for Education (case C-379/87) [1989] ECR 3967; [1990] 1 CMLR
  401 . . . . 29, 73, 91
Grogan (case C-159/90) [1991] 3 CMLR 849 31
Gul v Regierungsprasident Dusseldorf (case 131/85) [1986] ECR 1573; [1987] 1 CMLR
  501 72
Haegeman (case 181/73) [1974] ECR 449; [1975] 1 CMLR 515 233
Hag 11. See SA CNL-Sucal Nv v Hag GF AG (case 10/89) 41
Hakvoort (case 348/88) [1990] ECR I-1647; [1991] 2 CMLR 689 230
Hamill v Commission (case 180/87) [1988] ECR 6141 98
Harz v Deutsche Tradex (case 79/83) [1984] ECR 1921; [1986] 2 CMLR 430 . . . . . . 39, 118, 230
Hauer Case 44/79, [1979] ECR 3727; [1981] EHRR 140 8
Hettrich v Commission (case T-134/89) (unreported judgment, 17 October 1990) 28
Heylens v UNECTEF (case 222/86) [1987] ECR 4097; [1989] 1 CMLR 901 . . . . 41, 42,
                                                                                  48, 240, 243
Hoeck v Openbaar Centrum voor Mattschappelijk Welzijnkalmthout (case 249/83)
  [1985] ECR 973; [1987] 3 CMLR 638 84
Hoekstra (nee Unger) v Bestuur der Bedrijsvereniging voor Detailhandel en Ambachten
  (case 75/63) [1964] ECR 177; [1964] CMLR 319 68
Holtz and Willemsen Case 134/74 [1974] ECR 1 7
Hurd v Jones (case 44/84) [1986] ECR 29; [1986] 2 CMLR 1 233
Imm Zwartfeld (case C-2/88) [1990] 3 CMLR 457 233
International Agreement on Natural Rubber (Opinion 1/78) [1979] ECR 2871; [1979] 3
  CMLR 639 28
Iorio v Azienda Autonoma delle Ferovie dello Stato (case 298/84) [1986] ECR 247;
  [1986] 3 CMLR 665 70

Irish Creamery Milk Supplies v An Taoiseach [1981] ECR 735; [1981] 2 CMLR 455
    (joined cases 36, 71/80) 226
Jenkins v Kingsgate (case 96/80) [1981] ECR 911 112
Johnston v Chief Constable of the Royal Ulster Constabulary (case 222/84) [1986] ECR
    1651; [1986] 3 CMLR 240 .... 39, 41, 48, 114, 117, 222, 240, 243, 248, 279
Jongeneel Kaas (case 237/82) [1984] ECR 483; [1985] 2 CMLR 53 243
Just v Danish Ministry for Fiscal Affairs (case 68/79) [1980] ECR 501; [1987] 1 CMLR
    764 120
Kempf v Staatssecretaris van Justitie (case 139/85) [1986] ECR 1741; [1987] 1 CMLR
    764 .... 69, 81
Kjeldsen, Busk Madsen and Pedersen v Denmark (Series A no 23); [1979–80] 1 EHRR
    711 80
Kipgen v Secretaire D'Etat a l'Agriculture et a la Viticulture (joined case 201, 202/85)
    [1986] ECR 3477; [1988] 1 CMLR 151 242
Kramer (joined cases 3, 4, 6/76) [1976] ECR 1279; [1976] 1 CMLR 440 53
Kolpinghuis Nijmegen (case 80/86) [1987] ECR 3969; [1989] 2 CMLR 18 .... 37, 39,
                                                                              242, 248
Kowalska v Frie und Hansestadt Hamburg (case C-33/89) [1990] ECR I-2591 .... 112, 113
Kupferberg (case 104/81) [1982] ECR 3641; [1983] 1 CMLR 1 233
Kziber (case C-18/90) (unreported judgment, 13 January 1991) 233
Lair v Universitat Hannover (case 39/86) [1988] ECR 3161; [1989] 3 CMLR 545 ...... 69, 82,
                                                                                   86
Lawrie-Blum v Land Baden-Wurttemberg (case 66/85) [1986] ECR 2121; [1987] 3
    CMLR 389 .... 68, 77, 82, 92, 94, 95, 96, 100
Levin v Staatssecretaris van Justitie (case 53/81) [1982] ECR 1035; [1982] 2 CMLR
    454 .... 68, 81
Liefting et al v Directie van het Academish Ziekenhuis bij de Univeriteit van Amsterdam
    (case 23/83) [1984] ECR 3225; [1984] 3 CMLR 702 112
Litster v Forth Dry Dock and Engineering Co Ltd [1989] 2 CMLR 194 40
Luck (case 34/67) [1968] ECR 245 38
Ludwigshafener Walzmuhle (joined cases 197–200, 243, 245, 247/80) [1981] ECR 1041 . 7
Luisi and Carbone v Ministero del Tesoro (joined cases 286/82, 26/83) [1984] ECR 377;
    [1985] 2 CMLR 57 .... 84, 89, 122
Lutticke GmbH (case 4/69) [1971] ECR 325 7
Luxembourg v Parliament (case 230/81) [1983] ECR 255; [1983] 2 CMLR 726 233
Macarthys v Smith (case 129/79) [1980] ECR 1275; [1980] 2 CMLR 205 112
McDermott and Cotter, no 1 (case 286/85) [1987] ECR 1453; [1987] 2 CMLR 607 ..... 46, 119,
                                                                                   254
McDermott and Cotter, no 2 (case C-377/89); [1991] 3 CMLR 507 .... 46, 119
McWhirter v Attorney General [1972] CMLR 882 217
Marleasing SA v La Commercial Internacional de Alimentacion SA (case C-106/89)
    [1990] ECR I-4135 .... 7, 39, 40, 48, 49, 117, 119, 222,
                                                       230, 247, 249, 250, 251, 252, 253
Marshall v Southampton and South West Hampshire Area Health Authority (case
    152/84) [1986] ECR 723; [1986] 1 CMLR 688 .... 37, 39, 115, 222, 247, 248, 249, 252
Marsman v Rosskamp (case 44/72) [1972] ECR 1243; [1973] CMLR 501 73
Masgio (case C-10/90) (judgment, 7 March 1991) 89
Matteucci v Communaute Francaise de Belgique (case 235/87) [1988] ECR 6589; [1989]
    1 CMLR 357 86
Mecanarte-Metalurgica (case C-348/89) (unreported judgment, 27 June 1991) 231
Merci Convenzionali Porto di Genova SpA v Siderurgica Gabrielli SpA (case 179/90)
    (unreported judgment, 10 December 1991) 15
Milasi v Italy (1988) 10 EHRR 333 196
Ministerie Public v Even (case 207/78) [1979] ECR 2019; [1980] 2 CMLR 71 74
Ministere Public v Marchandise, Chapuyis and Trafitex SA (case 332/89) (unreported
    judgment, 28 February 1991) 224
Ministere Public v Mutsch (case 137/84) [1985] ECR 2681; [1986] 1 CMLR 648 74
Ministere Public and Chambre Syndicate des Agents Artistiques et Impresari de Belgi-
    que v Van Wesemael et al (joined cases 110, 111/78) [1979] ECR 35; [1990] 1
    CMLR 656 123
Mooreman (case 190/87) [1988] ECR 4689 230
Murphy (case 157/86) [1988] ECR 673; [1988] 1 CMLR 879 39

page

(Natural Rubber) (Opinion 1/78) [1979] ECR 2871; [1979] 3 CMLR 6391 230
Netherlands v Reed (case 59/85) [1986] ECR 1283; [1987] 2 CMLR 448 72
Nicolo [1990] 1 CMLR 173 26
Nijman (case 125/88) [1989] ECR 3533; [1991] 1 CMLR 92 230
Nimz (case C-184/89) (unreported judgment, 7 February 1991) 113
Norddeutsches Vieh-und Fleischkontor v Balm (joined cases 213–215/81) [1982] ECR
    3583 242
Norris (Series A no 142) ECHR (26 October 1988) 235
Organon Laboratories v Department of Health [1990] 2 CMLR 49 230
Parliament v Council (case 13/83) [1985] ECR 1513; [1986] 1 CMLR 138 128
Parliament v Council ('Comitology') (case 302/87) [1988] ECR 5615, 5637 64
Parliament v Council (Post Chernobyl) (case 70/88) [1992] 1 CMLR 91 . . . . 8, 27, 64
Parti Ecologiste 'Les Verts' v Parliament (case 294/1983) [1986] ECR 1339; [1987] 2
    CMLR 343 . . . . 8, 30, 240, 243
Pecastaing v Belgium (case 98/79) [1980] ECR 691; [1980] 3 CMLR 685 76
Pecsca Valentia [1988] ECR 33; [1988] 1 CMLR 888 61
Physical Protection of Nuclear Materials (case 1/78) [1978] ECR 2151; [1979] 1 CMLR
    131 230
Pickstone v Freemans [1988] 3 CMLR 221 222
Pigs and Bacon Commission v McCarren (case 177/78) [1979] ECR 2161; [1979] 3
    CMLR 389 230
Pigs Marketing Board v Redmond (case 83/78) [1978] ECR 2347; [1979] 1 CMLR 177 . 230
Pinna (case 41/84) [1986] ECR 1; [1988] 1 CMLR 350 102
Pleck (case 157/79) [1990] ECR 2171; [1980] 3 CMLR 220 243
Pluimveeslachterij Midden-Nederland and Pluimveeslachterij Van Miert (joined cases
    47, 48/83) [1984] ECR 172 131
Pretore di Salo v X (case 14/86) [1987] ECR 2545; [1989] 1 CMLR 71 248
Procureur du Roi v Debauve et al (case 52/79) [1979] 2 CMLR 592 . . . . 123, 126
Publico Ministero v Ratti (case 148/78) [1979] ECR 1629; [1980] 1 CMLR 96 . . . . 222, 230, 247
Queen v Immigration Appeal Tribunal ex parte Antonissen (case C-292/89); [1991] 2
    CMLR 373 . . . . 69, 81
R v Minister for Agriculture, Fisheries, Food ex parte Agegate Limited (case C-3/87)
    [1989] ECR 4459; [1990] 1 CMLR 366; [1991] 1 All ER 6 . . . . 57, 58, 59, 60, 62, 64
Queen v Minister for Agriculture, Fisheries and Food, ex parte Jaderow Limited (case
    C-216/87) [1989] ECR 4509; [1991] 2 CMLR 556 . . . . 57, 58, 60, 62, 64
R v Minister of Agriculture, Fisheries and Food, ex parte Bostock [1991] 1 CMLR 687 . . 223
R v Bouchereau (case 30/77) [1977] ECR 1999; [1978] QB 732 76
R v Immigration Appeal Tribunal ex parte Antonissen (case C-292/89) (unreported
    judgment, 26 February 1991) 69
R v Ministry for Agriculture, Fisheries and Food, ex parte Agegate [1987] 3 CMLR 939 . 226, 227
R v Ministry for Agriculture, Fisheries and Food, ex parte Bell Lines [1984] 2 CMLR 502: 225
R v Pharmaceutical Society of Great Britain, ex parte Association of Pharmaceutical
    Importers (API) [1987] 3 CMLR 951 . . . . 226, 227
R v Secretary of State ex parte Factortame [1990] 3 CMLR 375 . . . . 26, 225
R v Secretary of State for Transport, ex parte Factortame Ltd and Ors (case 213/89)
    [1990] 3 CMLR 1 . . . . 223, 249, 268
R v Secretary of State for Home Affairs, ex parte Santillo (case 131/79) [1980]
    1 CMLR 47 76
R v Saunders (case 175/78) [1979] ECR 1129; [1979] 2 CMLR 216; [1979] 2 All ER
    267 70
Raulin v Minister for Education and Science (case C-357/89) OJ 1990 C11/4 82
Razzouk and Beydoun v Commission (joined cases 75, 117/82) [1984] ECR 1509 110
Reina v Landeskreditbank Baden-Wurttemberg (case 65/81) [1982] ECR 33; [1982]
    1 CMLR 744 74
Retter (Case 130/87) [1989] ECR 865 10
Rewe v Hauptzollamt Kiel (case 158/80) [1981] ECR 1805; [1985] 3 CMLR 449 36
Rewe-Zentral AG v Director of the Landwirtschaftskammer Rheinland (case 37/83)
    [1984] ECR 1229; [1985] 2 CMLR 586 . . . . 130, 132
Rewe-Zentral AG v Bundesmonopolverwaltung fur Branntwein (case 120/78) [1979]
    ECR 649; [1979] 3 CMLR 494 121
Rewe Zentralfinanz EG v Landswirtschaftskammer fur das Saarland (case 33/76) [1976]
    ECR 1989, 2003, 2043, 2053; [1977] 1 CMLR 533 . . . . 35, 38, 39, 48, 234

page

Reyners v Belgium (case 2/74) [1974] ECR 631; [1974] 2 CMLR 305 .... 92, 93, 132
Rheinmuhlen (case 166/73) [1974] ECR 33;[1974] 1 CMLR 523 267
Ringeisen (16 July 1971) CEDH A vol 13; (1979–80) 1 EHRR 455 279
Rinner-Kuhn v FWW Spezial-Gebauderreinigung GmbH (case 171/88) [1989] ECR
    2743 .... 112, 113
Romkes (case 46/86) [1987] ECR 2671; [1988] 3 CMLR 524 61
Royer (case 48/75) [1976] ECR 497; [1976] 2 CMLR 619 71
Rush Portuguesa Lda v Office National d'Immigration (case C-113/89) [1990] ECR
    I-1417; [1991] 2 CMLR 818 124
Russo v AIMA (case 60/75) [1976] ECR 45 44
Rutili v Minister for the Interior (case 36/75) [1975] ECR 1219; [1976] 1 CMLR 140 . 75, 92, 242
SA CNL-Sucal NV v Hag GF AG (Case 10/89) [1990] ECR I-3711 41
Sabbatini v European Parliament (case 20/71) [1972] ECR 345; [1972] CMLR 945 108
Spa SAGE v Ministry for Finance of the Italian Republic (case 33/70) [1970] ECR
    1213; [1971] CMLR 123 .... 36, 222
Sager v Dennemeyer (case C-76/90) (unreported judgment, 21 February 1991) 123
Salabiaku v France (24 May 1988) (Series A no 133) (1991) 13 EHRR 379 200
Salgoil SA v Italy (case 13/68) [1968] ECR 453; [1969] CMLR 181 38
Schul v Inspecteur der Invoerrechten en Accijnzen (case 15/81) [1982] ECR 1409;
    [1982] 3 CMLR 229 122
Scrivener v Centre Public d'Aide Social de Chastre (case 122/84) [1985] ECR 1027;
    [1987] 3 CMLR 638 84
Seco et al v EVI (joined cases 62, 63/81) [1982] ECR 223 123
Simmenthal (case 106/77) [1978] ECR 629; [1978] 3 CMLR 263 .... 231, 265, 266, 267
Societe Generale Alascienne de Banque v Koestler (case 15/78) [1978] ECR 1971; [1979]
    1 CMLR 89 123
Societe SMANOR et Syndicat National des Produits Surgeles (CE 19 November 1986)
    [1986] Rec LEBON 260 263
Society for the Protection of Unborn Children Ireland Ltd v S Grogan et al (case
    C-159/90) [1991] 3 CMLR 849 123
Sotgiu v Deutsche Bundespost (case 152/73) [1974] ECR 153 .... 69, 73, 77, 92, 101, 103
Southampton and South West Hampshire Area Health Authority v Marshall (case
    C-271/91) (pending); [1986] 1 CMLR 506; [1986] 2 WLR 367 .... 47, 49
Stanley Adams v Commission (case 145/83) [1985] ECR 3651 98
State (Netherlands) v Federatie Nedelandse Vokbeweging (case 71/85) [1986] ECR
    3855; [1987] 3 CMLR 767 119
Steenkolenmijnen (case 30/59) [1961] ECR 48 230
Steymann v Staatssecretaris van Justitie (case 196/87) [1988] ECR 6159; [1989]
    1 CMLR 449 70
Stichting Collective Antennevoorziening Gouda et al v Commissariaat voor de Media
    (case C-288/89) (unreported judgment, 25 July 1991) 121, 123,
                                                    124, 125, 126, 129, 131, 132
Stoeckel (case C-345/89) (unreported judgment, 25 July 1991) 115, 257
Sudmilch v Ugliola (case 15/69) [1969] ECR 363; [1990] CMLR 194 73
Synacomex (case 34/70) [1976] ECR 1233 .... 258, 263
Testa (joined cases 41, 121, 796/79) [1980] ECR 1979; [1981] 2 CMLR 552 242
Timex v Council (case 264/82) [1985] ECR 849; [1985] 3 CMLR 550 240
Torfaen Borough Council v B & Q plc (case C-145/88) [1989] ECR 3851; [1990]
    1 CMLR 337 .... 29, 129
Transocean Marine Plant (case 17/74) [1974] ECR 1063; [1974] 2 CMLR 459 240
Uglioa (case 15/69) [1969] ECR 363; [1970] CMLR 194 92
Union Departmentale des Syndicats CGT de l'Aisne v SIDEF Conforama and others
    (case 312/89) (unreported judgment, 28 February 1991) 224
Van Binsbergen v Bestuur van de Bedrijfsvereniging voor de Metaalnijverheid (case
    33/74) [1974] ECR 1299; [1975] 1 CMLR 298 .... 125, 126, 127, 129
Van den Broeck v Commission (case 37/74) [1975] ECR 235 109
Van Duyn v Home Office (case 41/74) [1974] ECR 1337; [1975] 1 CMLR 1 . 75, 92, 126, 221, 265
Van Gend en Loos (case 26/62) [1963] ECR 1 6
Van Miert (joined cases 47, 48/83) [1984] ECR 1721 244
Verhooen (case 87/90–89/90) (unreported judgment, 29 May 1991) 230
Vlassopoulou v Ministerium fur Justiz, Bundes-und Europaangelgenheiten Baden-
    Wurttemberg (case C-340/89) (unreported judgment, 28 November 1990) 132

Von Colson and Kamann v Land Nordhein Westfalen (case 14/83) [1984] ECR 1891;
  [1986] 2 CMLR 430 .... 7, 39, 118, 220, 230, 249, 250, 252
Von Kempis v Geldof (cass civ) [1976] 2 CMLR 152; [1976] Dalbz Jur 33   262
Wachauf v Bundeamt fur Ernahrung und Forstwirstchaft (case 5/88) [1989] ECR 2609;
  [1991] 1 CMLR 328 .... 27, 232, 242
Walrave and Koch v Association Union Cycliste Internationale (case 36/74) [1974]
  ECR 1405; [1975] 1 CMLR 320   69
Watson and Belmann (case 118/75) [1976] ECR 1185; [1976] 2 CMLR 552 .... 69, 243
Webb (case 279/80) [1981] ECR 3305; [1982] 1 CMLR 719   123
Worringham and Humphreys v Lloyd's Bank (case 69/80) [1981] ECR 767; [1981]
  2 CMLR 1   112
X v UK (case 5124/71) ECHR 135   200
Zuckerfabrik Suderdithmarschen AG (joined cases C-143/88, C-92/89) (unreported
  judgment, 21 February 1991) 42, 223

Table of Statutes

EC PRIMARY LEGISLATION
European Coal and Steel Community 1951 Treaty (ECSC Treaty)
art 31 4
   56 79
European Atomic Energy Community 1957 Treaty (Euratom Treaty)
art 2(*a*) 79
arts 4–11 79
art 136 4
European Economic Community 1957 Treaty (EEC Treaty)
art 2 .... 70, 121
   3(*c*) 121
   5 .... 35, 36, 37, 41, 45, 131, 231, 248, 250, 251
   7 .... 53, 56, 62, 63, 85, 86, 89
   8(7) 127
   12 6
arts 30–36 130
art 30 .... 15, 129, 225, 243, 258
   31 258
   34 65
   36 .... 28, 29, 243
   38 60
   41(*a*) 79
arts 48–51 89
art 48 .... 16, 68, 69, 70, 71, 72, 75, 81, 82, 83, 86, 89, 90, 104
   (1) 93, 100
   (2) 68, 93, 101, 102, 104
   (3) 28, 69, 74, 75, 77, 93, 96, 102, 126
   (4) 77, 89, 90, 91, 92, 93, 94, 95, 96, 97, 98, 99, 100, 101, 102, 103, 104, 105, 106
arts 52–58 89
art 52 .... 62, 63, 132
   55 .... 77, 90, 91, 93, 94, 97
   56 .... 124, 126, 128
   (1) 129, 130
   57 127
   58 63
arts 59–66 89
art 59 .... 68, 121, 122, 123, 124, 125, 126, 127, 128, 129, 132
arts 60–66 121
art 60 .... 84, 125, 126
   63 .... 125, 126, 127, 129, 130
   65 130
   66 .... 90, 125, 126, 129, 130
   85 225
   86 .... 15, 225

European Economic Community 1957 Treaty (EEC Treaty)—*contd*
art 90 15
   (3) 15
   100A 15
   113 230
   119 .... 107, 108, 109, 110, 111, 112, 113, 114, 238
   128 .... 79, 85
   130R(4) 22
   130(*f*) 79
      (*q*) 79
   164 .... 4, 26, 48
arts 169–170 232
   169–171 5
art 169 .... 5, 6, 7, 16, 28, 29, 34, 98, 126, 130
   170 .... 5, 6, 7, 29, 34
   171 .... 33, 34
arts 173–176 5
art 173 .... 5, 7, 8, 27, 30
   175 .... 5, 8, 127
   177 .... 5, 6, 7, 16, 27, 34, 130, 231, 232, 249, 251, 268
      (2) 226
      (3) 227
   178 .... 5, 6, 7
   181 6
   184 5
   185 43
   189 .... 29, 37, 247, 248, 249, 250, 251, 252, 265
      (3) 39
   191 265
   210 6
   211 6
   215 .... 6, 46
   221 .... 62, 63
   227 264
   228 .... 3, 5, 28
Act of Accession 1972
   art 2 217
   arts 100–103 53
Act of Accession 1985
   arts 56–59 61
   art 56 57
      66 54
   arts 156–164 61
      156–166 54
   art 168(4) 57
   arts 346–353 54
Single European Act 1986 .... 79, 139, 160

OTHER INTERNATIONAL CONVENTIONS

Universal Declaration of Human Rights 1948
   art 11 .... 197, 200
      (2) 194
European Convention of Human Rights 1950
   art 2 80
      (4) 264
      6 41
      (1) 196
      (2) 197, 200
      (3) 197
      7(2) 194

European Convention of Human Rights—*contd*

art 8 .... 162, 277

9 276

10 .... 186, 276

13 41

International Covenant on Civil and Political Rights 1966

art 6 264

9(3) 196

14(7) 200

15.1 194

African Charter on Human and Peoples, Rights

art 7 197

SECONDARY EC LEGISLATION

Directives

Directive 64/221 (OJ 1963 L 117) 76, 126

art 3 74

Directive 68/151 (OJ 1968 L 65/8)

art 11 .... 40, 249, 250, 251, 252

Directive 68/360 (OJ 1968 L 257) 71

art 3 81

4 81

Directive 70/157 228

Directive 71/320 228

Directive 73/148 71

Directive 76/207 (OJ L 39/40) 47, 111, 116

art 2(2) 114, 115, 117

(3) 114, 115

3(1) 117

4(1) 117

5(1) 115, 116, 118

6 118

Directive 77/249 (OJ 1978 L 17) 122

art 5 122

Directive 79/7 (OJ 1979 L 6/24) 115, 119, 253

art 4(1) 119, 120, 254

Directive 80/987 (L 283) 43, 44

Directive 85/374 (OJ 1985 L 210/29) 252, 253

Directive 90/366 (OJ 1990 L 180/30) 84

Regulations

Regulation 1612/68 (OJ 1968 L 257) 71, 72, 83

art 3(1) 73

7(2) 81, 86, 87

(3) 81

10 .... 71, 83

12 .... 83, 87, 88

Regulation 1251/70 (OJ 1970 L 142)

art 1 81

2 81

7 81

Regulation 2170/70 (OJ 1970 L 236/1) 53

Regulation 1408/71 (OJ 1971 L 149) 84

Regulation 574/72 (OJ 1972 L 74) 84, 98

Regulation 101/76 (OJ 1976 L 20/19) 52, 53, 56, 61

Regulation 170/83 (OJ 1983 L 24/1) 53, 59, 61, 62, 64

art 8(3) 54

Regulation 2908/83 (OJ 1983 L 290/1) 61

Regulation 1914/87 (OJ 1987 L 183/5) 43

IRELAND

CONSTITUTION

Constitution of Saorstat Éireann
art 2 145
Constitution of Ireland 1937 (*Bunreacht na hÉireann*)
art 1 146
2 .... 145, 146
3 145
6 146
6.1 145
6.2 145
15 146
.4 169
.5 193
18 139
26 .... 146, 147, 151, 152, 155, 169, 170
.2 171
28 .... 138, 151
.3 138
29.1.3 241
.4.3 .... 229, 231
.6 233
30 138
34 .... 146, 155, 240
.3.1 141
.4.3 201
36.3.3 .... 170, 171
38.1 .... 198, 199
.5 215
40 .... 140, 147, 238
.1 237
.3 .... 140, 141, 142, 148, 186, 187, 198
.3.1 .... 182, 190
.3.2 182
.4 198
.6.1(*i*) 185, 186, 187, 188, 190
43 148
.1 148
44.1 139
46 137
50 .... 169, 174, 175
.1 215
51 .... 137, 138
58 145
Constitutional First Amendment Act 1941 138
Second Amendment Act 1941 138
Third Amendent Act 1972 139
Fourth Amendment Act 1973 139
Fifth Amendment Act 1973 139
Sixth Amendment Act 1979 139
Seventh Amendment Act 1979 139
Eighth Amendment Act 1983 139
Ninth Amendment Act 1984 139
Tenth Amendment Act 1987 139

LEGISLATION

Broadcasting Authority Act 1960 (no 10 of 1960)
s 31 187
(1) 205

Broadcasting Authority (Amendment) Act 1976 (no 37 of 1976)
s 16 205
Censorship of Publications Act 1929 (no 21 of 1929)
s 6 191
Censorship of Publications Act 1946 (no 1 of 1946)
Children Act 1908
Part V 205
Criminal Justice (Legal Aid) Act 1962 198
Criminal Procedure Act 1967 (no 12 of 1967)
s 18 202
Courts of Justice Act 1936 (no 48 of 1936)
s 62 .... 201, 202
Courts Act 1988 (no 2 of 1988)
s 1(3) 198
Criminal Justice Act 1951 (no 2 of 1951)
s 2(2)(*a*)(ii) 210
Criminal Justice (Legal Aid) Act 1962 (no 12 1962) 203
Emergencies Powers Act 1976 (no 33 of 1976) 138
Fisheries (Amendment) Act 1983
s 2 55
Fisheries (Consolidation) Act 1959 (no 14 1959)
s 222B 55
Health (Fluoridation of Water Supplies) Act 1960 140
Juries Act (no 23 of 1927) 1927 214
Larcency Act 1916 (6 & 7 Geo V c 60)
s 33(1) 215
Local Government (Planning & Development) Act 1963 (no 28 of 1963)
s 26 208
   (4) 209
   (5) 209
   82(3a) 209
Local Government (Planning & Development) Act 1979 (no 20 of 1976) 209
Offences against the State Act 1939 (no 13 of 1939)
s 34 202
   39(2) 199
   (3) 199, 200
Petty Sessions (Ireland) Act 1851
s 27 176
Pigs Bacon Act 1935 (no 24 of 1935) 176
Pigs Bacon Act 1937 (no 23 of 1937) 176
Statute of Limitations Act 1957 (no 6 of 1957)
s 11(2)(*b*) 172, 173
Trade Disputes Act 1906 .... 175, 176
Unfair Dismissals Act (no 10 of 1977) 1977
s 10(4) 214
Vagrancy Act 1824
s 4 193

Statutory Instruments

Garda Siochana (Discipline) Regulations 1971 (SI 316/1971 201
Sea Fishing Boat Regulations 1985 (SI 289/1986) 65
Rules of the Superior Courts 1986
order 60 207
   84 208
      rule 18(2) 207
         (19) 207
      21(1) 254
      26(4) 211

UNITED KINGDOM

European Communities Act 1972
s 2 .... 220, 250
  (1) 220
  (4) 220
s 3 220
  (1) 220
  (2) 220
s 5 220
  6 220
  7 220
  8 220
  9 220
  11 220
Housing (Homeless Persons) Act 1977 .... 284, 287, 293
s 3 285
Merchant Shipping Act 1988 .... 62, 224
Shops Act 1950
s 47 224
Solicitors Act 1974 292
Special Roads Act 1947
sch 1, paras 14–16 287
Statute of Limitation Act England 172
Supreme Courts Act 1981
s 31 286

BELGIUM

Constitution
art 6 93

FRANCE

Constitution 1958 258
art 3(1) 258
  37(1) 263
  54 269
  55 .... 259, 261, 264, 265, 267
  61(2) 261
  62(2) 261
  89 265
Civil Code
art 544 148
  545 148
Penal Code
art 127 259

NETHERLANDS

Constitution
art 7 276

PORTUGAL

Constitution 1976
art 32.2 196

SCOTLAND

Acquisition of Land (Authorisation Procedure) (Scotland) Act 1947
sch 1, para 15 287
16 287
Court of Session Act 1868
s 91 283
Town and Country Planning (Scotland) Act 1972
s 232 287
233 287

Statutory Instruments

Rules of the Court of Sessions (SI 1985 no 500) 283

SPAIN

Constitution 1978
art 24.2 196
25.1 194

SWITZERLAND

Civil Code
art 1 166

UNITED STATES OF AMERICA

American Convention on Human Rights
art 8(2) 197

Part 1

European Community Law

1 A Constitutional Court for the European Communities

Ole Due

The idea of establishing a separate 'Constitutional Court' was voiced at the very beginning of the Intergovernmental Conference on the creation of a European Political Union. The idea was initially closely linked with the proposal to introduce the 'Subsidiarity-principle' in the Treaties. Clearly, the model was the French 'Conseil Constitutionnel'. By a procedure similar to that prescribed in Article 228, second paragraph, of the EEC Treaty for obtaining an opinion on the compatibility of an international agreement to be concluded by the Community with the provisions of the Treaty, the envisaged court should have jurisdiction to decide, before the entry into force of an act adopted by a Community institution, whether this act was compatible with the said principle. This would certainly create difficult problems of delimitation in respect of the action for annulment on (other) grounds of incompetence.

Even if the idea of setting up a separate court for this specific purpose has been abandoned, the notion of a specialized court for questions of a constitutional character still seems to exert some attraction, in particular when the jurisdictions of the Court of Justice and the new Court of First Instance respectively are discussed.

These ideas have raised a number of questions within the Court of Justice, which until then had not occupied the minds of the Members and which puzzled in particular those coming from Member States without a specialized Constitutional Court: What really is a Constitutional Court? – Does the Court of Justice already exercise the functions of a Constitutional Court? – Should other functions of a constitutional character be added to those already exercised by the Court? – Is it possible to use the constitutional character of the matter in dispute as a criterion for the delimitation of jurisdiction?[1]

It is not my intention to treat all these questions or even to try to give a full answer to those which I shall treat. I shall simply put forward some reflections which may help to clarify the present situation.

I intend first to examine to what extent the Court of Justice exercises functions which are characteristic of a Constitutional Court. I shall then see whether it is possible to isolate such functions from the remainder of the Court's jurisdiction.

---

[1] A number of these questions have been treated by Advocate General Jean Mischo in his article 'Un rôle nouveau pour la Cour de Justice', 342 *Reveue du Marché Commun* (1990), 681 ss.

Does the Court of Justice exercise the functions of a Constitutional Court?

This question immediately poses a problem of definition. What is a constitutional court and what are its functions? It may be possible by means of a comparative study of the rules governing the judicial bodies which, in the different States, are considered to be constitutional courts, to arrive at a relatively precise definition, but such a study clearly falls outside the scope of this modest contribution. However, a minimal condition for qualifying a judicial body as a constitutional court must be that it has jurisdiction to interpret and apply the provisions of the national Constitution or to define and apply the constitutional principles where no written constitution exists.

According to Article 164 of the EEC Treaty and Article 136 of the Euratom Treaty, the terms of which are almost identical to those of Article 31 of the ECSC Treaty: 'The Court of Justice shall ensure that in the interpretation and application of this Treaty the law is observed'. Thus, the general task of the Court of Justice is to interpret and apply the Treaties in conformity with general legal principles. This begs the next question. Do the Treaties form a 'Constitution' for the Communities?

In this respect it is, of course, totally irrelevant to discuss whether the notion of a Constitution should be reserved for national States. The question of establishing a Constitutional court has been raised in relation to the Communities. They do not at present form a federal State, nor will they do so, at least in the short run, as a result of the Union Treaty signed in Maastricht. Thus, it is sufficient to examine whether, in relation to the Communities in their present shape, the Treaties play a role equivalent to that played by a Constitution of a national State.

They certainly do. The Treaties not only define the tasks of the Communities; they also set out the general principles to be respected by the Member States as well as by the Community Institutions; they establish the Institutions and provide them with the powers necessary for performing the tasks of the Communities; they install a complicated system of checks and balances between the Institutions; they define the relations between the Communities, their component States, third countries and international organizations; they regulate the effect of Community acts within the internal legal order of the component State and they authorize the Community Institutions to make rules and take decisions directly binding on the individual subjects of these States. In so doing, they go much further than normal treaties establishing international organizations and they perform, in fact, the same functions as the Constitution of a federal State.

The Treaties thus being, in fact, a Constitution for the Communities, nothing prevents the Court of Justice from being a Constitutional Court. However, it still remains to be seen whether it actually exercises the functions of such a court.

In the absence of the above-mentioned comparative study of the functions normally performed by constitutional courts in national States, I feel confident in following the old saying that an elephant may be hard to define, but that it is relatively easy to recognize the animal when you see it.

I shall therefore in the following try to describe the essential functions attributed to the Court by the Treaties and the manner in which the Court has actually exercised these functions. We shall then see whether, at the end of this description, it is possible to recognize the elephant, that is the Constitutional Court.

Among the three Communities, the EEC is by far the most general in its scope. Therefore, it seems reasonable to limit the examination to the Treaty establishing this Community. Also, going through the provisions of this Treaty enumerating the types of action falling under the jurisdiction of the Court, only the action for breach of the Treaty (Articles 169–171), the actions for annulment and for inactivity (Articles 173–176), the reference for a preliminary ruling (Article 177) and, eventually, the action for compensation in case of non-contractual liability (Article 178) seem to be relevant for the present purpose. The above-mentioned jurisdiction under Article 228, second paragraph, is certainly of a constitutional character, but it is too specific in its purpose and too extraordinary in its application to give a general indication as to the character of the Court.

The fact that one Member State may take another to court for breach of its Treaty obligations (Article 170) in no way distinguishes the Court of Justice from an international court. In principle, this type of action does not confer any constitutional function on the Court of Justice. It is more unusual that an Institution of the Community, the Commission, in pursuit of its duty to ensure compliance with the Treaty, may institute legal proceedings against a Member State before the Court (Article 169). Such cases may certainly raise issues of a constitutional character, for instance questions of distribution of powers. But even this system is known in international law, for instance under the European Convention for the Protection of Human Rights. In any event, natural or legal persons have no standing to bring direct actions against Member States of the Community.

For our purpose, the actions for annulment and for inactivity are of far greater interest. Legal disputes between Community institutions and actions introduced by Member States or even by natural or legal persons against the Council or the Commission may certainly present the Court with issues of a constitutional character, especially when an action for annulment is based on grounds of lack of competence. The Court's jurisdiction under Articles 173 and 175 clearly is part of the system of checks and balances provided for in the Treaty.

The provision on actions of annulment is fashioned after the model of the jurisdiction of national administrative courts. However, it also applies in respect of acts of a legislative character and may therefore give rise to actions comparable to the judicial review of legislation well known from national Constitutional Courts. In this respect, its importance is, nevertheless, considerably reduced by the limitations on the right of action of natural and legal persons. Although bound by the rules of a regulation, such an applicant is only admitted to bring an action for annulment if, in fact, this regulation contains a decision of direct and individual concern to him (Article 173, second paragraph). Only when the regulation is applied by a Community Institution addressing a decision to the natural or legal person, he has an unlimited right to invoke the inapplicability of that regulation (Article 184).

The reference for a preliminary ruling under Article 177 bears some resemblance to the system of references from an ordinary court to the Constitutional Court in some countries. In particular where the question concerns the interpretation of the Treaty or the validity of an act of an Institution, it may present the Court with issues of a constitutional character, but the importance of Article 177 in this respect depends solely on the use which the national courts or tribunals are willing to make of it and on the willingness of the Court of Justice to admit such questions.

The Community having legal personality as well as legal capacity in the Member States (Articles 210 and 211), it may become liable for damages, contractual as well as non-contractual. Except for the existence of an arbitration clause (Article 181), the Court only has jurisdiction in disputes relating to non-contractual damage (Articles 178 and 215, second paragraph). To the extent that the Court admits, under this jurisdiction, actions for compensation for damage caused by the norm-creating activity of the Institutions, even if such an action is brought by a natural or legal person who has no standing under the second paragraph of Article 173 in respect of the act challenged, Article 178 could indirectly form the basis for judicial review of legislative acts. However, this possibility also depends on the factual behaviour of the Court of Justice.

Thus, during the textual examination of the Treaty provisions on the jurisdiction of the Court, one occasionally catches a glimpse of what may be a pachyderm hiding in the forest. Whether it is possible to bring the animal into sight depends, however, on the use actually made of the different types of action.

In this respect, the most interesting object for examination is the way in which the Court has handled the limitations on the right to bring actions which may present it with issues of a constitutional character.

As we have seen, the Treaty does not provide for any action brought before the Court by a natural or legal person against a Member State for breach of the Treaty or of acts emanating from a Community Institution. Nevertheless, such a person may have a vital interest in being able to force the national authorities to respect the obligations imposed on the Member State by the Treaty or by such acts.

This problem was first squarely presented to the Court by the Dutch Tariefcommissie in the case *van Gend en Loos* from 1962.[2] A modification of the Benelux customs tariff possibly violated the stand-still provision of Article 12 of the Treaty, but this provision clearly was addressed to the Member States. The question was whether it not only created obligations for the Member States but also conferred rights upon individuals like the applicant firm in the main proceedings, rights which the national courts had the duty to protect. The answer to this question was by no means obvious. Some of the Member States held the dualist view of the relationship between international Treaties and the internal legal order, others were partisans of the monist perspective. The three Governments who presented written observations to the Court took the view that the authors of the Treaty had not intended to create individual rights as against the Member States and that a possible violation of Article 12 could therefore only be established by an action under Article 169 or 170. The Court, however, decided otherwise. It thereby stressed that the Treaty establishing the Community was no ordinary international treaty and, at the same time, made the citizens of the Community and the individual firms as well as the national courts and tribunals allies of the Commission and of the Court in their task of surveying the application of the Treaty by the Member States.

Since then, the case-law of the Court has developed to a point where every

---

[2] Case 26/62, [1963] ECR 1.

Treaty provision imposing obligations on the Member States which are unconditional and sufficiently precise to be directly implemented by the national authorities, may be relied upon by individuals and must be applied by the national courts and tribunals.

The control thus imposed on the national jurisdictions could, of course, not be completely effective, unless Community law was given precedence over conflicting national rules. This was done expressly by the Court in its preliminary judgment in the case *Costa v ENEL* from 1964[3] and even more precisely in its *Simmenthal* judgment from 1978.[4] According to this case-law, confirmed by numerous later judgments, any Community provision having direct effect in the internal legal order of the Member States automatically supersedes all existing national rules to the contrary and prevents any later national legislation from taking effect contrary to the Community provision.

Later judgments have even conceded the power of national jurisdictions to control the implementation of directives although, by definition, their provisions find no direct application in the normal sense of this expression. Unconditional and sufficiently precise provisions of a directive which has not been duly implemented in a Member State, may be invoked before the national jurisdiction by an individual citizen or firm[5] and even such directives with no provisions of this kind impose the duty on national authorities, courts and tribunals included, to achieve, within the scope of the powers conferred on them by national law, the result aimed at by the directive.[6]

Thus the Court has found a remedy for the lack of standing of individuals to bring direct actions before the Court against a Member State and it has instituted, in close collaboration with the jurisdictions of the Member States, a judicial control of the conformity of national law with Community law which supplements the control provided for in Articles 169 and 170 of the Treaty and which, in practice, has provided it with the opportunity to decide a great number of important issues concerning this relationship, one which clearly is of a constitutional character.

Turning to the actions for annulment or inactivity, we find that the Court has applied strictly the limitations on the right of the individual to bring such actions in respect of acts of a legislative character.[7] On the contrary, the Court has considered actions for compensation as a completely autonomous type of action, which is in no way dependent on the right of the individual to apply for annulment of the act having caused the eventual damage.[8] In the same way, the Court has not declared inadmissible any of the many preliminary questions put to it concerning the validity of Community Acts of a legislative character. Thus, the Court has judicially reviewed such acts on the basis of Articles 177 and 178, thereby providing a remedy for the absence of such an action under the second paragraph of Article 173. At the same time, the Court

---

[3] Case 6/64, [1964] ECR 585.
[4] Case 106/77, [1978] ECR 630.
[5] See, for instance, judgment in Case 8/81, *Becker* [1982] ECR 53.
[6] Case 14/83, *von Colson and Kamann* [1984] ECR 1891, and Case C-106/89, *Marleasing* [1990] ECR I-4135.
[7] Case 307/81, *Alusuisse Italia SpA* [1982] ECR 3463 and Case 134/74, *Holtz and Willemsen* [1974] ECR 1.
[8] Case 4/69, *Lütticke GmbH* [1971] ECR 325 and Case 5/71, *Aktien-Zuckerfabrik Schöppenstedt* [1971] ECR 975. See also, Joined Cases 197–200, 243, 245 and 247/80, *Ludwigshafener Walzmühle* [1981] ECR 3211.

has made provision for a filter either through the national courts or tribunals or through the requirement that damage be caused by the act.

Such judicial review goes further than would be expected when looking at the grounds for annulment enumerated in Article 173. This is the consequence of the case-law of the Court concerning the protection of the fundamental rights of the individual.

The principle of precedence prevents national courts from measuring Community rules with the yardstick of the fundamental rights expressed in the national Constitutions. On the other hand, except for provisions prohibiting discrimination, the Treaty itself does not set out fundamental rights to be respected by the Community institutions in their legislative and executive activities. Therefore, the Court of Justice has undertaken to ensure the respect by Community institutions as well as by Member States in areas regulated by Community law, of the fundamental rights of the individual on the basis of the common constitutional traditions of the Member States and of the international agreements to which all the Member States are parties. In this way, the Court has been able to exercise a full judicial review comparable to that carried out by the Constitutional Court of a Federal State.[9]

As already mentioned, articles 173 and 175 form part of the system of checks and balances between the Community institutions and between these institutions and the Member States. There are, however, loopholes in this system as provided for by the Treaty. Thus, contrary to the ECSC Treaty, Article 173 does not provide for actions against acts of the Parliament. On the other hand, the Parliament is not mentioned among the so-called 'privileged applicants' in the first paragraph of Article 173, and the second paragraph conferring a limited right of action on natural and legal persons is ill-suited to be applied to this institution.

However, also in these respects the Court has found a remedy to the deficiencies of the Treaty text. Recalling the extension of the powers vested in the Parliament, which has taken place since the initial Treaty, and stressing the need for a complete judicial protection within the Community, the Court has admitted actions for annulment against acts of the Parliament capable of affecting the legal position of third parties.[10] In the same way, this time basing itself on the function of the Court as arbiter between the other institutions in order to safeguard the system of checks and balances, the Court has admitted actions brought by the Parliament for the annulment of acts adopted in violation of the rights to be consulted or to cooperate in the legislative process, which the Treaty has conferred on the Parliament.[11]

It is possible to conclude from this short examination of the case law that the Court of Justice has found ways and means for filling the gaps in the judicial system of the Treaty text so as to provide full judicial protection of Member States, Community institutions and individuals against encroachment upon their rights and to offer opportunities for the Court to decide on practically any issue of a constitutional character which may arise in a Community context. Without any doubt, the Court exercises the functions of a Constitutional Court for the Communities.

[9] See, for instance, Case 44/79, *Hauer* [1979] ECR 3727.
[10] Case 294/83, '*Les Verts*' *v Parliament* [1986] ECR 1339 and Case 34/86, *Council v Parliament* [1986] ECR 2155.
[11] Case 70/88, *Parliament v Council* ('*Post Chernobyl*') [1990] ECR I–2041.

So the Court has itself brought the elephant into full view – with trunk, tusks and big flapping ears. A further examination of the case law in order to see how the functions have been exercised in order to decide issues of substance would show that the elephant is a lively one, sometimes even aggressive. However, such an examination falls clearly outside the scope of this contribution. Besides, the so-called 'judicial activism' of the Court has been widely commentated upon in the legal literature, highly praised or criticised as the case may be.

Is it possible to use the constitutional character of a case as criterion for division of jurisdiction?

Seen in relation to the total number of cases brought before the Court of Justice, the amount of constitutional issues to be decided in these cases is surprisingly high. One of the explanations certainly is the novelty of the Communities. Their legal system is still very much a system under creation and there are few comparable systems from which legal experiences may be drawn. Another explanation is that the Community system contains many areas of tension and that it does not always provide efficient political procedures for relieving the tension. When negotiations drag on without any political solution in sight, it is tempting to bring the matter before the Court if the Treaty, completed by the case law of the Court, offers a type of action which makes it possible to arrive at a legal solution. In this respect, the Court certainly is the victim of its own success.

All the types of actions mentioned above may present issues of a constitutional character although the aspect of these issues differs. Actions for breach of Treaty obligations may raise questions concerning the distribution of power between the Communities and the Member States. So do actions for annulment brought by Member States, while such actions brought by individuals and actions for compensation more often concern the respect by the institutions of fundamental rights. Actions for annulment or for inactivity brought by a Community institution nearly always raise questions of principle relating to the balance of power between the institutions. Finally, preliminary questions may raise all types of constitutional issues, but more especially problems concerning the relationship between Community law and national law. Therefore, a division of jurisdiction based on the constitutional character of the case will not coincide with a division based on the type of action.

Neither can an attempt to isolate cases of a constitutional character be based on the area of Community law giving rise to the dispute. Even sectors of Community law which in general only generate trivial cases to be solved by the application of well established criteria to the particular facts may occasionally give rise to problems of a clearly constitutional nature. So, for instance, the customs classification of goods,[12] the settling of accounts of the Agricultural Fund[13] or the control of other expenses partially financed by the Community.[14]

That the nature and object of the main proceedings giving rise to a preliminary question cannot offer a reliable criterion in this respect is clearly

---

[12] Case C–231/89, *Gmurzynska-Bscher* [1990] ECR I–4003.
[13] Case C–342/89, *Germany v Commission* – judgment of 17 October 1991, not yet reported in ECR.
[14] Case C–303/90, *France v Commission* – judgment of 13 November 1991, not yet reported in ECR.

shown, for instance, by the *Costa v ENEL* case,[15] where the object of the action brought before the Italian *Praetore* was the payment of a minimal electricity bill.

Thus, if cases raising issues of a constitutional character have to be isolated from other cases, this can only be done on a case by case basis after an examination of the merits of each particular case.

For direct actions, such an examination can only be carried out at the end of the written procedure. In the case of references for a preliminary ruling, the wording of the questions should, in principle, provide a sufficient basis for the examination. However, the national judge normally drafts his questions with the sole purpose of obtaining the information necessary for deciding the particular case pending before him. He may therefore overlook that, in Community law, his question forms part of a context raising a general problem of a constitutional character. Quite often, this problem is first spotted by the Commission or by a Member State presenting observations to the Court. It even happens, in direct actions as well as in the case of references for a preliminary ruling, that the real nature of the problem only emerges at the oral hearing or even during the drafting of the opinion by the Advocate General or during the discussion between the judges – with the result that the oral hearing has to be reopened.[16]

If it is deemed desirable that the constitutional character of a case be used as a criterion for the division of jurisdiction between judicial bodies in the Community system, it could hardly be done in any other way than by introducing a system of references from the other bodies to the Court of Justice, a system like that known from national constitutional courts. However, at the present stage of development of Community law, the number of references will be much higher, in relation to the total number of cases introduced before the Community judiciary, than is the case in any national legal system.

In conclusion, the Community system seems to be far from ripe for the installation of a specialized Constitutional Court. It is better served by the present two-tier system, where the division of jurisdiction is based on other and more simple criteria and where the necessary safeguard is provided by the right of appeal on points of law in general.

Also in this respect it is hardly worth elaborating an abstract definition of the elephant; it is sufficient to handle it, when it actually comes into view.

---

[15] Case 6/64, [1964] ECR 585.
[16] See, for instance, Case C–2/90, *Commission v Belgium*, pending, and Case 130/87, *Retter* [1989] ECR 865.

2 Joining the Threads: the Influences Creating a European Union

Peter D. Sutherland

The considerable debate, in the United Kingdom in particular, on the issue of the erosion of national sovereignty during the period leading up to the Maastricht Conferences at least had the positive value of laying to rest the argument that the process of European integration is being conducted as a clandestine operation. Looking back over the last forty years it is fair to say that if there was inadequate public debate on the evolution of the European Community this was because most national politicians (and indeed lawyers) chose to ignore what was obviously happening.

In constitutional terms what has been achieved during those forty years has been quite remarkable – particularly as the original treaties lacked many of the essential attributes of a constitution. They did not, for an example, provide real fiscal powers or an adequate federal executive structure. In this they have been compared to the Articles of Confederation of the original thirteen states of the United States.[1] However whatever their deficiencies the treaties did create an entity which whilst less than a federation was something more than simply intergovernmental association of states – the neologism 'supranational' has been appropriately used to describe it. The potential for the evolutionary development of the Community's supranational character was to be found primarily in the parts of the treaties dealing with the legal and judicial system. On the other hand the area of final political decision-making, and the structures to accommodate that decision-making, were essentially intergovernmental in that the Council of Ministers that ultimately adopts legislation is an institution which in the main serves to co-ordinate a co-operative process between the Member States.[2]

The treaties have gradually assumed a constitutional character largely through the interpretative process to which they have been subjected.[3] However the 'constitutionalisation' of the treaties did not happen automatically nor did it occur in a political vacuum. While it required an activist judiciary to develop the authority of the treaties as a higher law[4] that judiciary could only

[1] Cappelletti and Golay. *Judicial Branch in the Federal and Transnational Union:* European University Institute p. 307.
[2] J. Weiler *The Community System: The Dual Character of Supranationalism* IYB Eur. p. 267, 271–273 (1981)).
[3] Hartley *Federalism Courts and legal Systems: the Emerging Constitution of the European Community*. The American Journal of Comparative Law 1986 vol s4 p. 231.
[4] Cappelletti and Golay *supra* p. 309.

have adopted and maintained its interpretative approach with a minimum of political consent. The relationship between the ebb and flow of politics and the development of constitutional jurisprudence has been of central importance to the process of integration.

The first and one of the great presidents of the European Commission Walter Halstein commonly referred to the fact that the Community did not have divisions; it could only be sustained by respect for the rule of law. This respect has been won by a combination of factors. The first and most important of these was the broad political acceptance by the peoples of Europe that the Community necessarily involved an entirely new type of relationship between states. In the second place the pace and nature of judicial innovation by the European Court of Justice would have to be politically astute and carefully modulated to the tempo of changing political realities without nonetheless compromising on central principles. These realities were influenced by a number of political movements which assisted in establishing an environment where dramatic constitutional advance was attainable.

It is clear that even though the political protagonists of a more united Europe saw separate routes leading to their objective very few recognised the role that the European Court of Justice could and would play. Even the federalist Altiero Spinelli constantly underestimated the role the court could play.

Spinelli had of course indicated his desire for a new European order even before the end of World War II and was to remain a committed federalist for nearly 50 years. A primary influence on his thinking were the essays by British federalists that he read in 1939 together with those of Einaudi that had been published in Corriere della Sera at the end of 1918. (Einaudi was later to play a crucial role in Italy as President of the Republic in the enactment of the Treaty of Paris). None of these focussed however on the judicial influence on federal development.

It is instructive today to read the *Ventotene Manifesto* which was written by Spinelli and Ernesto Rossi whilst in captivity in 1941/42.[5] They concluded then that the real problem facing the organisation of international relationships was that 'the absolute sovereignty of national states had led to the desire of each of them to dominate since each felt threatened by the strength of the others' and that only the creation of a supranational entity could provide a solution. Another passage from the Manifesto indicates the contemporary relevance of their thinking: 'The multiple problems which today poison international life on the continent have proved insoluble: tracing boundaries through areas inhabited by mixed populations, defence of alien minorities, seaports for landlocked countries, the Balkan questions, the Irish problem and so on. All matters which would find easy solutions in the European Federation just as corresponding problems suffered by the small states which became part of a vaster national unity, lost their harshness as they were turned into problems of realtionships between various provinces'. Today there might be many more who would accept the essential thesis that nationalist and ethnic conflict can only be effectively restrained under some form of constitutional supranational umbrella and whilst the solutions may not be 'easily found' even under such an umbrella they are at least conceivable whereas otherwise often they are not.

---

[5] Published by the Altiero Spinelli Institute for Federalist Studies, Ventotene Italy.

Spinelli constantly sought to enhance the supranational character of the Community through institutional reform but that reform was envisaged primarily in the area of decision-making rather than in 'normative supranationalism' (as Weiler describes the judicial process). Certainly the initiative taken by Spinelli in June 1980 to relaunch the process of fundamental constitutional reform, and which set much of the agenda for the debates which were to follow, was not focussed on the Community legal system's role. For Spinelli institutional reform and the attempt to achieve European Union were 'one and the same thing'[6] but that institutional reform was directed primarily at enhancing the powers of the Parliament and Commission. This is evident not merely from the draft Treaty for European Union (proposed by the European Parliament in 1984) but also from Spinelli's influence on the paper prepared by the European Commission prior to the Tindemans Report of 1976.

The European Parliament, particularly through its institutional Affairs Committee (chaired in the first half of the '80s by Spinelli), has remained an essentially federalist voice in the ongoing debate on Community constitutional reform but again has been less interested in the development of the Community legal system than might have been expected. Furthermore the Commission, which is acutely aware of Parliaments' concerns, has been less conscious of the need to address the central constitutional issue of the effectiveness and enforcement of the law. The creation of a Court of First Instance represented only a minimal reaction to the real needs and demands of the European Court of Justice itself.

Since the death of Spinelli the pure federalist position has had no comparable authoritative or forceful individual at its head but there has been an increasingly catholic, informed and numerous representation of the movement within the European Parliament. When one recalls that Spinelli's circular of June 1980 relaunching the European Union debate only elicited responses from eight MEPs and compares that situation to the current interest amongst MEPs in institutional affairs generally the attitudinal changes wrought in a decade are clearly demonstrated.

A second force working towards integration might be described as the functionalists (following the theory formulated by Mitrany in 1946).[7] The most forceful advocate of this approach was Jean Monnet whose pragmatism and rejection of utopian visions led him into some conflict with Spinelli. The admirable study of the two conflicting political approaches to the building of Europe contained in *'Federalism and European Union'* by Michael Burgess demonstrates in fact their complementarity.[8] As Burgess points out while 'Monnet and Spinelli are usually depicted as opposing forces in the quest for close union yet, though their paths diverged en route, in their separate journeys they travelled towards the same destination'.

Monnet was almost Anglo-Saxon in his rejection of a visionary approach to the development of the Community. His memoirs attest to his distrust of 'general ideas' and his concern with 'practical things'.[9] In a sense Monnet, whose primary objective was peace, started his rationalisation from a different point to most federalists or constitutional lawyers. He looked firstly at the

---

[6] Spinelli *The European Adventure* p. 176.
[7] D. Mitrany *A Working Peace System* Royal Institute for International Affairs.
[8] Michael Burgess *Federalism and European Union. Political Ideas, Influences and Strategies in the European Community 1972–1987.* Routledge 1989.
[9] J. Monnet *Memoirs.* Doubleday, New York 1978, p. 519.

activities of man which cause conflict and he sought then to create a new environment or context in which to place those activities in order to reduce tension. He recognised that problem solving in itself was not an answer to the need for conflict resolution. Plainly economic integration was a primary means whereby the context of relationships could be so altered so as to avoid conflict and, in consequence, he looked to this area first rather than to a constitutional theory.

Monnet's functionalism is perhaps better described as incremental federalism. He believed in moving forward in small steps and in taking them in a manner that did not directly confront entrenched views on national sovereignty except where it was absolutely unavoidable. He recognised of course that institutional development would be a vital part of this process but essentially he believed in permitting the institutions to grow out of change rather than to precipitate change. His rejection of Adenaur's approach in March 1950 to Franco–German union and later his scepticism about the proposed Defence Union may be cited in evidence of his caution. When Monnet had to confront national sovereignty he sought to do so in limited and clearly defined circumstances and thus to gradually build a relationship between peoples that would open the door to further progress. Thus he wrote of a 'de facto solidarity from which a federation would gradually emerge' and of the 'pragmatic method . . . leading to a federation'. His basic political instincts were often proved to be quite right.

In reality the difference between the functionalist approach of Monnet and the federalist approach of Spinelli appears to be less profound than many of their stated views might suggest. Undoubtedly they did emphasise different methods of development but fundamentally they both recognised the essential debate as being that between the intergovernmentalists and those who sought the development of supranational power.

No study of the political evolution of the United States could ignore, as a central theme, the influence of the Supreme Court in shaping the federal state. Similarly no one looking at the EC today could ignore the decisive influence of the European Court of Justice. Just as the principles of the powers of judicial review enunciated in *Madison v Marbury* created a debate about government by the judiciary that has persisted into this century in the United States (particularly through Boudin's attack in 1932) so also in the European Community one may hear similar criticisms often from surprising quarters. This is particularly the case in France where the courts have been viewed with some suspicion since the French Revolution. Indeed the *Conseil d'Etat* only finally conceded the principle of the supremacy of Community law in 1989.[10]

The doctrines of pre-emption, supremacy of community law and direct effect have arguably done more to transform the EC into a supranational power than anything done legislatively since its foundation. Furthermore 'the competences of the Community have been extending in a material sense through the judicial doctrine of implied powers'.[11] But there has been a perceptible connection, it seems to me, between the periods of significant judicial activism in pushing out the boundaries of Community authority and the periods when the political momentum for increasing integration has been most evident.

---

[10] L'arrêt du 20 Octobre 1989, Nicolo. req. 108243. Conseil d'Etat Francais.
[11] *Integration Through Law*. European University Institute vol 1 book 1 p. 34.

Thus during the period since 1985 the European Court of Justice has made a number of decisions which have potentially enormous implications. Take for an example its decision on Article 90 of the Treaty of Rome in the *Terminal Equipment* case.[12] Article 90 forbids Member States from adopting or maintaining in force measures contrary to the Treaty in regard to public undertakings and undertakings granted special or exclusive rights. The Commission claimed the rights under Article 90(3) to issue a directive to the Member States to ensure the application of Article 90 in the telecommunications field and this right was upheld. This has been viewed in some quarters as creating a legislative power for the Commission although it does nothing of the sort. It has however opened up a really formidable legal mechanism with which the Commission may face Member States with their responsibilities. (The fact that, for the moment, the Commission has preferred not to use Article 90(30) to introduce competition into the energy sector and to use Article 100A instead is a measure of the political sensitivity of the use of Article 90(3)). There have been other recent cases concerning Article 90. In the Port of Genoa case the Court of Justice indicated that Article 90 in combination with Article 30 on free movement of goods, Article 48 on the prohibition of discrimination against workers on grounds of nationality and Article 86 on abuses of a dominant position create rights for individuals which national courts must protect.[13] However this area is only one where the supranational character of the Community has been reinforced. One may look also at the implications of the *Factortame* case on the obligation to provide effective interim protection of putative rights under Community law when no such protection is available under national law to see how hallowed principles of great significance have been publicly confronted.[14]

It has been postulated that one reason why the Court of Justice in the early days was able to successfully develop its authority and that of the Commission was the belief amongst the intergovernmentalists that the Member States ultimately could protect their interests through the Council. They therefore felt no absolute need to challenge the Court of Justice. In other words what was there to fear when the Member States could simply stop the Court in its tracks by denying it the legislation needed to provide a base for its action?' Whatever about the validity of this argument in the era prior to the Single European Act it is markedly less valid today. Apart from the fact that majority voting has been introduced over a far wider area the use of the veto under the Luxembourg Accord of 1966 has become politically more difficult. Furthermore the Commission has become significantly more willing to seek expansive interpretations of the original treaty in order to force Member States to comply with the fundamental objectives of the Community. Thus in the area of competition policy the threat of direct action under the Treaty acted as one element in bringing the Council to agree on the first liberalisation package on air transport in 1986.

Joseph Weiler, who has written extensively on the subject, has accurately commented that the Court has gone much further than simply playing an

---

[12] Case C–202/88, *France v Commission*, 19 March 1991 unreported ('the terminal equipment case').
[13] Case 179/90, *Merci Convenzionali Porto di Genova SpA v Siderurgica Gabrielli SpA*, 10 December 1991 unreported.
[14] Case C–213/89, *Factortame v Sec of State for Transport* [1982] 2 WLR; [1990] ECR I-2433.

'instrumental–technical role'. It is playing a vital part in the constitutional evolution of the Community 'and has a very immediate connection with its political philosophy'. In a sense this wider role has been imposed on the Court by the Treaties but it is not without risk. The initial reaction to the principle of supremacy of Community law by the *Conseil d'Etat* previously mentioned emphasises the point. Had any Member State absolutely and continuously rejected the principle then the whole edifice would have been threatened. Fortunately this fear has for the moment at least receded.

Of course the passage of time has reinforced the authority of the Court. This re-inforcement has above all been assisted by the careful development of jurisprudence in the interpretation and application of Article 177 which has created a necessary nexus between the national courts and the Community institutions. This connection in effect creates the type of unitary system of law that distinguishes the Community supranational legal order from that of international law and allows it to develop. Above all however the involvement of national courts, under a measure of direction in interpretation from Luxembourg, has imbued Community law with the authority established by the national legal systems and with 'the habit of obedience' that attaches to those systems. Recent case law on issues such as the right of individuals to claim damages from Member States for failure to transpose Community law into municipal legislation adds to this process of legal integration and significantly adds to the limited sanction of Article 169 proceedings.

The European Court of Justice of course usually acts as a result of a step being taken by the Commission through the exercise of its exclusive power of initiative or in implementing the law. As a quasi political body the Commission should be sensitive to the political limits at any given time of Community action and this sensitivity should act as a factor that reduces the risk of real conflict developing between the Member States and the European Court of Justice. However sometimes the risk of conflict appears to have induced paralysis on the part of the Commission. As guardian of the treaties the Commission has a responsibility to enforce the law. In retaining a principled discretion on when and whether it ought to act it ought not constantly take the easy option of compromise. Increasingly it does not.

So in looking at the various influences that have shaped the evolution of a disparate and divided Europe to a more integrated one certain broad conclusions may be drawn. First it may be said that the federalist and functionalist approaches to increasing integration have each contributed positively to developing the supranational character of the Community inter alia through the Court of Justice. The functionalists effectively gave Europe, through the original treaties, a framework which enabled the first tentative steps to be taken towards creating a supranational Europe. Whilst an analysis of the original intent of the framers of the Treaty of Rome fails to establish a full appreciation of how the interpretation of the treaties by the European Court of Justice would develop, the principle that the framers intended the effective implementation of the words agreed can hardly be disputed. One suspects that Monnet today would have been happy with what has been achieved through the 'constitutionalisation' process. It would be seen by him as changing the context of relationships in a way that increasingly presents opportunities for the further and deeper integration that is required to enable the Community to withstand the shock of a significant number of new members. Likewise the federalists have through their vision and ambition pushed out the limits of debate to horizons far beyond those contemplated by more pragmatic politicians concerned with day to day realities. The momentum for change stimulated by the federalists has made it conceivable to imagine the limited constitutional changes that have come from the various intergovernmental conferences since the mid '80s. Furthermore the European Court of Justice and the Commission could only have made the remarkable progress that has been made in asserting and defending the Community interest against vested national interests with a minimum of real consent. The sometimes grudging acquiescence in the sovereignty of the Community has been hard won. It has been won by the increasing respect for the fairness and legitimacy of the decision-making processes and for the European Court of Justice itself. Above all it has been won by the increasing conviction of ordinary Europeans that only through a sharing of sovereignty can we avoid constantly reliving the worst moments of our history.

3 Subsidiarity – A Busted Flush?

Lord Mackenzie-Stuart

It is not to be assumed that all readers of *Festschriften* are necessarily committed players of poker. A 'Busted Flush' describes the situation where an initially promising hand is rendered worthless by the turn of the cards. The object of this note is to suggest that the promising concept, or apparently promising, concept of subsidiarity has been reduced to little value by the approach of the current Intergovernmental Conference on Political Union.

Two preliminary points must be made. First, it is by no means certain that the Conference will have completed its work by the time these words appear in print, still less that the appropriate treaty will have been signed. It may thus be that in the end some or all of this note will have been superseded by a change of substance. Secondly, it has been remarkably difficult to ascertain in precise terms the proposals under consideration by the Intergovernmental Conference. Confidentiality cannot be the problem since there has been no shortage of nebulous statements in the Press but the release of a text which can be the object of serious study is another matter altogether. Leaving aside the abortive Dutch proposals which were rejected by a meeting of the Foreign Ministers of the Member States on 30 September, as of the autumn of 1991 the best that is available is the Luxembourg Government text of 20 June 1991 and this is available only through the private enterprise medium of Agence Europe. There is here an aspect of the 'Democratic Deficit' which demands further comment.

The doctrine or principle of subsidiarity is, of course, a short-hand name for the proposition that, in government, decision-making powers should be exercised as close to those affected as may reasonably be possible. That is to say, higher echelons should not legislate, even when they may competently do so, where action by lower echelons is equally competent and more appropriate. It is fashionable to see the origins of this proposition in the Papal Encyclical Letter *Quadragesimo Anno* of 1931 but it is surely much older than that. Indeed, is it more than a self-evident maxim of good government? Without retracing one's steps to Aristotle, as some commentators have done, is it not more apposite to look at the debates leading to the drafting of the American Constitution of 1787 and its subsequent ratification? The essence of the antifederalist argument turned on 'subsidiarity'.

'Within a large territory the various regions would strive against one another, different climates, products, interests, manners, habits, laws, would lead to discord.

How to legislate uniformly for a land so diverse? A law which suited one part might oppress another. Therefore the major functions of government must be exercised at the local or state levels, and a confederation alone would preserve freedom.'[1]

It is also worth observing, since he has received no credit for it, that the then President of the Commission, Lord Jenkins of Hillhead, affirmed in his 1979 Dimbleby lecture, 'You are against unnecessary centralisation and bureaucracy. You want to devolve decision-making wherever you sensibly can.'[2]

This short note, however, is not the place to embark upon a discussion on the history and scope of the principle of subsidiarity. The principle has already been the subject of two interesting and valuable discussion papers produced, respectively, on behalf of the Royal Institute of International Affairs and the Institute of Economic Affairs.[3] It has also been fully discussed in a report by the Select Committee of the House of Lords on the European Communities.[4] It was penetratingly analyzed by Judge Kapteyn in a lecture given in London in November 1990[5] and was the subject of a conference held at Maastricht in March 1991 by the European Institute of Public Administration. At this colloquium papers were presented by M. Jacques Santer, Prime Minister of Luxembourg and President in Office of the Council of Ministers, M. Jacques Delors, President of the Commission, and M. Panayotis Roumeliotis of the European Parliament and a member of the committee, presided over by M. Giscard d'Estaing, which had reported on subsidiarity and allied matters to the Parliament in 1990.[6]

Given this constellation of talent is there anything more that can be said? Inevitably, yes. Not all the authors mentioned speak with the same voice and within the Community and even more outside it events do not stand still.

It is most appropriate, given his distinguished contribution in the field both in Ireland and in Luxembourg, that Judge O'Higgins should be honoured with a volume on the theme of the role of the judge as constitutional interpreter. It is the constitutional aspect of the principle of subsidiarity with which this note is concerned. Can and should subsidiarity be elevated to a constitutional principle? If so, how should it be defined and how may it be enforced?

The principle, as has been said, is widely accepted as a precept of good administration. This being so it is perhaps right that those who legislate for the Community and those who administer it should have the precept firmly before their eyes. As Dr Adonis has put it in his IEA paper:

> 'subsidiarity has a part to play as a slogan for the pursuit of an essentially decentralist rather than a centralist approach. As Jacques Delors put it to the European Parliament in January 1990, subsidiarity should serve as a "constant counterweight to the natural tendency of the centre to accumulate power".'[7]

Dr Adonis continues, however, by arguing strongly that 'it would be a serious

---

[1] Jackson Turner Main *The Antifederalists* New York 1974, p. 129.

[2] Roy Jenkins *A Life at the Centre* London 1991, p. 519.

[3] Marc Wilke and Helen Wallace *Subsidiarity: Approaches to Power-Sharing in the European Community* Chatham House, London, 1990; Andrew Adonis and Andrew Tyrie *Subsidiarity* IEA, London 1990.

[4] Session 1989–90, 27th Report, published 30 October 1990.

[5] *Revue des Affaires Europeennes* No. 2, 1991, p. 35.

[6] Proceedings published by the Institute, '*Subsidiarity: the Challenge of Change*', October 1991.

[7] IEA Discussion Paper, above, p. 5.

error to attempt to convert the slogan into a general legal principle for inclusion in a new Community Treaty'.

Be that as it may, there is little doubt, or so it is suggested, that far too much has been made of the principle. It has been invested with some magical quality and regarded as a sort of Community juju or totem-pole. M. Delors in addressing the College d'Europe at Bruges in October 1989 said that the principle of subsidiarity was:

> 'the inspiration to reconcile that which seemed to many to be irreconcilable: the emergence of a united Europe and fidelity to our own country; the need for a European power equal to the problems of our times and the vital imperative to preserve our motherland and regions'.

Other politicians, denouncing the loss of national sovereignty – itself a much misused word – have found in subsidiarity a prophylactic against the contagion of Brussels. To others, particularly to those from a Member State having a federal structure, subsidiarity is invoked to preserve the rights of the component parts. There has, too, been much comment on the paradox that in the United Kingdom those most enthusiastic in advancing the principle of subsidiarity in the Community are the least keen to see it applied in domestic matters.

It is thus not surprising that in the first published agenda of the Intergovernmental Conference 'subsidiarity' appeared in its own right as a topic to be discussed. What is surprising is that so little has been said, or said publicly, of the principle of subsidiarity as the work of the Intergovernmental Conference progressed but, as the terms of the Luxembourg and Netherlands draft treaties demonstrate, the *Times* went too far when it produced the engaging head-line '"Eurocrats bury a buzz word only a Pope could understand"'.[8] According to the article which followed the difficulty was one of definition.

> 'The treaty drafters have been unable to agree on a clear legal "test" which a court could use to see whether, say, a proposal on minimum animal welfare standards for Europe's zoos violates the principle of subsidiarity by interfering with national responsibilities or not.'

That there were drafting difficulties is not to be questioned. The discussion papers already mentioned and the House of Lords report amply demonstrate how many possible definitions there can be of the principle. At the Maastricht Conference the representatives of the three Community political institutions not only failed to agree among themselves on a definition but no legal definition worth the name emerged. Broadly speaking, however, the possible definitions reduce to a choice between two opposing ideas. The first, which may be described as the necessity test, predicates that the Community will take action only when it is necessary so to do. That is to say, The Community will only act when it is not possible for action to be taken at the level of the Member States or, indeed, at local level. The other, which may be called the effectiveness test, permits the Community to legislate if it can be shown that action is more effective at Community level. Each test, of course, can be and has been expressed in a variety of ways but it is clear that the 'necessity' test is

[8] 23 June 1991.

more restrictive of Community competence than the 'effectiveness' test.

As is well known, the only treaty text which has attempted a definition of subsidiarity is Article 130R(4) of the Treaty of Rome and which was introduced by the Single European Act. The text is as follows—

> 'The Community shall take action relating to the environment to the extent to which the objectives . . . can be attained better at the Community level that at the level of individual Member States'.

Here the test is plainly one of effectiveness. In the Luxembourg text of 20 June we find a refinement. Article 3b reads:—

> 'In the areas which do not fall within its exclusive jurisdiction, the Community shall only take action, in accordance with the principle of subsidiarity, if and insofar as those objectives can be better achieved by the Community than by the Member States acting separately because of the scale or effects of the proposed action.'

The abandoned text put forward by the Netherlands repeated this formula except that it added the word 'only', that is to say it read ' "*Only* if and insofar as those objectives can be better attained . . ." ' It is not clear how this addition was intended to improve the text.

Be it noted that this paragraph does seek to define the principle of subsidiarity which is left as a hanging parenthesis. Moreover, even if an objective can be better achieved at Community level the Community must not take action unless the 'scale or effects' of the proposed action make this necessary. One *or* the other will suffice. The scope for debate in any given instance is enormous.

Taking the Luxembourg text at its face value the Court of Justice may have to face countless challenges – probably for the most part by Member States who have lost the battle within the Council of Ministers – alleging that a Directive or Regulation, or whatever new instrument may be devised, has an objective which can equally well be attained at the level of a Member State and, that even if this be incorrect, the proposed action is warranted by neither its scale nor its effects.

Assuming that such a challenge be mounted how is the dispute to be resolved? It has been suggested by Dr Tyrie[9] that to adjudicate on whether or not a proposal satisfies the subsidiarity test there are three or more 'plausible' solutions. The two which Dr Tyrie lists, the Court apart, are ' "the Council of Ministers, perhaps with some administrative agency to carry some of the work load" ' and some new institution set up specifically to adjudicate on subsidiarity, 'either of "wise men", or of national parliamentarians.' There are serious constitutional objections to both these proposals. If the doctrine of subsidiarity is elevated to a legal principle it is the duty of the Court of Justice under Article 164, and no-one else, to see that the law is observed. Neither of the two treaty drafts, however, suggest that the arbiter should be other than the Court.

The fundamental question remains. Is subsidiarity truly a justiciable question? If the responsibility is thrust upon it no doubt the Court will rise to the occasion. It will not be the first time that the Court has had to make sense, by

---

[9] IEA Discussion Paper, above, p. 27.

interpretation and by extrapolation, of ambiguous and difficult texts. Nonetheless, in the last analysis, 'subsidiarity' reflects a political choice and not a principle of law. Despite accusations in the past of political prejudice, and the last echo has not yet died away, the Court has amply demonstrated its independence of Member State and Community Institution alike. Is it not foolish to give the Court a task which could so easily lay it open to charges, however unfounded they might be, of political motivation? It is not just the reputation of the Court that is at stake. The Court is the cement which holds the Community together. Weaken the Court and the whole structure is in danger.

The House of Lords Select Committee saw the problem with great clarity,

> '"The Committee do not believe that subsidiarity can be used as a precise measure against which to judge legislation. The test of subsidiarity can never be wholly objective or consistent over time – different people regard collective action as more effective than individual action in different circumstances. Properly used, subsidiarity should determine not only whether Community legislation is necessary or appropriate at all, but also the extent to which it should regulate and harmonise national divergences, and how it should be enforced. But to leave legislation open to annulment or revision by the European Court on such subjective grounds would lead to immense confusion and uncertainty in Community law."'

For all these reasons, if the principle of subsidiarity is to find its place in the Treaties let it first be given a workable definition and second and more importantly let it find its proper place – in the Preamble. The principle of subsidiarity is a valuable concept provided that its limitations are clearly understood. It is a political maxim not a legal one. To attempt, as do the current drafts, to transform a political goal into a constitutional imperative is both to devalue a sound principle of administration and to endanger the reputation and status of the Court of Justice. In short, 'A Busted Flush'.

Note
This note was written before the Report of the House of Lords Select Committee on Political Union, Law-making Powers and Procedures (Session 1990–91, 17th Report) and the text of the subsequent debate (Hansard, House of Lords, Monday, 21 October 1991) became available. Fortunately, they strengthen the argument developed above.

Further Note
The version which has now emerged from Maastricht reads as follows:–

> 'In the areas which do not fall within its exclusive jurisdiction' the Community shall take action, in accordance with the principle of subsidiarity, only if and insofar as the objectives of the proposed action cannot be sufficiently achieved by the Member States and can therefore, by reason of the scale or effects of proposed action, be better achieved by the Community.
>
> Any action by the Community shall not go beyond what is necessary to achieve the objectives of the Treaty'.

There is nothing in the Maastricht text to suggest that this Article is not justiciable nor that the Court does not have power to interpret the words quoted. Its task will be an unenviable one. It would appear that the words following 'the principle of subsidiarity' are intended as a definition, although this is not clear. What is new, however, is the addition of the final sentence – 'ruin upon ruin, rout on rout, confusion worse confounded'. Far from having made a choice between the tests of 'effectiveness' and 'necessity' the Court will somehow have to reconcile the two.

4 Is the Court of Justice of the European Communities a Constitutional Court?

F. G. Jacobs

The purpose of this contribution is to examine the extent to which the Court of Justice of the European Communities may properly be considered a constitutional court.[1] I shall begin by identifying some of the fundamental characteristics of a constitutional court. I shall then consider whether, in the light of the functions it performs in the Community system, the Court of Justice can be said to possess those characteristics.

What is a Constitutional Court?

This is not the place for a detailed examination of the general rôle of Constitutional Courts. However, the term 'Constitutional Court' is usually used to designate a specialized tribunal whose jurisdiction is limited to constitutional issues. Perhaps most typically, its tasks include judicial review of legislation to ensure its conformity with the constitution or other fundamental law; and in particular to ensure the observance of fundamental rights. More generally, it may also adjudicate in disputes over the respective powers of the organs of the State. Where, as in a federal system, power is divided between central authorities and those of the component States or regions, the respective limits to the powers of those authorities will also be considered a constitutional issue.

Responsibility for adjudicating on issues such as these, however, is not always conferred on a specialized constitutional court. In the United States, which provides early examples both of a system providing for judicial review of legislation ('constitutional review'), and of a developed federal system, it is significant that no constitutional court in this sense exists. The US Supreme Court may, independently of its constitutional rôle, also act as a final court of appeal in cases which raise no specifically constitutional issues. Indeed that Court has a remarkably wide jurisdiction, being the highest court in the federal system and also having appellate jurisdiction in cases involving federal law that arise in the State courts.

---

[1] See further the contribution of President Due to this volume; J. Mischo, 'Un rôle nouveau pour la Cour de justice?' (1990) RMC 681; J. Temple Lang, 'The development of European Community constitutional law' (1991) 25 *The International lawyer* 455; G. F. Mancini, 'The making of a constitution for Europe' in *The New European Community*, ed. Keohane and Hoffmann, Westview 1991, 177.

In Europe, specialized Constitutional Courts have developed relatively recently, particularly in countries which have emerged from totalitarian régimes. In other countries with written constitutions, such as Ireland, constitutional review is the function of non-specialized courts, although certain courts may have special functions in relation to constitutional review: in Ireland, for example, the Supreme Court has special functions.[2]

In many European countries, however, the compatibility of legislation with the Constitution is not in general susceptible to judicial review. But it should be noted that even in countries which fall within this group, legislation may be subject to judicial review in the Member States of the Community where it is alleged that a provision of national law is incompatible with the EEC Treaty.[3] Thus the EEC Treaty may have a 'constitutional' status in the courts of all the Community's Member States. To anticipate a point which will be developed below, it can be said that, where the courts of the Member States, in reviewing national legislation for compatibility with Community law, apply Community law as interpreted by the Court of Justice, the Court is fulfilling, albeit indirectly, the function of a Constitutional Court.

The jurisdiction of the Court of Justice

In the Community, the Court of Justice is not of course a specialized constitutional court. Its function is broadly described in Article 164 of the EEC Treaty as being to ensure that in the interpretation and application of the Treaty, the law is observed. The various heads of jurisdiction are then spelt out, but the practical effect of the Treaty provisions is to give the Court jurisdiction over virtually all questions of Community law. In some circumstances, however, that jurisdiction is shared with the national courts of the Member States. It is clear that disputes which the Court of Justice has jurisdiction to hear do not all raise issues of a constitutional nature, even if that term is used very broadly. The EEC Treaty, the most far-reaching of the founding treaties, certainly has some aspects of a Constitution: in particular, it allocates powers between the Community and its constituent Member States and lays down the conditions under which the legislative powers enjoyed by the Community institutions are to be exercised. In many respects, however, the Treaty does not have the character of a constitution. First, it does not contain many of the general provisions usually found in national Constitutions. In particular, although it guarantees particular social and economic rights, such as the right of men and women to equal pay for equal work and the right of workers and the self-employed to move freely between the Member States, the Treaty does not contain a comprehensive catalogue of fundamental rights. Secondly, the Treaty contains many provisions which would not traditionally be regarded as being of a constitutional character, such as substantive rules on competition.

There is therefore no formal criterion for identifying constitutional issues in Community law: it cannot be said, for example, that review of Community or

---

[2] See J. P. Casey, 'The Development of Constitutional Law under Chief Justice O'Higgins', *The Irish Jurist*, 1986, p. 7.

[3] See e.g. in relation to the United Kingdom, the decision of the House of Lords in *R v Secretary of State, ex parte Factortame* [1990] 3 CMLR 375; and in relation to France, the decision of the *Conseil d'Etat* dated 20 October 1989 in the *Nicolo* case, [1990] 1 CMLR 173.

Member State legislation for compatibility with the Treaty is necessarily a jurisdiction of a constitutional type. It should also be noted that judicial review of Member State action for compatibility with Community law does not result in the national measure being struck down, as would normally be the case with constitutional review. Instead, the national authorities, including the national courts, are simply required to draw the appropriate consequences from the Court's ruling and to repeal, in the case of the legislature, or to 'disapply' in the case of the administration and the courts, the contested national measure.

Nor can constitutional issues be identified by reference to the different heads of jurisdiction expressly conferred on the Court. Judicial review of Community action under Article 173 of the Treaty may involve review of a constitutional nature, but it may be confined to review of administrative action; and the principles governing such review are the same in both cases. The same is true of review under Article 177 of the validity of Community action.

All such cases may give rise to 'constitutional' issues, but these often arise incidentally. By way of example, a reference on the interpretation of Community law, which ostensibly raises a pure question of interpretation, may be found to raise the issue of conformity of Community measures, or implementing measures taken by Member States, with fundamental rights.[4] More generally, it might even be said that any question of interpretation of Community law may give rise to the application of fundamental principles which might be regarded as having a constitutional character. Again, from this point of view, it seems to make no difference whether the question is of the interpretation or of the validity of the Community measure. In either case, constitutional principles may be invoked either to render the Community measure invalid or to govern its proper interpretation.

One source of constitutional issues which has proved fruitful in recent years is litigation between the Council, the Commission and the Parliament concerning the determination of their respective powers. Thus the Council has challenged the exercise by the Parliament of its powers over non-compulsory expenditure in the Community budget;[5] more recently, the Council has raised before the Court the long-standing issue whether the Parliament also has any competence in respect of the revenue provisions of the budget.[6] The Parliament for its part has brought proceedings against the Council alleging a failure to act in respect of the common transport policy;[7] and has also challenged Council measures which the Parliament alleges infringed the latter's prerogatives. The Court, having initially denied the Parliament standing under Article 173,[8] more recently accepted a limited standing, despite the absence of any Treaty provision to that effect, where the Parliament's own prerogatives were in issue.[9]

It may be observed that such inter-institutional proceedings are unfamiliar in national legal systems which have no Constitutional Court, but are less novel under, for example, the French and German constitutions, where the *Conseil Constitutionnel* and the *Bundesverfassungsgericht* respectively may be called upon to adjudicate at the instance of parliamentary organs.

[4] See e.g. Case 5/88, *Wachauf v Bundesamt für Ernährung und Forstwirtschaft* [1989] ECR 2609.
[5] Case 34/86, *Council v Parliament* [1986] ECR 2155.
[6] Case C-284/90, *Council v Parliament*, pending before the Court.
[7] Case 13/83, *Parliament v Council* [1985] ECR 1513.
[8] Case 302/87, *Parliament v Council* [1988] ECR 5615.
[9] Case C-70/88, *Parliament v Council*, judgment of 22 May 1990.

Yet, once again, the existence of an inter-institutional case is not necessarily a sign of a truly constitutional issue. The Commission has in recent years brought a number of cases against the Council on the ground that the Council has adopted a measure on the incorrect Treaty basis, an issue which can well be described as constitutional, especially since it may have implications for the rôle of the European Parliament, and for the question whether such a measure can be adopted by majority voting in the Council rather than by unanimity. But other actions between the same parties have related to more mundane matters such as the remuneration of Community officials, matters which will not usually be regarded as having a constitutional dimension.[10] Indeed, identical issues could and do arise in cases brought by officials before the Court of First Instance.[11]

One context in which issues of a constitutional nature are liable to be raised directly is provided by requests under Article 228 of the Treaty for the opinion of the Court on whether an agreement which the Community proposes to conclude with one or more third countries or with an international organization is compatible with the Treaty. That question can be regarded as a form of judicial review of the constitutionality of the agreement. Sometimes, the question also arises in such proceedings whether the Community has exclusive competence to conclude the agreement or whether the agreement falls partly within the competence of the Member States.[12] In that event, the issue of constitutionality goes further and extends to the issue of the division of powers between the Community and the Member States.

Occasionally constitutional issues may arise in proceedings brought against a Member State by the Commission under Article 169 of the Treaty. A striking illustration is provided by a decision in which the Court applied the principle of pre-emption, familiar to lawyers in federal systems and particularly in the United States. In the usual case, pre-emption precludes the States from acting once the central authority has 'occupied the field'. But in a case brought by the Commission against the United Kingdom concerning fishery conservation measures in the North Sea, the Court held that Member States were no longer free to enact conservation measures, even though no Community measures had been taken.[13]

Often, however, issues of the division of powers between the Community and the Member States present themselves less clearly. From one perspective, many questions of Treaty interpretation can be regarded as raising the issue of the balance between the Community and the Member States: this is illustrated by the many cases where Member States seek to justify national measures under the exception clauses of the Treaty, such as Article 36 and Article 48(3). Where the Member States concerned are unsuccessful, these cases result in the Treaty right becoming, in effect, a constitutional right, protected against all conflicting national measures. The principles of direct effect and primacy of Community law give these rights an 'entrenched' status.

Other cases, by contrast, raise very clearly the issue whether a fundamental interest of a Member State should be protected against the incursions of

---

[10] See most recently Case C-301/90, *Commission v Council*, pending before the Court.
[11] Case T-134/89, *Hettrich v Commission*, not yet reported.
[12] See e.g. Opinion 1/78, *International Agreement on Natural Rubber* [1979] ECR 2871.
[13] Case 804/79, *Commission v United Kingdom* [1981] ECR 1045.

Community law: in *R v Thompson*,[14] for example, the Court recognised in the context of Article 36 the fundamental interest of Member States in protecting the right to mint coinage. Similarly, in *Torfaen Borough Council v B & Q plc*[15] the Court acknowledged, again in the context of the free movement of goods, that national rules governing the opening hours of retail premises reflected

> 'certain political and economic choices in so far as their purpose is to ensure that working and non-working hours are so arranged as to accord with national or regional socio-cultural characteristics, and that, in the present state of Community law, is a matter for the Member States.'

In *Groener v Minister for Education*[16] the Court accepted, this time in relation to the free movement of workers, that, subject to certain conditions, the Treaty did not prohibit 'the adoption of a policy for the protection and promotion of a language of a Member State which is both the national language and the first official language.'

As President Due points out elsewhere in this volume, it is therefore relatively rare for issues to come before the Court with labels attached to them identifying them as constitutional. It is more common for such issues to emerge only in the course of argument before the Court, sometimes when specifically raised by Member States or by the Commission: sometimes they may emerge only at the stage when the Advocate General delivers his opinion or even, it might be said, during the judges' deliberations. Commentators may sometimes claim that the presence of constitutional issues has escaped the Court entirely. Where such a claim is made, it is some consolation that the issue will probably also have escaped the Member States and the other institutions, not to mention the parties to the case.

The approach of the Court of Justice to constitutional issues

Given the developed nature of the Community legal system and the existence of a Court of multifarious jurisdiction, the fact that the Treaty lacks many features of a Constitution could not prevent many issues of a constitutional character from arising; thus the Court has often had to work out the solution without much guidance from the texts. In fact, it could be said that it is precisely where the features of a written constitution are lacking in the Treaty that the Court has most obviously fulfilled the rôle of a Constitutional Court.

A first example may be taken from the review of measures of Member States.

Although the legality of national measures may be brought before the Court directly by the Commission under Article 169 of the Treaty, or even by another Member State under Article 170, it is inevitable, given the decentralized system of Community administration, that disputes concerning the conformity of national measures with Community law often arise before the national courts. Such disputes will necessarily give rise to issues concerning the relationship between Community law and national law. But, apart from the provisions of Article 189 of the Treaty on the effects of regulations,

---

[14] Case 7/78, [1978] ECR 2247.
[15] Case C-145/88, [1989] ECR 3851.
[16] Case C-379/87, [1989] ECR 3967.

directives and decisions, the Treaty is silent on that relationship, and it was left to the Court to work out the details. The well known principles of the direct effect and primacy of Community law, developed in the early case-law of the Court, are clearly principles of a constitutional character. The result of that case-law is often to make the rights created by Community law rights of a constitutional character, enforceable in the national courts and prevailing over any conflicting national measures. In such proceedings, it is the national courts which are essentially responsible for judicial review of national measures, in application of rulings on interpretation of Community law given by the Court of Justice. The constitutional protection of Community rights is thus the joint responsibility of the Court of Justice and the national courts, a possibly unique constitutional arrangement.

A second example can be taken from the review of Community measures. Here the rôle of the national courts is limited to raising before the Court of Justice the question of the validity of Community measures, where such a question arises in the national proceedings. The Court of Justice alone can declare a Community measure invalid:[17] a consequence that again can be seen as following from the need for Community law to be applied uniformly in all the Member States.

The approach of the Court of Justice to constitutional issues can be seen most clearly, however, in the review of Community measures arising in a direct action under Article 173 of the Treaty. According to the terms of Article 173, such review is limited to measures taken by the Council and the Commission; the Court's ruling in *Les Verts*[18] that measures taken by the European Parliament could also be challenged under Article 173 was a consequence of applying a fundamental constitutional principle that the Community was based on the rule of law, so that no measures either of the Community institutions or of the Member States could escape judicial review.

The Court's reference to the Treaty in *Les Verts* as a 'constitutional charter' has a particular significance here. The Court's approach was based on the need to see the Treaty provisions in the light of the Community's development. Thus the Court expressly justified its decision on the ground that, when the Treaty was drawn up, the Parliament did not have powers whose exercise called for judicial review. This dynamic interpretation of the Treaty is an approach characteristic of the interpretation of a constitutional text, which by its nature cannot readily be amended, and which therefore calls for a more flexible approach to interpretation than would be appropriate in the case of ordinary legislation.

The *Les Verts* case also provides a good illustration of the Court's approach to the various judicial remedies provided for by the Treaty. The Court has striven to ensure that these make up a coherent system of remedies, and its approach appears to have been designed to eliminate gaps and inconsistencies in the system. The elaboration of this approach would require a separate paper, but it can be regarded as the application of a constitutional principle. Indeed in the *Les Verts* judgment the Court explicitly based that approach on its characterisation of the Treaty as the basic constitutional charter of the Community.

A third example can be taken from the substantive principles governing

---

[17] Case 314/85, *Foto-Frost* [1987] ECR 4199.
[18] See Case 294/83, *Les Verts v European Parliament* [1986] ECR 1339.

judicial review. As noted earlier, the tasks of a Constitutional Court typically include review designed to ensure observance of fundamental rights. Although the Treaty contains no references to fundamental rights, with limited exceptions such as those already mentioned, the development in the activities of the Communities has led the Court to conclude that in the exercise of their powers the Community institutions are bound by the principle of respect for fundamental rights, in much the same way as are the authorities of the Member States under their own constitutional provisions. Moreover, in its more recent case-law, the Court of Justice has applied similar principles to the review of measures taken by the Member States when acting within the field of the Treaty.[19]

The principle of respect for fundamental rights is only one illustration of the 'general principles of law' to which the Court has resorted both in interpreting Community provisions and in assessing their validity. Other such principles include the principle of non-discrimination, which the Court has extrapolated, from specific references in the Treaty, into a universal principle; and the principle of proportionality, which has served as a yardstick to test the necessity and appropriateness of any measure imposing burdens on the individual.

The fundamental character of such principles is evidenced by the fact that they prevail over any measure, from whatever source it originates within the legal hierarchy (unless of course it is a Treaty provision), and by the fact that they apply to Community and to national measures implementing Community provisions, in the same way. Their applicability across the entire spectrum of the Community legal system would seem to justify their being regarded as constitutional principles.

Conclusions

A number of conclusions can be drawn from this discussion. First, it is clear that, while the Court of Justice can certainly not be regarded as a constitutional court in the sense of the specialized Constitutional Courts found in some of the Member States, it was endowed by the Treaties with certain constitutional functions. But while certain heads of jurisdiction are more obviously constitutional in character than others, constitutional issues can arise in almost any type of proceedings before the Court, and the label 'constitutional' is not particularly helpful in analysing the Court's various heads of jurisdiction.

Nevertheless, in at least two respects, the epithet 'constitutional' may be appropriate to the work of the Court. In the first place, certain of the Court's functions are incontestably constitutional. The clearest examples are, on the one hand, cases in which the Court must adjudicate on the respective powers of the other, 'political' institutions – the Council, Commission and European Parliament; on the other hand, cases involving the delimitation of competence between the Community and the Member States. It also seems likely that issues of the latter kind will be increasingly significant in future years as the

[19] See Case C-260/89, *ERT*, judgment of 18 June 1991; compare Joined Cases 60 and 61/84, *Cinéthèque v Fédération Nationale des Cinémas Français* [1985] ECR 2605 and, most recently, Case C-159/90, *Grogan*, judgment of 4 October 1991.

Community assumes and exercises new powers. The Court will have a difficult but essential rôle in preserving the balance between the Community and the Member States.

On these issues the Court performs, sometimes directly, sometimes indirectly, the tasks of a Constitutional Court.

Secondly, and also of increasing significance, there is the emergence through the case-law of many principles of a constitutional character. These include not only the historic principles of direct effect and primacy, governing the relationship between Community law and national law, but also the more recently emerging principles governing the scope of judicial review itself: the requirement that, the Community being subject to the rule of law, all Community and national measures must be subject to judicial review, and the requirement that such review must ensure conformity with substantive standards including respect for fundamental rights and such principles as non-discrimination and proportionality.

In these respects it is appropriate to speak of the constitutional jurisprudence of the Court.

If, then, the Court sometimes performs the tasks of a constitutional court, and if it has developed constitutional principles in its case-law, we can understand why, in some quarters, the Court's activities have been misunderstood. The Court has sometimes been criticised as a 'political' court. Such criticisms are probably based on unfamiliarity with the very notion of constitutional jurisprudence, which, as we have seen, is not familiar in all the Member States, and which requires what may seem novel judicial techniques, different approaches to interpretation, even a different conception of the law. Yet, in the Community system, which is based on the notion of a division of powers, some form of constitutional adjudication is inescapable, if indeed the Community is to be based, as its founders intended, and as the Court has recognized, on the rule of law. By establishing a Court of Justice, the founders of the Community intended that disputes, even constitutional disputes, should thenceforth be resolved by judicial settlement, rather than by the methods which had been tried, often unsuccessfully, sometimes disastrously, in the past.

5 The Decentralised Enforcement of Community Law Rights. Judicial Snakes and Ladders

Deirdre Curtin

Introduction

It has been clearly recognised for some considerable time now that European Union, whatever form it takes, will lack any force if it is based upon rules that impose neither obligations nor sanctions upon Member States in their relations with one another or with individuals.[1] The legal gap in the Treaty of Rome is that it does not expressly provide for any effective sanction against a State which fails to respect its obligations, to the detriment of those States which do, jeopardised the rule of law in the Communities.[2] Post-litigation non-compliance, especially in cases holding that Member States have failed to fulfill their obligations under the Treaty in implementing directives, spread dramatically in recent years,[3] the danger being that 'if a court is forced to condone the wholesale violation of a norm, that norm can no longer be termed law'.[4] The question of sanctions in Community law was finally the subject of intergovernmental debate and agreement at the Maastricht Summit in December 1991, resulting in the inclusion of a new second paragraph additional to the existing text of Article 171 of the Treaty of Rome.[5] This paragraph empowers the Court to, at the initiative of the Commission, impose a lump sum or penalty payment on a Member State which has failed to take the necessary measures to comply with a judgment of the Court within the time limit laid down by the Commission.

---

[1] See, *Suggestions of the Court of Justice on European Union*, Bulletin of the European Communities (1975), Supplement 9/75 at 17.

[2] The central place of the rule of law as the very basis of the Community legal order was expressed most recently by the Court in Opinion 1/91, *Draft Agreement between the Community and the Countries of EFTA relating to the Creation of the European Economic Area*, Opinion of 14 December 1991, not yet reported, consideration 21.

[3] See, Weiler '*The White Paper and the Application of Community Law*' in Bieber, Dehousse, Pinder and Weiler (eds.) *1992: One European Market?*, (Baden-Baden, 1988), 337, 342. See also, Curtin '*Directives: the Effectiveness of Judicial Protection of Individual Rights*' 27 CML Rev. (1990) 709, 710. See also, the annual reports to the European Parliament on Commission monitoring of Community law.

[4] Cappelletti, Seccombe and Weiler, 'A general introduction' in *Integration through law* vol. 1 (1986), 38.

[5] *Treaty on European Union*, published in *Agence Europe* 7 February 1992.

Although premature,[6] the prediction can be ventured that this new remedial power of the Court of Justice is bound to contribute substantially to the effectiveness of the Court's direct jurisdictional bases against the action or inaction of Member States (vis. Articles 169, 170 and 171). However the requirements of a genuine rule of law cannot be satisfied by means of the (amended) centralised enforcement mechanism only. It is, sadly, a truism that the Commission is unable (in terms of available staff) or unwilling (for political reasons) to initiate infringement actions systematically in all those cases where Community law has been violated by a Member State.[7] It clearly operates a selective litigation strategy.[8] In this context it is obvious that the essential complement to the centralized enforcement of Community law is and remains the horizontal decentralized action which takes place in national courts and reaches the Court of Justice indirectly by way of Article 177.[9] Not only does this system have the advantage the Court recognized in *Van Gend en Loos*[10] of placing every individual affected by Community law in the position of a vigilante but it removes the possibility of non-compliance since a State cannot defy its own courts.[11]

Under the Community system of decentralized control every national judge is considered to be a Community judge[12] and is empowered to question the Community validity of national laws. Community law has become in this way part of the legal culture of Member States while at the same time remaining a dependent legal order in the sense that it relies heavily on the legal orders of the Member States for enforcement.[13] Advocate General Warner saw the situation as one in which: 'Community law and national law operate in combination, the latter taking over where the former leaves off, and working out its conse-

[6] The Treaty on European Union still has to be ratified by Member States before it enters into force.
[7] See, Ehlermann, 'Ein Playdoyer fur die dezentrale Kontrolle der Anwendung des Gemeinschaftsrecht durch die Mitgliedstaaten' in *Liber Amicorum Piere Pescatore*, (Baden-Baden, 1986), 205, 207. Nor indeed is it under a legal obligation to do so.
[8] For what amounts to a very clear admission on the part of the Commission that this is the case see the answer to Written Question No. 1226/87, O.J. 1988 C 325 and to Written Question No. 1070/86, O.J. 1987 C 149. This is so despite its 'new' approach of systematically monitoring the incorporation of directives into national law resulting in the immediate initiation of infringement procedures as soon as deadlines are reached: see, *Seventh annual report to the European Paliament on Commission monitoring of the application of Community law* –1989, O.J. 1990, C 232/1, 6. Such monitoring is in any event superficial in that it does not include in systematic fashion the monitoring of the substantive content of implementing measures.
[9] See also, Weiler, op. cit. note 3 at 357 and Weatherill, 'National Remedies and Equal Access to Public Procurement' 10 *Yearbook of European Law* (1990) 243, 245. In the field of competition law see *Thirteenth Report on Competition Policy* (1983) at paragraph 217 and *Fourteenth Report on Competition Law* at paragraph 47. The Commission is understood at present to be drafting a 'Notice on the application of EEC Competition rules by national courts' in order to focus the attention of potential complainants on the fact that only national courts can provide what will often be the most effective possible remedy for a Treaty infringement (i.e. damages or interim injunctions). The philosophy behind this drive to encourage individuals to bring private actions in national courts is understood to be to allow the efficiency of the centralised enforcement mechanism to be enhanced by focussing resources and prioritising certain types of cases.
[10] Case 26/62, [1963] ECR 1.
[11] See also, Weiler, op. cit. at 358.
[12] See, Kovar, 'Voies de droit ouverte aux individus devant les instances nationales en cas de violation des normes et decisions du droit communnautaire' in *Les recours des individus devant les instances nationales en cas de violation de droit europeenne* (Brussels, 1978) 245.
[13] See, in general terms, Bridge *Procedural aspects of the enforcement of European Community law through the legal systems of the Member States*' (1983) El Rev. 28.

quences.'[14] This has posed an immense challenge to integration in the form of procedural and remedial barriers to the enforcement of substantive Community rights. For although the text of the law may read the same in two countries, the substantive rights granted by the law to the citizens of those same countries will differ if their courts are unequally available for the vindication of those rights.[15] These national differences bring with them a risk of inequality and unfairness in the protection of individual rights conferred by Community law and inevitably have a disintegrating effect.

A vital part of the Court of Justice's constitutionalisation of the Treaty of Rome[16] has depended upon the elaboration of increasingly far-reaching obligations on national judges in the context of their Community law mandate. This development confirms the rôle of the national judge as the *maitre d'oeuvre* of European integration. The source of the obligations placed upon the national judge is the principle of co-operation laid down in Article 5 of the Treaty, namely the obligation to 'take all appropriate measures, whether general or particular, to ensure fulfilment of the obligations arising out of this Treaty or resulting from action taken by the institutions of the Community'. This has been traditionally interpreted by the Court to oblige national courts to ensure the legal protection which citizens derive from the direct effect of the provisions of Community law.[17]

The performance by the national judge of his role in the Community legal order, as conceived by the Court of Justice, entails a delicate balancing exercise between the constraints imposed by two strands of the Court's well-established case-law. The twin constitutional principles[18] of the supremacy of Community law over national law and the direct effect of Community law in certain circumstances, while giving the national judge effective jurisdiction to apply Community rules in his national legal order, suffer from serious deficiencies. Neither provided the national judge with any practical legal assistance in terms of the content of remedies or procedures or guidance on jurisdictional matters on the basis that the national legal system was to be regarded as procedurally and institutionally autonomous. The philosophy is that where Community law confines itself to forbidding this or that kind of act on the part of a Member State and to saying that private individuals are entitled to rely on the prohibition in their national courts, without prescribing the remedies or procedures available to them for that purpose, there is no real alternative to the application of the remedies and procedures prescribed by national law.[19] This lack of interaction between the existence of a right and its specific remedial context together with the shortcomings specific to the principle of direct effect of directives will be referred to as the 'snakes' of judicial decentralisation.

The purpose of this article is to highlight the fact that the Court of Justice

---

[14] *Ibid.*

[15] See in particular, Kovar, *supra* at 251. See also, Capelletti and Golay, op. cit. at 265.

[16] Mancini *The making of a Constitution for Europe* 26 CML Rev. (1989) 595.

[17] See, Case 45/76, *Comet* [1976] ECR 1989, 1997 and Case 33/76, *Rewe* [1976] ECR 2043, 2053. See also, Constantinesco, 'L'article 5 CEE, de la bonne foi a la loyaute communautaire' in *Liber Amicorum Pierre Pescatore*, op. cit. 97, 111.

[18] The phrase is used advisedly. See, the Court's use of the phrase 'constitutional charter' to describe the Treaty of Rome in opinion 1/91, *supra* at consideration 21.

[19] Advocate General Warner in Case 33/76, *Rewe Zentralfinanz eG. v Landswirtschaftskammer für das Saarland* [1976] ECR 1989, 2003.

seems to have changed course in some recent cases, giving substantive guidance as to what precisely Community law requires of judicial procedure and national legal remedies, even where the Community law provisions do not enjoy direct effect. It will be argued that the Court's role in providing a Community wide approach to problems of judicial procedure and remedies has been to construct a number of 'ladders', escaping the 'snakes' of its own earlier case-law and helping individual litigants to effectively enforce their Community law rights before their national courts. Using only its powers to construe the effectiveness of Community law and the obligations inherent upon national courts by virtue of the – general provisions – of Article 5 of the Treaty, the Court in *Francovich and Bonifaci v Italy*[20] asserted and shaped a remedy which was denied to (Italian) national courts by national law.[21] This is a development of fundamental constitutional importance which confirms the role of the Court of Justice as the living oracle of Community law, to coin a phrase of Blackstone.

The snakes hinder the uniform applicability of Community law

Snake 1: Limited direct effect of directives

The doctrine of direct effect was developed by the Court of Justice in the early 1960s in relation to Treaty articles as an important constitutional tool designed to recognize the aptitude of Community law to confer rights and impose duties on individuals. Recourse was had to the 'spirit and general scheme' of the Treaty to discover that vocation.[22] The existence of the principle of direct effect in the Community framework is thus the product of judicial creativeness. The Court adjudicated that individual rights thus created, after certain criteria had been satisfied, had to be protected by the national courts. In other words these subjective rights had to be safeguarded by proceedings brought before the competent national courts. The direct effect of Community law which was at the beginning regarded as exceptional, quickly turned out to be what was described as the normal state of the law,[23] with one exception – directives. Unfortunately, this is a critical and far-reaching exception. As Judge Mancini has put it, the hopes of seeing Europe growing institutionally, in matters of social relationships and in terms of quality of life, rests to a large extent on the adoption and the implementation of directives.[24]

In the 1970s the Court extended a limited direct effect to provisions of directives as long as they met the conditions already laid down by the Court in relation to Treaty articles.[25] This is not the place for a detailed consideration of

---

[20] Joined Cases C-6/90 and C-9/90, judgment of 19 November 1991, not yet reported.
[21] Thereby definitively overruling the Court's contrary statement in Case 158/80, *Rewe v Hauptzollamt Kiel* [1981] ECR 1805.
[22] See further, Barav '*The Court of Justice of the European Communities*' in *The Role of Courts in Society*, Shetreet (ed), Nijhoff, 1989, 590, 596.
[23] Pescatore *The Doctrine of Direct Effect: an Infant Disease of Community Law* EL Rev. (1983) 155.
[24] Mancini *The making of a Constitution for Europe* 26 CML Rev. (1989) 595, 601.
[25] See, in particular, Case 9/70, *Grad* [1970] ECR 825; Case 33/70, *SACE* [1970] ECR 1213; Case 41/74, *van Duyn* [1974] ECR 1337. For a discussion of the different theoretical bases justifying the recognition that provisions of directives can possess direct effect see, Curtin *The Province of Government: Delimiting the Direct Effect of Directives in the Common Law Context* in 15 EL Rev. (1990) 195, 197.

the formidable problem in making provisions of directives immediately enforceable. Very briefly, the distinguishing feature of directives is that, unlike Treaty articles (or indeed Regulations), Directives are addressed to Member States and are binding on them only as to the *result* to be achieved. In *Marshall v Southampton and South West Hampshire Area Health Authority*[26] the Court linked the possibility of relying on an unconditional and sufficiently precise provision of a directive against a Member State to the failure of the Member State to implement the directive into national law correctly and at the proper time. Thus, if an individual asserts before a national court a right vis a vis the Member State which is not available under national law but which would have been available if the Member State had implemented the directive into national law then the individual is entitled to have the case adjudged as if the Member State had performed its Treaty obligations. The rationale, confirmed recently in *Emmott v Minister for Social Welfare*,[27] is the overriding one of a desire to prevent the Member State in question from deriving any advantage whatsoever from its failure to comply with Community law. The legal basis is a combination of Articles 5 and 189 of the Treaty. Furthermore, the Court has indicated that the effect of Community legislation in the form of directives is uni-directional[28] in the sense that 'the State cannot plead its own wrong' by seeking to rely on the terms of a directive (as opposed to unimplemented national law) to its own advantage[29] *vis a vis* private parties.[30]

The direct effect of provisions of directives can be invoked not only against central government but also against any organ or 'emanation' of the State, as widely interpreted by the Court,[31] irrespective of the fact whether the latter are responsible or otherwise for the failure to implement the directive in question.

Why should this case-law be categorized as a 'snake'? Primarily because individuals who are meant to benefit from the substance of a Community directive and who fall within its scope *ratione personae* find themselves, in the absence of implementing legislation by a Member State, having to return to base, unable to enforce their substantive rights before a national court where the defendant happens to be a private party, say, a private sector employer or counterparty of an agreement of any type. It is only the largely fortuitous fact that the defending party before the national court happens to be the State or an organ or emanation thereof that will enable them to rely on the terms of the directive in question before a national court.

In *Foster v British Gas plc*[32] the Court went some way towards providing guidelines to national courts as to what types of bodies can be considered synonymous with public authorities for the purposes of the vertical direct effect of directives. The *Foster* test provides national courts with a starting

---

[26] Case 152/84, [1986] ECR 723.
[27] Case C-208/90, judgment of 25 July 1991, not yet reported.
[28] See, Mustill LJ in *Doughty v Rolls Royce plc*, judgment of the Court of Appeal of 19 December 1991, not yet reported.
[29] See, Advocate General van Gerven in Case C-188/89, *Foster and Others v British Gas plc* opinion of 8 May 1990, [1990] ECR 1–3326.
[30] Case 80/86, *Kolpinghuis* [1986] ECR 3969.
[31] See, Case 188/89, *Foster v British Gas*, [1990] ECR 3313. See, however, the view of the English Court of Appeal in *Doughty supra* where it concluded that Rolls Royce Ltd where the Government was at the relevant time sole shareholder could not be considered as an emanation of the State.
[32] Case C-188/89, *supra*.

point in future cases but still leaves many grey areas[33]: what happens where the public service provided is unquestionably a classic duty of the State but is provided in a constitutionally independent manner? Are private contractors performing public services subject to the obligations contained in a directive where their freedom of operation is subject to regulatory control? What about bodies funded by or only partially regulated by the State? Or commercial undertakings where the State acquires a total or partial share-holding?[34] Or newly privatised companies where the State retains a 'golden share' on such matters as take-over bids or dividend policy or the appointment and removal of directors? Or the purely commercial activities of a body also performing a public function under some control from the State?

The answer to such questions are delicate enough to formulate within the legal system of one country; it is however extremely difficult within the Community firmament to develop a principled test which can be universally applied in all the Member States. It is submitted that the Court in *Foster* realised *sotte voce* the limitations of its own approach to delimiting the province of the private and public sector respectively for the purposes of the direct effect or otherwise of directives. The Court in fact soon side-stepped its case-law on this matter and constructed a 'ladder' which would nevertheless allow private litigants to reach their goal of enforcing their Community law rights deriving from unimplemented directives (see further, *infra*).

Snake 2: Institutional and procedural autonomy

The protection of the directly effective rights conferred on individuals by Community law is ensured by the national courts of the Member States. These courts are required to afford a 'direct and immediate' protection to affected individuals[35] which involves setting aside inconsistent national legislation as well as the recognition of the right to recover payments made in contravention of Community law. The orthodox understanding is that Community law requires no more than that national courts must ensure that individual rights conferred by it are indeed effectively protected, leaving it to the national courts themselves to apply whichever they consider to be the most appropriate of the various remedies and procedures available under national law for that purpose.[36] Whereas this presupposes that national law must provide procedures for the protection of rights arising from Community rules, it at the same time subjects directly effective rights to the vicissitudes of national law.

The only Community-wide principles developed by the Court of Justice were strictly *minimum* ones to the effect that the proceedings in which Community law is enforced must be no less favourable to the petitioner than the proceedings applicable to similar matters of national law (the 'non-discrimination principle').[37] Moreover, the enforcement of Community law must not be precluded or made virtually impossible (the 'effectiveness prin-

---

[33] See further, Szyszyzak, annotation of *Foster* in 27 CML Rev. (1990) 859.
[34] See, the judgment in this respect of the Court of Appeal in *Doughty v Rolls Royce plc, supra* note 28 which decided in the negative without referring preliminary questions to the Court. See however the view of Advocate General van Gerven on this point in his opinion in *Foster*.
[35] Case 13/68, *Salgoil SA v Italy* [1968] ECR 661.
[36] Case 34/67, *Luck* [1968] ECR 245.
[37] See, for example, Case 33/76 and Case 45/76 *supra*.

ciple').[38] However, how can national law practicably satisfy such minimum standards when Community law gives no guidance to national courts on such critical issues as standing, time limitations (other than the nebulous statement that they must be 'reasonable'), the scope of judicial review and the proper content of judicial remedies? The consequence of this approach was that national authorities could *inter alia* rely upon national time limitation periods to defeat rights claimed on the basis of Community law.[39] The same is true with regard to the availability of remedies and rights of action generally.

The Court constructs ladders to assist litigants gain access to justice

Ladder 1: Indirect effect of directives

The Court found a convenient way of avoiding the denial of access to justice inherent in its *Marshall* line of case-law. It was to effectively categorize the direct effect of directives as an *ultima ratio*[40] only to be resorted to where no other judicial technique can be applied to ensure the effectiveness of the terms of directives envisaged in Article 189(3) of the Treaty of Rome. The Court shifted focus from enforceable rights of individuals to the obligation on national courts to interpret the terms of their national law in the light of the requirements of Community law. At issue in these cases is not the 'active' direct effect of the Community directive in question as between individuals but with the natural effect of national law as interpreted by the national courts in accordance with Community law.[41] In practice it is the pertinent provisions of the national law which, interpreted in conformity with Community law, will have direct effect in horizontal litigation.

This obligation on the part of the national judiciaries has had a gestation period during which its scope has expanded. It was first elaborated in *von Colson and Kamann v Land Nordhein Westfalen*[42] in 1984 and has been reiterated and expanded upon since.[43] In particular the Court's judgment of recent vintage in *Marleasing SA v La Commercial Internacional de Alimentacion SA*[44] clarified many of the contentious issues surrounding this obligation on national courts. In the first place this judgment decided the contentious issue whether this mandate to national courts applied equally to *pre-existing* national

---

[38] *Ibid.*
[39] Compare, for example, Case 33/76 and Case 45/76, cited in note 17. In the former case the applicable national period of limitation was one month or, in certain circumstances, one year; in the latter case the applicable Dutch statute on administrative jurisdiction prescribed an absolute period of limitation of 30 days.
[40] See, the Advocate-General's opinion in Joined Cases C-177/88 and 179/88, *Dekker* and *Hertz* [1990] ECR 3941, 3956.
[41] See, the opinions of Advocate General Darmon in Cases 177/78 and 179/88, *ibid.* and Opinion of Advocate General van Gerven in Case C-262/88, *Barber v Guardian Royal Exchange Assurance Group* [1990] ECR 1889, 1912.
[42] Case 14/83, [1984] ECR 1891 and in the practically identical judgment in Case 79/83, *Harz v Deutsche Tradex* [1984] ECR 1921.
[43] See, Case 222/84, *Johnston* [1986] ECR 1651; Case 80/86, *Kolpinghuis* [1987] ECR 3969; Case 157/86, *Murphy* [1988] ECR 673; Case 125/88, *Nijman* [1989] ECR; Case C-322/88, *Grimaldi* [1989] ECR 4407.
[44] Case C-106/89, [1990] ECR 4135.

legislation (i.e. legislation not enacted specifically to implement a Community obligation, for example, a directive).[45] The Court ruled explicitly in the affirmative. In this manner the Court gives effective content to the mandate of the supremacy of Community law over *all* provisions of national law.

The Court indicated in the second place however the outer limits of the obligation on the national court: it was only obliged to strain the meaning of the words used in the national law so as to comply with Community law 'as far as possible'. This must be contrasted with the previous formula that the Court had used namely that the national judge should seek a conform interpretation 'in so far as it is given discretion to do so under national law'. This latter dictum made the fulfillment of the Community law mandate by the national judge dependent on the content of national law. The Court corrected this position in *Marleasing* making it quite clear that the national judge is fulfilling a Community law function when he seeks the conform interpretation of national law with a Community directive and that Community law itself prescribes the limits of this obligation on and the techniques that must be used. Community law requires that the consistency between the Community norm and the national norm be sought no matter how wide the departure from the *prima facie* meaning of the language used. The words 'as far as possible' refer, it is submitted, to the nature of the judicial function *per se* – the Court of Justice naturally enough did not require national judges to assume a legislative task by rewriting the terms of their national law completely. National judges may do so if they wish (as the House of Lords did in *Litster v Forth Dry Dock and Engineering Co Ltd*)[46] – that is a matter for their total discretion as to what they feel is possible – but they are not *obliged* to do violence to the language used in the sense of rewriting it entirely or compelled to give an interpretation *contra legem*. That seems to be the Court's bottom line.

That is the theory at least. In *Marleasing* itself the Court left the national court with no discretion and determined in its reply precisely how the national court had to, *in concreto*, interpret the relevant provision of national law (the Spanish Civil Code) in order to comply with the terms of the First Company Law Directive, which had not been implemented at all into Spanish law.[47] The end result was that the Spanish tribunal was *obliged* to interpret the provisions of the Spanish Civil Code in a manner so as to preclude a declaration of nullity of a public limited company based on a ground different from those set out in Article 11 of the (unimplemented) First Company Law Directive. To achieve this result the national court had to in practice 'disapply' or exclude the relevant provision of national law which effectively allowed the declaration of the nullity of a company where there was no consideration (not a ground permitted by the terms of Article 11 of the Directive).

The interesting point about the Court's judgment in *Marleasing* for present purposes is that the Court in practice has proceeded far down the road of actually placing obligations contained in directives on *private parties*, albeit after transforming them, via creative judicial interpretation, into obligations

---

[45] Contentious in particular for the British because of their sacro-sanct doctrine of the sovereignty of Parliament. See, the views of Lord Templeman in *Duke v Greater Reliance Systems Ltd* [1988] QB 108. See also, *Finnegan v Clowney Youth Training Programme Ltd* [1990] 2 CMLR 859.

[46] [1989] 2 CMLR 194.

[47] See ground 9 and the operative part. See Stuyck and Wytinck, annotation of Case C-106/89, *Marleasing* 27 CML Rev. 205, 210. See also, Finlay *infra*.

of national law.[48] In other words, the Court of Justice has provided the national courts with the necessary ladder for litigants to assure that horizontal rights and obligations enshrined in directives can have the force of law between individuals without a specific domestic legislative process. This jurisprudential development can be equated with indirect horizontal effect as opposed to full horizontal direct effect which would have entailed the Court explicitly overruling its own decision in *Marshall* which it has not been willing to do to date.[49]

Ladder 2: obligation to amend national remedies and to apply Community remedies

The Court has in recent years elevated the principle of the effectiveness of judicial protection in Community law to the rank of a fundamental principle of Community law.[50] The principle of the effective protection of individual rights has been used by the Court to require national courts to amend in certain circumstances the (existing) remedies offered by national law to enforce Community rights. Thus in *Johnston v Chief Constable of the RUC*[51] the Court, clearly motivated by a desire to ensure respect for the rule of law which is at the very basis of the Community legal order, linked the requirement of effective judicial control to a general principle of law which underlines the constitutional traditions common to the Member States as well as to Articles 6 and 13 of the European Convention of Human Rights. As a result a certificate issued by a national authority, stating that the conditions for derogating from the principle of equal treatment for men and women for the purposes of protecting public safety are satisfied, could not be treated as conclusive evidence so as to exclude the exercise of any power of review by the courts. It follows from this case that a national court cannot, without infringing Article 5 of the Treaty, hold itself bound by a provision of national law which purports to exclude on the grounds of a presumption that the requirements of public order (or *a fortiori* on any other grounds) all judicial review of the implementation of Community legislation (including on human rights grounds which forms part of the Community legal order). For this reason it is suggested that this case represents the nascence of what subsequently became a tendency in the Court's case-law effectively conferring national courts with jurisdiction as a matter of Community law to review certain actions of the State in circumstances where the applicable national law clearly would not have allowed it to do so.

The next step along the road to interference by the Court of Justice with the

---

[48] Stuyck and Wytinck, op. cit. at 212 have suggested that it may be possible to equate this jurisprudential development with a type of 'passive' horizontal direct effect. The passive element comes in because the individual litigant does not seek to impose *obligations* on another individual but merely to safeguard rights which the directive endows upon him.

[49] The possibility of it doing so at some future date should not be completely ruled out. Recent cases have confirmed that the Court does not consider itself bound irretractably by the doctrine of *stare decisis*. See, for example, Case C-10/89, *Hag 11* [1990] ECR I-3711.

[50] See, in particular, Case 222/84, *Johnston v Chief Constable of the Royal Ulster Constabulary* [1986] ECR 1651 and Case 22/86, *Heylens v UNECTEF* [1987] ECR 4097. See also, Prechal *Remedies after Marshall* 27 CML Rev 451, 468.

[51] Case 222/84, [1986] ECR 1651.

institutional autonomy of Member States came in *Heylens v UNECTEF*[52] where the Court ruled to the effect that where national rules did not *require* but simply *authorised* the competent administrative authorities in a Member State to state reasons for (final) decisions of refusal (*in casu* to recognise equivalence of qualifications in relation to the free movement of persons) then (directly effective) Community law dictated that a statement of reasons must mandatorily be given. The reason for this requirement that the national court tinker with the existing national remedy is the concern that a satisfactory remedy of a judicial nature be available in the national legal system for the effective vindication of a Community right.

Factortame 1 set the stage for potentially far-reaching interference by the Court of Justice with the competences and obligations of national courts in ensuring the effective protection of Community rights. It follows from this judgment that Community law requires national courts, in the context of interim proceedings, to suspend the application of a national measure allegedly in violation of Community law, even if under national law the national judge does not have the power to grant injunctions leading to the suspension of the national rules in question. Some commentators interpreted this judgment to mean that the Court had implicitly held that Community law itself directly conferred national judges with the competence to 'create' new remedies in the context of their own legal systems if this was necessary to ensure the effective protection of Community rights[53] although this view was by no means unanimous.[54] The reason why this judgment was taken as an indication *sotto voce* that the Court had implicitly recognized that Community law could, in certain circumstances, dictate to national judges a new remedy unavailable under national law (interim injunctive relief against the Crown) was the factual premise that under English law there was no positive rule preventing national courts from granting interim relief against the Crown but rather the courts simply enjoyed no jurisdiction in that respect. The ultimate result of the judgment was arguably therefore the imposition of a 'new' remedy in a Community law context. However, not alone did the Court seek to hide this result by deliberately phrasing its judgment in terms of a mandate to the national judges of 'disapplication' of contrary national rules (repeating *verbatim* the *Simmenthal* formula), neatly side-stepping the problem that national courts had no jurisdiction under national law to apply the remedy in question, but it even more deliberately eschewed providing any indication, in response to the House of Lords' explicit question in that respect, as to the substantive conditions under which the remedy at issue was to be granted.

The fear that the Court would systematically refuse to provide any substantive guidance to national courts as to the remedies Community law required them to provide was considerably abated in its subsequent judgment in *Zuckerfabrik Suderdithmarschen AG*.[55] This time the Court chose to respond to the

---

[52] Case 22/86, [1987] ECR 4097.
[53] See, Toth CML Rev. (1990) 573; Barav and Simon RMC (1990) 591; Simon *Journal du droit international* (1991) 447; Ross EL Rev. (1991) 476 and Curtin CML Rev. (1990) 709. See also, Advocate General Mischo in his opinion of 29 May 1991 in Joined Cases C-6 and 9/90, *Francovich and Bonifaci*, judgment of 19 November 1991, not yet reported.
[54] Le Mire, (1990) *Actualite juridique. Droit Administratif* 834. Weatherill, (1990) *Yearbook of European Law* 265.
[55] Joined Cases C-143/88 and C-92/89, judgment of 21 February 1991, not yet reported. See also, Case C-177/88, *Dekker* [1990] ECR I-3941.

explicit questions of a national court as to the conditions according to which the interlocutory relief in question had to be granted.[56]

The Court of Justice first confirmed that national courts have the power to suspend the execution of a national administrative measure adopted on the basis of a Community Regulation since:

> 'the interim protection assured to litigants before national courts may not vary, according to whether they contest the compatability of the provisions of national law with Community law (which was at issue in *Factortame 1*) or the validity of Community secondary legislation, since in both cases the challenge is based on Community law itself.'[57]

Traditionally the Court would then have proceeded to insist on the institutional autonomy of the national legal systems as to the substantive conditions which had to be fulfilled prior to the grant of the interim relief by the national court, subject only to the principles of effectiveness and non-discrimination. Instead the Court began by explicitly stressing the fact that the national laws of Member States diverged so much in this respect that their application would threaten the uniformity of application of Community law, one of the fundamental leitmotif's running through the Court's case-law. This meant therefore that uniform conditions had to be defined in order to overcome the hurdle of different national procedural rules. This the Court proceeded to do by applying by analogy the conditions which it had developed in relation to its own competence to grant interim measures under Article 185 of the Treaty.

In *Zuckerfabrik* the Court explicitly countenanced the imposition of Community-wide conditions for the grant of interim measures suspending the operation of national administrative decisions. This detailing of the substantive parameters of the proposed remedy is precisely the step the Court would not take in *Factortame 1* some eight months earlier. The other step it fought shy of in *Factortame 1* was to recognize explicitly that where a national judge did not have any power under national law to provide a particular remedy for the enforcement of a Community law right then Community law itself conferred the requisite competence. Some sixteen months after *Factortame 1* the Court vigorously propelled the Community legal order down this road in *Francovich and Bonifaci v Italy*, pushing aside some sacred cows in the process.

Space does not permit exhaustive consideration of this important case.[58] Briefly, the facts were that Italy failed to implement Council Directive 80/987 of 20 October 1980 on the approximation of the laws of the Member States

---

[56] To recoup higher than expected losses in the sugar sector, Council Regulation 1914/87 (OJ 1987 L 183/5) required sugar manufactures to pay a special elimination levy where their losses for 1986/1987 marketing year were not entirely covered by the production levies owed. The German customs authorities sought to levy substantial sums on the plaintiffs by virtue of Council Regulation 1914/87. The plaintiffs, on the basis that the Regulation was invalid as a matter of Community law, sought orders in the German courts suspending the execution of the payment orders. The competent German courts referred preliminary questions whether interim relief should be available as a matter of Community law and if so, under what conditions.

[57] Consideration 20. Provisional translation.

[58] But see the excellent opinion of Advocate General Mischo of 29 May 1991, *supra*. For annotations of this case see, Barav, 'Damages against the state for failure to implement EC Directives', *New Law Journal*, (1991) 1584, and Curtin, 'State Liability under Community Law: a New Remedy for Private Parties', (1992) *Industrial Law Journal*, 74.

relating to the protection of employees in the event of the insolvency of their employer.[59] It should have set up a 'guarantee institution' by 23 October 1983 which, in the event of an employers insolvency, would guarantee the payment of the employees outstanding employment related claims. The Commission successfully brought infringement proceedings against Italy. Italy still failed to implement the terms of the Directive into national law. Towards the end of 1989, two actions were commenced in the Italian courts by former employees who were owed roughly 254 million lira in arrears of pay by their respective insolvent employers. All attempts to obtain the moneys from the employers having failed, legal proceedings were brought against the Italian State seeking payment of the sums owed. This claim arose from the provisions of the Directive and depended on the acknowledgement that its provisions were directly effective and could be enforced as against the Italian State. In the alternative an order was sought against the State seeking the payment of compensation for the injury sustained by the plaintiffs on account of the failure to give effect to Directive 80/987.

Preliminary questions were referred to the Court of Justice. The Court disposed of the direct effect point by concluding on an analysis of the relevant provision of the Directive that, since the Member States were given a discretion to establish a privately financed guarantee institution, it could not be assumed for the purposes of the operation of the direct effect doctrine that they would have opted to have the institution financed by the public authorities. Therefore the Member State could not be obliged to guarantee the payment of arrears of salary in the absence of the establishment of the appropriate 'guarantee institution'. The question which then fell to be considered was whether the employees nevertheless had the right to be compensated by the State in damages for the loss they had suffered (in terms of the guaranteed payment of their arrears of salary) as a result of the State's failure to implement the terms of the directive into national law? In Italy (as in virtually all Member States there was no basis in national law for an action in damages against the State for what effectively amounted to a failure to legislate) the success of the plaintiffs submission thus depended on the willingness of the Court of Justice to rule that the liability in damages in question had its source in *Community* law.[60]

The Court began its reasoning by recalling in very general terms the nature of the Community legal system as an autonomous legal system capable of conferring rights on individuals. It explained, citing well-established case-law, the central role of national courts in assuring the effective respect of these

---

[59] OJ 1980 L 283/23.

[60] This is a novel point. However, there is some authority in the case-law for the proposition that the interest of having a judgment by the Court of Justice in the context of proceedings under Article 169 of the Treaty is that it may establish the basis of the *liability* the State may occur, in particular towards individuals as a result of a breach of its obligations: see, Case 39/72, *Commission v Italy* [1973] ECR 101; Case 309/84, *Commission v Italy* [1986] ECR 599; Case 103/84, *Commission v Italy* [1986] ECR 1759; Case 154/85, *Commission v Italy* [1987] ECR 2717. In the context of an action concerning a Member States failure to correctly transpose a directive into national law see, Case C-287/87, *Commission v Greece* [1990] ECR 125. The proposition that damages should be awarded under national law to those individuals who suffer loss as a result of a Member States breach of Community law received some support in Case 60/75, *Russo v AIMA* [1976] ECR 45. See further Green and Barav, 'Damages in the National Courts for Breach of Community Law' (1987) *Yearbook of European Law* 55 and Durand 'Enforceable Community Rights and National Remedies' (1987) *Denning Law Journal* 43.

rights. Motivated overtly by the concern that *l'effet utile* of Community law
would be threatened and the protection of Community law rights weakened,
the Court discovered another unenumerated right for private parties which
formed an integral part of the Community legal system. This was the right of
private parties to obtain compensation from a Member State where that
Member State is responsible for a violation of Community law rights. The
Court stressed that the existence of this right of action in damages against a
defaulting Member State was particularly necessary where the failure by a
Member State (*in casu*, to implement the provisions of a non-directly effective
directive into national law) meant that private parties were unable to enforce
the Community legal provisions directly before a national court.

The Court went on to confirm its discovery of this right for private parties
as embedded in the general scheme and structure of the Community legal
order. It referred in support to the ubiquitous Treaty article – article 5.
According to the Court's extensive interpretation of the terms of this Treaty
Article, Member States are under an obligation to eliminate the illegal consequences of a violation of Community law. Part and parcel of that obligation is
the principle of State liability for any damage suffered by private parties as a
result of the State's illegal behaviour.

The Court then proceeded – of its own motion – to detail the substantive
conditions attaching to this Community remedy against a Member State as
tortfeasor where what was at issue was the State's failure to implement the
terms of a directive into national law. First, the objective of the directive must
include the creation of *rights* for individuals. Second, the *content* of those rights
must be ascertainable from the terms of the directive itself. Third, a *causal link*
must exist between the violation by the State of its duty to implement the terms
of the directive into national law and the loss sustained by the affected private
parties.

These then were the substantive parameters of the newly created Community remedy which private parties could avail of against the State. Implicit
in the elaboration of this remedy was the obligation for national courts to
ensure that this remedy was effectively applied for the benefit of private
parties. With regard to detailed matters such as the calculation of damage, the
award of interest and the courts competent to apply the Community remedy, it
seems that the principle of 'institutional autonomy' still has a rôle with each
national court applying the rules of its national law in this respect,[61] subject, of
course, to the principles of effectiveness and of non-discrimination.[62]

The anomalous result however of the Court's creativity in *Francovich* is not
only the risk that the Community law litigant is effectively placed in a superior
position to the purely domestic litigant but also the fact that the litigant
seeking damages from a Member State is in a considerably better position than
the litigant seeking damages from a Community institution under Article 215
of the Treaty. Can it be right that a Member State should be liable in damages
in circumstances where the Community would be protected, as Oliver LJ (in
the minority) in *Bourgoin v Minister of Agriculture, Fisheries and Food*[63] believed?[64]

---

[61] See, the wording of consideration 42 of the Court's judgment in *Francovich*.
[62] See, consideration 43.
[63] [1986] QB 716.
[64] See also, Weatherill, op. cit. at 286.

The prediction is ventured that the Court may respond in time by lowering the obstacles to a successful Article 215 action.[65]

Ladder 3: the obligation not to apply national time limits

One matter not touched upon in *Francovich* is the question of time limits. Upon reading the Court's judgment in isolation it might reasonably be assumed that such procedural matters survived *Francovich* intact and are still a matter of discretion for national law. That this is not a correct assumption is clear from a judgment of the Court some four months earlier in an Irish case, *Emmott v The Minister for Social Welfare.*[66] The facts in this case concerned the situation where the plaintiff did not become aware that she had a directly effective right under a Community Directive which had not been correctly implemented into Irish law until the Court of Justice gave judgment in *McDermott and Cotter (No. 1)*,[67] a factually similar case. The problem was that by the time she had become aware that she had a right and acted upon it, the three month time limit for bringing judicial review proceedings had expired. Moreover, on the facts of that particular case it transpired that the relevant Government department had misled the claimant by assuring her that her case would be resolved once the Court of Justice had given judgment in *McDermott and Cotter (No. 1)*. Instead, when the time came it relied on the fact that she had not brought her claim within three months of the directly effective right coming into *existence* (i.e. the date the Directive should have been correctly implemented into Irish law, 23 December 1984) to defeat her claim and despite the fact that the existence of this right was only *established* by the Court some three years later in its judgment in *McDermott and Cotter (No. 1)*. The problem thus was the lack of contemporaneity between two points in time, namely the point when the right comes into existence and the point (later on) when the existence of the right is (definitively) established.[68]

The Court could have adopted the narrow approach prompted by the factual context of *Emmott* of a test based on *knowledge*, actual or constructive, by the claimant of the existence of a directly effective right. This was essentially the approach of Advocate General Mischo who suggested that the time limit for initiation of (judicial review) proceedings should only commence from the date the claimant could reasonably have been assumed to have acquired knowledge as to the existence of Community law rights, provided that the exercise of the claimant's rights had not been made virtually impossible by the competent authority. The approach of the Court on the other hand was much wider than it needed to be on the facts of *Emmott*. It formulated an extremely wide and inclusive general rule in the following terms:

---

[65] See also, Barav *Damages in the domestic courts for breach of Community law by national public authorities* in Schermers, Heukels, and Mead (eds.), *Non-Contractual Liability of the European Communities*, (Nijhoff, 1988), 149, 165–6.

[66] Case C-208/90, judgment of 25 July 1991, not yet reported. The Court has also held that a 'Member State which has not implemented a directive adequately may not be allowed to rely on national law principles (*in casu* the principle of unjust enrichment) to defeat the operation of directly effective rights: Case C-377/89, *McDermott and Cotter (No. 2)*, judgment of 13 March 1991, not yet reported. See further, Banks, *infra*.

[67] Case 286/85, [1987] ECR 1453.

[68] This was also the problem in Case C-213/89, *Factortame 1, supra*. See, in particular Advocate General Tesauro's opinion of 17 May 1990, [1990] ECR 2433, 2455.

'until such time as a directive has been properly transposed, a defaulting Member State may not rely on an individual's delay in initiating proceedings against it in order to protect rights conferred upon him by the provisions of the directive and that a period laid down by national law within which proceedings must be initiated cannot begin to run before that time.'[69]

The Court explained its approach on the basis that individuals are unable to ascertain the full extent of their rights so long as a directive has not been properly transposed into national law. Only the proper implementation of the directive will bring the state of uncertainty to an end and it is only that implementation which brings about the requisite legal certainty which must exist if individuals are to be required to assert their rights. This means that whereas in principle it is for national law to lay down the procedural condi-tions governing actions at law intended to ensure the protection of rights which individuals derive from the direct effect of Community law, provided that the conditions of principles of non-discrimination and effectiveness are fulfilled, time limits can never be reasonable if they expire before a Member State has eliminated the situation of legal uncertainty brought about by its failure to correctly implement a Directive into national law. It follows that domestic time limits – including any statute of limitations – do not apply to claims brought under EEC law until (it has been established that) the relevant provisions of EEC law have been implemented into national legislation. It seems from the actual wording used by the Court that this applies across the board to all litigation and not merely to vertical litigation involving the State. This is extremely broad indeed. Suppose that the outcome of the House of Lord's reference to the Court in *Southampton and South West Hampshire Area Health Authority v Marshall*[70] is that the British legislation purporting to imple-ment the terms of the Equal Treatment Directive[71] into national law is defective because the limit on compensation is found to be inadequate. This opens a potentially large window of opportunity, effectively permitting claims to be brought without any reference to national time limits with regard to all those acts of discrimination taking place from the date the Directive was supposed to have been correctly implemented, August 1978. Time would not begin to run against potential claimants until new – adequate – legislation had been adopted after which the ordinary time limits under the applicable (or equivalent) domestic legislation would apply – in the UK and Ireland that is three months.

The way the Court formulated its broad brush approach in *Emmott* renders its reasoning equally applicable in an action for damages against the State for failure to implement as well as the situation where what is at issue is the direct effect of certain provisions of an incorrectly implemented directive (the situation in *Emmott*). It follows that a Member State which has not correctly implemented the terms of a directive into national law, cannot seek to defend itself against a private party's action in damages by arguing that the latter's delay in bringing the action makes it time-barred as a matter of national law.[72] This is the case across the entire Community and with regard to

---

[69] See, consideration 23, *ibid.*
[70] Case C-271/91, still pending.
[71] Directive 76/207 of 9 February 1976, OJ L 39/40.
[72] It is also significant in this respect that the Court did not follow the suggestion of its Advocate General and impose a limitation on the retroactive effect of its judgment in *Francovich*.

unimplemented directives or incorrectly implemented directives with regard to which the requisite elements of proof can be established. Its effect is to penalise Member States for their failure to implement directives on time and to deprive them of the fruits of their recalcatrance.

Conclusion

One reason which has been advanced as to why the Court traditionally did not take a more active role in promoting a Community-wide approach to the problems of judicial procedure is its belief that issues such as standing and judicial procedure so clearly affects the limits of judicial power that they are best resolved by other Community institutions which have less at stake.[73] Indeed the Court has itself clearly stated that the problems stemming from the disparities in national remedies and procedures could be tempered by the adoption of Community legislation harmonizing national remedies and procedures relating to actions based on Community rights.[74] In *Express Dairy Food v IBAPI*[75] the Court went so far to speak of the 'regrettable absence of Community provisions harmonising procedure and time-limits'.

The absence of Community rules undermines the authority, integrity and uniformity of Community law, as well as obstructing the realisation of Community objectives.[76] What can the Court of Justice do when the political system fails to address a very real problem hindering something as fundamental as the uniform applicablity of Community law? Of course, not every problem of European integration can be reduced to something justiciable.[77] But the remedies and procedures available for the effective judicial protection of individuals under national law can *par excellence* be reduced to the justiciable. Motivated by a desire to avoid disharmony and serious inefficiency in the proper application of Community law, the Court during the time span in which Judge O'Higgins was a member, has used its powers of interpretation to lay down uniform rules relating to the substance of remedies. In this manner it has admirably sought to fulfil its task of ensuring 'that in the interpretation and application of the Treaty the law is observed'.[78]

The Court has gradually built up momentum in promoting a Community-wide approach to problems of judicial procedure. All the relevant 'ladders' were constructed during the period of Judge O'Higgin's tenure. The Court's quest for procedural justice started in cases such as *Johnston* and *Heylens* and continued through *Marleasing* to *Factortame*: Community law dictates that national courts are obliged to reshape existing remedies under national law so that they comply with the minimum requirements of Community law. Moreover, *Marleasing* indicated clearly for the first time that national courts cannot rely on *national* techniques of interpretation in providing a benevolent interpretation of national law. In *Emmott* the Court opened a 'window of opportunity' regarding the non-applicability of national time limits in certain circumstances, thereby effectively sanctioning Member States for their tardiness.

---

[73] Cappelletti and Golay, op. cit. at 337.
[74] See, *Rewe* and *Comet, supra.*
[75] Case 130/79, [1980] ECR 1887.
[76] *Bridge, supra.* note 13, at 41.
[77] Koopmans *The role of law in the next stage of European integration* 35 ICLQ (1986) 925, 231.
[78] Article 164 of the Treaty of Rome.

Francovich was the logical (and some would argue, inevitable) culmination of this process as a whole. In this case the Court overtly asserted that it possesses the judicial power to make Community rights accessible as such throughout the Member States, even if in some (ancillary) respects it remains dependant on national law.

Moreover, in access to justice terms, the Court has significantly narrowed a previously existing gap in the decentralized judicial protection of private parties under Community law. Prior to *Francovich* private parties who suffered loss as a result of a Member State's failure to implement the terms of a directive into national law only had a (private law) remedy to the extent that they could enforce any directly effective rights against the State or an 'emanation of the State', as broadly construed (*Foster*). The limitation inherent in the attempt by the Court in *Marleasing v La Commercial*[79] to grant some further access to justice to those private parties seeking to rely on provisions of Community directives as against other private parties lies in the fact that the national judge is obliged to engage in the interpretative exercise only 'to the extent that it is at all possible'. The denial of a remedy may therefore occur where the national judge concludes, at his own discretion, that the conflict between the Community law provision and the national law provision is entirely unambiguous and that he cannot therefore 'interpret' national law in the light of Community law. After *Francovich* individuals who find themselves denied a remedy in such circumstances – or in any other, since *a fortiori* the ruling of the Court extends to all breaches of the Treaty – can sue the State directly in damages for the loss sustained.

It will be surprising, when the extent of the Court's involvement in reshaping national remedies and creating a Community remedy filters through to national lawyers and judges, if we do not witness over the coming decade a cascade of challenges to the national laws of remedies and procedures on grounds of incompatibility with Community law.[80] This will certainly serve to highlight the inherent limitations of an exclusively judicial solution to this type of disintegration problem. This is because issues reach the Court on an *ad hoc* basis and because the Court can, in any event, only outline the parameters of what Community law requires of national remedies and procedures without detailing every related matter of substance. It is suggested that the Court has done enough trouble-shooting in some of its recent case-law in this field to provoke the Community legislator to consider and adopt long-overdue Community legislation harmonising national procedures and time limits relating to actions based on Community law rights as a matter of some urgency.[81]

[79] Case C-106/89, op. cit.
[80] Case C-208/90, *Emmott, supra* was the first of this new wave of actions. See also, the recent reference (14 October 1991) from the House of Lords in Case C-271/91, *Southampton and South West Hampshire Area Health Authority v Marshall*, still pending. See also, the decision of the English EAT in *Livingstone v Hepworth Refractories Limited*, reported in *The Times*, 23 December 1991.
[81] This leaves to one side the difficult question whether the Community legislator actually posseses competence at present to adopt such a harmonising measure and its legal basis or whether a Treaty amendment conferring specific competence would be required.

6 Judicial Review and the Common Fisheries Policy in Community Law

James O'Reilly

Introduction

Litigants, it would seem, have always litigated about fish and fisheries. This is illustrated by one of the earliest series of Irish law reports dealing with the common law edited by Sir John Davies, the King's Attorney General of his day in the early years of the 17th century.[1] That case dealt with a several fishery but the potential for growth was there. Nothing has changed much in the intervening period of almost 400 years. Ireland's unique position in being placed in the centre of the richest fishing grounds in Western Europe set the scene for future fisheries litigation. Most recently, this has arisen in the context of the common fisheries policy.[2] Before the accession of Spain and Portugal to the European Communities, the common fisheries policy had achieved a permanence which the Commission had laboured long to establish. One of the most difficult problems which had confronted the Commission, the Council and the Member States was the adoption of effective measures to deal with the problem caused by over-fishing and the need to conserve fish stocks. What was intended by the Commission at the time as one of the means to achieve this objective was the introduction of national quotas allocated by the Commission to the various Member States from a Community total allowable catch. This short paper discusses recent litigation that has come before the Court of Justice which has highlighted hitherto unforeseen consequences of the manner in which these matters were provided for in the common fisheries policy. Not only has the whole area of national quotas been undermined but the apparent consequences of the most recent cases raise the most important of issues for the manner in which Member States may maintain their national shipping registers. Before the accession of Spain and Portugal, which took effect from 1 January 1986, both of these Member States had accepted a strict Community regime which was to apply to fisheries. While this required concessions on the part of these Member States, they were apparently accepted in the context of the Treaty of Accession negotiated with the Commission and the other Member States. Notwithstanding this acceptance of the status quo, there followed a number of legal challenges in the national courts of Ireland and the

---

[1] *The Case of the Royal Fishery of the Banne* Davies' Reports, 147. This case was determined by the King's Courts in Ireland in Michaelmas term in the eighth year of the reign of James I in 1610.
[2] See Churchill *EEC Fisheries Law* (1987) at pp. 11–16, 23–31, 25–81, 100–112 and 243–244.

United Kingdom by undertakings with substantial Spanish investments. The object of this litigation was to ensure that such 'Irish' or 'United Kingdom' sea fishing boats registered on the Irish or UK register and crewed almost exclusively by Spanish nationals could fish against the Irish or UK nation quota while operating, by and large, out of the well established sea fishing ports of North Western Spain.

The outcome of this litigation suggests that not sufficient care or foresight was taken by the Commission and the Member States in negotiating the provisions of the common fisheries policy upon which so much reliance had been placed and in particular the Community legislation providing for national quotas. The cases also act as a reminder of the importance that attaches at all times to the constitutional provisions of the EEC Treaty. They will take priority over secondary community legislation, including in this context the common fisheries policy, unless appropriate amendments are made. With the benefit of hindsight, it would appear that the provisions of the EEC Treaty concerning agriculture ought to have been amended to make special provision for the common fisheries policy. After all, the rules of competition only apply in the agricultural field to the extent that they are incorporated by the Treaty. Fisheries ought to have merited the same treatment. However, what is even more surprising is the extent to which the Commission stood back and allowed the structure it had carefully set in place over a period of many years to be worn away by this new tide of litigation. It was even more surprising, towards the end of this process, to see the Commission actually take the initiative against those Member States who wished to protect national quotas against what they saw as 'quota hopping'. While the judgments of the Court of Justice discussed in this paper may accord with the basic principles of Community law found in the Treaties, they raise, at the same time, the most serious issues for the Member States and the Commission to face over the whole area of fisheries.

The inevitability of such Community litigation was contributed to by the Hague Resolution of 3 November 1976.[3] This Resolution is described as a 'Council Resolution on Certain External Aspects of the Creation of a 200-Mile Fishing Zone in the Community with effect from January 1, 1977'. This was the effect of the resolution. Overnight, three and twelve mile fishery limits were extended to 200 miles from baselines. It was adopted in the context of a changing pattern that had asserted itself in public international law whereby maritime states were extending their fishing zones to 200 miles. Overnight the rich fishing resources of an extended community came under the closer attention of Community lawyers.

Any Constitutional Court can only deal with the cases coming before it. The Court of Justice is no exception. In viewing the fishery cases that have recently come before the court those dealt with in the 1970s into the early 1980s were concerned with the establishment of Community competence in conservation matters including protection of the fishing grounds and conservation of the biological resources of the sea. The common fisheries policy itself evolved over a number of years. One of the first items of Community legislation to attract the repeated attention of the court was Council Regulation No. 101/76 laying

---

[3] 'Council Resolution on Certain External Aspects of the Creation of a 200-mile Fishing Zone in the Community with effect from January 1, 1977', OJ 1981, C 105/1; see also Churchill, *EEC Fisheries Law* (1987), at pp. 69–72.

down a common structural policy for the fishing industry.[4] Constitutional decisions of the first rank were delivered in the judgments of the court dealing with such matters as discrimination and the scheme of things under the developing common fisheries policy and the extent to which the competence of the Member States in certain matters, notably dealing with conservation, had been transferred to the institutions of the Communities, notably the Commission.[5]

There can be little doubt that such precedents were used by the Commission as a justification for one of the most controversial and difficult aspect of the common fisheries policy, namely the adoption of Community measures dealing with the protection and conservation of the biological resources of the sea. The need to adopt such legislation had been anticipated in the 1972 Act of Accession for Denmark, Ireland and the United Kingdom.[6] This legislation was not adopted until 25 January 1983. This was Council Regulation 170/83 establishing a Community system for the conservation and management of fishery resources.[7] Now, for the first time there was to be an enforceable limit on the catch for those quota species covered by an annual regulation. A Community reserve was established for each such species – the total allowable catch – and a portion of this, in turn, allocated to each of the Member States. It would seem that the quotas allocated initially to each Member State were based on an historical catch for the species concerned. The measure was unpopular with fishing interests in the various Member States as it imposed a strict limitation structure on their fishing activities. The fact that the regulation took a period of almost eight years to negotiate underlines the difficulties encountered. Each of the Member States with maritime populations therefore looked to this legislation as guaranteeing a national quota for the fishermen establishment within their respective jurisdictions.

This article attempts to deal with some of the more recent fisheries litigation before the Court of Justice in which the question of 'quota hopping' has been raised. Invariably, these cases have involved Irish, UK and Spanish fishing interests both at a time when Spain was a third country and, latterly in its status as a Member State. These cases have led one of the leading commentators in this area to suggest that the common fisheries policy itself has been 'wrongfooted' in the process.[8] What better fare could there be for the role of the judge as a constitutional interpreter?

---

[4] OJ 1976, L 20/19. This legislation replaced Council Regulation 2170/70 of 20 October 1970 laying down a common structural policy for the fishing industry: OJ 1970, L 236/1.
[5] See, by way of example, Case 61/77 *Commission v Ireland* [1978] ECR 417, at 450–451, paras 78–80 dealing with discrimination. The court stated that '. . . not only overt discrimination by reason of nationality but also to all covert forms of discrimination which, by the application of other criteria of differentiation, lead in fact to the same result.' This portion of the judgment was expressed in the context of Art. 7 of the EEC Treaty and the then relevant Community secondary legislation. The same judgment is also authority for the principle repeated continually in other fishery litigation during this period that '[t]he power to establish permanent rules for fishing belongs therefore to the Community as such and, according to the settled case law of the court . . . this power is an exclusive one' [1978] ECR 417 at 448 para. 61. Case 22/70, *Commission v Council* [1971] ECR 363 and joined cases 3, 4 and 6/76, *Kramer* [1976] ECR 1279 are just two further examples from many such cases.
[6] See Arts. 100–103 of the 1972 Act of Accession.
[7] OJ 1983, L 24/1.
[8] Churchill, *Quota Hopping: The Common Fisheries Policy Wrongfooted?* 27 CML Rev. (1990), 209–247.

The Common Fisheries Policy and 'quota hopping'

The earlier fisheries litigation before the Court of Justice had raised and settled the question of competence between the Member States and the Communities concerning the adoption of measures necessary to ensure protection of the fishing grounds and the conservation of the biological resources of the sea. The competence argument was answered conclusively in favour of the Commission. Spain has the largest fishing fleet in the European Communities. In the 1985 Treaty of Accession for the Kingdom of Spain and Portuguese Republic,[9] a special regime was laid down for the fishing interests of these states. These are set forth, respectively, in Articles 156–166 and 346–353 of the 1985 Act of Accession. Under these regimes strict rules were laid down as to the number of Spanish and Portuguese fishing vessels which could fish in Community waters during a specially provided for transitional period. The details of the provisions extended to a schedule of list of vessels so entitled. The actual regimes themselves are to apply until 31 December 2002.[10] The most recent fisheries litigation has dealt with the question of access to the national fishing quotas allocated to Member States. All Member States, with the sole exception of Spain, who have been parties to this litigation saw these cases as raising, squarely, the problem of 'quota hopping'. The answer to date of the Court of Justice has been much less clear cut than the earlier referred to fisheries litigation. It remains to be seen how the problem resolves itself over the coming decade during which period some new arrangement will have to be made by the Commission or the Court if the Commission's conservation policy is to succeed.

Quota hopping is referred to in passing in *Factortame II*[11]. A more detailed description is given by Dr R R Churchill as follows:

> 'Quota hopping refers to the situation where, because of the relative liberality of the laws of a Member State governing the conditions under which vessels may have the nationality of that Member State, it is possible for what are in reality foreign, or predominantly foreign, interests, either from another Member State or a third state, to register vessels they own under the flag of the first Member State (thereby obtaining its nationality) and thus for such foreign-owned vessels to fish for quotas allocated to that Member State.'[12]

[9] OJ 1985, L 302/9.

[10] Article 66 of the 1985 Act of Accession in the case of Spain states that the regime defined '. . . shall remain in force until the date of expiry of the period laid down in Article 8(3) of Regulation (EEC) No. 170/83'. The article 8(3) referred to describes the aforesaid date of expiry as '. . . during the 10th year following 31 December 1992'.

[11] Case C-221/89, *The Queen v Secretary of State for Transport, ex parte Factortame Limited & Others* [1991] ECR I, not yet reported. In paragraph 4 of the judgment, the Court referred to the UK pleadings as follows:
> 'It is common ground that the United Kingdom amended the previous legislation in order to put a stop to the practice known as 'quota hopping' whereby, according to the United Kingdom, its fishing quotas are 'plundered' by vessels flying the British flag but lacking any genuine link with the United Kingdom.'

[12] Churchill *Quota Hopping: The Common Fisheries Policy Wrongfooted?* 27 CML Rev. (1990), 209 at 210.

While the earlier judgment in *Factortame I*[13] is of great importance so far as the jurisdictions of national courts are concerned where reliance is placed on Community law to suspend the operation of a national measure pending the outcome of a reference to the Court of Justice, my interest is with the judgments which have dealt with the question of quota hopping and some of the differing views that emerged in this process.

This approach reflects, essentially, the concerns of a practising lawyer presented with starkly conflicting views on what should be the correct approach to this issue. This concerns the significance of national quotas under the common fisheries policy and, more particularly, the annual regulation providing for the total allowable catch for quota species of certain fish stocks and their subsequent distribution between the member states. The scarcity of fish (including quota species fish) makes future litigation and legislation inevitable. The fact that quotas are being reduced in certain instances and some species of fish are under threat makes all the more necessary a clear cut resolution of this matter.

Quota Hopping and Third Countries

No problems are caused now by third countries as the Court of Justice has confirmed the competence of the Member States to impose restrictions on third country nationals. While no doubt can attach to the exercise of such power by a Member State, the manner of its determination is illustrative of difficulties in this area. In *Pesca Valentia Limited v Ministry for Fisheries and Forestry, Ireland and the Attorney General*,[14] The Irish courts were faced with a challenge to the State's competence to impose a requirement in a licensing system for sea fishing boats on the Irish register that 75% of the crew must be nationals of a Member State of the European Communities. Pesca Valentia was a joint venture company between Irish and Spanish fishing interests. It owned three fishing vessels which previously had been registered in Spain. They were taken off the Spanish register and subsequently registered on the Irish register. The members of the crew were entirely Spanish and the vessels operated for most of the time out of fishing ports in Galicia in north western Spain. After the coming into operation of the Community regime for the conservation and management of fishery resources, Ireland enacted specific legislation giving the relevant minister of government power to impose conditions on sea fishing licences.[15] While a crewing requirement of 75% Community nationality was imposed in the licences granted the company's three

---

[13] Case C-213/89, *The Queen v The Secretary of State for Transport, ex parte Factortame Limited & Others* [1990] ECR I–2433. The Supreme Court of Ireland applying identical principles of constitutional jurisprudence granted an interlocutory injunction restraining the Irish authorities from enforcing a 75% EC nationality crewing requirement against Spanish nationals before Spain joined the European Communities in *Pesca Valentia Limited v Minister for Fisheries and Forestry, Ireland and the Attorney General* [1985] IR 195. The Irish Supreme Court judgment was delivered some five years before the decision of the Court of Justice in *Factortame I*. Interim measures were also ordered by the Court of Justice in a related case on the application of the Commission after the reference from the House of Lords in *Factortame I*: see case C-246/89, R, *Commission v United Kingdom* [1989] ECR 3125.

[14] [1985] IR 193.

[15] Fisheries (Amendment) Act 1983, s 2. This inserted an additional section 222B into the Fisheries (Consolidation) Act 1959.

fishing vessels in 1983 and 1984, Pesca Valentia was informed that the Irish authorities would postpone the application of the Community nationality provisions to them until late 1984.

However, Pesca Valentia never complied with these conditions and continued to fish with an exclusively Spanish crew. Following the arrest of one of their vessels, the 'Monte Marin', on 11 September 1984, legal proceedings were issued on behalf of the joint venture company against the relevant Irish authorities challenging their competence to impose such a Community crewing requirement. It was alleged that only Community institutions had power to impose such restrictions after the end of the transitional period for fisheries on the 31 December 1982 and that the Irish legislation was discriminatory and in breach of Community law. Spain was a third country when these proceedings were instituted and the court dealt with the issues involved on the basis that Spanish nationals were nationals of a third country. On the 12 March 1985 the High Court of Ireland granted an interlocutory injunction restraining the Irish authorities from enforcing this crewing requirement until the determination of the High Court action.[16] Subsequently, after a reference from the High Court in the plenary action, the Court of Justice rule that the Community law argument raised by Pesca Valentia failed. The Court of Justice ruled that under Regulation 101/76 laying down a common structural policy for the fishing industry, the conditions for 'flying the flag' of a Member State or 'registered' in that State were left to be defined in the legislation of that Member State.[17]

The Court of Justice delivered an emphatic ruling on the competence of a Member State to determine the conditions under which vessels were entitled to fly its flag. This was in accord with accepted principles of public international law whereby the maintenance of State's shipping register was regarded as an aspect of national sovereignty. The Court of Justice appeared to concur in this view. Having reviewed the provisions of Community legislation dealing with the common structural policy for the fishing industry, the court reached the following conclusion:

'However, it is clear from the provisions of the regulation (Regulation No. 101/76) that, pending the entry into force of such Community measures, the Member States may apply their own rules in respect of fishing in the maritime waters coming under their sovereignty or within their jurisdiction (Article 2) and define their structural policy for the fishing industry (Article 1). Furthermore, it should be noted that the provisions of the regulation refer to fishing vessels 'flying the flag' of a Member State or 'registered' there, leaving these terms to be defined in the legislation of the Member States.'[18]

Emphasis is laid upon this passage as the Court of Justice would appear to have introduced a new requirement in the *Factortame II* litigation which is not referred to at all in *Pesca Valentia*. I refer to the newly found reliance upon Article 7 and the requirement that there should be no discrimination on the grounds of nationality.

---

[16] This injunction was granted on constitutional principles in Irish law reflecting what was said subsequently by the court in Case C-213/89, *Factortame I* [1990] ECR 1–2433. The later High Court judgment which made the reference is reported at [1987] 1 CMLR 856.

[17] [1988] ECR 83 at p. 107, para 13; see also Case C-221/89, *Factortame II* [1991] ECR at para 13.

[18] Case 223/86, *Pesca Valentia* [1988] ECR 83, at p. 107, para 13.

The judgment of the Court of Justice in *Pesca Valentia* was delivered on 19 January 1988. Subsequently in the resumed High Court proceedings, Pesca Velentia was unsuccessful in its claim in reliance upon the other arguments that had been advanced.[19] However, by that stage references had been made by the High Court of Justice of England and Wales in *Agegate*[20] and *Jaderow*.[21] Separate proceedings were instituted on behalf of Pesca Valentia raising identical issues to those in the *Agegate* and *Jaderow* cases. An interlocutory injunction was obtained from the Irish High Court preventing the application of the 75% crewing requirement excluding Spanish nationals, this time on the basis that as nationals of a Member State, it was unlawful to exclude them from working on such vessels until the 1 January 1993 in reliance upon Article 56 of the 1985 Act of Accession. Thus the Spanish fishing interests represented in the Irish joint venture successfully avoided the application of the Community crewing requirement to its vessels throughout the entire period when Spain was a third country and thereafter when Spain became a Member State under the 1985 Act of Accession.

Pesca Valentia, Jaderow and *Agegate* may be seen as part and parcel of a continuum whereby constitutional arguments advanced in reliance upon Community law successfully challenged the scheme of things apparently accepted by Spain under the 1985 Act of Accession. It is interesting to note that the vessel giving rise to *Pesca Valentia*, the 'Monte Marin', merits an individual mention in the 1985 Act of Accession as a joint venture vessel which secured the special benefits of Article 168(4) of the 1985 Act of Accession whereby the produce of such vessels was not to be subjected to a restrictive regime that otherwise applied to Spanish fishery products during a transitional period.[22]

Quota Hopping and the Member States

The issue that did not have to be decided in *Pesca Valentia* was raised in the subsequent litigation commencing with *Agegate* and *Jaderow* and subsequently involving the *Factortame I* and *Factortame II* group of cases. The issue to be decided in these cases concerned the validity of licensing conditions imposed by the United Kingdom on its vessels intended to deal with the problem of quota hopping and to ensure a closer economic link between a vessel entered on the UK Register and that jurisdiction.

It is interesting to observe the contrasting approaches of the Court of Justice and the Advocate General[23] to this issue. There seems to be little doubt that the crucial judgments are those delivered in *Agegate* and *Jaderow* and of these two *Agegate* would appear to be the more important. *Agegate* concerned licensing conditions imposed with effect from 1 January 1986 which (a) required

---

[19] *Pesca Valentia Limited v Minister for Fisheries and Forestry, Ireland and the Attorney General* [1990] 1 CMLR 707.

[20] Case C-3/87, *The Queen v Minister for Agriculture, Fisheries and Food, ex parte Agegate Limited* [1989] ECR 4459.

[21] Case C-216/87 *The Queen v Minister for Agriculture, Fisheries and Food, ex parte Jaderow Limited* [1989] ECR 4509.

[22] See 1985 Act of Accession, Art. 168(4) and Annex 2 for such joint venture companies: OJ 1985, L 302/1 at 74 and 274.

[23] A. G. Mischo.

75% Community nationality of crew excluding Greek, Spanish and Portuguese nationals to that period in their respective Acts of Accession concerning free movement of workers; (b) imposed a residential requirement in the United Kingdom; and (c) imposed a requirement that the skipper and crew make contributions to the social security scheme of that Member State.

Jaderow concerned the operating conditions imposed in the UK licensing system with effect from the same date. This required the vessel concerned to land at least 50% by weight of its catch in a United Kingdom port and to operate on at least four days out of fifteen from a UK port. After the institution of the proceedings in *Agegate* and *Jaderow*, applications were brought on behalf of the many undertakings represented in those proceedings for interlocutory injunctions restraining the UK authorities from enforcing these conditions. A compromise was reached between the parties to this litigation as a consequence whereof, pending the resolution of the Community law issues raised, the UK authorities permitted the Anglo-Spanish vessels to operate much as they had previously, subject to strict reporting conditions. At the same time, proceedings were instituted before the Irish courts seeking identical relief to enable those same vessels to fish against the UK quota in waters coming within the maritime jurisdiction of Ireland. The English proceedings operated as a springboard for the Irish proceedings. The Irish High Court granted interlocutory injunctions restraining the Irish authorities from enforcing similar requirements on such vessels.[24]

The oral hearings in the references in *Agegate* and *Jaderow* took place on the 26 October 1988. The Advocate General delivered his opinion some three weeks later on 18 November 1988. While the issues seemed clear cut to the Advocate General raising important issues about the status of national quotas in Community law and the problem of dwindling fish stocks, the Court of Justice had much greater difficulty in dealing with the cases. The judgments of the court were not delivered until 14 December 1989, almost thirteen months after the Advocate General's opinion.[25] The judgments are not clear cut and are difficult to understand so far as their practical application is concerned.[26]

The judgments of the Court of Justice in *Factortame II*[27] and *Commission v United Kingdom*[28] give almost identical descriptions of the earlier litigation. The following passage is representative of the court's statement of its jurisprudence:

> 'It must be observed in the first place that, in its judgments in Case C-3/87 *Agegate* [1989] ECR 4459 and Case C-216/87, *Jaderow* [1989] ECR 4509, the Court stated that, when exercising the power granted to them to define the detailed rules for the utilisation of their quotas, the Member States may determine which vessels in their fishing fleets will be allowed to fish against their national quotas, provided that the

---

[24] *Decanos Fisheries Limited, Brigtal UK Limited and Ardar Fishing Co. Limited v The Minister for the Marine, Ireland and the Attorney General*, ex tempore judgment of the High Court of Ireland (Miss Justice Carroll), 4 June 1987. The High Court followed the Supreme Court judgment in *Pesca Valentia Limited v Minister for Fisheries and Forestry, Ireland and the Attorney General* [1985] IR 193.

[25] The reference in *Agegate* was received in the court on the 12 January 1987 and the reference in *Jaderow* on the 14 July 1987.

[26] See Churchill *Quota Hopping: The Common Fisheries Policy Wrongfooted?* 27 CML Rev. (1990) 109, 220–229 where the judgments are criticized.

[27] [1991] ECR I, not yet reported.

[28] [1991] ECR I, not yet reported.

criteria employed are compatible with Community law. In the second judgment cited above, the Court held in particular that a Member State was entitled to lay down conditions designed to ensure that the vessel has a real economic link with that State if that link concerns only the relations between that vessel's fishing operations and the population dependent on fisheries and related industries.'[29]

In *Agegate*, the Court of Justice had ruled that the relevant provisions of Community law[30] entitled Member States to stipulate the conditions under which vessels could fish against its national quota:

'In this regard, Member States may refuse to allow fishing vessels to fish against the national quotas unless certain conditions are fulfilled with regard to, for example, the size, age or state of the vessel, its equipment, the number of fishermen on board, accommodation and mess facilities for the crew, sanitary arrangements, safety matters and so forth, in so far as those conditions are not governed exclusively by Community legislation.[31]

This was stated in the context of the court's summary of the position prior to answering the individual questions raised in that reference. What is most difficult to follow is the court's treatment of the resident requirement in the UK licensing conditions. Having referred to various provisions of Community law including certain recitals in Regulation 170/83 emphasising the particular needs of regions where local populations are especially dependent on fisheries and related industries, the court continued as follows:

'It follows from the foregoing that the aim of the quotas is to assure to each Member State a share of the Community's total allowable catch, determined essentially on the basis of the catches from which traditional fishing activities, the local populations dependent on fisheries and related industries of that Member State benefitted before the quota system was established.'[32]

One would have thought that such a residence requirement gives effect to that policy. However this was rejected by the Court:

'In that context a residence requirement such as the one in point in this case is irrelevant to the aim of the quota system and cannot therefore be justified by that aim.
    The answer to this question must therefore be that Community law precludes a Member State from requiring, as a condition for authorising one of its vessels to fish against its quota, that 75% of the crew of the vessel in question must reside ashore in that Member State.'[33]

It could be argued that the resident requirement imposed in the UK operating conditions were of too general a nature. Would the same answer be given by the Court if an effort was made to link that residence to a maritime region of the

[29] Case C-246/89, *Commission v UK* [1991] ECR I, para 35; Case C-246/89, *Factortame II* [1991] ECR I, para 40.
[30] Regulation 170/83, Art 5(2) which provides as follows: 'Member States shall determine, in accordance with the applicable related provisions the detailed rules for the utilisation of the quotas allocated to them'.
[31] [1989] ECR 4459, at p. 4500, para 18.
[32] [1989] ECR 4459, at p. 4502, para 24.
[33] [1989] ECR 4459, at p. 4503, paras 25–26.

Member State concerned which was dependent on fisheries? Such a condition might acquire even greater efficacy if it was part and parcel of a further effort to establish a real economic link between the fishing vessel or vessels concerned and the coastal population dependent on fisheries in the Member State in question.

In *Jaderow* the court was concerned with certain operating conditions. On the system of quotas the court adopted some of the language used in *Agegate*. A rubric in the court's judgment dealing with quotas is entitled '[a] *real economic link* between the vessel and the Member State'. Having repeated much of what had been said immediately before in *Agegate*, the Court in *Jaderow* answered the general question on 'real economic link' by stating that the answer:

> · '. . . must be that Community law as it now stands does not preclude a Member State, in authorising one of its vessels to fish against national quotas, from laying down conditions designed to ensure that the vessel has a real economic link with that State if that link concerns only the relation between the vessel's fishing operations and the populations dependent on fisheries and related industries.'[34]

In the light of the importance attached to the traditional fishing activities and local populations dependent on fisheries and related industries, the residence requirement struck down by the Court of Justice on the facts disclosed in these references would appear intended to achieve that very aim. Certainly, if that condition had stipulated residence in a maritime region, so as to provide for the population dependent on fisheries, would the court have reached the same conclusion?

Another view

The Advocate General in *Agegate* and *Jaderow* reached a different conclusion. The oral hearing in both of these cases set the pattern for the oral hearing in the subsequent *Factortame II* group of cases. The Commission and Spain supported the Anglo-Spanish companies, the applicants in the UK references. Ireland and the United Kingdom, as the only two other maritime jurisdictions concerned, supported the respondent UK authorities. The approach of the Advocate General in *Agegate* illustrates a contrasting approach to the topic of national quotas.

The essential difference between the analysis of the Advocate General and that of the Court in *Agegate* related to the residence requirement. Having analyzed and examined the unique features attaching to the market in fish and fish products, the opinion was expressed that Community law did not preclude the imposition of such a condition in the context of a 75% Community crewing requirement.[35] Fish are a unique agricultural product. They clearly come within the definition of 'agricultural products' under Article 38 of the EEC Treaty. 'Fish, crustaceans and molluscs' is the expression used in Annex II to the Treaty. However, there the similarity with other agricultural products ends. All of the other products listed in the Treaty are not in scarce supply.

---

[34] [1989] ECR 4509, at p. 4544, para 27.
[35] [1989] ECR 4459, at pp. 4481–4490, paras 41–104.

Indeed, the opposite is the case. It is common case with fisheries that there has been over fishing of stocks of the main species. Indeed, this is one of the principal reasons why the Communities adopted Regulation 170/83 and imposed a Community and national licensing system which is reflected in the annual TAC regulation made under this regulation apportioning national quotas between the various Member States. The following would appear to be factors which influenced the Advocate General in his opinion.

The restructuring regulations whereby the Member States under multi-annual guidance programmes are to reduce their gross registered tonnage in their fleets.[36] There is a huge over capacity in all of the Member States which the Commission wishes to have reduced. Further, the special provisions in Articles 156 to 164 of the 1985 Act of Accession concerning the number of Spanish fishing vessels which may fish within Community waters falling within the jurisdiction of the old Member States. A list of such vessels was appended to the Act of Accession. In addition, the judgment in *Pesca Valentia* had left it to Member States to define the application of appropriate principles to vessels 'flying the flag' of a Member State or 'registered' in a Member State. This is to avoid flags of convenience.[37]

Apart from the above, the Advocate General expressed the view that further considerations justified a Member State in adopting measures to ensure that the catches of new vessels entering the register mainly benefit the fishermen residing in its territory. So far as Spanish nationals were concerned, the Advocate General was of the view that they could not comply with the 75% nationality crewing requirement until 1 January 1993. This was to comply with the special provisions of Articles 56 to 59 of the 1985 Act of Accession which provides for a derogation from the principle of free movement of workers in the case of such nationals until that date.

So far as national quotas were concerned, these reflected the Community's policy of trying to deal with the difficulties and problems caused by the over fishing of the main species of fish to the extent that this had jeopardised the standards of living of those dependent upon the fishing industry. The scarcity of fish, therefore, justified a derogation from the principle of free access otherwise provided for under Community law and, in particular, Regulation 101/76.The quota system was justified '. . . because it apportions on an objective basis the sacrifices to be made by the *fishermen* of each member State'.[38] Apart from this consideration, the Advocate General took into account various recitals in Regulation 101/76 to the effect that those who lived by the fishing industry should be assured of a fair standard of living and the recognition that sea fisheries have their own social structure and fish under special conditions.[39] This led the Advocate General to conclude that the residence condition included in the UK licence:

---

[36] Council Regulation 2908/83 on a common measure for restructuring, modernizing and developing the fishing industry and for developing aquaculture: OJ 1983, L 290/1; see also Council Regulation 4028/86 on Community measures to improve and adapt structures in the fisheries and aquaculture sectors: OJ 1996, L 376/7.

[37] [1988] ECR 83, at p. 107, para 13.

[38] [1989] ECR 4459, at p. 4485, para 73. Case 46/86, *Romkes* [1987] ECR 2671 was the first judgment to refer to the concept of equality of sacrifice among fishermen.

[39] Regulation 101/76, 5th and 2nd recital respectively.

'. . . constitutes the corollary, so to speak, of the derogation from certain rules of Community law entailed in the quota system itself.'[40]

The Advocate General also stated that the 1985 Act of Accession had given Treaty status to the quota system.[41] This was confirmed in the Advocate General's opinion in *Jaderow*.

Some Consequences of *Agegate, Jaderow,* and *Factortame*

The commentator referred to at the start of this article expressed the view after *Agegate* and *Jaderow* that the common fisheries policy has in all probability been 'wrongfooted'. However he felt that an element of doubt remained as the problem of quota hopping was also raised in the *Factortame II* litigation. The judgments of the Court of Justice were delivered on 25 July 1991[42] and 4 October 1991.[43] *Factortame II* had the effect of declaring invalid those provisions of the UK Merchant Shipping Act 1988 which had imposed a 75% British nationality requirement on the ownership of fishing vessels on the UK register. The Court declared that the United Kingdom had thereby failed to fulfil its obligations under Articles 7, 52 and 221 of the EEC Treaty.

In the fisheries litigation that came before the Court of Justice in the 1970s and early 1980s, the Commission had argued for its exclusive competence in those areas concerning the protection of fishing grounds and the conservation of the biological resources of the sea. The Commission eventually succeeded and used its competence as a central justification for Regulation 170/83. This regulation was viewed by the Member States as the keystone of the common fisheries policy. If there had to be sacrifices, they were to be equally shared among all the fishermen of the Member States and the respective interests of those fishermen were protected by the system of national quotas introduced in this regulation. That regulation was based on a Commission proposal which in turn provided for both the Community total allowable catch and the respective national quotas. Having secured that competence, the Commission has failed to deal effectively or at all with the problem of quota hopping. As Dr Churchill has observed in his article, the Commission has been considering this issue as long ago as 1983. No concrete proposals have emerged from this institution. Its principal response has been a somewhat anodyne communication published in the Official Journal in 1989 entitled '*Commission Communication on a Community Framework for Access to Fishing Quotas*'.[44]

So far as quota hopping itself is concerned, the Commission in the recent litigation has intervened in support of parties who are seen as representing the quota hoppers. In addition, it has instituted direct actions against those maritime Member States – notably Ireland and the United Kingdom – which have endeavoured to deal with this problem in the absence of any Community measure. It is paradoxical that an institution should fight so doggedly to establish its competence in fisheries and conservation matters and, having

[40] [1989] ECR 4459, at p. 4486, para 82.
[41] [1989] ECR 4459, at p. 4488, para 91.
[42] Case C-221/98, *Factortame II* [1991] ECR I, not yet reported.
[43] Case C-246/89, *Commission v United Kingdom* [1991] ECR I, not yet reported. Case C-98/89, *Commission v Ireland* [1991] ECR I, not yet reported.
[44] OJ 1989, C 224/3.

achieved that end, make no effective proposal to deal with a crucial conservation issue.

There is a crisis in the fishing industry. Any interested party will tell of dwindling fish stocks. The extent of the problem is described in general terms in the communication from the Commission to the Council and the European Parliament on the common fisheries policy.[45] This mentions the serious imbalance between available resources and fishing capacity. It also deals with the threat to fish stocks. However, there is no discussion of any reform of national quotas or any recognition of quota hopping as a problem that requires urgent consideration.

The accepted practice on the manner in which Member States have maintained their shipping registers and invariably applied a nationality requirement has now been thrown into question by the judgment of the court in *Commission v United Kingdom*.[46] The Court of Justice commences by repeating in general terms its ruling in *Pesca Valentia* concerning the competence of Member States to determine the conditions upon which a vessel may fly its flag.[47] However, there the similarity ends because the Court adds a new requirement in reliance upon Articles 7, 52 and 221 of the EEC Treaty. The Court referred to a recent judgment[48] whereby Article 7 was held applicable to the activities comprised within Article 52 of the Treaty. Having observed that the concept of the nationality of ships is different from that of the nationality of natural persons within the meaning of the Treaty concerning the right of establishment, the Court went on to declare that the registers of the Member States could not discriminate on grounds of nationality:

'The prohibition on discrimination on grounds of nationality which sets out in particular, as regards the right of establishment, in Article 52 of the Treaty, is concerned with differences and treatment as between natural persons who are nationals of Member States and between companies that are treated in the same way as such persons by virtue of Article 58.

Consequently, in exercising the powers for the purposes of defining the conditions for the grant of its "nationality" to a ship, each Member State must comply with the prohibition of discrimination against nationals of Member States on grounds of their nationality.

It follows from the foregoing that the contested nationality requirements, according to which natural persons who own or charter a vessel and, in the case of a company, its shareholders and directors, must have British nationality in order to enable a vessel to be registered in the British register of fishing vessels, are contrary to Article 52 of the Treaty.'[49]

It is not difficult to envisage the consequences of this judgment so far as national quotas under the common fisheries policy are concerned. This judgment stands in contrast to the earlier declaration of the Court of Justice in *Pesca Valentia* that it was left to the Member States to determine the registration conditions applicable to fishing vessels who wish to enter its register. All of the Member States at that time would have maintained registers reflecting the nationality of that jurisdiction. That in turn would have been reflected in the

---

[45] SEC (90) 2244 final, Brussels, 6 December 1990.
[46] Case C-246/89, *Commission v United Kingdom*.
[47] See paragraphs 11–12 of judgment.
[48] Case 305/87, *Commission v Hellenic Republic* [1989] ECR 146, paragraphs 12–13.
[49] Case C-246/89, *Commission v United Kingdom* [1991] ECR I, paragraphs 29–31, not yet reported.

national quotas allocated to that state under the common fisheries policy. There has been a marked change in direction with the judgment in *Commission v United Kingdom* which has now stated that, in respect of a national shipping register, there may be no discrimination between nationals of Member States on the ground of nationality when it comes to the exercise of a right of establishment by nationals of another Member State who wish to be registered on that latter state's shipping register. No Member State agreeing to national quotas in Regulation 170/83 could have foreseen this subsequent development.

There may also be other factors involved. One of the distinguishing features in the oral hearing in the *Factortame II* litigation was the number of other Member States which intervened in support of the position taken by United Kingdom on the entitlement of a state to maintain its shipping register as heretofore. Each of those Member States saw a challenge or threat to its own shipping register in a way that had not seemed apparent or possible until after the judgments of the court in *Agegate* and *Jaderow* and the arguments advanced by the Commission in the *Factortame II* litigation.[50]

Throughout this most recent litigation the Commission has concentrated exclusively on principles of Community law. It has not advanced any theory on quotas or on quota hopping generally other than an assertion that whatever proposals or scheme is adopted in the future to deal with fisheries any such proposal must comply with fundamental principles of Community law. Judges determine matters and questions of law. The Directorate General for Fisheries is supposed to determine questions of fishery policy. One of the unique features of Community law is the extent to which economic and related arguments find reflection in the law. In this context one would have expected from the Commission a response which would take into account the unique features of fisheries and the problem facing that sector as reflected in the common fisheries policy. This has not occurred to date. What has happened is that the Commission has stepped aside and allowed the structure of national quotas carefully negotiated over a lengthy period under its aegis and direction to be worn away and undermined by subsequent litigation. No effective steps or proposals have been advanced by the Commission to date to remedy this situation.

If the general situation continues to disimprove and no effective measures are taken by the Commission to deal with quota hopping, might not a different situation arise? As already stated, the determination of any case before a constitutional court is influenced by the facts. The Court of Justice has on occasions departed from earlier decisions if it feels that this is justified. Precedent does not have the same binding effect in Community law as in other legal systems, notably the common law system.[51] It would be interesting to see the fate of a Commission application for interim measures in a future case if that institution continues to do nothing effective about quota hopping. Viewed from the perspective of the Member States most affected, the imposition of an adapted residence requirement would meet the objectives of the common

---

[50] The United Kingdom was supported, in the main, by the Governments of Belgium, Denmark, Germany, Greece and Ireland. The Commission and Spain supported *Factortame Limited & Others*. By way of contrast, Ireland, Spain and the United Kingdom were the only Member States to intervene in the *Agegate* and *Jaderow* litigation.

[51] Case 302/87, *Parliament v Council ('Comitology')* [1988] ECR 5637 and Case C-70/88, *Parliament v Council ("Chernobyl")* [1990] ECR I–2041, for a recent example where the court did not follow a judgment delivered some eighteen months previously on a similar principle.

fisheries policy in securing the requirements of local populations dependent on fisheries and related industries.[52]

Ireland has a reputation as a country where there is great game fishing. Salmon and sea trout have been the kings of such river and estuary fishing especially in the West of Ireland. In very recent years, the sea trout has virtually disappeared. There was no warning. Suddenly, approximately three seasons ago, the fish failed to return from the Atlantic to spawn in Irish rivers in the manner they had done for millennia. There have been various suggestions advanced but no conclusive reason has yet been produced. Looking at sea fisheries generally, the success or failure of the present litigation should be seen not only in jurisprudential terms concerning the interpretation of Community law but its effect on the agricultural produce concerned – fisheries. If the situation should further disimprove and quota species of fish either disappear or reach near extinction, what response would the Court of Justice give to a direct action by the Commission against a maritime Member State which sought to apply licencing conditions imposing a residence requirement in its maritime regions so as to provide for the local population dependent on fisheries? This may not be a remote possibility. During the oral hearing in *Agegate* and *Jaderow*, it was represented by leading counsel on behalf of these companies that the Spanish fishermen engaged on these vessels would, if necessary, take up residence in the United Kingdom. This assertion might be put to the test if Member States subsequently adapt their legislation so as to reflect the needs of coastal communities dependent on fisheries and to establish a genuine economic link with those regions.

---

[52] There remain two direct actions before the Court of Justice in the context of the common fisheries policy which raise the application of the principles decided in the earlier litigation: see Case C-279/89, *Commission v United Kingdom* and Case C-280/89, *Commission v Ireland*. The United Kingdom proceedings raise the question of the compatibility of the operating conditions impliedly approved of by the Court of Justice in *Jaderow* with Article 34 of the EEC Treaty. The Irish proceedings concern a challenge to the earlier English operating conditions which were reflected in the Sea Fishing Boat Regulations 1986 (SI No. 289 of 1986).

7 The Free Movement of Workers in the Case-Law of the European Court of Justice

G. Federico Mancini

In this article I wish to examine the free movement of workers in the light of the case-law of the Court of Justice. By concentrating on more recent judgments, I intend to outline the direction taken by the Court in this area. I also intend to keep to a minimum my treatment of primary and secondary law so as to avoid the theoretical debates to which their interpretation has given rise.

According to Charles Evans Hughes, the celebrated American scholar and judge, 'the Constitution is what the judges say it is'. If we replace the word 'Constitution' by 'Treaty of Rome', the phrase retains its relevance. This is so because the document which established the European Economic Community suffers from numerous lacunae and also because until recently Luxembourg was a byword for unrestrained judicial activism. It is true that in the field of labour-related matters, such activism has frequently been motivated by a desire to consolidate the jurisdiction of the Court and at the same time to ensure the full and effective functioning of the Common Market. It is, however, also true that the judges of the Court have approached the human problems associated with the free movement of workers in a very sensitive manner. If it can be said to be a good thing that our Europe is not merely a Europe of commercial interests, it is the judges who must take much of the credit.

Since the foundation of the EEC the free movement of workers has given rise to an extensive body of case-law: more than 300 judgments out of 3000 delivered by the Court of Justice up to the end of 1991. This figure includes cases dealing with social security which I have excluded from the present article. The movement within the Common Market of workers from Member States is now slowing down. However, immigration from the Third World and Eastern Europe is on the increase, and this is a matter which has given rise to serious problems for Member States and the Community as a whole. Nonetheless, these developments have not led to a reduction in the number of cases referred to Luxembourg for preliminary rulings. It has to be added that the three accessions to the Community have also increased the potential for conflict, if only because of the peculiarities of the Common Law systems and the transitional measures applicable to Greece, Spain and Portugal.

I would like to make one further general point. The Court has shown that it pursues a two-fold aim when dealing with the free movement of workers. The Court's first aim is to derive directly effective subjective rights from the principle of free movement of workers, rights upon which the migrant worker can rely against the authorities in proceedings before the courts of the Member State in which he works. Secondly, the Court aims to guarantee uniform application of Community law, thereby abolishing the many forms of direct and indirect discrimination which existed within the legal and administrative procedures of Member States even before the Treaty was signed and which continue to be applied in ever more subtle ways today.

As we shall examine later in more detail, in order to realize its first objective, the European Court recognized the direct effect of Article 48 of the Treaty and subsequently of numerous provisions of the two directives covering this subject. This bold approach met, at least initially, with stubborn resistance from certain major national legal systems and also provoked harsh criticism in political circles (the former French Prime Minister Michel Debré declared that the Court in Luxembourg was suffering from 'morbid megalomania'). Moreover, the Court conferred on itself what we might describe as a hermeneutic monopoly for the purpose of counteracting the unequal and discriminatory application of the rules on freedom of movement. Thus, it decided that it was not a matter for national legislation to define key concepts such as employed persons, social advantage, public policy etc. These definitions would have to be elaborated at Community level (as was done in 1964 in the judgment in *Unger*).[1]

The remainder of this article will be divided into three parts. In the first, I will identify the ambit of the practical and material application of the rules relating to the movement of workers. In the second, I shall examine the content of such provisions; and in the third I will analyse the two restrictions which the Treaty imposes on the freedom of movement.

The scope of the rules relating to free movement of workers

I have already mentioned that the free movement of workers is established by Article 48 of the Treaty. However, neither that article nor the regulations and directives detailing its content and governing its application expressly define the term 'worker'. From the elements mentioned in Article 48(2) ('employment', 'remuneration' and 'other conditions of work and employment') one can, by contrasting them with the terms used in Article 52 ('activities as self-employed persons') and in Article 59 ('freedom to provide services'), deduce that a 'worker' is any Community national who carries out an 'activity as an employed person'. However, the true scope of these terms remains unspecified.

The Court did not formally answer this question until 1986. As was stated in the judgment in *Lawrie-Blum*,[2] a worker is 'any person performing for remuneration work the nature of which is not determined by himself for and under the control of another, regardless of the legal nature of the employment relationship.' However, this definition is not complete. In 1982, in its judgment in *Levin*,[3] the Court had stated that the work also had to be an 'effective and genuine economic activity'. The Court, therefore, had limited itself by

---

[1] Case 75/63, *Hoekstra (née Unger) v Bestuur der Bedrijfsvereniging voor Detailhandel en Ambachten* [1964] ECR 177.

[2] Case 66/85, *Lawrie-Blum v Land Baden-Württemberg* [1986] ECR 2121.

[3] Case 53/81, *Levin v Staatssecretaris van Justitie* [1982] ECR 1035.

drawing conclusions based upon the particular facts of the case, as it has done previously. In 1974, for example, in *Sotgiu*,[4] the Court had ruled that factors such as the professional title of the worker (wage-earner, white collar employee, manager) and the public or private nature of the contractual relationship were irrelevant. Other judgments also delimited the scope of the employment relationship in a series of more or less problematic situations, such as in the case of the au pair girls.[5] The same occurred in the cases of the middle-distance cycle pacemakers[6] and the professional footballers.[7]

Having stressed the importance of a precise definition, let us now look at how the Court has clarified a few of the elements of this definition before and after the judgment in *Lawrie-Blum*. First, according to the Court, the extent and duration of the work done and the legal nature of the employment relationship are irrelevant. In line with the judgment given in *Levin*, in particular, a worker can be someone who engages or intends to engage in a part-time activity and consequently is or will be paid less than the minimum wage guaranteed by law and under the contracts of employment applicable to that particular activity. Accordingly, both a teacher employed for only 12 hours a week who supplements his income with social security benefits[8] and a university student who briefly takes on employment connected with his studies in order to finance the latter[9] may benefit from the rules on freedom of movement.

Consequently, it is not necessary that the work be continuous or full-time. However, the Court has gone beyond this conclusion, significant though it is, by ruling that a national of a Member State need not be working at the material time in order for him to be entitled to rely on Article 48. It is sufficient that a person is in the course of preparing to be a worker (as was the plaintiff in *Lawrie-Blum*, who had moved from England to Germany in order to work as a trainee teacher) or that he had been a worker and remained in the country in which he worked in order to pursue studies related to his previous experience.[10] More significantly, the judgments in *Levin* and *Adoui and Cornuaille*[11] refer to the rights of those who 'intend to carry out work' or 'wish to seek work'. This was given clear expression in *Antonissen*.[12] In holding that it was not contrary to the provisions governing the free movement of workers for a Member State to provide that a non-national may be required to leave its territory if he has not found employment there after six months, unless he can show he is continuing to seek work and has a genuine chance of being employed, the Court held that Article 48(3) must be interpreted as enumerating, in a non-exhaustive way, certain rights benefitting nationals of Member States in the context of the free movement of workers. That freedom includes the right for nationals of Member States to move freely and stay within the territory of other Member States for the purposes of seeking employment.

[4] Case 152/73, *Sotgiu v Deutsche Bundespost* [1974] ECR 153.
[5] Case 118/75, *Watson and Belmann* [1976] ECR 1185.
[6] Case 36/74, *Walrave and Koch v Association Union Cycliste Internationale* [1974] ECR 1405.
[7] Case 13/76, *Donà v Mantero* [1976] ECR 1333.
[8] Case 139/85, *Kempf v Staatssecretaris van Justitie* [1986] ECR 1741.
[9] Case 197/86, *Brown v Secretary of State for Scotland* [1988] ECR 3205.
[10] Case 39/86, *Lair v Universität Hannover* [1988] ECR 3161.
[11] Joined Cases 115 and 116/81, *Adoui and Cornuaille v Belgium* [1982] ECR 1665.
[12] Case C-292/89, *R v Immigration Appeal Tribunal ex parte Antonissen*, judgment 26 February 1991, not yet reported in ECR.

The apparent broadening of the principle in the judgments cited above may appear to be at variance with the requirement that the work should have an economic relevance, as stipulated in Levin. This discrepancy, however, is only apparent when one considers that, as stated in Article 2 of the Treaty, the founding fathers of the Community attributed to the Treaty the material objectives of progress (a harmonious development of economic activities, a continuous and balanced expansion, an increase in stability and an accelerated raising of the standard of living). Moreover, the Court has done all within its powers to dilute the concept of 'economic activity'. It has even applied it to cases where the work was carried out in the context of activities like prayer and meditation. In *Steymann*,[13] for example, the Court ruled that the support given by a religious or philosophical community to its members may be regarded as the indirect quid pro quo for genuine and effective work.

·On the other hand, the judges in *Bettray*[14] reached a different conclusion. A German drug addict worked for a Dutch undertaking under a public programme designed to re-educate and re-integrate such people into society. In line with its previous case-law, the Court did not consider the low productivity of the worker or the public source of his remuneration. However, it took the view that the purpose of the scheme and the reason why the plaintiff had been employed made it impossible to describe his work as an 'economic activity'. Accordingly, this activity did not allow the Court to guarantee the rights inherent in the free movement of workers.

Bettray, however, is an extreme case. Apart from it, the only cases where the Court systematically excludes the applicability of Article 48 are those which are known as 'domestic' cases. The judgment in *Saunders*[15] is a good example. Mrs Saunders, a UK national, was prosecuted before an English court for refusing to obey an order to move to Northern Ireland and not return to England or Wales for a period of three years. The question whether Mrs Saunders was protected by the rules on free movement of workers was referred to the Court of Justice. The Court replied in the negative. According to the judgment, rights laid down in the Treaty cannot be applied to circumstances where there is no factor connecting them to any of the situations envisaged by Community law. A sentence or penalty for an act committed within the territory of a Member State, which deprives or restricts the freedom of movement of such national, is a'wholly domestic situation' and Community law cannot interfere in its application.

Saunders was followed by many similar judgments. I shall limit myself to citing only those in *Morson*[16] and *Iorio*.[17] In the former, the Government of the Netherlands was found to have acted lawfully in refusing entry into its territory to nationals of a non-member country. These nationals of a non-member country were relatives of Dutch nationals, but they had never worked in any other Member State. The second judgment was to the effect that Community law did not prohibit the Italian railway authorities from limiting access to certain trains to passengers holding tickets for a minimum number of

---

[13] Case 196/87, *Steymann v Staatssecretaris van Justitie* [1988] ECR 6159.
[14] Case 344/87, *Bettray v Staatssecretaris van Justitie* [1989] ECR 1621.
[15] Case 175/78, *R v Saunders* [1979] ECR 1129.
[16] Joined Cases 35 and 36/82, *Morson and Jhanjan v Netherlands* [1982] ECR 3723.
[17] Case 298/84, *Iorio v Azienda Autonoma delle Ferrovie dello Stato* [1986] ECR 247.

kilometres, provided that this restriction was applied without discrimination on grounds of nationality.

The substance of the guarantee of free movement of workers

Let us now deal with the contents of the guarantee, beginning with the rights which it enshrines: entry and residence. The Treaty sets them out in a general manner, while the secondary legislation which regulates their application is very detailed. Directives 68/360 and 73/148 respectively oblige Member States to grant to nationals of those States the right to leave their territory in order to take up activities as employed persons in another Member State and to allow entry into their territory to nationals of other Member States on production of a valid identity card or passport, and to issue them with a residence permit. If one looks back a little more than 30 years and recalls the many formalities that a migrant worker had then to go through, one will undoubtedly appreciate the valuable progress which these new rules represent. Moreover, the Court has interpreted them in such a way as to highlight their emancipatory scope.

The basis of this jurisprudence is the case of *Commission v France*,[18] in which the Court ruled that Article 48 and Regulation No 1612/68 had direct effect. From this the Court was to draw a very important inference. As stated in *Royer*,[19] the right of residence does not flow from the issue of a residence permit. It is a right which is vested in migrant workers by virtue of Community law. The issue of a permit is thus reduced to a mere formality. The worker who neither applies nor is in possession of one may be penalized, but any such penalty must not be disproportionate to the aim or interest to be protected and cannot therefore jeopardize his freedom of movement. In other words, a worker cannot be deported nor, it seems, imprisoned on these grounds.

The subject of entry and residence also has an important social aspect. According to Article 48, these rights belong only to the worker. Article 10 of Regulation No 1612/68, however, extends the benefits to relatives of the worker; more precisely, to the spouse and descendants who are under the age of 21 or are dependants thereon, and to dependent relatives in the ascending line of the worker and his spouse. The nationality of the relatives is irrelevant. Nevertheless, in order for family members to obtain residence permits, the worker must have available for them 'housing considered as normal' for national workers in the region where he is employed. It is obvious that we are dealing here with progressive rules, not to say generous ones. The Court's interpretation of these rules is equally commendable. In *Commission v Germany*,[20] it ruled that the requirement of normal housing applied only to the time at which the relatives join the worker in the Member State in which he is employed. Consequently, it is incompatible with Community law for the national authorities of a Member State to refuse to renew a residence permit on

---

[18] Case 167/73, *Commission v France* [1974] ECR 359.
[19] Case 48/75, *Royer* [1976] ECR 497.
[20] Case 249/86, *Commission v Germany* [1989] ECR 1263.

the ground that the housing is no longer suitable for reasons such as an increase in the number of family members.

Even more interesting, in view of the light which they shed on the moral-political stance of the Court, are the judgments which define the term 'spouse'. In *Diatta*[21] it was held that a woman separated from a migrant worker had a right of residence even if both parties had demonstrated an intention to divorce. This was so because until a competent authority had made an official announcement the marital relationship could not be regarded as dissolved. The existence of such a relationship, however, is essential. It implies, as the Court affirmed in *Reed*,[22] that the right cannot be guaranteed to the unmarried partner of a worker, at least not until such time as social evolution has brought about the legal recognition in all Member States of cohabitation *more uxorio*. The reader will, I hope, agree that in a multinational community such as ours in which the electorate of one of the Member States, Ireland, has expressly demonstrated its opposition to the legalization of divorce this reservation constitutes proof of liberalism in the strongest sense of the word.

It has been said that once migrant workers have been allowed to enter into a Member State for the purpose of working, they – and, since the judgment in *Gül*,[23] their relatives – must be treated in the same way as nationals of that Member State.

This observation is correct. Yet, one can speak of equality in two senses: formal and substantive. Is it possible to say that Community law recognises the second meaning of equality, that is to allow for discrimination in favour of the weak and consequently in favour of the foreigner? Some writers point out that, by limiting the prohibition of discrimination to 'nationality . . ., as regards employment, remuneration and other conditions of work and employment', Article 48 does not go far enough. I would agree with this opinion. The guarantee of free movement excludes any form of affirmative action, as the American courts call it. On the other hand, there is no sign of a move from formal to substantive protection – not even in Regulation No 1612/68, which expands the provisions of the Treaty by means of sharper and more robust arrangements.

Neither has the Court of Justice made this move. On the contrary, it has declared that the equality of treatment guaranteed to migrant workers may also benefit national workers in that it protects them against the risk that wages or working conditions inferior to those guaranteed under national law may be offered to migrant workers. Nevertheless, one must not underestimate the contribution of the Court's case-law to this area. Whilst not taking the 'affirmative action' route, the Court has attempted to distil as much equality as possible from the Treaty and secondary legislation. This is shown by two lines of judgments.

The first group consists of those judgments which have recognised the rules on equality of treatment as being directly effective, with the result that they can be invoked before national courts in the State of employment. Those rules, therefore, also take precedence over any national provisions to the contrary, be they legislative, administrative or contractual.[24] The second group includes

[21] Case 267/83, *Diatta v Land Berlin* [1985] ECR 567.
[22] Case 59/85, *Netherlands v Reed* [1986] ECR 1283.
[23] Case 131/85, *Gül v Regierungspräsident Düsseldorf* [1986] ECR 1573.
[24] Case 9/74, *Casagrande v Landeshauptstadt München* [1974] ECR 773.

those judgments which have given a wide interpretation to the concept of 'working conditions'. In particular, the Court has declared that, when nationals of the host State enjoy similar gurantees, the migrant worker has the right: (a) to have the periods of his military service taken into account in the calculation of his seniority in the undertaking in which he works;[25] (b) to have special protection against dismissal if he is disabled;[26] (c) to receive compensation if assigned to work in an area different from that in which he resides;[27] and, (d) to receive aid granted for the acquisition and use of immovable property.[28]

More problematic is the position taken by the Court with regard to the discrimination against foreign workers on linguistic grounds. The final subparagraph of Article 3(1) of Regulation No 1612/68 refers to the possibility that national rules requiring a linguistic ability may be imposed on the migrant worker, when such knowledge is required by reason of the nature of the post to be filled. Ireland requires teaching staff in public vocational education institutions to hold a certificate providing adequate knowledge of the Irish language, defined in the Constitution as the 'national language' and 'first official language' of the State. It is a fact, however, that the vast majority of Irish people do not use Irish and that even teaching in the Republic is normally carried out through the medium of English.

The case of *Groener*[29] falls within this context. Mrs Groener, a Dutch national, was an art teacher in a third-level education institution in Dublin and possessed a high level of fluency in English. She was refused a permanent position because she did not have the above-mentioned certificate. She took her case to the Irish High Court, and it in turn referred to Luxembourg the question whether the relevant legislation was compatible with Community law. In what was evidently a very difficult case, the Court of Justice replied in the affirmative. The Court held that in Ireland there is a policy to promote the use of Irish, which has special historical roots, and this policy cannot be questioned from the point of view of Community law. Consequently, it is not unreasonable to require that teachers should have a knowledge of the language, given the obvious importance of their rôle in the education of each new generation. However, this policy cannot be applied in a manner disproportionate in relation to the aim pursued nor can it give rise to discrimination. For example, it would not be legitimate to require, as Irish law does, that the linguistic knowledge must have been acquired within the national territory.

It is a truism that 'welfare state' legislation which is found to a greater or lesser extent in all Member States, guarantees to its workers a series of social and tax advantages. Regulation No 1612/68 provides that the principle of equal treatment also applies to these advantages. The credit must go to the Court for having defined the ambit of these rules in general terms – all those rights 'which, whether or not linked to a contract of employment, are generally granted to national workers . . . and the extension of which to workers who are nationals of other Member States therefore seems suitable to facilitate their

---

[25] Case 15/69, *Südmilch v Ugliola* [1969] ECR 363.
[26] Case 44/72, *Marsman v Rosskamp* [1972] ECR 1243.
[27] Case 152/73, [1979] ECR 153.
[28] Case 305/87, *Commission v Greece* [1989] ECR 1461.
[29] Case C-379/87, *Groener v Minister for Education and the City of Dublin Vocational Education Committee* [1989] ECR 3967.

mobility'[30] – and for having included in such terms rights with or without an economic content, which in any event have a very tenuous link with the situation of a migrant worker. In this way, as the judgment in *Reed*, cited above, demonstrates, the Court overcame the problem of not being able to equate the partner in cohabitation *more uxorio* with a spouse, for the purpose of granting a residence permit, by proceeding on the basis of a 'social advantage' for the worker.

If *Reed* can be regarded, so to speak, as an exercise in judicial acrobatics, other judgments confine themselves to demonstrating the strong social sensibility so characteristic of the case-law of the Luxembourg Court, as I have shown in earlier examples. I will cite a few at random. The right to a minimum income for dependent relatives in the ascending line of the worker has been treated as a social advantage[31] as have university grants for the benefit of one's own child;[32] the payment of reduced rail fares by large families grants;[33] interest-free, State-assisted, long-term loans by a German bank for the purpose of stimulating the birth rate;[34] the opportunity to use one's native tongue in legal proceedings if the law of the State grants this right to nationals living in different areas of the country.[35]

Restrictions imposed on free movement of workers

Having discussed the content, let us now examine the restrictions. As we shall see, the right to free movement disappears each time public interest rears its head. The right may be limited 'on grounds of *public* policy, *public* security or *public* health' and does not apply to 'employment in the *public* service' or to activities connected with the exercise of official authority.

Let us first deal with the exception based on public policy. The formula set out above is contained in Article 48(3), but to interpret it one should look at Directive 64/221. In effect, Article 3 of the Directive has extensively enhanced the Treaty formula by providing that the national measures adopted in the name of public order must be based on the 'personal conduct of the individual' to whom they are to apply. Therefore, a measure adopted with the general purpose of prevention or as an example to others will be unlawful. The reader will agree that this is not only a commendable rule, but also one which is extremely difficult to implement. It is far from easy to justify the danger of certain behaviour in purely personal terms when, as is almost always the case, the danger in view is the risk of imitation by others and the fact that the actions in question are repugnant to society as a whole.

This difficulty explains why the Court may have initially hesitated between a liberal and conservative position on this matter. Few notions are so closely linked as the public policy to the political history and customs of the Member States. This confirms, as the English judge Lord Burrough commented last century, that public policy is 'an unruly horse to ride'. *Bonsignore*[36] is among the

---

[30] Case 207/78, *Ministère Public v Even* [1979] ECR 2019.
[31] Case 261/83, *Castelli v ONPTS* [1984] ECR 3199.
[32] Joined Cases 389 and 390/87, *Echternach and Moritz v Netherlands Minister for Education and Science* [1989] ECR 723.
[33] Case 32/75, *Cristini v SNCF* [1975] ECR 1085.
[34] Case 65/81, *Reina v Landeskreditbank Baden-Württemberg* [1982] ECR 33.
[35] Case 137/84, *Ministère Public v Mutsch* [1985] ECR 2681.
[36] Case 67/74, *Bonsignore v Oberstadtdirektor der Stadt Köln* [1975] ECR 297.

least conservative of the Court's judgments. Bonsignore was an Italian national resident in Germany, where he was found guilty of manslaughter and the illegal possession of firearms. After passing sentence, the German authorities deported him. In so doing they applied a national measure which was regarded by German law as a deterrent, and which therefore excluded the necessary link with the personal conduct of the person in question. The Court held that the measure was incompatible with Community law. The reservation contained in Article 48(3), it declared, was an exception which had to be strictly construed. The concept of 'personal conduct' implied that deportation could only be allowed if the accused person had specifically and directly breached public order and security.

The *Van Duyn*[37] judgment was inspired by a different philosophy. It is worth looking at the case in detail. A Dutch national moved to the UK to work as a secretary for the Church of Scientology, a bizarre pseudo-religious movement. The authorities in England refused her entry, claiming that the activities of the sect were harmful to society. Miss Van Duyn alleged that the decision forcing her to return to the Netherlands constituted an infringement of Article 48. The High Court in London referred to the Court of Justice the question whether membership by a Community national of a particular group could in itself constitute 'personal conduct' capable of justifying measures restricting the right to free movement.

The Court answered that question in the affirmative. Participation in the activities of an organised group, as well as identification with its aims and designs, was, the Court said, a voluntary act on the part of the person concerned. Consequently, it fulfilled the requirement of the Directive with regard to the issue of personal conduct. This reply is highly questionable and merits the criticism to which it has been subjected. Although the English courts regarded this religion as antisocial, there was in fact no legislation which actually prohibited the activities of the Church of Scientology. The Court of Justice considered such an anomaly to be irrelevant for the purposes of Community law. Perhaps it did not appreciate that such a decision exposed the Court to the accusation that it had disregarded the principle of equality. It is clear that this aspect of English law discriminates between British citizens, upon whom the provision has no effect, and all other Community nationals wishing to work in the UK, to whom the provision applies.

The Court of Justice quickly recovered from this slip by adopting a more open approach, as may be seen in the case of *Rutili*.[38] Rutili was a worker resident in France and, as one often finds in the case of Italians, a standard bearer in the class struggle. He was refused entry into four departments, among them the one in which he lived with his wife. The Court found that, since the measure in question did not equally apply to French nationals in respect of trade union matters, it had to be considered as unlawful. So, Rutili was able to return home, where he was euphorically welcomed by his friends and received, so I have been told, a more guarded reception from his wife.

The principle established in *Adoui and Cornuaille*, is similar to the above. It was there held that Belgium was not entitled to deport waitress-prostitutes who were nationals of another Member State, if it did not apply an equally severe sanction to Belgian prostitutes. In other words, the Belgian authorities

---

[37] Case 41/74, *Van Duyn v Home Office* [1974] ECR 1337.
[38] Case 36/75, *Rutili v Minister for the Interior* [1975] ECR 1219.

had the right to suppress the oldest profession in the world, but this right was limited by the prohibition of discrimination. Consequently, it was unlawful to expel foreign workers from, as the somewhat Victorian language of the Court put it, 'a bar which was suspect from the point of view of morals'.

However, the culmination of the development I have attempted to outline is the judgment in *Bouchereau*.[39] In *Bonsignore* it was established that in order to justify a restrictive measure, there had to be a real threat to public order. *Rutili* and *Adoui* developed this principle by requiring that the values detrimentally affected by the conduct of a foreign worker had to be universally held. *Bouchereau* identified in very narrow terms the values which merit protection. It was not enough, the Court held, that the measure had been adopted in reaction to the 'perturbation of the social order which any infringement of the law involves'. Public policy is infringed only by 'a sufficiently serious threat . . . affecting one of the fundamental interests of society'. Long gone are the days when membership of a marginal sect was enough to justify refusal of entry to a Member State.

Let us now move on to the procedural guarantees. In order to avoid abuse in the application of these measures to the migrant worker, and in order to ensure respect for the substantive restrictions already mentioned, Directive 64/221 obliges Member States: (*a*) to grant or refuse a first residence permit not later than six months from the date of application, during which time the person concerned shall be allowed to remain in the territory pending the decision; (*b*) not to permit a restrictive decision to be taken by the administrative authority until an opinion has been obtained from a competent authority of the host country before which the person concerned enjoys such rights of defence and of assistance and representation as the domestic law of that country provides for; and (*c*) to notify the person concerned of the decision and allow the same legal remedies in respect of that decision as are available to nationals of the State in question.

With regard to these obligations, the Court's contribution reflects once again a high degree of liberalism. In effect, the Court has: (*a*) declared that the relevant provisions have direct effect in the domestic arena;[40] (*b*) ruled that decisions to deport or refuse a residence permit must provide adequate and precise details (*Rutili, Adoui and Cornuaille*, cited above); (*c*) held that a foreign national may not in general be deported before he has had an opportunity to lodge an appeal (*Royer*, cited above) and that deportation may subsequently be carried out only on condition that the person concerned is in a position, despite his absence, to obtain a fair hearing and to present his defence in full.[41]

The judges have set out the criteria against which the independence of the body taking the decision on the restrictive action must be measured. They have stated that this decision must be taken immediately before deportation is carried out. Since the decision must be based on personal conduct, the threat to society posed by the foreigner can change in the course of time. That is why it must be assessed at that point in time which reduces the possibility that new factors may be taken into consideration to a minimum, thus leading to an unjustified expulsion (*Santillo*, cited above).

Finally, I would refer briefly to the second exception to the freedom of

---

[39] Case 30/77, *R v Bouchereau* [1977] ECR 1999.
[40] Case 131/79, *R v Secretary of State for Home Affairs, ex parte Santillo* [1980] ECR 1585.
[41] Case 98/79, *Pecastaing v Belgium* [1980] ECR 691.

movement. As I have already mentioned, Article 48(4) provides that the freedom does not apply to employment in the public service. This provision, however, does not define the concept of public service. Neither does Article 55, which excludes activities connected with the exercise of official authority. Consequently, the Court has been obliged to use the 'hermeneutic monopoly' to which I referred earlier in order to affirm that, in Community law, employment in the public service consists in the direct or indirect participation in the exercise of public policy, or the carrying out of tasks with the aim of protecting the general interests of the State (*Sotgiu*, cited above, and six other judgments, among them *Lawrie-Blum*).

There is not much to say about the first requirement, namely that set out in Article 55. I find it more interesting to examine the implications of the second. Why is it necessary that the activities of the worker be in defence or promotion of the *general* interest? It is not difficult to answer that question. As we know, the public authorities in many Member States have taken on broader economic and social responsibilities and tasks which correspond less and less to the traditional functions of public administration. If, consequently, the exception contained in Article 48 were extended to all employment where such responsibilities are assumed and such tasks carried out, the Treaty would cease to be apply to a large number of workers. Worse still, significant differences in treatment would emerge as between Member States, given that all intervene in different ways and to varying degrees in their respective economies.

That said, I must stress that the case-law of the Court has been unable to overcome, except to a modest extent and only in relation to the lower and middle levels of employment (nursing staff, railway workers, university researchers, secondary level teachers etc.), the resistance on the part of States to the employment of foreigners in public administration. This resistance, however, is hardly surprising if one takes account of the widespread view that the functioning of the public service is an exercise of full State sovereignty, and if one bears in mind the importance, particularly in times of high unemployment, of maintaining an adequate reserve of places. I would add that the practice of reserving public administration posts for nationals is imposed in some States (Belgium, France, Italy, the Netherlands) by the Constitution. More generally, this has its roots in xenophobic, sentiments which may not be evident on the surface but undoubtedly exists at all levels of national bureaucracy.

The above factors explain why the Commission proposed some years ago to develop Article 48(4) by means of a directive. There was serious doubt about such a proposal, including the view that Member States would take advantage of it to restrict the right of movement and deprive the decided case-law of its full effect. The principal danger that I perceive in a possible legislative intervention is different, namely the ossification of a process which, since it is linked to the objective of political union of the Member States, should be allowed to continue in as unrestricted a manner as possible. Thus, it is preferable that the matter should be entrusted to the Court of Justice and that the political organs of the Community strive towards the creation of a 'citizens Europe' by establishing an area free of borders in which all Community nationals, and not only workers and providers of services, may be able to circulate freely.

8 Wandering Students: Their Rights under Community Law

Philippa Watson*

Daniel O'Connell (1775–1847), one of Ireland's greatest statesmen, was the most formidable Irish barrister of his time. He was educated by a hedge-schoolmaster, in Father Harrington's school at Cobh in County Cork, at the English Colleges of St Omer and Douai in Northern France and at Lincoln's Inn London. This pattern of education was not altogether unusual at that point in time: up until the twentieth century movement of persons in Europe was relatively unrestricted.

It was only in the course of this century that countries began to impose stringent conditions upon the entry and movement of aliens within their territory. This resulted in the nationalisation of education, unfortunately to the detriment of scholarship.

When the European Community was set up, starting in 1952 with the European Coal and Steel Community, proceeding in 1957 to the creation of the European Atomic Energy Community and the European Economic Community, although a common market in which goods, persons, services and capital moved without hinderance was envisaged, little mention was made of education.

Apart from Article 128 in the EEC Treaty which empowers the Council to 'lay down general principles for implementing a common vocational training policy' and the more specific provision of vocational training measures for agricultural workers[1] the original EEC Treaty is silent on the question of education, although Articles 130*f* to 139*q*, inserted into the EEC Treaty by the Single European Act, provide for the funding of research and technological projects.

More specific are the provisions of the ECSC Treaty[2] and the Euratom Treaty. The promotion of research is one of the main tasks of Euratom.[3]

The Community Treaties, in providing only for that type of education which is closely associated with employment thus linked to the free movement of workers and the economic objectives of the Treaty, reflected the traditional

---

* Some of the ideas to be found in this paper were first expressed by the author at a conference organised by the European Law Students Association (Ireland) in Dublin on 18–20 April 1991, entitled 'Free Movement of Persons – Towards a Common European Home.'
[1] Article 41(*a*) EEC Treaty.
[2] Article 56.
[3] Articles 2(*a*) and 4–11 Euratom Treaty.

view that education was a matter for the Member States to regulate according to national cultural, religious and philosophical norms.[4]

Educational policy, in general, is therefore not considered to be a matter of concern for the Communities, a view recently endorsed by the Court of Justice.[5] This however does not justify the absence in either the Community Treaties or implementing legislation of any provision enabling students to move within the Community to avail themselves of educational opportunities outside their own Member State. Such movement would not interfere with the educational policy of the Member States any more than the free movement of workers affects the terms and conditions of employment prevailing within the Member States.

In fact it could be argued that a pluralist education is necessary for the successful creation of a single integrated market in that it spawns the cross fertilisation of ideas amongst the peoples of the Member States which generates the degree of mutual understanding required for harmonious social and economic co-existence.

Whatever the inherent merits of encouraging the Community's youth to pursue their studies outside their home town or country the Community's legislative bodies, until recently and then only in the wake of a considerable body of case-law of the Court of Justice establishing the right of students to a Community-wide education of a vocational nature, have done little to encourage the movement of students.

What rights students have to move in pursuit of learning outside their own Member State derives from the case-law of the Court over the past eight years.[6] Since this body of rights has evolved on a case by case basis it is complex and incomplete as is evidenced by the continuing flow of references for preliminary rulings from the Member States.

Essentially to-day's student, unlike his ancestors, who wishes to pursue post-school studies in a Member State other than his own, must complete what can be described as an obstacle race in the course of which he must successfully surmount three main barriers.

He must firstly, have the right to enter and take up residence in the Member State in which he chooses to study; he must gain acceptance at a university or other educational establishment and finally he must overcome what may be his greatest obstacle: the financing of his studies.

The extent of his rights with respect to the above-mentioned matters will depend upon his status – whether he is a migrant worker, a member of the family of a migrant worker, or a Community citizen simply wishing to take

---

[4] Although the European Convention on Human Rights in Article 2 of its First Protocol outlined the rights of children and parents in relation to the provision of education, the Court of Human Rights in *Kjeldsen, Busk Madsen and Pedersen* Eur Court HR (1976) Ser. A No 23 made it clear that the State had primary responsibility for education subject to teaching controversial subjects 'in an objective and pluralistic manner' and respecting the rights of parents as regards religious and philosophical convictions and the rights of children.

[5] Case 293/83, *Gravier v City of Liege* [1985] ECR 595: '. . . educational organisation and policy are not as such included in the spheres which the Treaty has entrusted to the Community institutions . . .'.

[6] A considerable body of literature exists on this subject: J. Lonbay, *Education and the Law: The Community Context* 14 EL Rev. (1989) 363–388; B De Witte (ed.) *European Community Law of Education*, (Nomos, Baden Baden, 1989); J Flynn 'Vocational Training in Community Law and Practice' 8 *Yearbook of European Law* (1988) pp. 59–85. E. Hennis 'Access to Education in the European Communities', 3 *Leiden Journal of International Law* (1990 pp. 35–44).

advantage of educational opportunities outside his home country and the nature of the studies he wishes to pursue.

Entry and Residence

(i) The Migrant Worker

A migrant worker has the right to enter and take up residence in a Member State in order to look for and take up employment there.[7] Once in employment he must be granted the right, under the same conditions as nationals of that Member State to vocational training.[8] In addition, he has the right to 'the same social and tax advantages' in the host Member State as nationals of that Member State[9] which in turn, gives him the right to pursue studies of a vocational training nature in that Member State and to continue to reside there for that purpose even after ceasing to work. Similarly, retired workers who have been employed in that host Member State for a certain period of time have the right to continue to reside on the territory of that State and to continue to enjoy the right to equality of treatment prescribed in Regulation 1612/68.[10]

But who is a worker for these purposes? Are there any restrictions on either the nature of the employment or the length of time during which it must have been pursued before a person can obtain the rights to remain in the host Member State for educational purposes? And does he cease to have the status of worker when he gives up work to pursue his studies on a full-time basis?

The concept of worker has been generously interpreted by the Court of Justice as extending '. . . to any person who pursues an activity which is effective and genuine, to the exclusion of other activities on such a small scale as to be regarded as purely marginal and ancillary'.[11] The essential characteristics of an employment relationship is that for a certain period of time a person performs services for, and under the direction of, another person in

---

[7] Articles 3 and 4 of Directive 68/360 on the abolition of restrictions on movement and residence within the Community for workers of Member States and their families (OJ 1968 L 257). Article 3 gives the right to Community nationals to enter a Member State for the purposes of taking up employment there simply on the production of a valid passport or identity card. Article 4 gives such a person the right to reside in that Member State provided he can produce, inter alia, a confirmation of engagement from his employer or a certificate of employment. Although neither Article 48 of the EEC Treaty nor Directive 68/360 make any mention of the right of Community citizens to enter a Member State to look for work, the Court of Justice in Case C-292/89 *The Queen v The Immigration Appeal Tribunal ex parte Antonissen*, judgment of 26 February 1991 held that a national of a Member State has the right to move freely within the Community and to stay in another Member State in order to seek employment there. Such a right however is limited in time: the Court considered a period of six months was 'not insufficient to enable the persons concerned to apprise themselves . . . of offers of employment corresponding to their occupational qualifications'. However, if after the expiry of that period, the persons concerned provides evidence that he is seeking employment and that he has genuine chances of being engaged, he cannot be required to leave the territory of the host Member State.

[8] Article 7(3) of Regulation 1612/68 on the Free Movement of Workers within the Community OJ 1968 L 257.

[9] Regulation 1612/68, Article 7(2).

[10] Regulation 1251/70 OJ 1970 L 142, Article 1, 2, and 7.

[11] Case 53/81, *Levin v Staatssecretaris van Justitie* [1982] ECR 1035; case 139/85, *Kempf v Staatssecretaris van Justitie* [1986] ECR 1741; Case 197/86, *Brown v The Secretary of State for Scotland* [1988] ECR 3205.

return for which he receives remuneration.[12] Consequently a trainee teacher who gives lessons whilst training to be a teacher is to be regarded as a worker within the meaning of Article 48 of the EEC Treaty,[13] as is a person employed for eight months in a country with a view to undertaking subsequent university studies in that country.[14] A worker does not lose his status as such simply because he ceases to be employed and starts to study[15] nor does the duration of his employment determine his status as a worker.[16] However there must be a link between the previous occupational activity and the studies in question.[17]

An official of the European Communities and his family are to be regarded as coming within the scope of the EEC Treaty provisions on free movement and must therefore enjoy all the benefits flowing therefrom.[18]

The conclusion to be drawn from this case law is therefore that a person who has been employed in a Member State, even if such employment is for a short duration and for the express purpose of subsequently undertaking studies in the host Member State retains that status, and continues to have the right to reside in that Member State provided that there is a link between the employment pursued and the course of studies proposed to be followed. There must be temporal continuity also: a lengthy lapse between the cessation of employment and the taking up of studies may break the chain of continuity required for a person to maintain the status of a migrant worker.

(ii) Members of the Family of the Migrant Worker

The members of the family of a migrant worker, that is his spouse, and their descendants under the age of 21 and any dependent descendants of whatever age and the dependent relatives in the ascending line of the worker or his

---

[12] Case 66/85, *Lawrie – Blum v Land Baden – Wurttemberg* [1986] ECR 2121.

[13] Case 39/86, *Lair v Universitat Hannover* [1988] ECR 3161 '. . . a national of another Member State who had undertaken university studies in the host Member State leading to a professional qualification, having engaged in occupational activity in that State must be regarded as having retained his status as a worker . . . (judgment para 39).

[14] *Brown v Secretary of State for Scotland*, op. cit. *supra* note 10.

[15] In *Lair* op. cit. note 10 the Court held: 'Persons who have previously pursued in the host Member State an effective and genuine activity as an employed person . . . but are no longer employed are nevertheless to be considered to be workers . . . it is therefore clear that migrant workers are guaranteed certain rights linked to the status of worker even when they are no longer in an employment relationship (Judgment paras 33 and 36).

[16] *Lair* op. cit. note 12 judgment at paras 33 and 36. Although it can be questioned whether a person who has worked for only a short period before he seeks entry into an educational establishment is genuinely a worker. Did he take up employment because he wished to work and then subsequently became either involuntarily unemployed or decided to improve his qualifications or career prospects by undertaking further education or training or was the underlying motive behind his taking up employment to gain the right to reside and the right to pursue studies in the host Member State on the same terms as nationals of that Member State? Two cases currently pending before the Court raise the question of whether someone who has worked for only a short period of time is a worker or not – Case C-357/89, *Raulin v Minister for Education and Science*, OJ 1990 C11/4, and Case C-3/90, *Bernini v Minister for Education and Science* OJ 1990 C 35/13.

[17] *Lair* and *Brown supra* notes 10 and 11. But such continuity may not be required where the migrant has become involuntarily unemployed and is obliged by current employment conditions to undertake occupational retraining in another field of activity.

[18] Case 152/82, *Forcheri v Belgian State* [1983] ECR 2323. Consequently the Court held that a Member State could not require an enrolment fee in respect of a vocational training course from a national of another Member State lawfully established in the first State (in this case the Italian wife of a Community official) which it did not require of its own nationals.

spouse have the right to enter and reside in the host Member State with him.[19]

However of all these members of the family, only the children of the migrant are granted specific educational rights under Regulation 1612/68.

The child of the migrant worker has the right to be admitted to the host State's '. . . general educational, apprenticeship and vocational training courses under the same conditions as nationals of that State.'[20] This includes '. . . any form of education including university courses in economics and advanced studies at a technical college'.[21] It also includes educational opportunities granted by the host Member State to its nationals to study abroad.[22] The spouse and other members of the family of the migrant worker are not granted any comparable rights but since they are persons to whom the EEC Treaty applies they can claim the right of access to studies of a vocational training nature on equal terms with nationals of the host Member State. This point is dealt with in more detail below.

Since the child of the migrant worker derives his status from his parent does this mean that when the parent ceases to be a migrant worker the rights of the child also terminate? This question arose in the case of *Echternach and Moritz*.[23] The Court held a child of a migrant worker retains that status and so conserves the right to continue to reside and to pursue his studies even when his parents from whom he derived his status returned to the Member State of origin. In coming to this conclusion the Court was influenced by the fundamental aim of Article 12 of Regulation 1612/68 which is to ensure 'as complete an integration as possible of workers and members of their families in the host country'. Such integration requires that the children of migrant workers must have the possibility of going to school and pursuing their studies in the host Member State and to complete their education there even after the parent from whom they derive their rights returns to the Member State of origin.

However there are limits to this right: the child of a migrant worker is not marked indelibly with this status: In *Brown v Secretary of State for Scotland*[24] the Court held that a child born after his parents had ceased to work and reside in the United Kingdom could not be regarded as a member of a worker's family. The Court did not state for how long the child must have lived or been educated in the host Member State. Presumably there must be no perceptible break in the child's education in the host Member State:[25] any integration into the educational system of another Member State will terminate any rights he can claim under Article 12 of Regulation 1612/68. The only right the child of a migrant worker has is to remain in the educational system of the host Member State into which he was integrated when his parent departed from that State.

(iii) The Community Citizen

The right of a Community citizen, who is not exercising his right to free movement under Article 48, to enter and take up residence in a Member State

---

[19] Regulation 1612/68, Article 10.
[20] Regulation 1612/68. Article 12.
[21] Joined Cases 389 and 390/87, *Echternach and Moritz v Minister for Education and Science* [1989] ECR 723.
[22] Case C-308/89, *Di Leo v Land Berlin*, judgment of 13 November 1990.
[23] Op. cit. note 22.
[24] See note 12 above.
[25] *Ecternach and Moritz* op. cit. note judgment at para 23.

in which he wishes to pursue his studies has only been recently established and is somewhat more restricted than that of either the migrant worker or his family.

Directive 90/366 on the right of residence for students,[26] makes the right of residence of a student, his spouse and their dependent children, conditional upon proof that he has sufficient resources to avoid becoming a burden on the social assistance system[27] of the host Member State and that the family as a whole are covered by sickness insurance for all the risks in the host Member State.[28]

This Directive appears to be the only basis in Community law as it stands at present, on which a Community citizen who is neither a migrant worker nor a member of the family of a migrant worker, can claim the right to enter and take up residence in a Member State for educational purposes. He cannot claim such rights as a recipient of services[29] since education has been held not to be a service within the meaning of Article 60 of the EEC Treaty.[30]

Access to Educational Establishments

Students who are nationals of a Member State have the right to equality of access to vocational training courses: there must be no discrimination between

[26] OJ 1990 L 180/30.

[27] The migrant worker can claim social and medical assistance for himself and for the members of his family who reside with him, from the host Member State on the basis of Article 7(2) of Regulation 1612/68. Case 261/83, *Castelli v ONPTS [1984] 3199; Case 249/83, Hoeckx v Openbaar Centrum voor Maatschappelijk Welzijn* [1985] ECR 973; Case 122/84, *Scrivener v Centre public d'Aide social de Chástre* [1985] ECR 1027; Case 157/84, *Frascogna v Caisse des Depots et consignations* [1985] ECR 1739.

[28] This requirement to have adequate sickness insurance may be difficult to satisfy in practice. Regulation 1408/71 (OJ 1971 L 149) and Regulation 574/72 (OJ 1972 L 74) which co-ordinates the social security systems of the Member States apply only to employed and self employed persons, their families and survivors, refugees and stateless persons. Students who do not fall within these categories of persons are outside the scope of the Regulation. This means that the sickness insurance system to which they have been affiliated in their Member State of origin is not required, by Community law, to provide coverage for illness occurring in the host country. It may of course do so either under its own domestic legislation or by virtue of a bilateral or multilateral agreement with the host Member State. If this is not the case the student will have to try to insure himself in the host Member State. That Member State may refuse to insure him, offer him partial insurance only, charge him relatively high contributions and will almost invariably ask him to complete a waiting period (a period of time in which contributions are paid but no title to benefit arises) only at the end of which will he be entitled to benefits. Meanwhile the student in such a situation has no sickness insurance and so cannot satisfy the requirements of Directive 90/366 (except perhaps by taking out private insurance but these schemes are frequently linked to, and dependent, upon affiliation to a state social security system). The Commission is currently working on a proposal to extend the scope of Regulation 1408/71 to students. Until this proposal becomes law some students will have difficulties in satisfying the conditions required to establish a right of residence in the Member State in which they wish to pursue their studies on the basis of Directive 90/366.

[29] Joined Cases 286/82 and 26/83, *Luisi and Carbone v Ministero del Tesoro* [1984] ECR 377; Case 186/87, *Cowan v Tresor Public* [1989] ECR 195.

[30] Case 262/86, *Belgian State v Humbel* [1988] ECR 5365 ; '. . . The first paragraph of Article 60 of the EEC Treaty provides that only services 'normally provided for remuneration' are to be considered to be 'services within the meaning of the Treaty . . . The essential characteristic of remuneration thus lies in the fact that it constitutes consideration for the service in question . . . That characteristic is, however, absent in the case of courses provided under the national educational system. First of all the State in establishing and maintaining (a national educational system) is not seeking to engage in gainful activity but is fulfilling its duties towards its own population in the social, cultural and educational fields . . . secondly the system in question is as a general rule funded from the public purse and not by pupils or their parents.'

nationals and non-nationals with respect to conditions for enrolment on these courses. In particular non-nationals cannot be required to pay fees over and above those levied on national students. Similarly where a numerus clausus system exists in respect of a particular faculty or course the criteria applied in operating that system must be objective i.e. unrelated to nationality.

The principle of equality of access to vocational training courses was established in the case of *Forcheri v Belgian State*[31] in which the Court ruled that '. . . although educational and vocational training policy is not as such part of the areas which the Treaty has allotted to the competence of the Community institutions . . .' the Treaty did in Article 128 empower the Council to lay down general principles for implementing a common vocational training policy. Such a policy had been laid down in a Council decision adopted in 1963.[32]

'Consequently if a Member State organizes educational courses relating in particular to vocational training, to require a national of another Member State lawfully established in the first Member State an enrolment fee which is not required of its own nationals in order to take part in such courses constitutes discrimination by reason of nationality, which is prohibited by Article 7 of the Treaty.'[33]

Subsequent case-law has clarified the precise scope of the concept of vocational training and hence the ambit of the right to equality of treatment. In *Gravier v City of Liege*[34] the Court defined vocational training as '. . . any form of education which prepares for a qualification for a particular profession, trade or employment or which provides the necessary skills for such a professional trade or employment is vocational training whatever the age and level of the pupil or student'.

Some years after the *Gravier* decision the Court, in *Blaizot v University of Liege*,[35] further refined its thinking on the concept of vocational training holding that it not only encompassed studies where the final academic examination directly provided the required qualification for a particular profession, trade or employment but also where those studies equip a person with the knowledge needed for the pursuit of a profession, trade or employment even if no legislative or administrative measures make that knowledge a pre-requisite for that purpose. In general, the Court concluded, that university studies fulfil these criteria. The only exception to this general principle would be

'. . . certain courses of study which, because of their particular nature, are intended for persons wishing to improve their general knowledge rather than prepare themselves for an occupation.'[36]

In assessing whether a particular course of studies is of a vocational training nature or not, the Court has insisted that it must be considered as a whole: the various years of a study programme which forms 'a single coherent entity'

[31] Case 152/82, [1983] ECR 2323.
[32] Decision No 63/266 of 2 April 1963 laying down general principles for implementing a common vocational training policy OJ Eng Sp Ed. 1963/64 p. 25.
[33] *Ibid.* judgment para 18.
[34] Case 293/83 [1985] ECR 606.
[35] Case 24/86 [1988] ECR 355.
[36] *Ibid.* judgment at para 20; see also Case 242/87, *Commission v Council* [1989] ECR 1425.

cannot be split up into 'academic years' and 'vocational training years'.[37] It is for the national courts to determine whether a particular course of study is or is not such a single coherent entity.

Financing of Studies: Grants and Scholarships

Entitlement of non-nationals to grants or scholarships from the host Member State on the same terms as nationals of that Member State will depend firstly, on the purpose of the grant or scholarship and secondly, as in the case with the right to enter and reside within the host Member State described above, upon the status of the student in question.

Financial assistance for the purpose of meeting the cost of registration and other fees charged for access to vocational training courses must be granted to non-nationals on the same terms as nationals; such grants form part of the conditions of access to vocational training, they are within the scope of the Treaty and so discrimination on the grounds of nationality is prohibited under Article 7 of the EEC Treaty.[38]

The right of the non-national to maintenance and training grants is more complex: the migrant worker may claim a grant from the host Member State on the basis of Article 7(2) of Regulation 1612/68 which, it will be recalled gives him the right to the same 'social and tax advantages' as nationals of that State. This principle was first established in the case of *Lair*. However it is subject to two conditions. Firstly there must, in general, be 'some continuity between the previous occupation and the course of study' and secondly the employment which endows the student with the status of 'worker' and hence to claim equality of treatment under the law of the host Member State with respect to social and tax advantages, must have been undertaken independently of the course of study for which the maintenance or training grant is requested.[39] Where a student becomes employed for the subsequent pursuing of the studies in question, that employment being '. . . merely ancillary to the studies to be financed by the grant' does not entitle him to receive by virtue of Article 7(2) of Regulation 1612/68 the same maintenance allowance as is payable to students who are nationals of the host Member State.[40]

The right to a maintenance and training grant under Article 7(2) of Regulation 1612/68 includes the right to grants for study abroad. In *Matteucci* the

---

[37] *Blaizot* op. cit. supra note 20 and Case 263/86, *Belgian State v Humbel* [1988] ECR 5365.

[38] Case 39/86, *Lair v Universitat Hannover* op. cit. *supra* judgment at para 14 'It is only to the extent to which asistance of that kind is intended to cover registration and other fees, in particular tuition fees charged for access to education . . . falls . . . within the scope of the EEC Treaty and that, consequently, the prohibition of discrimination on the grounds of nationality laid down by Article 7 of the EEC Treaty is applicable.'

[39] In *Lair* op. cit. *supra* the Court held that the right to social advantages provided for in Article 7(2) of Regulation 1612/68 could not be made conditional upon the completion of a minimum period of employment in the host Member State.

[40] This ruling has potentially wide ramifications. It departs from general approach adopted hitherto of treating a person who is a worker within the meaning of Article 48 as being entitled to all the rights given to workers under other Treaty provisions on free movement and implementing legislation. It seems that there are two types of worker: those whose employment is ancillary to some other type of activity or which is merely a means to another unrelated objective and whose rights to equal treatment are correspondingly reduced and those workers whose employment is an end in itself and who therefore as 'genuine' workers are entitled to the full range of rights and benefits granted under Community law to migrant workers.

child of an Italian migrant worker, born and brought up in Belgium, where she subsequently taught rhythmics was refused a scholarship to study singing and voice production in Berlin. The scholarship in question was provided for under a bilateral cultural agreement between Belgium and Germany and was expressed to be available only to nationals of either of those countries. The Court held that Article 7(2) of Regulation 1612/68 lays down a general rule which imposes responsibility in the social sphere on each Member State with regard to every worker who is a national of another Member State and established in its territory as far as equality of treatment with national workers is concerned. Consequently, where a Member State gives its national workers the opportunity of pursuing training provided in another Member State, that opportunity must be extended to Community workers established in its territory. Consequently:

> '. . . a bilateral agreement which reserves the scholarships in question for nationals of the two Member States which are parties to the agreement cannot prevent the application of the principle of equality of treatment between national and Community workers established in the territory of one of those two Member States.'[41]

The child of a migrant worker has the same right to all types of educational grants, whatever their purpose, as nationals of the host Member State. In *Casagrande v Landeshauptstadt Munchen*[42] and *Alaimo v Prefet du Rhone*[43] the Court held that Article 12 of Regulation 1612/68, giving the child of a migrant worker the right to be admitted to that State's general educational, apprenticeship and vocational training courses under the same conditions as nationals of that State providing that he is residing in there, refers not only to rules relating to the admission to educational courses but also to other educational facilities such as educational grants. In both of these cases, Italian migrant workers were refused grants in respect of their school-going dependent children solely on the ground that those children were not nationals of the host State. Some fifteen years later the Court re-iterated this ruling in *Echternach and Moritz*.[44] It held, further that the concept of education in Article 12 was broad, comprising 'any form of education, including university courses in economics and advanced vocational training at a technical college.'

In *Belgian State v Humbel*[45] the Court emphasised that Article 12 of Regulation 1612/68 binds only the Member State in which the migrant worker resides: even though a student may be the child of a migrant worker he can only claim educational rights under Article 12 in the Member State in which his parents are residing.[46] But such rights may be claimed in respect of courses of study to be pursued in another Member State. Thus in *di Leo v Land Berlin*[47] the Court held that where a Member State, in this case Germany, awarded grants to its nationals for study abroad, it was obliged also to give them to the children of migrant workers resident upon its territory since by virtue of

---

[41] *Ibid.* judgment para 23.
[42] Case 9/74 [1974] ECR 773.
[43] Case 68/74 [1975] ECR 109.
[44] Case 389/87, [1989] ECR 723.
[45] Case 263/86, [1988] ECR 5365.
[46] Consequently Frederic Humbel, the child of a French father working and residing in Luxembourg could be required to pay an enrolment fee as a condition for admission to a Belgian school even where a Belgian child could not be obliged to pay such a fee.
[47] Case C-308/89, judgment of 13 November 1990.

Article 12 of Regulation 1612/68 these children were assimilated to nationals.

From the Court's case law discussed above it can be concluded that students do have the right to move freely within the Community in pursuit of their studies. However the precise scope of their rights will depend upon their status. Migrant workers have a generous bundle of rights, followed by their children. But all have the right to enter a Member State in order to pursue studies there and the right of equal access to educational institutions in that Member State.

Inspired by the Court's case-law the Community legislature has created and financed a number of programmes, some general, some specific, which are designed to promote co-operation between the Member States in third level education and to facilitate the movement of both students and their professors. They arc, by all accounts extremely successful enabling millions of students to spend time in universities and other third-level educational institutions. The Community it seems has been successful in dismantling those barriers which have nationalized education in this century and has helped to reinstate the scholarly environment of a European dimension of past centuries. In doing so it has surely made a significant contribution to the creation of a single integrated market.

9 Judicial Interpretation of the Public Service Exception to the Free Movement of Workers

David O'Keeffe*

The free movement of persons is one of the areas where the European Court has been most active in interpreting the constitutional document which is the EEC Treaty. This article examines the judicial interpretation which has been given to the public service clause contained in Article 48(4) of the Treaty.[1]

The Treaty provides for the free movement of persons in Articles 48–51 (workers), 52–58 (self-employed) and 59–66 (providers of services).[2] The Treaty articles provide in the case of employed persons and their families for the right to accept offers of employment actually made, to move freely within the territory of the Member States for this purpose, to stay in a Member State for the purpose of employment and to remain in a Member State after having been employed there. The freedom of movement entails the abolition of any discrimination on grounds of nationality, the general principle enshrined in Article 7 and which is given specific application in the provisions relating to free movement.[3] Similar provisions exist in the case of the self-employed and providers of services. These positive rights are subject to two categories of exceptions, the first concerns exceptions to the free movement of persons which may be justified on grounds of public policy, public security or public health. The second exception concerns employment in the public service.

Article 48(4) of the EEC Treaty, relating to employed persons, provides that 'the provisions of this Treaty shall not apply to employment in the public service'.

Article 48 does not specify what is meant by the concept 'public service'. It

---

* The writer directs a project on the free movement of persons and the single market for the UK Economic and Social Research Council within the framework of the ESRC's initiative on the evolution of rules for the single European market.
[1] See Jacques Ziller *Egalité et Merite, L'accès à la Fonction Publique dans les Etats de la Communauté Européenne* (Bruylant, Brussels 1988), especially pp. 280–6; Brigitte Lenz 'The Public Service in Article 48(4) EEC with Special Reference to the Law in England and in the Federal Republic of Germany', 1989/2 *Legal Issues of European Integration*; John Handoll '*Article 48(4) EEC and Non-National Access to Public Employment*' 313 EL Rev (1988) pp. 223–241; Louis Dubois '*La Notion d'emplois dans l'administration publique* (art. 48 para 4 traité C.E.E.) et l'accès des ressortissants communautaires aux emplois publiques', 3 *Revue française de droit administratif* (1987) pp. 949–962.
[2] The Court has included recipients of services in the category of persons enjoying rights under the Treaty. See Case 186/87, *Cowan* [1989] ECR 195 and Joined Cases 286/82 and 26/83, *Luisi and Carbone* [1984] ECR 377.
[3] See Case C-213/90, *ASTI*, preliminary ruling of 4 July 1991 and Case C-10/90, *Masgio*, preliminary ruling of 7 March 1991, not yet reported in the European Court Reports.

therefore was left to the courts to determine the content of that concept and thus the scope of Article 48(4).

By contrast, Article 55 of the Treaty, relating to the self-employed, provides as follows:

'The provisions of this Chapter shall not apply, so far as any given Member State is concerned, to activities which in that State are connected, even occasionally, with the exercise of official authority.

The Council may, acting by a qualified majority on a proposal from the Commission, rule that the provisions of this Chapter shall not apply to certain activities'.

By virtue of Article 66 of the Treaty, the provisions of Article 55 shall apply to the providers of services.[4]

Purpose of Public Service Exception

The first question which arises is why the public service exception was provided for. The tenor of the Treaty provisions on free movement is liberal, and the other exceptions they contain, relating to public policy, public security or public health, are the necessary bare minimum.

The reasons for the public exception are not hard to find. Every Member State is concerned, to a greater or lesser degree, that certain activities carried out by or in the name of the State should be performed only by its own nationals. Moreover, every State has its own conception of the public service, and of what is signified by the status of its officials, be it an Irish civil servant, a French *fonctionnaire* or a German *Beamte*.

The State has traditionally carried out functions relating to defence, policing and the maintenance of order, justice, finance and taxes, and foreign affairs. It has also taken on roles in relation to local government (at state, regional and local level), the health service, education, public utilities or public transport. Moreover, as the social and economic organisation of society altered, so too did patterns of ownership and activity, as the State assumed responsibility in sectors where previously it had not been present, operating through semi-State or State-owned bodies, often governed by public law, or created by Statute or Charter. In this guise, the State carries out economic or commercial activities of an entrepreneurial character, in which it acts *qua* economic or commercial actor rather than *qua* State. The participation of the State in such activities, and the degree of its involvement varies from one Member State to another, depending on the way in which economic life is organised in the different Member States.

The Court has already dealt with this phenomenon in other areas of Community law. It is remarkable that there has been no spill-over effect, and the interpretation of Article 48(4) does not appear to have been influenced by, or have had an influence on, the Court's jurisprudence in cases presenting analogous problems. In *Commission v Italy* (tobacco monopoly),[5] the Court recognised that the State may carry out an entrepreneurial function and provided convincing criteria to determine when the State was acting as the

[4] This article does not deal with the case-law relating to Article 55 of the Treaty.
[5] Case 118/85, *Commission v Italy* [1987] ECR 2599.

State and when it was engaging in a commercial activity. In *Foster v British Gas*,[6] the Court was able to give guidelines for establishing when an entity is to be deemed an emanation of the State which it held to be 'a body, whatever its legal form, which has been made responsible, pursuant to a measure adopted by the State, for providing a public service under the control of the State and has for that purpose special powers beyond those which result from the normal rules applicable in relations between individuals'.[7]

It is for each State to determine the status of the employees who carry out activities on its behalf, attributing to them or not, as the case may be, the status of civil servant or the equivalent status in the national system. Likewise, national law may stipulate that candidates for recruitment to the public service of a State should possess the nationality of the State.[8]

In making such a determination, a State will be motivated by a number of factors. There is a deep-rooted conviction that the public service is an area in which the State should exercise full sovereignty. There are considerations linked to national security in the case of security-sensitive positions. There may be imperative public policy considerations, where the State, acting as the State, should be represented by its own nationals (diplomacy is a good example). There may be situations where a bond of loyalty is necessary which can only be ensured by the employment of one's own nationals. Finally, and importantly, such an exception creates a *de facto* reserve of jobs to which Community nationals cannot accede by virtue of the other provisions; the public service sector thus constitutes a valuable reservoir of jobs for a Member State's own nationals.[9]

The Public Service Exception as a Concept of Community Law

Article 48(4) poses a number of inherent problems. If it is up to the Member States to delimit the notion of 'employment in the public service', the Member States may adopt a very wide interpretation, effectively limiting the scope of the free movement of workers. Moreover, the interpretation given to the concept of 'employment in the public service' may vary widely from one Member State to another, if the Member States remain free to determine the content of the exception.[10] This would be contrary to the notion of the common

---

[6] Case C-188/89, *Foster v British Gas* [1990] ECR I-3313.

[7] See Deidre Curtin The Province of Government: Delimiting the Direct Effect of Directives in the Common Law Context (1990) 15 EL Rev. 195 who rightly points out that the definition of public service developed in the context of Article 48(4) is not necessarily transposable to other areas of Community law, where different needs may be present, as in the case of Community estoppel.

[8] The State may impose other requirements such as a certain level of educational or professional qualifications, linguistic knowledge (cf. Case 379/87, *Groener v Minister for Education and the City of Dublin Vocational Educational Committee* [1989] ECR 3967), or general aptitude. See Dubois and Handoll, op. cit., note 1 above, at p. 960 and 236 respectively.

[9] Opinion of Advocate Geneal Mancini, as he then was, in Case 307/84, *Commission v France* [1986] ECR 1725 at p. 1728.

[10] In a Resolution of 17 January 1972, regarding the definition of the concepts of public service and public authority in Member States and the consequences of this definition in connexion with the application of Article 48(4) and 55 of the EEC Treaty, the European Parliament stated that 'Article 48(4) may be applied to any employment considered by a Member State as coming within its public service, regardless of the nature of the activities carried on within the framework of such employment'. The European Parliament stated the express wish that Member States would as far as possible limit the application of Article 48(4) to occupations which involved the exercise of public authority and noted that in fact many employments in the public service do not involve the exercise of public authority. OJ 1972, C 10, p. 4.

market: if the Treaty confers Community-wide rights of free movement, then the exceptions to these rights should be uniform throughout the Community.

Although therefore it was fairly clear that judicial interpretation of the notion of 'employment in the public service' would be necessary, the outcome of the interpretation was unclear, given the highly sensitive, and politically charged, nature of the problem. It should also be noted that most academic writers favoured an interpretation which depended on whether the employment relationship was one governed by public or private law.[11]

In *Sotgiu*,[12] the first case to deal with the exception, the Court held that the exceptions made by Article 48(4) cannot have a scope going beyond the aim in view of which this derogation was included. This is an early version of the approach very shortly afterwards adopted with regard to exceptions to the free movement of persons by the Court, to the effect that exceptions to the fundamental principle of freedom of movement for workers must be interpreted strictly,[13] which was subsequently extended to Article 48(4).[14]

The Court also dealt in *Sotgiu* with the problem whether the extent of the exception provided in Article 48(4) can be determined in terms of the designation of the legal relationship between the employee and the employing administration. The Court held that in the absence of any distinction in Article 48(4) itself, the *legal designation* of the employment (workman, clerk, official) and the nature of the legal relationship between the employee and the employing administration is immaterial. The Court held also that it was irrelevant whether the terms on which the worker was employed fell under *public or private law*. As the Court noted, such 'legal designations can be varied at the whim of the national legislatures and cannot therefore provide a criterion for interpretation appropriate to the requirements of Community law.'

In *Sotgiu*, the Court did not define the concept of 'employment in the public service' as a concept of Community law, but it is clear that this was implicit in its thinking. This decisive step was taken in *Commission v Belgium (No 1)*[15] in which the Court held that the concept of public service requiries uniform interpretation and application throughout the Community.

Conflict with National Laws

The Court had already held in *Sotgiu* that national legal designations were not appropriate to delimit the scope of 'employment in the public service'. A further step was taken in *Commission v Belgium (No 1)*, where it was argued before the Court that the constitutional laws of certain Member States specifically excluded, with provision for derogations, the employment of non-

---

[11] See the authorities quoted by Advocate General Mayras in his Opinion in *Commission v Belgium* [1980] ECR 3881 at pp. 3911–3912.

[12] Case 152/73, *Sotgiu v Deutsche Bundespost* [1974] ECR 153.

[13] Case 41/74, *Van Duyn v Home Office* [1974] ECR 1337. The restrictive interpretation line can be traced back to Case 15/69, *Ugliola* [1969] ECR 368. See also Case 36/75, *Rutili* [1975] ECR 1219 at p. 1231. To the same effect as in *Sotgiu*, with respect to the first paragraph of Article 55 of the Treaty, see Case 2/74, *Reyners* [1974] ECR 631, para 43.

[14] Case 66/85, *Lawrie-Blum v Land Baden Württemberg* [1986] ECR 2121.

[15] Interim judgment of the Court in Case 149/79, *Commission v Belgium* [1980] ECR 3881.

nationals in the public service.[16] The Court replied, as it had frequently held in other contexts, that recourse to provisions of the domestic legal systems to restrict the scope of the provisions of Community law would have the effect of impairing the unity and efficacy of that law, and consequently could not be accepted. The Court stressed that the demarcation of the concept cannot be left to the total discretion of the Member States and that interpretations of the concept of the public service which are based on national law alone and which would obstruct the application of Community rules may not restrict the effectiveness and scope of the Treaty provisions on freedom of movement for workers and equality of treatment of nationals of all Member States.

The Concept of Employment in the Public Service Outlined

In its interim judgment in *Commission v Belgium (No 1)*, the Court laid down broad guidelines for the operation of the public service exception. The Court gave two criteria to define the notion of 'employment in the public service' as set out in Article 48(4) of the Treaty. According to the Court, 'that provision removes from the ambit of Article 48(1) to (3) a series of posts which involve direct or indirect participation in the exercise of powers conferred by public law and duties designed to safeguard the general interests of the State or of other public authorities'. The Court explained that 'such posts in fact presume on the part of those occupying them the existence of a special relationship of allegiance to the State and reciprocity of rights and duties which form the foundation of the bond of nationality'.[17]

By holding that Article 48(4) referred to posts which involve direct or indirect participation in the exercise of powers conferred by public law, the Court was plainly borrowing from Article 55 of the Treaty which, less laconic than Article 48(4), excludes the application of the provisions on the right of establishment to 'activities which . . . are connected, even occasionally, with the exercise of official authority'.[18] The second criterion, that such posts must involve duties designed to safeguard the general interests of the State or of other public authorities is totally new.

This judicial inventiveness should be remarked on. In his Opinion, Advocate General Mayras had noted that even if the two provisions, Article 48(4) and 55, show a certain analogy they do not have the same sphere of application, the former applying to workers, the latter to the self-employed. The different content of the two provisions is accounted for in the situations envisaged: as the Commission explained in *Commission v Belgium (No. 1)*, it is evident that employed persons can only participate in the exercise of public authority when they occupy a public post whereas in the case of the self-employed, it was necessary to specify that the exception operates when an occupation comprises activities which may possibly be connected with or involve the exercise of official authority.

The Court's approach in adopting the two criteria should be noted: it avoids giving an abstract definition or a list of what may constitute posts involving the

---

[16] This was the case of Article 6 of the Belgian Constitution.

[17] *Commission v Belgium*, note 15 above, para 11 at p. 3900.

[18] For the historical background to the drafting of Article 55, see the Opinion of Advocate General Mayras in *Commission v Belgium (No 1)*, note 15 above, at p. 3915.

exercise of public authority. It relies on the very broad guidelines noted above, preferring a post by post evaluation. This approach has given rise to criticism in those countries where the public service is organized in careers rather than based on specific posts.[19]

Conditions for the Application of Article 48(4)

(i) The exercise of powers conferred by public law

The criteria set by the Court in *Commission v Belgium (No 1)* give rise to some problems of interpretation. The Court did not give an abstract definition of the meaning of 'direct . . . participation in the exercise of powers conferred by public law. In subsequent cases, both Advocates General Mayras and Mancini (as the latter then was) focused on the notion that the exercise of such powers implied powers of coercion over citizens.[20] As Advocate General Mancini put it: 'The duties [inherent in the post at issue] must involve acts of will which affect private individuals by requiring their obedience or, in the event of disobedience, by compelling them to comply'.[21]

On the other hand, it has been argued that the exception covers not only coercive powers but also covers the sorts of power affecting the individual which are exercised in the 'welfare' area. The test would therefore be whether the public servant exercises a power, discretionary or otherwise, which affects the position of individuals.[22]

However, in the final analysis it does not seem that there is much difference between the two views put forward above. Whereas coercive powers certainly are indicative of the exercise of public authority, so too are decisions taken which affect an individual, be they coercive or not.

The Court has also not explained what is meant by *indirect* participation in the exercise of powers conferred by public law, part of the first condition set by the Court for the application of Article 48(4). This is potentially a very wide category but it is to be presumed that it will be interpreted restrictively by the Court, and will be confined only to those who realistically are associated with the exercise of public authority even though they may not exercise it themselves. It is submitted that the Court could, if it wished, make use of the concept in Article 55 of the Treaty, of activities which are *connected* with the exercise of official authority, which implies a relationship with the exercise of public authority without necessarily denoting direct participation. In each case, the Court will have regard to the 'tasks and responsibilities involved' of a specific post.[23]

(ii) Safeguarding the general interests of the State

The scope of the second condition for the application of Article 48(4), duties designed to (or as the Court held in other cases the discharge of functions

---

[19] See Ziller, note 1 above, at p. 284.
[20] Advocate General Mayras in *Reyners*, note 13 above, and Advocate General Mancini in Case 307/84, *Commission v France* [1986] ECR 1725.
[21] Case 307/84, *Commission v France* [1986] ECR 1725, at p. 1732.
[22] Handoll, op. cit., note 1 above, at pp. 234–5.
[23] *Lawrie-Blum*, note 14 above, para 27, at p. 2147.

whose purpose is to)[24] safeguard the general interests of the State, has also been left without precise definition. There is the very strong persuasive authority of the Opinion of Advocate General Lenz in *Lawrie-Blum*, who, insisting on the cumulative nature of the two conditions, held that not all activities connected with the exercise of powers conferred by public law fall within the scope of the exception of Article 48(4): they must involve the exercise of powers for safeguarding the general interests of the State. Seen in this way, the first condition, the exercise of public authority, is the wider category of the two, and the condition relating to safeguarding the general interests of the State refines and limits its scope. This approach seems to me to be a sensible one, and consonant with the case-law of the Court to date. Obviously, much turns on whether the two conditions are cumulative or alternative, a point which is discussed below.

If one accepts the approach suggested by Advocate General Lenz, in a sense, the second condition can be read as introducing a *de minimis* consideration in the sense that not all posts in the public service which include participation in the exercise of official power constitute posts in the public service for the purposes of Article 48(4), but require a manifest connection between the post in question and the safeguarding of the general interests of the State. That appears to be a rather strict test, but the reality may be less restrictive: in *Commission v Italy*[25] the Court accepted that the duties of management in a National Research Council or of advising the State on scientific and technical questions could be described as employment in the public service within the meaning of Article 48(4). The Court did not elaborate; however it is submitted that to include senior posts in management in State bodies, and senior Government advisers in the public service exception is an unsurprising consequence of the two conditions for the application of Article 48(4) and one which would accord with the analysis for the application of the conditions suggested above.[26]

To date the Court has not specifically ruled on the application of Article 48(4) to national security, which is one of the classic justifications for the public service exception, and would certainly be covered by the second condition, safeguarding the general interests of the State. The point has arisen only once. In *Commission v Belgium (No 1)* the security argument was raised by Belgium which argued that the admission of foreign staff to work on the railways (such posts also being at issue in the case) could conceivably jeopardise national security. The Court held that 'such a line of argument is based on an hypothesis which has no connection with the legal context of that provision'. Presumably the Court had in mind no more than the consideration that the railway employees in question (drivers, shunter and the like) do not exercise powers conferred by public law and have responsibility for safeguarding the general interests of the State, and thus did not meet the test for the application of Article 48(4). It is submitted that this is the most plausible interpretation as presumably considerations of public safety and public security as

[24] In *Lawrie-Blum*, note 14 above, and in Case 33/88, *Allué and Coonan v Università degli studi di Venezia* [1989] ECR 1591. The wording varies in Case 307/84, *Commission v France* [1986] ECR 1725: responsibility for safeguarding. (There is no discrepancy between the French and English texts).

[25] Case 225/85, *Commission v Italy* [1987] ECR 2625.

[26] For another view, see Handoll, op. cit., note 1 above, at pp. 235–6 for a discussion of the scope of the Court's judgment.

regards the public service must be envisaged and protected by Article 48(4). It is suggested that reliance cannot be had on the exceptions based on public policy, public security and public health contained in Article 48(3), as these exceptions would seem to be related to the person of the worker, rather than to the nature of the post which he aspires to occupy. Moreover, Article 48(3) confers positive rights on the worker, and does not envisage the exclusion of migrant workers from a whole sector of the economy, which is the effect of the public service exception.

(iii)   Cumulative or alternative character of the conditions

The question which arises is whether the two requirements are cumulative rather than alternatives: a post falls within the public service exception only if the duties involved in the post entail the exercise of official authority *and* are designed to safeguard the general interests of the State or of other public authorities, including smaller territorial units. Though the Court has not ruled explicitly on this point, there is very strong persuasive authority from its Advocates General to the effect that the two conditions are cumulative.[27]

However, in *Commission v Italy*, discussed in more detail below, the Court held that it had not been established that the researchers employed at the National Research Council were 'responsible for exercising powers conferred by public law *or* for safeguarding the general interests of the State'. It held that only the duties of management or of advising the State on scientific and technical questions could be described as employment in the public service within the meaning of Article 48(4), but that these duties were not carried out by the researchers. It has been suggested that the combination of this reasoning, and the use of the word 'or', indicate that the two criteria identified by the Court in *Commission v Belgium (No 1)*, 'the exercise of powers conferred by public law' and 'duties designed to safeguard the general interests of the State or of other public authorities' are alternative and not cumulative. Thus, according to this view, advising the State on scientific and technical questions, which the Court admitted could fall within the Article 48(4) exception, could not fall under the criterion of 'exercise of powers conferred by public law' but would fall under the second criterion relating to the general interests of the State.[28]

However, it should be noted that in the cases decided after *Commission v Italy*, the Court did not present the two criteria as alternatives.[29] In the face of the persuasive authority of the Advocates General referred to above, and in the light of the subsequent case-law, the better view is therefore probably that the two conditions are cumulative, and not alternative.

---

[27] Opinion of Advocate General Mancini, *Commission v France* [1986] ECR 1725 at p. 1730. Opinions of Advocate General Lenz in *Lawrie-Blum*, note 14 above, at p. 2135 who states that the posts must meet both criteria '*at the same time*', and in *Commission v Italy*, note 25 above, at p. 2634 where he states that the Court had held in *Lawrie-Blum* that both conditions must be present at the same time. However, Handoll, op. cit., note 1 above at p. 234, believes that they are alternatives.

[28] See Handoll, op. cit., note 1 above, at p. 230 and 234.

[29] Case 33/88, *Allué* and *Coonan* [1989] ECR 1591 and Case C-4/91, *Bleis*, preliminary ruling of 27 November 1991, not yet reported in the European Court Reports.

(iv) Functional test

The two criteria make it clear that the judge-made test of what constitutes employment in the public service is a strict one. The concept of employment in the public service is to be appraised in functional terms, and in any event, it is of decisive importance to determine whether the activity at issue involves the exercise of official authority and protection of the general interests of the State or of other public authorities.[30] The test is therfore a material one, concentrating on the characteristics of the posts which it is sought to remove from the general ambit of the free movement of workers.

It should be noted that the Court rejected an institutional approach in favour of a functional one. The basis for the institutional approach is that Article 48(4) refers to the public service as an entity or institution. Thus all posts which fall within this institutional ambit must belong to the public service. The institutional argument often refers to the different wording of Articles 48 and 55: whereas the latter sought to deal with certain activities, the former is presumed to deal with the public service as an institution. Another argument is that the drafters of the Treaty intended by Article 48(4) to incorporate the rule existing in the different Member States excluding foreigners from the public service.[31]

More specific arguments, all of which have been raised in the case-law of the Court, turn on the characteristics of the public service as seen by the different Member States. Thus, France drew attention to the difficulties the functional test would cause for the French system of the public service which was based on a unitary concept and was founded on a comprehensive idea based on the requirement of French nationality as a condition for entry to any post in the public service, municipalities or other public establishments, without any possibility of making a distinction on the basis of the nature and the characteristics of the post in question.[32] Likewise, Member States have adverted to the difficulties which a functional test would create, restricting flexibility in transfers of officials, giving rise to discrimination as regards promotion, and causing many practical difficulties in implementation. Such arguments have as leitmotif that the concept of employment in the public service may vary from one Member State to another according to the laws or traditions of each of them. It is also common ground that employment in the public service calls for a special form of loyalty, 'a commitment and devotion which is more readily to be expected from nationals than from non-nationals'.[33] Finally, the proponents of the institutional view will argue that in fact in many cases, national law permits nationals of other Member States to enter into private law contracts in order to hold positions of employment vis-à-vis the State.

---

[30] See opinion of Advocate General Mancini, Case 307/84, *Commission v France* [1986] ECR 1725 at p. 1729.

[31] See Dubois, op. cit., note 1 above, pp. 951–2.

[32] In its observations in Case C-4/91, *Bleis*, note 29 above, the French government stated that the French Council of Ministers had accepted a draft law modifying the existing rules in order to give access to the public service in France to Commuity nationals as regards posts which do not involve direct or indirect participation in the exercise of powers conferred by public law or other public authorities.

[33] Intervention of the Government of the United Kingdom in *Commission v Belgium (No 1)*, note 15 above, [1980] ECR 3881 at pp. 3892–3.

Characteristics of the Public Service

In *Commission v Belgium (No 1)*, the Court referred to the difficulties of defining the sphere of application of Article 48(4). It noted that in the various Member States, authorities acting under powers conferred by public law have assumed responsibilities of an economic and social nature or are involved in activities which are not identifiable with the functions which are typical of the public service yet which by their nature still come under the sphere of application of the Treaty.

In order to avoid disparities which might arise from one Member State to another, according to the different ways in which the State and certain sectors of economic life are organized, the Court or the national courts must examine whether certain posts may fall within the concept of public service. In *Commission v Belgium (No 1)*, the Court admitted that the application of the test for the application of Article 48(4) could give rise to problems of appraisal and demarcation in specific cases, as such a classification depends on whether or not the posts in question are typical of the specific activities of the public service in so far as the exercise of powers conferred by public law and responsibility for safeguarding the general interests of the State are vested in it.

Notoriously, the Court in *Commission v Belgium (No 1)* did not feel able to make a sufficiently accurate appraisal of the actual nature of the duties involved in the posts at issue so as to determine whether such posts properly fell within Article 48(4) or not, (although its Advocate General did make such an appraisal).[34] The parties were invited by the Court to re-examine the issue between them taking account of the principles of interpretation defined by the Court and having regard to the characteristics of each post. In essence, therefore, the Court having provided sufficient legal guidelines, the parties were being asked by the Court to settle the case, along the lines familiar to common lawyers.

The Court manifestly did not wish to have to decide for itself whether particular posts fell within or outside the scope of Article 48(4), probably feeling that such would be time-consuming, fact-related and more properly left to the Commission, as guardian of the Treaties. The Court has used this tactic with success on other occasions in other areas,[35] but it must be admitted that it failed in the context of the Article 48(4) case-law. Nevertheless, whereas originally I felt that the Court was evading its responsibility, and should have decided the case on the facts before it,[36] I now feel that its approach was the correct one. On the basis of the very clear guidelines given in its judgment in *Commission v Belgium (No 1)*, it should have been possible for the parties to arrive at a solution, without compelling the Court to enter into issues of complex fact-finding.

Such an outcome moreover would have been auspicious for future pre-contentious Article 169 enquiries initiated by the Commission, which could

---

[34] Advocate General Mayras' view that certain posts might fall within the scope of Article 48(4) because they were covered by a special social security scheme for civil servants falling outside the application of Regulation 1408/71 looks like a classic case of allowing the tail to wag the dog. However, Advocate General Mayras was purporting to follow a dictum from previous case-law which Advocate General Mancini was later to characterize as a *lapsus calami* (see Opinion of Advocate General Mancini in Case 307/84, *Commission v France* [1986] ECR 1725).

[35] See Case 145/83, *Stanley Adams v Commission* [1985] ECR 3539 and Case 180/87, *Hamill v Commission* [1988] ECR 6141, as regards settling compensation between the parties.

[36] See my article, 'Practical Difficulties in the Application of Article 48 of the EEC Treaty' 1982 CML Rev. p. 35.

invite the Member States to adhere to the Court-set guidelines for the application of Article 48(4). The Court presumably had envisaged such a solution: moreover, the Court may also have had in mind that national courts too would be called upon to apply its criteria.[37]

However, as the parties in *Commission v Belgium (No 1)* were unable to agree, it fell to the Court in *Commission v Belgium (No 2)*[38] to examine whether the posts at issue fell within the scope of Article 48(4), as defined in its earlier, interim, judgment. The Court, rather tamely, it is submitted, accepted the Commission's acknowledgement that certain posts might have characteristics which bring them within the scope of Article 48(4): these posts were for employment with the City Council of Brussels and the *Commune* of Auderghem and concerned the following: head technical office supervisor, principal supervisor, works supervisor, stock controller and night watchman, and architects. It should be said that the Commission seems to have taken a very soft line indeed.[39] Likewise, the lack of reasoning used by the Court is striking. For the most part, referring laconically to 'the nature of the duties and responsibilities' of the posts at issue, without going into any detail beyond this purely global reference, it merely endorses the Commission's stance.

It is suggested that the outcome of this case should not be taken to reflect the Court's views on the characteristics of the specific activities of the public service; more likely, it reflects an uneasy accommodation with the partial settlement arrived at by the parties at the Court's invitation, which the Court was then disinclined to upset.

The Court has dealt with a number of other specific posts in the course of the case-law. It is sufficient here to refer to the case-law concerning nationality requirements for posts for nurses and teachers, which provide ample demonstration of the sureness of the Court in evolving a jurisprudence which applied the two criteria laid down in *Commission v Belgium (No 1)*.

Posts for hospital nurses and children's nurses were among those which had been at issue in *Commission v Belgium*.[40] In *Commission v France*,[41] the Court dealt

---

[37] In *Commission v Belgium (No 1)*, note 15 above, Advocate General Mayras regretted that the Commission did not intend to draft legislation to implement Article 48(4) because of its extreme complexity owing to the vast range of very diverse situations covered by the concept of employment in the public service. He tartly remarked ([1980] ECR 3881 at p. 3911): 'that complexity is at least as great for national courts and for the Court of Justice too'.

[38] Case 149/79, *Commission v Belgium* [1982] ECR 1845.

[39] As Advocate General Rozès pointed out in her Opinion in *Commission v Belgium (No 2)*, note 38 above, at p. 1854, the Commission had 'fallen into line' with the Opinion of Advocate General Mayras in the earlier case, who had ruled out several posts.

[40] There was some confusion. In his Opinion in *Commission v Belgium (No 1)*, note 15 above, Advocate General Mayras thought that as a result of the differences between the parties having been reduced during the proceedings, 'unless I am mistaken, the Commission no longer questions the offering of posts for . . . hospital and children's nurses'. However, in her Opinion in *Commission v Belgium (No 2)*, note 38 above, Advocate General Rozès specifically stated that such posts must be classified amongst the posts which Advocate General Mayras considered fell outside the concept of public service within the meaning of Article 48(4). In the operative part of its final judgment, the Court condemned Belgium for having made Belgian nationality a condition of entry for the posts referred to in the reports lodged by the parties, save those named posts which the Court accepted fell within the scope of Article 48(4). Since hospital and children's nurses are mentioned in such reports, it must be presumed that these posts were held by the Court to fall outside the scope of Article 48(4). In *Commission v France* [1986] ECR 1725, para 13 at p. 1739, the Court had no doubts that the posts of nurses in public hospitals had been covered by the judgment in *Commission v Belgium (No 2)*.

[41] Case 307/84, *Commission v France* [1986] ECR 1725.

with a provision under French law whereby the possession of French nationality was a precondition for appointment and establishment in permanent employment as a nurse in public hospitals.

The Court's judgment is interesting because, assisted by the brilliant conceptually orientated Opinion of Advocate General Mancini, it brought together the different strands of its previous case-law to dismiss justification of the French rule. Thus it cited *Sotgiu* to the effect that the legal designation of a post or the legal nature of the employment relationship is irrelevant, as this would allow Member States to determine the scope of the provision at will. The Court itself characterized as 'functional' its test in *Commission v Belgium (No 1)* and stated that the criterion for determining whether Article 48(4) is applicable must be functional and must take account of the nature of the tasks and responsibilities inherent in the post. Finally, it cited *Commission v Belgium (No. 2)* as authority for the proposition that in view of the nature of the functions and responsibilities which they involve, posts of nurse in public hospitals do not constitute employment in the public service within the meaning of Article 48(4).

In *Lawrie-Blum*,[42] the Court examined whether Article 48(4) applied in the case of a British national who, after passing an examination for the profession of teacher was refused admission, on the ground of her nationality, by the competent German local education authority, to a period of preparatory service leading to the Second State Examination, which qualifies successful candidates for appointment as teachers in Germany.[43]

The Court held that as a derogation from the fundamental principle that workers in the Community should enjoy freedom of movement and not suffer discrimination, Article 48(4) must be construed in such a way as to limit its scope to what is *strictly necessary* for safeguarding the interests which that provision allows the Member States to protect. The Court then restated its earlier case-law and held that the posts excluded from the ambit of Article 48(4) are confined to those which, having regard to the tasks and responsibilities involved, are apt to display the characteristics of the specific activities of the public service. The Court qualified these conditions as being 'very strict'.

The *Lawrie-Blum* judgment, decided by the full Court (*petit plenum*), has become part of the constant case-law, having been adopted by a Chamber of five in *Allué*[44] (concerning discriminatory treatment of foreign-language assistants at the University of Venice) and most recently by a Chamber of three in *Bleis* (concerning the requirement of French nationality for posts of secondary school teachers).[45] In both cases, the Court contented itself by repeating the criteria from *Lawrie-Blum*, and noted that these very strict conditions were not fulfilled in the case of posts for foreign-language assistants or for a secondary school teacher.

---

[42] *Lawrie-Blum v Land Baden-Württemberg*, note 14 above.

[43] The Court first held that she must be considered as a worker within the meaning of Article 48(1). It reasoned that a trainee teacher who, under the direction and supervision of the school authorities, is undergoing a period of service in preparation for the teaching profession during which he provides services by giving lessons and receives remuneration must be regarded as a worker within the meaning of Article 48(1), irrespective of the legal nature of the employment relationship.

[44] See note 29 above.

[45] *Idem.*

Employees under Contract and the Public Service

As noted above, one of the arguments used to justify the institutional rather than the functional approach is the consideration that nationals of other Member States may in fact occupy posts in the public administration, not as established officials or civil servants, but as agents under contracts, normally governed by public law. The Court has dealt with this situation in a number of cases, including *Sotgiu* and *Allué*, but it has been most explicit in *Commission v France* and *Commission v Italy*. In *Commission v France*, attention should be drawn to the very particular manner in which the Court proceeded.

After having determined that the posts of nurses in public hospitals fell outside the scope of Article 48(4), rather than simply conclude with this finding, the Court instead proceeded to inquire whether the contested French nationality requirement led to discrimination of the kind prohibited by Article 48(2). This patently was to deal with the French Government's claim that access to employment as a nurse in public hospitals was open to the nationals of other Member States as they could be recruited as employees under contract as opposed to members of the established staff. At the material time, French public hospitals employed 89,000 nurses of whom 86,000 were established in their posts and 3000 were employees under contract. Fewer than 5% of the employees under contract were nationals of other Member States. The argument was rejected by the Court as France had not:

'established that all posts as nurses offered in public hospitals were equally accessible to the nationals of other Member States and that when such nationals were recruited they enjoyed conditions – with the exception of the possibility of promotion to posts in the public service within the meaning of the Treaty – advantages and safeguards which were in every respect equivalent to those deriving from the status of members of the established staff, which is reserved to French nationals'.[46]

It is suggested that this approach – although benign as to the result in the present case – is dangerous. If France had indeed been able to show that nationals of other Member States were able to be recruited as nurses under contract and enjoy conditions, advantages and safeguards which were in every respect equivalent to those deriving from the status of members of the established staff, it is clear that the Court would have found that there was no discrimination. This approach drives a coach and four through the earlier jurisprudence: effectively it would allow a Member State to exclude nationals of other Member States from employment in a series of posts designated by it as falling within the public service, but which do not fall within the ambit of the exclusion contained in Article 48(4). Such posts could be reserved to the Member State's own nationals, and a separate category of post, giving rise to employment on a different basis, probably governed by private law contract, could be created for non-nationals. The question which arises is whether this really matters, as for such an arrangement to satisfy the requirements of the Court's judgment in *Commission v France*, the migrant workers must enjoy the conditions, advantages and safeguards which are in every respect equivalent to those deriving from the status enjoyed by nationals of the host State.

The answer must be that this does indeed matter; even if no material

[46] *Commission v France*, note 41 above, para 16 at p. 1738.

difference presently derives from the fact that a given employment in the public sector is only open to non-nationals on a different basis to that in the case of nationals of the host State (for example, the difference between established and contractual posts for nurses in public hospitals as in *Commission v France*), such a difference may appear in the future. It is fundamental that there is an inherent difference between the duration of established posts and contractual ones.[47] But most of all, such an approach destroys the principle that all posts within the Community should be available to any Community national, subject to the exceptions contained in Article 48(3) and (4), which must be interpreted strictly. The approach implied by the Court in *Commission v France* would add another exception. The consequences for the individual migrant worker may not be immediately substantially disadvantageous (though one should bear in mind my earlier comments regarding the duration of contractual appointments), but it would represent a retrograde step in that it partitions the labour market and makes it less transparent.

Such an approach is open to criticism for another major reason. It gives to nationality a privilege which the Treaty provisions on the free movement of workers had denied. Article 48(4) is intended to cover those posts which as the Court pointed out in *Commission v Belgium (No 1)*, presume on the part of the post-holders the existence of a special relationship of allegiance to the State and reciprocity of rights and duties which form the foundation of the bond of nationality. Apart from this, the Treaty provisions do not allow the granting of a privileged status to a host country's own nationals.

The reply, based on *Commission v France*, to this line of argument, would be that no privileged status is at issue. However, it is submitted that in fact the *different treatment* envisaged by that case is contrary to the principles enshrined in the Treaty and in the Court's own case-law, the tendency of which is to assimilate own nationals and Community migrant workers. Arguably, since the approach suggested by the Court would add to the disparities existing between the nationals of the host State and Community migrants, the principle of non-discrimination on the ground of nationality would be violated.[48]

The reasoning used by the Court in *Commission v France* concerning the issue of the different status of contractual employees, non-nationals of the host State, as opposed to the established staff, the latter category being reserved to its own nationals, was followed in *Commission v Italy*. The case concerned discrimination as regards job security, promotion prospects, pay and pensions in the case of researchers who were nationals of other Member States working for the *Consiglio nazionale delle ricerche* (National Research Council) who were nationals of other Member States.

The approach is interesting. The Court has introduced the notion of discrimination under Article 48(2) which may be justified by Article 48(4). In both cases, employment in the disputed professions was not entirely closed to nationals from other Member States, but they were given a different status as compared with the nationals of the host State. Hence the Court enquires whether the foreign nationals do not in fact enjoy advantages and guarantees equivalent to those deriving from the status of the host State's own nationals.

---

[47] See *Dubois*, op. cit., note 1 above at p. 959, who remarks 'qui, aujourd'hui, récuserait cette appréciation portée sur la stabilité de l'emploi!'

[48] It is submitted that this line of reasoning would accord with that used by the Court in Case 41/84, *Pinna* [1986] ECR 1.

The Court's approach to this problem of different statuses has been summarized as holding that 'any distinction had to be one without a difference'.[49] However, for the reasons given above, I feel that such a result is not possible, and that this development in the case-law is to be deplored.

Promotion and Other Conditions of Employment

The issue of recruitment to the public service has always been closely linked to the problem of nationals of Member States who are employed in the public service of another Member State, and who find themselves disadvantaged by their nationality in their subsequent career as regards promotion and other conditions of employment.

The problem first arose in *Sotgiu*. In that case, an Italian national was employed, under a private law contact of employment, by the Federal German Post Office, which under national law, formed part of the public service. The Court held that Article 48(4) cannot justify discriminatory measures with regard to remuneration or other conditions of employment against workers once they have been admitted to the public service. The Court added that the very fact that they have been admitted shows that those interests which justify the exceptions to the principle of non-discrimination permitted by Article 48(4) are not at issue.

Member States have argued that the exclusion of foreign workers from posts which do not at the outset involve any participation in the exercise of powers conferred by public law becomes necessary if a foreign national who has been recruited to a post is eligible for a career which in the higher grades involves duties and responsibilities involving the exercise of powers conferred by public law.[50] Likewise, Member States have maintained that such an exclusion is also necessitated by the fact that flexibility in assignment to posts is a characteristic of the public service and the duties and responsibilities of an employee may consequently change, not only on promotion, but also after a transfer within the same branch, or to a different branch at the same level.[51]

Responding to these arguments, the Court has held that Article 48(4) allows Member States to reserve to their nationals by appropriate rules entry to posts involving the exercise of such powers and such responsibilities within the same grade, the same branch or the same class.[52]

As regards the argument that any exclusion of nationals of other Member States from promotion or transfer to certain posts in the public service would have the effect of creating discrimination within such service, the Court has observed that this would have the effect of debarring those nationals from the totality of posts in the public service, and would involve a restriction on the rights of such nationals which goes further than is necessary to ensure observance of the objectives of Article 48(4).[53] The ruling is an application of the principle of proportionality.

---

[49] Handoll, op. cit., note 1 above, at p. 228.
[50] Arguments of the Belgian and French Governments in *Commission v Belgium (No 1)*, note 15 above.
[51] Arguments of the German and British Governments, *ibid.*
[52] *Idem.*
[53] *Idem.*

In *Commission v France*, the Court specifically excluded the possibility of promotion to posts in the public service within the meaning of Article 48(4) from the equality of conditions advantages and safeguards which it held must apply as between members of the established staff and foreign nationals employed under contract.

This case-law now seems to have stabilized, and to have become part of the constant jurisprudence of the Court. The Court's approach is coherent. By allowing Member States to reserve for its own nationals those posts which meet the two criteria for the application of Article 48(4), the Court has effectively safeguarded the legitimate interests of the States. At the same time, by ruling that the exclusion of foreign nationals from promotion or transfer on this account should not constitute grounds for a general exclusion from the public service, the Court has rightly focused on the exceptional nature of Article 48(4), and has avoided the temptation of letting specific difficulties have an influence on, or indeed replace, the general rule.

The principle of non-discrimination governs the position of workers from other Member States once they have been admitted to the public service in so far as posts meeting the conditions for the application of Article 48(4) are not involved. Where this is the case, Article 48(4) cannot justify discriminatory treatment with regard to remuneration or other conditions of employment. This is conceptually correct, as only the exceptions contained in Article 48 can prevent the application of the rule prohibiting non-discrimination contained in Article 48(2) of the Treaty.

The implication of this case-law is that it imposes a heavy burden on the Member States who employ nationals of other Member States in their public service. In order to ensure that such employees do not enter posts which meet the conditions for the application of Article 48(4), such States must examine the position of the non-national at each stage of his or her career, whether on promotion, transfer or alteration of his or her job functions, to ensure that it does not admit him or her to a post within the meaning of Article 48(4). Moreover, some posts will be very difficult to classify. Indeed, this has been one of the sticking points for the Member States, which see the unity of their public service endangered. Nevertheless, this is the price to be paid for the public service exception, in seeking to balance the legitimate interests of the State with the principle of non-discrimination.

Commission Programme

The Commission has issued an action plan for the elimination of restrictions on grounds of nationality to access to posts in parts of the public sector.[54] The Commission does not intend to introduce legislation[55] or produce a list of posts to which Article 48 applies. Rather, adhering strictly to the case-law of the Court, it refers in general terms to categories of posts which it considers fall

---

[54] 'Freedom of movement of workers and access to employment in the public service of the Member States. Commission action in respect of the application of Article 48(4) of the EEC Treaty,' OJ 1988, C 72, p. 2.

[55] The Commission had originally considered legislation, and had prepared an (unpublished) draft directive. See Ziller, op. cit., note 1 above at pp. 282–3. See also note 37 above.

within the public service exception,[56] and to those which do not, where action will be taken on a sectoral basis.[57]

Implications of the Internal Market and European Integration

There is an inherent conflict between Article 48(4) on the one hand and the creation of the internal market and increased European integration on the other. The public service exception is geared to a conception of the State performing certain essential activities related to its function as the State, where the legitimate interests of the State can best be served and protected by the recruitment of the State's own nationals to perform certain tasks on its behalf.

However, this view of the public service exception is founded on a conception of nationality which may face increasing strain. It is based upon a very traditional notion of loyalty to the State and finds its parallel in the denial to foreigners of political rights.[58] The very recent Court decision censuring a national law which excluded foreign workers from voting for elections to their professional body takes a very restrictive view of the socio-civic rights which may be denied to migrants.[59]

At the Maastricht summit, the foundations for citizenship of the European Union were agreed upon. The new provisions confer substantial political rights on Community migrants in another Member State, including the right to move and reside freely within the territory of the Member States to vote and to stand as a candidate in municipal elections and in elections for the European Parliament. In addition, every Member State citizen shall, in the territory of a third country in which the State of which he is a citizen is not represented, be entitled to protection by the diplomatic or consular authorities of any Member State. Citizenship of the Union, which is additional to citizenship of a Member State, is a dynamic concept, as the adoption of provisions to strengthen or to add to the rights laid down by the new provisions is envisaged.[60]

It is clear that these provisions will alter the perceptions of Member States concerning nationals of other Member States. They blur the distinction between the State's own nationals and nationals of other Member States in several ways which go to the heart of the concept of nationality. Previously, Community law, and in particular the case-law of the Court of Justice,[61] had

[56] The armed forces, the police and other forces for the maintenance of order, the judiciary, the tax authorities and the diplomatic corps. It also includes posts in state ministries, local and regional authorities and other public bodies where the duties of the post involve the exercise of State authority such as the preparation of legal acts, their implementation and the monitoring of their application, and the supervision of subordinate bodies.

[57] The following activities are envisaged: commercial services (public transport, airlines and shipping companies, posts and telecommunications, radio and television companies, electricity and gas supply), public health services, teaching in State educational establishments and research for non-military purposes in public establishments.

[58] See *Dubois*, op. cit., note 1 above, at pp. 955–6.

[59] Case C-213/90, *ASTI*, note 3 above.

[60] Article 8e 1759/60 (7 February 1992). See text of *Treaty on Political Union* published by *Europe*, Documents no 1759/60 (7 February 1992).

[61] See the Opinion of Advocate General Mancini in *Commission v France*, note 41 above, at p. 1731 where he states that 'in order to guarantee full freedom of movement it would be necessary to remove the obstacles deriving from the existence of different nationalities and to create a Community citizenship, which is no longer metaphorical, in the sense currently reflected in the judgments of this Court, but real'. See also G. F. Mancini 'The Making of a Constitution for Europe' 1989 CML Rev. 595.

concentrated on the economic and social integration of Community migrants (viewed as economic actors by the Treaty)[62] in order to create a Community citizenship. As Community nationals are now to enjoy political rights deriving from Community law, it will become progressively more difficult to justify a different treatment of them as regards employment in the public service, which is founded upon political considerations.[63] However, it is suggested that although the application of the Court's criteria for the operation of Article 48(4) may become more stringent, only true European integration will make that provision redundant, as far as nationals of Member States are concerned, by altering the perceptions of the sovereignty of the independent Member States and of the concept of nationality upon which the public service exception is based.

Conclusion

The Court has provided convincing criteria which may be applied on a case-by-case basis in order to determine whether a given post in the public administration falls within the public service exception provided by Article 48(4). The approach it has chosen in dealing with this issue, by giving broad guidelines rather than abstract definitions, is helpful for both national courts and the Commission, which must apply the criteria.

The Court's case-law appears constant and, with the exception of the treatment of nationals of other Member States who are employed under contract as opposed to being appointed civil servants, satisfactory.

However, both the case-law and the provision contained in Article 48(4) will be put under increasing conceptual strain by the achievement of the internal market and the evolution of citizenship of the European Union. Should true integration be achieved, it must be doubted whether the public service exception may survive as regards nationals of the Member States.

---

[62] I have discussed this at some length in 'Trends in the Free Movement of Persons', in James O'Reilly (ed.), *Essays for Brian Walsh* (Round Hall Press, Dublin, 1992).

[63] See Constantin A Stephanou, '*Identité et Citoyenneté Européennes*', 1991 *Revenue du marché commun* (no 341) p. 30 at p. 36 who perceptively notes: 'L'accès à la fonction publique constitue un cas intéressant de "spill-over" de l'économique au politique'.

10 Constitutional Implications of Community Sex Equality Law

Karen Banks

Introduction

Most lawyers probably think of that part of Community law concerning sex discrimination as a rather specialized area with little or no general relevance. This is a mistaken view, for it ignores the fact that this domain is rich in principles of a constitutional nature, and therefore in possible lessons for other areas of Community law. The idea of the right to equal treatment as between the sexes as a fundamental personal right known to Community law has been accepted by the Court of Justice since the 1970s. It has led the Court to strike down sex-based differences of treatment in the Staff Regulations governing the conditions of work of Community officials, and has had important consequences for the Court's interpretation of different provisions of Community law. Rights have been construed broadly and exceptions narrowly. In the sphere of indirect discriminations, the Court is extremely exacting in relation to the criteria for justification of a measure bearing more harshly on women than on men. The idea that a fundamental right was at stake appears even to have played some role in encouraging the Court to declare the direct effectiveness of Article 119.

Other principles of a constitutional character have been developed in this domain which are equally applicable elsewhere. The intricacies of the direct effect of Directives, the obligation of the national courts to interpret their legislation so as to bring it into conformity as far as possible with the requirements of Community law, the need for effective remedies to sanction breaches of Community-commanded national law, all these figure prominently in the case-law of the Court concerning equality between the sexes. Recent cases also bear on the relationship between Community law and provisions of national law which would impede the full availability of a right based on Community law.

A final point of constitutional interest which has arisen more than once in the case-law relating to equal treatment between the sexes concerns the possibility for the Court to limit the effect in time of a judgment in which it *interprets* a provision of Community law. In *Defrenne No 2*[1] the Court declared the direct effect of Article 119 but limited the possibility of relying on it (except

---

[1] Case 43/75, *Defrenne v Sabena* [1976]ECR 455.

for those who had already brought claims) to periods subsequent to the judgment. In *Barber*,[2] the Court declared the applicability of Article 119 to pensions paid under private 'contracted-out' pension schemes, but stated that (again, save for those who had already commenced proceedings) the direct effect of Article 119 could not be relied upon in order to claim entitlement to a pension with effect from a date prior to that of the judgment. The constitutional importance of this type of action on the part of the Court is obvious, since it may be wondered whether it does not transform its role from that of interpreter of laws to that of lawmaker. An examination of the appropriateness of such initiatives on the part of the Court would however require a detailed and analytical study which is beyond the scope of this paper. This question is therefore mentioned only in passing, while the other matters referred to above are now dealt with more fully.

The right to equal treatment as a fundamental right

In *Defrenne No 2*, the Court had occasion to analyze the nature of the guarantee of equal *pay* contained in Article 119. It declared the principle of equal pay to form 'part of the foundations of the Community', and went on, largely inspired it seems by this idea, to declare the direct effect of Article 119 (see in this regard particularly grounds 7–12). It was not until *Defrenne No 3*[3] however, that the Court was called upon to say whether, apart from the specific provisions concerning equal pay, Community law contained any general principle prohibiting discrimination based on sex in relation to *working conditions*. The Court recalled that:

> '. . . respect for fundamental personal human rights is one of the general principles of Community law, the observance of which it has a duty to ensure' (ground 26),

and declared:

> 'There can be no doubt that the elimination of discrimination based on sex forms part of those fundamental rights' (ground 27).

The Court noted that the same concepts are recognized by the European Social Charter of 18 November 1961 and by Convention No 111 of the International Labour Organization of 25 June 1968 concerning discrimination in respect of employment and occupation.

Here then was the clear recognition of a fundamental human right to equal treatment as between the sexes. What are the practical consequences in Community law of the existence of such a right? The most clear-cut consequences have appeared in the context of cases concerning claims brought by members of the staff of Community institutions against their employers. In two staff cases prior to *Defrenne No 3*, the Court had already struck down a provision of the Staff Regulations which discriminated according to sex. In *Sabbatini*[4] and *Bauduin*[5] the provisions at issue were those which prescribed the

---

[2] Case C-262/88, *Barber v Guardian Royal Exchange Assurance Group* [1990] ECR I-1889.
[3] Case 149/77, *Defrenne v Sabena* [1978] ECR 1365.
[4] Case 20/71, *Sabbatini v European Parliament* [1972] ECR 345.
[5] Case 32/71, *Bauduin v Commission* [1972] ECR 363.

withdrawal of an official's expatriation allowance upon marriage to a person not qualifying for the allowance unless the official thereby became a head of household, and which defined the term 'head of household' in such a way that a woman would rarely be considered to be one. The purpose of the expatriation allowance is to compensate for the expenses and other disadvantages resulting from entry into the service of the Community for those officials who are thereby obliged to change their place of residence. It is not at all clear on what basis the authors of the Staff Regulations considered that these problems could be diminished by marriage, and even less why their diminution or continued existence should depend on whether one was a head of household or not. However that may be, the one thing that is clear is that women officials were massively disfavoured by the method of definition of 'head of household'. The Court noted that the Staff Regulations had created an arbitrary difference of treatment between officials. They were to that extent unlawful and incapable of founding the decisions which had been taken to withdraw the expatriation allowances of Mrs Sabbatini and Mrs Bauduin. Those decisions were therefore annulled.

In two further staff cases decided before *Defrenne No 3*, the Court was able to avoid annulling any provision of the Staff Regulations by *interpreting* them in the light of the principle of equal treatment. In *Airola*[6] and *Van den Broeck*,[7] the expatriation allowance paid to most Community officials again held centre stage. The problem in these cases arose from the acquisition by female officials of the nationality of their husbands. If their marriage caused them to acquire the nationality of their country of work, they would lose their expatriation allowance (or never gain one, as the case might be). This evidently gave rise to an unequal situation as between male and female officials, since a male official would never find himself in such a position. The Court decreed that 'payment of the expatriation allowance must be determined by considerations which are uniform and disregard the difference in sex' (ground 9 of both judgments). It therefore decreed that the concept of an official's nationality, for the purposes of the relevant provision of the Staff Regulations, had to be defined as excluding nationality imposed by law on a female official upon her marriage with a national of another State, when she has no possibility of renouncing it. In *Airola*, this was the case, and therefore the imposed nationality was to be disregarded. In *van den Broeck*, on the other hand, the relevant national law would have allowed renunciation of the husband's nationality, but the official in question chose not to take advantage of this possibility. The Court therefore took the view that there were no reasons associated with equal treatment why her new nationality should be disregarded for the purposes of the expatriation allowance.

In none of these cases did the Court refer to the notion of fundamental rights. It simply appeared to take it for granted that relations between the Community institutions and their officials must be governed by the principle of equality of the sexes. The only possible source of such a principle however was the fundamental right to equal treatment. Article 119, which was mentioned by the applicants in some of the cases as a ground upon which the institution's decisions could be attacked, is in fact not applicable in relations between Community institutions and their officials, being addressed to the

---

[6] Case 21/74, *Airola v Commission* [1975] ECR 221.
[7] Case 37/74, *Van den Broeck v Commission* [1975] ECR 235.

Member States and concerned with situations governed by national law. In none of its judgments in these cases did the Court refer to Article 119. It was clearly basing itself, albeit tacitly, on a superior principle of law from which the Staff Regulations could not derogate.

A year and a half after the judgment in *Defrenne No 3*, yet another staff case came before the Court concerning loss of the expatriation allowance on marriage.[8] Here again the applicant had had the possibility of renouncing her husband's nationality but had not done so. Following its earlier approach the Court therefore found that there was no unwarranted difference of treatment based on sex. What is interesting about this judgment however is that for the first time in a staff case, the Court refers to a 'general principle' prohibiting any such unwarranted difference of treatment. It also explicitly attributes its earlier decision in *Airola* to the existence of this principle.

It was not until 1984 however that the Court chose to state clearly that the fundamental right to equal treatment as between the sexes which it had recognized in *Defrenne No 3* could be directly relied upon so as to render inapplicable a discriminatory provision of the Staff Regulations. This was in the case of *Razzouk and Beydoun*,[9] and the problem on this occasion arose from the fundamentally different treatment accorded by the Staff Regulations to the widows and widowers of officials. The widow of a male official in general automatically received a pension, whereas the widower of a female official could only receive a (smaller) pension in extremely limited circumstances (permanent incapacity for work and destitution). There were also other differences in treatment. The Regulations in fact, as the Court observed, provided for two fundamentally different survivor's pension schemes according to whether the deceased official was male or female.

This was the occasion for the Court to recall the status of 'the principle of equal treatment for both sexes' as forming part of the fundamental rights protected by the Court and to state unequivocally that provisions of the Staff Regulations which were contrary to the fundamental right in question were not to be applied. In the course of its judgment, it stated that:

'. . . . in relations between the Community institutions, on the one hand, and their employees and the dependants of employees, on the other, the requirements imposed by the principle of equal treatment are in no way limited to those resulting from Article 119 of the EEC Treaty or from the Community directives adopted in this field' (ground 17).

Put another way, Article 119 and the directives cannot be relied upon in an action against a Community institution, and they are not needed, for they are only the detailed expressions in a particular context of a general principle, a fundamental right, which may be relied upon directly in such an action. The Court will not allow a Community instrument to breach a fundamental right nor a Community institution to ignore one. They are both subject to general principles of law of which the Court is the guarantor.

[8] Case 257/78, *Devred v Commission* [1979] ECR 3767.
[9] Joined Cases 75 and 117/82, *Razzouk and Beydoun v Commission* [1984] ECR 1509.

The national context

The situation is rather different when a complaint of discrimination arises in a context governed by the national law of a Member State. In *Defrenne No 3* itself, the complaint concerned the insertion in the contract of employment of an air hostess of a clause bringing the contract to an end when she reached the age of 40, no such limit being attached to the contracts of male cabin attendants who did the same work. At the time in question, there was as yet no Community directive governing the application of the principle of equal treatment between men and women in relation to working conditions other than pay.[10] The Court therefore, while specifically acknowledging the existence of the fundamental right to equal treatment, declared that the matter before the Belgian courts had to be dealt with according to the law for the time being in force in Belgium. In other words, the mere fact that a fundamental right is recognized in Community law does not mean that it can be relied upon *as an independent element of that law*, in order to invalidate a contrary national provision, or to fill a gap in national law. It is one thing for the Court to insist on reading Community texts in the light of fundamental rights norms and even to strike down those *Community* provisions which are incapable of being read so as to make them conform to such principles. It would be another thing altogether for the Court, *independently of the existence of a Community instrument*, to apply notions of fundamental rights in order to judge the correctness of national law. To do so would amount to expanding the scope of Community law beyond that agreed upon by the authors of the Treaty and later settled by the Community legislator. Moreover, for the Court to judge national laws by the bare standard of norms of fundamental rights would cause it to encroach upon the domain of other jurisdictions specifically created for this purpose. This it has steadfastly refused to do.

What then can be expected of the Court in the context of national laws? It can be expected to construe Article 119 of the Treaty and Community directives concerning sex equality, with which national law must comply, in a manner which takes full account of the importance of the principle of equality enshrined in those texts. This indeed it has done with a will. By taking a generous approach to the definition of the rights conferred, and a restrictive one to all exceptions and derogations, the Court ensures, albeit indirectly, that national law in this area reflects the fundamental nature of the right at stake.

Article 119

The Court's generous attitude in the area of equal pay has attracted attention recently because of its judgment in *Barber*,[11] whereby it decreed that even 'contracted-out' occupational pension schemes (closely linked to State pensions) were 'pay' for the purposes of Article 119. However, the Court's open-handed approach in this area is of long standing. The text of Article 119 itself gives a fairly generous definition of 'pay'. It covers not only wages or

---

[10] See now Council Directive 76/207 of 9 February 1976 on the implementation of the principle of equal treatment for men and women as regards access to employment, vocational training and promotion and working conditions, OJ 1976, L 39/40.

[11] *Supra* note 2.

salary, but also 'any other consideration, whether in cash or in kind, which the worker receives, directly or indirectly, in respect of his employment from his employer'. The Court's approach has been equally broad. It has included in the idea of 'pay' advantages such as retirement pensions,[12] contributions to an occupational pension scheme paid by an employer on behalf of employees and producing certain effects,[13] temporary payments paid by an employer to an ex-employee after the cessation of the work relationship,[14] maintenance of salary in case of sickness[15] as well as other payments such as a severance allowance[16] and even benefits voluntarily accorded by an employer to his ex-employees.[17]

The employer in this last case was a transport undertaking which, without being contractually obliged to do so, continued after the retirement of its male employees to grant them special travel facilities for themselves, their wives and their dependent children. The Court found that the fact of not granting the same facilities to former female workers was a discrimination within the meaning of Article 119. What was at stake was of course a payment in kind, made by the employer to the worker *in respect of his employment*, even if that employment had been terminated.

Another aspect of the Court's broad approach to defining the content of Article 119 is the development of its case-law in the area of indirect discrimination. Indirect discrimination arises where a rule applicable to both men and women workers in fact prejudices many more workers of one sex than of the other. Such a rule will be unlawful unless it can be justified by reference to reasons having nothing to do with sex discrimination. This type of discrimination is not limited to equal pay cases; it can also arise in the area of access to jobs, for instance. However, it is dealt with here in the context of equal pay because of the abundance of case-law in this domain, relating to pay for part-time work.

The evolution of the Court's approach to cases of indirect discrimination has been remarkable. The Court showed early doubts about the possibility of Article 119 applying directly to such cases.[18] However, in *Jenkins v Kingsgate*,[19] just a year after the judgment in *Macarthys v Smith*, the Court admitted this possibility. The case concerned hourly rates of pay in an undertaking which were lower for part-time workers, the quasi-totality of part-time workers being women. No doubt the Court was influenced by the fact that the same employer had previously paid men and women at different rates, and by the suspicion that the replacement of this directly discriminatory system by an apparently neutral method of remuneration was simply a charade. Nevertheless, it was circumspect in its conclusion. It said that:

'A difference in pay between full-time workers and part-time workers does not amount to discrimination prohibited by Article 119 of the Treaty unless it is in

---

[12] Case 80/70, *Defrenne No 1* [1971] ECR 445; Case 170/84, *Bilka Kaufhaus v Weber* [1986] ECR 1607; Case C-262/88, *Barber, ibid.*
[13] Case 69/80, *Worringham and Humphreys v Lloyds' Bank* [1981] ECR 767.
[14] Case C-33/89, *Kowalska v Freie und Hansestadt Hamburg* [1990] ECR I-2591.
[15] Case 171/88, *Rinner-Kühn v FWW Spezial-Gebäuderreinigung GmbH* [1989] ECR 2743.
[16] Case 69/80, *Worringham and Humphreys* op. cit.; Case 23/83, *Liefting et al v Directie van het Academisch Ziekenhuis bij de Univrsiteit van Amsterdam* [1984] ECR 3225.
[17] Case 12/81, *Garland v British Rail* [1982] ECR 359.
[18] Case 129/79, *Macarthys v Smith* [1980] ECR 1275.
[19] Case 96/80, *Jenkins v Kingsgate* [1981] ECR 911.

reality merely an indirect way of reducing the pay of part-time workers on the ground that the group of workers is composed exclusively or predominantly of women',

and that:

'Where the national court is able, using the criteria of equal work and equal pay, without the operation of Community or national measures, to establish that the payment of lower hourly rates of remuneration for part-time work than for full-time work represents discrimination based on difference of sex the provisions of Article 119 of the Treaty apply directly to such a situation.'

The intention of the employer was clearly something to which the Court gave importance at this stage (see also ground 14 of the judgment). Moreover, the negative manner of framing the ruling might have been thought to betoken a somewhat restrictive attitude. This element in the Court's approach has, however, quite disappeared in the meantime.

In *Bilka Kaufhaus*,[20] the Court decided that Article 119 is infringed by an undertaking which excludes part-time employees from its occupational pension scheme, where that exclusion affects a far greater number of women than of men, *unless the undertaking shows* that the exclusion is based on objectively justified factors unrelated to any discrimination on grounds of sex. The justification put forward for the difference in treatment of full-time and part-time workers (such as an objective of deterring part-time workers) must be related to a real need of the enterprise, and the difference in treatment must be appropriate and necessary with a view to achieving the undertaking's objective.

This stricter attitude on the part of the Court has been maintained and even reinforced. In *Rinner-Kühn*[21] the problem arose from German *legislation* which allowed employers to exclude from the system of paid sick-leave part-time workers working less than a certain number of hours per week or per month. Again, this was a measure affecting many more women than men. The Court held that such a measure was contrary to Article 119 *unless the State* responsible for the legislation could show that it was justified by objective and non-discriminatory considerations.

Two other cases have concerned indirectly discriminatory provisions affecting part-time workers, on these occasions clauses contained in collective agreements. In *Kowalska*,[22] the agreement allowed employers not to pay part-time workers a temporary benefit payable to full-time workers on the termination of the employment relationship. In *Nimz*,[23] the agreement provided for a much slower system of adaptation of pay for persons working between half-time and three-quarters time. In both cases again, the disfavoured group was composed predominantly of women. Again, the Court took the view that in those circumstances the provision in question infringed Article 119 unless the employer could establish an objective and non-discriminatory justification for it. If no such justification was found by the national court, the question arose as to whether the national judge could immediately bring the discrimi-

---

[20] Case 170/84, *supra* note 12.
[21] Case 171/88, *supra* note 15.
[22] Case C-33/89, *supra* note 14.
[23] Case C-184/89, judgment of 7 February 1991, not yet reported in ECR.

nation to an end. The Court was undaunted by the argument that the principle of the autonomy of the social partners required that the national court await the amendment of the collective agreement along egalitarian lines. It pointed out that, as it had said as long ago as 1976, in *Defrenne No 2*, Article 119 is sufficiently clear and precise to be relied upon before a national court in order to ask it to set aside a discriminatory provision, including one contained in a collective agreement. The Court therefore decreed that, as long as a collective agreement contained discriminatory terms, the persons discriminated against were entitled to have applied to them the more beneficial terms reserved to the favoured group, this being the only relevant point of reference.

It may be seen therefore that the Court now adopts a vigorous attitude in relation to cases of alleged indirect discrimination. Its early doubts appear to be a thing of the past. Any measure which impacts more severely on women than on men must be closely scrutinized as to its justification, and the criteria for justification are not easy to meet. Nor will the Court be deterred from its severity by arguments about the autonomy of the social partners, or indeed, as far as one can tell, by anything else. The clear impression which emerges from the case-law is of a determined drive by the Court to achieve progress in an area of fundamental personal rights.

The exceptions provided for by the Directives

The Court's tendency to construe narrowly the exceptions it finds in the 'equality' directives has already been mentioned. Of course, it may be said that it is a general rule of construction that exceptions to a norm are to be construed so as to take away as little as possible from the norm. However, one cannot help feeling that the particular enthusiasm shown by the Court for this rule in the context of equal treatment as between the sexes must reflect its sense of the fundamental nature of the right at stake. Thus, Article 2(2) of Directive 76/207 provides that the directive is without prejudice to the right of the Member States to exclude from its field of application those occupational activities for which 'by reason of their nature or the context in which they are carried out, the sex of the worker constitutes a determining factor'. The Court has been at pains to point out that Article 2(2) refers to occupational *activities*, and not to jobs.[24] In principle, this means that a Member State cannot exclude women from doing certain jobs only because *some* of the activities associated with those jobs may legitimately be reserved to men. Thus, as the Court pointed out in *Johnston*,[25] the fact that a security situation may legitimately lead to a decision to allow only male policemen to carry guns and to perform certain police duties for which guns are regarded as necessary, does not of itself justify the total exclusion of women from access to the police force. The principle of proportionality requires that the exclusion should go no further than is objectively necessary for the attainment of the security objective in view. In other words, Mrs Johnston's contract with the RUC should have been renewed if it was operationally feasible to allocate duties to women which could be performed without fire-arms.

Article 2(3) of the Directive provides that the latter is without prejudice to

---

[24] Case 318/86, *Commission v France* [1988] ECR 3559.
[25] Case 222/84, *Johnston v Royal Ulster Constabulary* [1986] ECR 1651.

provisions concerning the protection of women, particularly as regards pregnancy and maternity. In *Johnston* the Court pointed out that Article 2(3), like Article 2(2), must be interpreted strictly. It regarded it as being clear from the express reference in that provision to pregnancy and maternity that the directive's purpose was to allow protection of a woman's biological condition and the special relationship which exists between a woman and her child. It did not therefore allow women to be excluded from a certain type of employment only because public opinion expected women to be given greater protection than men against risks which affect men and women in the same way (such as the risk of being shot).

This judgment appears therefore to indicate that women may lawfully only be granted special protection where their condition as women specifically requires it. This has also been the approach of the Court in its most recent case-law, relating to nightwork,[26] where it pointed out that, apart from the situation of pregnancy and its after-effects, the problems associated with nightwork were common to men and women. There was therefore no justification for a generalized ban on nightwork for women only.

The Court's narrow approach to exceptions was again in evidence in the famous *Marshall* case.[27] This case concerned the relationship between the prohibition of discrimination based on sex in relation to conditions governing dismissals contained in Article 5(1) of Directive 76/207, and the exception to the rule of equality allowed by Directive 79/7/EEC on the progressive implementation of the principle of equal treatment for men and women in matters of social security,[28] which permits the Member States to have different pensionable ages for men and women in relation to State pensions.

In the UK, State pensionable age for men is 65 and for women is 60. In *Marshall*, the problem was that Ms Marshall's employer had a policy of obliging its employees to retire at the State pensionable age. This obviously meant that women were forced to retire at an earlier age than men. This retirement policy was occasionally waived for a certain period, and in fact Ms Marshall was allowed to go on working until she was 62. However, this was still three years short of the age at which a man would have to have retired, and Ms Marshall was aggrieved at not being allowed to go on working until she was 65. She challenged the discriminatory nature of her dismissal, and the Court of Justice was asked whether such a dismissal was contrary to Directive 76/207. The Court said that it was. It pointed out that the term 'dismissal' used in Article 5(1) of the Directive (in relation to which all discrimination between the sexes is forbidden) must be construed broadly. Consequently, an age limit for the compulsory dismissal of workers pursuant to an employer's general policy concerning retirement falls within that term, even if the dismissal involves the grant of a pension. Since the problem was therefore one of dismissal of men and women at different ages, it was covered by Article 5(1). The fact that Directive 79/7 allowed different ages to be fixed for access to a State pension did not mean that compulsory dismissals could lawfully be effected at different ages.

---

[26] Case C-345/89, *Stoeckel*, judgment of 25 July 1991, not yet reported in ECR.
[27] Case 152/84, *Marshall v Southampton and South West Hampshire Area Health Authority* [1986] ECR 723.
[28] OJ 1979, L 6/24.

The Court took the same approach in another judgment given the same day in a Dutch case, *Beets-Proper v Lanschot Bankiers*.[29]

Aspects of direct effect developed in the case-law on equality

The difference between *Marshall* and *Beets-Proper* was that the Dutch law implementing Directive 76/207 was capable of being interpreted in conformity with the requirements of the Directive, whereas the British law was not. The question therefore arose as to whether Ms Marshall could rely directly on Article 5(1) before the UK courts. This involved two questions: is Article 5(1) sufficiently precise and unconditional to enable it to be relied on before national courts, and if so, may it be relied úpon as against all defendants or only as against the State which has failed to implement it properly?

As regards the first of these questions, the Court gave a positive answer. The prohibition of discrimination in relation to working conditions, including the conditions governing dismissal, is general and unequivocal. The exceptions to the principle of equal treatment allowed by the Directive (e.g. specific provisions for the protection of women; positive action to promote equal opportunity) do not take away from its unconditionality in the areas in which it applies. Article 5(1) is therefore by its nature capable of being relied on before national courts.

It is the Court's answer to the second question which has proved more controversial. It held that, since a directive is addressed to the Member States, its 'binding nature' (which is the basis for allowing reliance on it) exists only in relation to them. A directive cannot therefore of itself impose obligations on an individual. In other words, a provision of a directive, however clear and precise, cannot be relied upon directly before a national court in an action against a private individual.

This ruling did not prevent Ms Marshall from relying on Article 5(1), since her employer was a public authority, which of course comes within the notion of 'State'. As to the argument of the UK that it should not be possible to rely on the provisions of the Directive against the State when it was acting in its capacity as an *employer*, because this would give rise to discrimination between public and private employees, the Court dealt with this in summary fashion by pointing out that the Member State could eliminate any such problem by legislating to implement the Directive properly.

The fact that the Court chose to clarify its position on the impossibility of relying on a provision of a directive as against an individual in a case in which that would not affect the outcome can only be taken as a sign of the importance attached by the Court to a settlement of this question. It clearly intended to lay down a rule of principle. It has not departed from this principle, although one can have doubts as to the conformity with it of the Court's judgment in *Dekker*.[30]

This case concerned a woman who was refused a job because she was pregnant. The reason the employer refused to take on Ms Dekker was not however an objection to her pregnancy as such. The problem was that Dutch law appeared to allow the employer's insurer to refuse to reimburse the

[29] Case 262/84, [1986] ECR 773.
[30] Case C-177/88, [1990] ECR I-3941.

amount it would be obliged to pay her during her maternity leave. Since it was a small employer, this would make it very difficult for it to hire a replacement for her. If it did so, it could find itself in financial difficulties.

The Commission took the view that the discrimination was to be found at the level of this legislation which put pressure on employers not to hire pregnant women. Since it is the Member States which are responsible for the implementation of directives in their national legal order, the Commission thought that the Netherlands, and not the employer, should be regarded as being in breach of Directive 76/207. The Court did not agree. It decreed that an employer who refuses to engage a woman because she is pregnant commits an act of direct discrimination since pregnancy is a condition which can only affect women. Not only did the Court thus fix the employer with full responsibility for the discrimination, it further refused to examine questions of justification such as the difficulty caused by the Dutch law.

A private employer was therefore held bound by the provisions of Directive 76/207 even though its national law was defective. One can perhaps see this case as a strong encouragement given by the Court to the national jurisdiction to construe its law so as to conform with the Directive's requirements. In this way, the effect of the Directive would be deemed to have reached the employer via the national law. That approach would be consistent with the Court's most recent case-law which energetically confirms the obligation of the national judge to do his best to interpret his national law so as to meet Community law requirements.[31]

As for Directive 76/207, the Court has also declared the direct effect of Articles 3(1) and 4(1), prohibiting respectively all discrimination based on sex in relation to access to jobs and promotion on the one hand, and training courses on the other. This was in *Johnston*, the case we have already seen above in relation to Articles 2(2) and 2(3). Apart from declaring that Articles 3(1) and 4(1) could be relied upon before national jurisdictions, the Court also spelt out further the idea that a directly effective provision of a directive could be enforced as against any body which represented the State. The 'body' in question here was the Chief Constable of the Royal Ulster Constabulary. The UK tried to argue that the Directive should not be directly enforceable against the Chief Constable, on the ground that he was constitutionally independent in his functions, and could not therefore be regarded as part of the 'State'. The Court dismissed this argument firmly, saying:

> '. . . the Chief Constable is an official responsible for the direction of the police service. Whatever its relations may be with other organs of the State, such a public authority, charged by the State with the maintenance of public order and safety, does not act as a private individual. It may not take advantage of the failure of the State, of which it is an emanation, to comply with Community law.'

The question as to what types of body may be considered to be 'emanations of the State' was pursued further in *Foster and others v British Gas Plc*.[32] This case concerned a number of women who found themselves in the same position as Ms Marshall had done, in that they had been obliged to retire at age 60. Their employer was a statutory corporation which had a monopoly for the supply of

---

[31] Case C-106/89, *Marleasing v La Comercial Internacional de Alimentacion.* [1990] ECR I-4135.
[32] Case C-188/89, [1990] ECR I-3313.

gas in Great Britain. The competent Secretary of State had considerable powers of supervision over its activities. It maintained that it could not be treated as 'the State' for the purposes of direct effect, because it did not carry out any classic 'State' functions. The Court replied that Article 5(1) of Directive 76/207 could be relied upon in an action 'against a body, whatever its legal form, which has been made responsible, pursuant to a measure adopted by the State, for providing a public service under the control of the State and has for that purpose special powers going beyond those which result from the normal rules applicable in relations between individuals'.

It may be seen therefore that this area of the law has formed the background for the development of certain key ideas concerning the direct effect of directives. It has also furnished the material for the early development of the Court's efforts to ensure that even provisions of a directive which were not capable of having direct effect would nevertheless achieve their purpose as far as possible.

The obligation of the national court to construe its law so as to bring it into conformity with Community law

Von Colson[33] and *Harz*,[34] concerned the problem of an effective remedy for sex discrimination. Article 6 of Directive 76/207 requires the Member States to introduce into their national legal systems such measures as are necessary to enable all persons who consider themselves wronged by discrimination 'to pursue their claims by judicial process'. The Court has inferred from this provision that Member States are required to adopt measures which are sufficiently effective to achieve the objective of the directive and to ensure that those measures may in fact be relied upon before the national courts by the persons concerned. This implies that there must be an effective remedy for any breach of the principle of equal treatment which is within the scope of the Directive. The problem in *Van Colson* and *Harz* was that, in a case where a German court was satisfied that a female candidate for a job had been discriminated against on the ground of her sex, it appeared to be extremely limited by German law in relation to the amount of compensation it could award her. The only sanction which seems to have been available was a minimal amount of damages, just the sum of the expenses actually incurred in applying for the job. The Court pointed out that, although the Directive did not impose any particular sanction for a breach of the rule of equal treatment, it did require that whatever sanction was provided for by national law be such as to guarantee real and effective judicial protection. It must also have a real deterrent effect on the employer. It follows, said the Court, that where a Member State chooses to penalize the breach of the prohibition of discrimination by the award of compensation, that compensation must in any event be adequate in relation to the damage sustained. A nominal amount was not enough.

The question therefore arose as to what the German court could be required to do about this, in view of the apparent limitations of national law. The Court's answer was that:

---

[33] Case 14/83, *Von Colson and Kamann v Land Nodrhein-Westfalen* [1984] ECR 1891.
[34] Case 79/83, *Harz v Deutsche Tradax* [1984] ECR 1921.

'It is for the national court to interpret and apply the legislation adopted for the implementation of the directive in conformity with the requirements of Community law, *insofar as it is given discretion to do so under national law*' (emphasis added).

In other words, the national court should bend its national law *as far as possible* in order to make it conform with Community law. It is not, on the other hand, required to set aside clear provisions of national law only because they conflict with Community norms. This position does not appear to have been altered by the much-acclaimed recent judgment in *Marleasing*,[35] although this judgment does of course add the important clarification that the obligation to construe national law so as to give effect, as far as possible, to the intentions of the Community legislator applies to *all* national law, and not only that passed in order to give effect to a particular directive.

Rules of national law impeding access to a right based on Community law

It is in the context of Directive 79/7 concerning equal treatment in social security matters that a particular Member State has sought to assert two different types of national law in order to thwart efforts by individuals to assert Community law rights.

Article 4(1) of Directive 79/7, which prohibits all sex discrimination in matters of social security, has been declared on several occasions to have direct effect.[36] This implies that, in the absence of a correct transposition of the Directive into national law, individuals can rely directly on Article 4(1) before the national courts. Ireland was two years late in implementing the Directive, with the result that a large number of claims for equal treatment, directly based on Article 4(1), have been brought before the Irish courts. The Irish authorities have sought to put up two different kinds of defence. On the one hand, they have relied on national rules concerning time limits for bringing legal actions, and on the other they have claimed that equal treatment for women would lead to an infringement of a national law rule prohibiting unjust enrichment. The 'unjust enrichment' was said to arise from the circumstances that dependency payments would be paid to a woman in receipt of social security benefits (as they had been to a man) without any need for her to prove actual dependency of a spouse or of a child, and that in certain cases (where both spouses were receiving social security payments) this could lead to double benefits in the same family.

The alleged conflict between the Community law requirement of equal treatment and the national law notion of 'unjust enrichment' was brought before the Court in *McDermott and Cotter No 2*.[37] The Court, evidently unwilling to allow such a rule of national law to block access to the equal treatment prescribed by the Directive, gave it short shrift. Undeterred by the fact that it had allowed such a rule of national law to be effective as against other types of

---

[35] *Supra* note 31. See also, Curtin *supra* and Finlay *infra*.
[36] Case 71/85, *FNV* [1986] ECR 3855; Case 286/85, *McDermott and Cotter (No 1)* [1987] ECR 1453; Case 80/87, *Dik* [1988] ECR 1601.
[37] Case C-377/89, *McDermott and Cotter v Minister for Social Welfare and Attorney General*, [1991] 3 CMLR 507.

claim based on Community law,[38] the Court disallowed reliance on this type of rule in a context in which the problem of 'unjust enrichment' only arose because of the lateness in transposition of the Directive. Had the Irish authorities legislated on time, they could have avoided the whole problem of double payments etc. (as indeed they did for the future when they finally passed the necessary legislation). They could not therefore be allowed to raise a difficulty which they had (unlawfully) created for themselves in order to deprive Article 4(1) of its full effect.

As for the effort to deploy rules on time-limits to frustrate actions based on Article 4(1), the Court's manner of responding to this is dealt with in detail elsewhere in this book.[39] It is therefore only necessary here to record the Court's remarkable conclusion that:

> · 'until such time as a directive has been properly transposed, a defaulting Member State may not rely on an individual's delay in initiating proceedings against it in order to protect rights conferred upon him by the provisions of the directive and . . . a period laid down by national law within which proceedings must be initiated cannot begin to run before that time'.[40]

It is evident that this decision, like the generality of the case-law referred to above, has implications far beyond the area of sex discrimination. It is testimony to the Court's determination to prevent Member States, as far as possible, from gaining any advantage by failing to transpose a directive on time.[41]

Conclusion

As was suggested at the beginning of this article, the area of sex discrimination law is a fount of constitutional principles which are of importance to Community law as a whole, and to national law as it is touched ever more vitally by Community law. Whether looked at in the context of fundamental rights or of the interaction between Community and national legal orders, this is a domain the content of which is vastly more significant than the limits of its own borders might suggest.

---

[38] See the line of case-law relating to the recovery of taxes levied in breach of Community law, extending from Case 68/79, *Just v Danish Ministry for Fiscal Affairs* [1980] ECR 501, to Case 104/86, *Commission v Italy* [1988] ECR 1799.

[39] See *Curtin, supra.*

[40] Case C-208/90, *Emmott v Minister for Social Welfare and Attorney General* judgment of 25 July 1991, not yet reported.

[41] Further such testimony is to be found in a different context in the recent judgment in Joined Cases C-6 and C-9/90, *Francovich and Bonifaci v Italy* judgment of 19 November 1991, not yet reported in ECR.

11 Legislative Lacunae, the Court of Justice and Freedom to Provide Services*

Jean-Yves Art

Introduction

The recent *Gouda* judgment[1] clarifies the precise extent of freedom to provide services. In this area, the substance and the consequences of *Gouda* are comparable to those of *Cassis de Dijon*[2] in the field of free movement of goods. The impact which *Gouda* is likely to have on the establishment of the common market accordingly provides an opportunity to examine the role played by the Court of Justice in the process of integration.

This essay describes the place which the *Gouda* judgment takes in the Court's case-law on freedom to provide services and reviews the role of the Court of Justice in the establishment of the common market in services. It then examines the consequences which *Gouda* is likely to have on the future activity of both the Community and national legislatures.

Gouda, a landmark case

The background

Freedom to provide services is one of the foundations of the Community. As appears from Article 3(*c*) of the Treaty, this freedom is one of the constituents of the common market and consequently is indispensable to the achievement of the objectives of the Community listed in Article 2 of the Treaty. The freedom is set out in Article 59 of the Treaty in the following terms;

> '(within the framework of the provisions of Articles 60 to 66) restrictions on freedom to provide services within the Community shall be progressively abolished during the transitional period in respect of nationals of Member States who are established in a State of the Community other than that of the person for whom the services are intended'.

---

* The author is indebted to Dennis Burton for his linguistic comments.
[1] Judgment of 25 July 1991 in Case C-288/89, *Stichting Collectieve Antennevoorziening Gouda et al v Commissariaat voor de Media* (not yet reported in ECR).
[2] Case 120/78, *Rewe-Zentral AG v Bundesmonopolverwaltung für Branntwein* [1979] ECR 649.

For a supplier of services,[3] 'freedom to provide services' could have at least two distinct meanings.[4] On a narrow view, a person established in one Member State (the 'home country') may be regarded as free to provide services in another Member State (the 'host country') if the host country imposes no requirements on that person which do not apply to persons established within the host country. On this view, freedom to provide services would simply require the abolition of any discrimination based on the supplier's place of establishment. However the freedom concept may be given a much wider meaning: a supplier established in a given Member State may be considered free to provide services in other Member States if the fulfilment of the conditions imposed by the home country for the supply of services within its territory automatically entitles the supplier to provide similar services in other Member States without having to satisfy any additional requirements imposed by the host country.

A teleological interpretation of Article 59 of the Treaty supports this broader view. The Treaty provisions concerning freedom to provide services aim to establish a common market in services throughout the Community. As the Court of Justice indicated in *Schul v Inspecteur der Invoerrechten en Accijnzen*,[5] the establishment of the common market 'involves the elimination of all obstacles to intra-Community trade in order to merge the national markets into a single market bringing about conditions as close as possible to those of a genuine internal market'. The Court added that 'it is important that not only commerce as such but also private persons who happen to be conducting an economic transaction across national frontiers should be able to enjoy the benefits of that market'.[6]

If such an objective is to be achieved, the abolition of restrictions on freedom to provide services cannot be limited to the elimination of discriminatory host country requirements. The establishment of a common market in services, as defined in *Schul*, clearly requires the abolition of all legislative or administrative measures which hinder the inter-state provision of service and which are not justified by the general good. In addition, disparities between national legislation justified by reasons of general interest create obstacles to the inter-state provision of services. Therefore, the establishment of a common market in services also requires the harmonization of this legislation or, more generally, the adoption of Community rules to govern the provision of services in one Member State by persons established in other Member States in so far as these rules are indispensable to safeguard values of general interest compatible with Community law.[7]

---

[3] Recipients of services also benefit from the Treaty provisions concerning freedom to provide services. See Joined Cases 286/82 and 26/83, *Luisi and Carbone v Ministero del Tesoro* [1984] ECR 377 at 403, para 16, in which the Court ruled that 'the freedom to provide services includes the freedom, for the recipients of services, to go to another Member State in order to receive a service there, without being obstructed by restrictions, even in relation to payments'.

[4] On the various possible meanings of the freedom concept as used in the Treaty, see Kapteyn and VerLoren van Themaat *Introduction to the Law of the European Communities after the coming into force of the Single European Act* (1989) 2nd ed., pp. 356–357.

[5] Case 15/81, [1982] ECR 1409 at 1431–1432, para 33.

[6] *Ibid.*

[7] See, for instance, Council Directive 77/249/EEC of 22 March 1977 to facilitate the effective exercise by lawyers of freedom to provide services (OJ L 78, at p. 17). Article 5 of the Directive allows national legislation to require a lawyer who is established in another Member State and pursues within the host country activities relating to the representation of a client in legal

Before *Gouda*, several Advocates General had concluded that non-discriminatory host country requirements may amount to restrictions on freedom to provide services.[8] The position of the Court, however, remained ambiguous.[9] The Court had never stated expressly that Article 59 requires non-discriminatory regulations which are not justified by imperative reasons of general interest to be abolished. However, the non-discriminatory host country regulations which the Court has found compatible with the objectives of Article 59 seem to have been regarded as justified by imperative reasons of general interest.[10] Conversely, all the cases in which national measures have been held to be 'restrictions' within Article 59 seem to have involved an element of discrimination on the facts.

In some cases, discrimination resulted from the fact that suppliers established in other Member States ('foreign' suppliers) had to satisfy similar requirements twice (i.e. the requirements imposed by the home country in order to take up and pursue activities within its territory and similar requirements imposed by the host country in order to conduct activities in its territory by way of provision of services) whereas suppliers established in the host country ('domestic' suppliers) had to satisfy these requirements only once in order to provide services within the host country.[11] In other cases, although the host country requirements differed from those imposed by other Member States and applied also to domestic suppliers, their application to foreign

proceedings, to work in conjunction with a local lawyer. As indicated by the Court, the obligation to work in conjunction with a local lawyer is intended to provide the lawyer established in another Member State 'with the support necessary to enable him to act within a judicial system different from that to which he is accustomed and to assure the judical authority concerned that the lawyer providing services actually has that support and is thus in a position fully to comply with the procedural and ethical rules that apply' (Case 427/85, *Commission v Germany* [1988] ECR 1123, at 1161, para 23; see also, judgment of 10 July 1991 in Case C-294/89, *Commission v France* at paras 30–36, not yet reported in ECR). Furthermore this Directive shows that although freedom to provide services may be facilitated by the harmonization or the mutual recognition of conditions imposed by Member States for the taking up and the pursuit of economic activities by persons established within the national territory, such harmonization or mutual recognition is not indispensable to the liberalization of services.

[8] On the issue whether non-discriminatory host country requirements may amount to restrictions within the meaning of Article 59, the Court of Justice in *Gouda* followed the Opinion delivered by Advocate General Tesauro on 18 April 1991 (see paras 11–14; not yet reported in ECR). See also Opinion of Advocate General Warner in Case 52/79, *Procureur du Roi v Debauve et al* and Case 62/79, *Coditel et al v Ciné Vog et al* [1980] ECR 860, at 870–873 and 905, opinion of Advocate General Sir Gordon Slynn in Case 279/80, *Webb* [1981] ECR 3328, at 3331–3333, opinion delivered by Advocate General Lenz on 5 December 1990 in Case C-154/89, *Commission v France*, Case C-180/89, *Commission v Italy*, and Case C-198/89, *Commission v Greece*, at paras 26–30 unreported (not yet reported in ECR), opinion delivered by Advocate General Jacobs on 21 February 1991 in Case C-76/90 *Säger v Dennemeyer* at paras 23–29 (not yet reported in ECR) and opinion delivered by Advocate General Van Gerven on 11 June 1991 in Case C-159/90, *The Society for the Protection of Unborn Children Ireland Ltd v S Grogan et al* at paras 20–21 (not yet reported in ECR).

[9] See Opinion delivered by Advocate General Jacobs on 21 February 1991 in Case C-76/90 *Säger v Dennemeyer* at para 21–22 (not yet reported in ECR) and Opinion delivered by Advocate General Van Gerven on 11 June 1991 in Case C-159/90, *The Society for the Protection of Unborn Children Ireland Ltd v S Grogan et al* at para 20 (not yet reported in ECR).

[10] See in particular Case 15/78, *Société Générale Alsacienne de Banque v Koestler* [1978] ECR 1971 at 1981, para 5 and Case 52/79, *Procureur du Roi v Debauve et al* [1980] ECR 833 at 857, para 15.

[11] See, e.g., Joined Cases 110 and 111/78, *Ministère Public and Chambre Syndicale des Agents Artistiques et Impresiari de Belgique v Van Wesemael et al* [1979] ECR 35; Case 279/80, *Webb* [1981] ECR 3305, at 3308–3309; Joined Cases 62 and 63/81, *Seco et al v EVI* [1982] ECR 223 at 235, para 9.

suppliers amounted to the very negation of freedom to provide services[12] or affected foreign suppliers more severely than domestic suppliers.[13]

The Gouda judgment

Gouda concerned a Dutch law regulating the broadcasting of advertisements contained in radio and television programmes transmitted from abroad and intended specifically for the public in the Netherlands.[14] The Dutch Government emphasized that, in substance, these regulations imposed conditions identical to those applying to Dutch broadcasting organizations and to advertisements broadcast during their programmes.[15] The Court was asked whether, in these circumstances, requirements such as those imposed by Dutch law amounted to restrictions on freedom to provide services and, if so, whether such requirements must be justified by reasons of general interest and be proportionate to the objectives they seek to achieve.

The Court of Justice began its judgment with a general examination of Article 59 of the Treaty. The Court stated that Article 59 requires the abolition of any discrimination against a provider of services by reason of his nationality or of the fact that he is established in a Member State other than that where the service is provided. The Court recalled that discriminatory measures are compatible with Community law only if they can be brought within the scope of an express derogation, such as Article 56 of the Treaty. It continued:

'en l'absence d'harmonisation des règles applicables aux services, voire d'un régime d'équivalence, des entraves à la liberté garantie par le traité dans ce domaine peuvent . . . provenir de l'application de réglementations nationales, qui touchent toute personne établie sur le territoire national, à des prestataires établis sur le territoire d'un autre Etat membre, lesquels doivent déjà satisfaire aux prescriptions de la législation de cet Etat. Ainsi qu'il découle d'une jurisprudence constante . . . pareilles entraves tombent sous le coup de l'article 59 dès lors que l'application de la législation nationale aux prestataires étrangers n'est pas justifiée par des raisons impérieuses d'intérêt général ou que les exigences que traduit cette législation sont déjà satisfaites par les règles imposées à ces prestataires dans l'Etat membre où ils sont établis.'[16]

---

[12] This seems to be the consideration underlying the Court judgments in the *Tourist Guides* cases: see judgments of 26 February 1991 in Case C-154/89, *Commission v France* at paras 12, 13 and 19, Case C-180/89, *Commission v Italy* at paras 15, 16 and 22, and Case C-198/89, *Commission v Greece* at paras 16, 17 and 23 (not yet published in ECR).

[13] See, e.g., 1 Case 205/84, *Commission v Germany* [1986] ECR 3755 at 3803, para 28 and Case C-113/89 *Rush Portuguesa Lda v Office national d'immigration*; [1990] ECR I-1417, at I-1443, para 12.

[14] The Dutch law in question required: (1) that advertisements be produced by a legal person distinct from the producer of the programmes; (2) that broadcasters established in other Member States must not grant benefits to third parties; and (3) that advertising revenues be wholly allocated to the production of programmes. Furthermore, it provided: (1) that advertisements must be clearly identified and separated from the other parts of the programme; (2) that they may not be broadcast on Sundays; and (3) that their duration may not exceed 5% of the air time used.

[15] See paras 21 and 26 of the judgment.

[16] Paras 12 and 13. 'In the absence of harmonization of the rules applicable to services, or of a system of equivalence, obstacles to the freedom guaranteed by the Treaty in this area may . . . result from the application of national regulations, which affect any person established within the national territory, to providers established in the territory of another Member State who must also satisfy the requirements imposed by the legislation of that State. As appears from a

The Court added that the application of national regulations to providers established in other Member States must be appropriate to the achievement of the objectives which these regulations seek to attain and may not exceed what is necessary in order to achieve these objectives.[17]

On the specific questions raised, the Court found that conditions such as those imposed by Dutch law amounted to restrictions on freedom to provide services within the meaning of Article 59 of the Treaty and were not justified by imperative reasons of general interest.

The Court's role in establishing the common market in services

In establishing that non-discriminatory obstacles to the inter-state provision of services which are not justified by imperative reasons of general interest must be abolished, *Gouda* clarifies an issue which had been rendered particularly uncertain by the apparent divergence between the opinion of several Advocates General and the decision of the Court of Justice in earlier cases. Furthermore, *Gouda* makes it clear that the Court is prepared to review the compatibility of such obstacles with Community law. Consequently, the contribution of the Court to the establishment of a common market in services might become as significant as the role which it has been playing in the liberalization of the movement of goods throughout the Community since *Cassis de Dijon*.

This section first shows that *Gouda* is a natural development from the *Van Binsbergen* case.[18] It then discusses the compatibility of the role assumed by the Court with the Treaty.

The Van Binsbergen case

In *Van Binsbergen*, the Court held that the obligation to abolish restrictions on freedom to provide services became unconditional on the expiry of the transitional period and that:

> 'as regards at least the specific requirement of nationality or of residence, Articles 59 and 60 impose a well-defined obligation, the fulfilment of which by the Member States cannot be delayed or jeopardized by the absence of provisions which were to be adopted in pursuance of powers conferred under Articles 63 and 66'.[19]

This ruling calls for two comments.

First, once it is accepted that both discriminatory and non-discriminatory obstacles to the inter-state provision of services are 'restrictions' within the meaning of Article 59, there can be no objective justification for saying that non-discriminatory restrictions must be abolished only if targeted by direct-

consistent case-law . . . such obstacles fall within the ambit of Article 59 where the application of the national legislation in question to foreign providers is not justified by imperative reasons of general interest or where the requirements which such legislation reflects are already satisfied by the rules imposed on these providers in the Member State where they are established.' (our translation; the official translation of the judgment in English is not yet available).

[17] See para 15.
[18] Case 33/74, *Van Binsbergen v Bestuur van de Bedrijfsvereniging voor de Metaalnijverheid* [1974] ECR 1299.
[19] *Ibid.,* at 1311–1312, para 26.

ives adopted pursuant to Articles 63 and 66 of the Treaty, while discriminatory measures must be abolished even in the absence of specific Council directives.[20]

It is true that the rules governing the elimination of discriminatory and non-discriminatory obstacles at first sight seem quite different. The permitted derogations from the obligation to abolish discriminatory measures are listed in full in Article 56 of the Treaty, whereas the reasons which, in the present state of Community law, may justify non-discriminatory restrictions are not set out in the Treaty and the list of these reasons, given in *Gouda*, remains open.[21] In other words, the obligations imposed by Article 59 in relation to non-discriminatory restrictions appear much less clear and precise than those imposed by Articles 59 and 56 with respect to discriminatory measures.

Nevertheless it should be stressed that at the time of the *Van Binsbergen* judgment, the concepts of 'public policy, public security and public health' used in Article 56 were quite unclear.[22] Therefore, in holding that as regards discriminatory measures Article 59 imposes 'a well-defined obligation', the Court could not have been referring to the precision of the concepts used to formulate this obligation. Rather, the Court's ruling must be based on the consideration that even though the permitted derogations to Article 59 may be vaguely defined, reliance on these exceptions is subject to judicial control and the fulfilment of the obligation incumbent upon Member States does not depend on or involve any policy choice by them.[23]

As regards the abolition of non-discriminatory restrictions on freedom to provide services, the situation is identical. Therefore, the absence of a provision in the Treaty specifying the 'reasons of general interest' capable of justifying the enforcement of non-discriminatory restrictions on freedom to provide services cannot be regarded as precluding the extension to these restrictions of the Court's ruling in *Van Binsbergen*.[24]

Secondly, in holding in *Van Binsbergen* that Article 59 imposes on Member States a clear and unconditional obligation to abolish restrictions on freedom to provide services and that the fulfilment of this obligation is not subject to the issuing of directives in accordance with Articles 63 and 66, the Court paved the way to the institution of proceedings pursuant to Article 169 of the Treaty against Member States which maintain such restrictions in force. Furthermore,

---

[20] See Opinion of Advocate General Warner in Case 52/79, *Procureur du Roi v Debauve et al* [1980] ECR 833, at 873–874.

[21] See para 14 of the judgment.

[22] On 25 February 1964, the Council adopted Directive 64/221/EEC on the co-ordination of special measures concerning the movement and residence of foreign nationals which are justified on grounds of public policy, public security and public health (OJ English Special Edition 1963–64, p. 117). This directive specifies to a certain extent the circumstances in which the grounds of public policy, public security and public health may be relied on to limit the free movement of workers, freedom of establishment and freedom to provide services. However, most of the cases in which the Court has been called upon to interpret Directive 64/221/EEC, Article 56 of the Treaty or Article 48(3) of the Treaty – which provides that freedom of movement of workers is subject to limitations justified on grounds of public policy, public security or public health – have been decided after *Van Binsbergen*.

[23] See Case 41/74, *Van Duyn v Home Office* [1974] ECR 1337, at 1347, paras 6–7.

[24] This is confirmed by the fact that in *Van Binsbergen* the Court ruled that Article 60, third indent, of the Treaty also imposes on Member States a well-defined and unconditional obligation notwithstanding the fact that the obligation in question is subject to exceptions which are not listed in the Treaty.

as this ruling also implied that Article 59 has direct effect,[25] it opened the door to challenges to national regulations under Articles 59 before national courts and, as a consequence, to references to the Court of Justice for preliminary rulings on the interpretation of this provision.

Compatibility of Van Binsbergen and Gouda with the Treaty

The Court's role in the process of negative integration[26] in the field of freedom to provide services is, therefore, a direct consequence of *Van Binsbergen*. Nevertheless, whether this role is compatible with the duties of the Court, to ensure that the law is observed in the application and the interpretation of the Treaty,[27] is an issue that must be considered.

Article 8(7) and 59 of the Treaty show that the abolition of restrictions on freedom to provide services was intended to be effected by directives adopted by the Council pursuant to Articles 63 and 57, which had to be implemented at the latest on the expiry of the transitional period.[28] However, notwithstanding these requirements and the increasing importance of the service sector in the Community economy, the inter-state provision of services was far from being fully liberalized when the transitional period expired on 31 December 1969.[29]

Article 175 of the Treaty aims to induce the Council to fulfil its obligations by giving the other Community institutions, Member States and, in certain circumstances, natural and legal persons the possibility of instituting proceedings before the Court of Justice against the Council's failure to act. However, this mechanism does not guarantee the fulfilment of the Council's obligations. Indeed, it is particularly likely to be ineffective in the field of freedom to provide services since, although natural and legal persons are the main beneficiaries of the abolition of restrictions on freedom to provide services, an action brought by such persons against the Council's failure to adopt the necessary directives would be inadmissible.[30] This leaves the institution of procedings against the Council's failure to adopt such directives to applicants which are not the direct and immediate beneficiaries of the liberalization of services. In addition, as in other fields, even if a 'privileged applicant'[31] institutes proceedings against the Council's failure to act and these proceedings are

---

[25] [1974] ECR 1299, at 1312, para 27.

[26] The concept of negative integration is borrowed from Tinbergen, *International Economic Integration* (1965), 2nd ed., p. 76. Tinbergen defines negative integration as 'measures consisting of the abolition of a number of impediments to the proper operation of an integrated area'. He defines positive integration as 'the creation of new institutions and their instruments or the modification of existing instruments'.

[27] Article 164 of the Treaty.

[28] Since the concept of common market as used in Article 8(7) refers to a market similar to the domestic market of a single State, one must admit that, at least as regards freedom to provide services, Article 8A of the Treaty does not extend the date by which the common market in services had to be established. See *Kapteyn* and *VerLoren van Themaat*, op. cit., note 4, at p. 102.

[29] See Commission's White Paper *Completing the Internal Market* (COM (85) 310 final), pp. 26–27, at paras 95–100.

[30] Pursuant to Article 175, third indent, a natural or legal person may institute legal proceedings before the Court of Justice only against the failure by a Community institution 'to address *to that person* (an) act other than a recommendation or an opinion' (emphasis added).

[31] The term 'privileged applicant' designates applicants to whom the condition of admissibility which must be satisfied by natural and legal persons instituting proceedings under Article 175 of the Treaty does not apply. The privileged applicants are the institutions of the Community other than that which has failed to act and the Member States.

declared well-founded, they would merely result in a judgment that, in failing to ensure freedom to provide services, the Council is infringing the Treaty.[32] The Council would then be bound to take the necessary measures to comply with the judgment within a reasonable period.[33] If the Council's failure continues beyond the expiry of this reasonable period, the whole process could start again and continue indefinitely.

The fact that the Treaty does not provide explicitly for an adequate remedy to the Council's failure to act leads to a dilemma for the Court. On the one hand, the Court's duties mean that it cannot confine itself to declaring that the Council has failed to take measures indispensable to the completion of the common market in services and to the achievement of the objectives of the Community. On the other hand, observance of the law precludes the Court from substituting itself for the Council and entering into the policy-making process entrusted to other Community institutions. The Court's finding that Article 59 imposes on Member States a clear and unconditional obligation to repeal unjustified restrictions enables it to escape this dilemma to a certain extent.

As indicated above, the abolition of unjustified obstacles to freedom to provide services is a first step towards the establishment of a common market in services. The completion of the process of integration may further require the adoption of common rules governing the provision of services by foreign suppliers in so far as such rules are necessary in order to protect values of general interest. However, this second step involves policy choices which are a matter for the Council.[34] In such circumstances, the only position the Court may adopt is to recognize that, pending Community action, Member States remain entitled to subject the provision of services within their territory by foreign suppliers to requirements indispensable to the safeguard of values of general interest, even though protection of those values at a national level leads to disparities between the various national laws and, consequently, to obstacles to the inter-state provision of services by suppliers providing lawfully similar services in their home country.

It might be argued that the active role adopted by the Court requires it to make policy choices to the extent that it determines the reasons capable of justifying non-discriminatory restrictions on freedom to provide services. In practice, however, the Court appears to leave Member States a wide discretion which to date has been limited only by the requirement that these reasons be compatible with Community law.

It is true that in *Gouda* the Court seems to have ruled that economic aims are not capable of justifying non-discriminatory obstacles to freedom to provide services.[35] Nevertheless, it should be noted that the economic objective at issue in *Gouda* was the protection of the revenues of the Dutch foundation with a

---

[32] See, e.g., Case 13/83, *Parliament v Council* [1985] ECR 1513, at 1603.

[33] *Ibid.*, at 1600, para 69.

[34] In this respect, see Judgment of 18 April 1991 in Case C-63/89, *Assurances du Crédit and Compagnie Belge d'Assurance Crédit v Council and Commission* at paras 9–11 (not yet reported in ECR).

[35] See paragraph 29 in which the Court referred to paragraph 34 of the Judgment of 26 April 1988 in Case 352/85, *Bond van Adverteerders et al v Netherlands State* ([1988] ECR 2085) – in which it had ruled that economic aims cannot constitute grounds of public policy within the meaning of Article 56 of the Treaty, capable of justifying discriminatory host country requirements – in support of the conclusion that the (economic) objective pursued by the Dutch regulations at issue in *Gouda* cannot justify restrictions on freedom to provide services.

monopoly over the broadcasting of advertisements in the Netherlands and that the Dutch regulations sought to achieve this objective by restricting competition between that foundation and foreign broadcasting organizations.[36] Thus the regulations in question arguably pursued an objective which was not compatible with Community law.[37] Furthermore, in the context of the application of Article 30 of the Treaty, the Court considers that, provided the national measures in question apply to domestic and imported products without discrimination and the restrictive effect of these measures on the free movement of goods does not exceed the effects intrinsic to measures of that kind, the prohibition laid down in Article 30 does not apply to national measures which 'reflect certain political and economic choices' dictated by 'national or regional socio-cultural characteristics (that), in the present state of Community law, (are) a matter for the Member States'.[38] There seems to be no reason why the discretion enjoyed by Member States in the area of free circulation of goods should be wider than that left to them in the area of freedom to provide services.

The consequences of *Gouda* for Community and national legislatures

As pointed out above, by confining itself to ensuring that unjustified obstacles to freedom to provide services are abolished, the Court of Justice has avoided participating in the policy-making aspects of establishing a common market in services which are the responsibility of other Community institutions. The role played by the Court is, nevertheless, likely to have significant consequences for the Community legislator as well as national legislatures.

The Community legislator

While the contribution of the Court to the establishment of a common market in services might increase significantly, it should be emphasized that neither *Van Binsbregen* nor *Gouda* deprives the Community legislator of any of the powers conferred upon it by Articles 63 and 66 of the Treaty. The Court's recognition that Article 59 has direct effect does not discharge the Council from the obligations imposed by these provisions. The Council remains not only entitled but bound to adopt directives aimed at ensuring the abolition of unjustified obstacles to freedom to provide services. Further, the Court has confined itself to fostering the process of negative integration. This means that national legislation which is justified either on the basis of Article 56(1) of the Treaty or by imperative reasons of general interest, remains enforceable with respect to foreign providers of services. The abolition of obstacles to the

---

[36] See para 29 of the judgment.

[37] Whilst the grant of exclusive rights to an undertaking means that other undertakings established within the national territory are precluded from engaging in the reserved activity, the application to foreign undertakings conducting such an activity occasionally, by way of provision of services, of requirements aimed at protecting the revenues of the undertaking which enjoys exclusive rights exceeds the effects intrinsic to the grant of such rights and is at variance with one of the objectives of the Treaty, namely the establishment of a single market in which competition is not distorted. See Schwartz *Broadcasting and the EEC Treaty* 11 EL Rev 7, at 14–15.

[38] Case C-145/88, *Torfaen Borough Council v B & Q plc* [1989] ECR 3851, at 3889, para 14.

inter-state provision of services which may result from disparities between national legislation of this type requires the intervention of the Community legislator pursuant to Articles 63 and 66 of the Treaty.

Even though the Community legislator retains its powers under the Treaty, it will nevertheless have to take into account any prior intervention by the Court in the process of negative integration when it legislates to complete the process of positive integration.[39] Indeed, as the Court has emphasized in relation to Articles 30 to 36 of the Treaty, although these provisions apply primarily to unilateral measures adopted by the Member States, the Community institutions themselves must also have due regard to freedom of trade within the Community, which is a fundamental principle of the common market.[40]

This undoubtedly applies also to Article 59 of the Treaty. Accordingly, if the Court finds that a requirement imposed by the host country amounts to a restriction on freedom to provide services within the meaning of Article 59 on the ground, for instance, that this requirement is disproportionate to the legitimate objective which it seeks to attain, this would prevent the Council from introducing the same requirement at Community level through a directive adopted pursuant to Article 63 of the Treaty.

This does not mean however that the role which the Court plays in the process of negative integration limits the discretion which the Community legislator would otherwise enjoy. Rather, in interpreting Article 59 in the context of 169 or 177 proceedings, the Court throws light on various obstacles to freedom to provide services which the Community legislator might not have perceived and may thereby facilitate its task in the process of positive integration.

National legislatures

The main consequences of *Gouda* for national legislatures emerges from what has been said above. Pending Community action, national legislatures remain the protectors of values of general interest which are reflected in regulations concerning services, notwithstanding the fact that disparities between the national legislation which aims to protect such values may actually hinder the inter-state provision of services.

It is true that *Gouda* amounts to introducing in Community law a set of derogations from the prohibiton of restrictions on freedom to provide services, in addition to the derogations listed in Article 56(1) of the Treaty with respect to discriminatory measures. However, whilst the Treaty allows Member States to maintain in force restrictive national measures as long as such measures are not targeted by Council Directives adopted pursuant to Articles 63 and 66 of the Treaty,[41] the Treaty fails to address explicitly the conse-

---

[39] See Pescatore, 'La Carence du Législateur Communautaire et le Devoir du Juge', in *Rechtsvergleichung, Europarecht and Staatenintegration, Gedachtnisschrift fur Leontin-Jean Constantinesco* (1983), 559–580, at 580.

[40] See Case 37/83, *Rewe-Zentrale AG v Director of the Landwirtschaftskammer Rheinland* [1984] ECR 1229, at 1248–1249, para 18.

[41] It should however be noted that Article 65 of the Treaty lays down a 'most favoured treatment' rule applicable during the transitional period. See Council Decision of 18 December 1961 laying down the general programme for the abolition of restrictions on freedom to provide services, Title IV (OJ English Special Edition (2nd Series) IX, p. 3).

quences of the Community legislator's failure to complete the establishment of the common market in services by the end of the transitional period. In those circumstances, pending Community action, Member States must be entitled to retain or introduce national measures designed to safeguard values of general interest which might otherwise be affected by the unregulated inter-state provision of services.

The rule of reason which *Gouda* reflects should not be regarded, however, as a *lex praetoria* devoid of any legal basis in the Treaty. In an earlier case concerning the compatibility with Community law of national measures allegedly pursuing the aims of the common organization of the market, the Court observed that the Council had not enacted the rules needed to enable that organization to function normally and stated that:

> 'in those circumstances there cannot in principle be any objection to a Member State's retaining or introducing national measures designed to achieve in its own territory the aims of the market organization. . . .
> However . . . such measures must not be regarded as involving the exercise of the Member State's own powers, but as the fulfilment of the duty to cooperate in achieving the aims of the common organization of the market which, in a situation characterized by the inaction of the Community legislature, Article 5 of the Treaty imposes on them. Consequently, the measures adopted by the Member States may only be temporary and provisional in nature and they must cease to be applied as soon as Community measures are introduced'.[42]

If this ruling is applied to the field of freedom to provide services, it would seem that, in the absence of Community rules establishing the common market in services, national measures which lay down requirements necessary to safeguard the general good which these Community rules would aim to protect should be regarded as implementing the duty to cooperate in the achievement of the aims of the Community imposed on Member States by Article 5 of the Treaty.

As the Court pointed out in *Gouda*,[43] the exercise of the power thus conferred on Member States is subject to strict requirements.[44] It should be emphasized, however, that the limits which *Gouda* places on the powers of Member States relate exclusively to the provision of services by persons established outside the national territory. Subject to the provisions of the Treaty concerning freedom of establishment, Member States remain formally free to regulate the activities of domestic undertakings. The co-existence of two distinct sets of rules governing the provision of services by domestic undertakings and the provision of services by foreign undertakings results from the different conditions

---

[42] Joined Cases 47 and 48/83, *Pluimveeslachterij Midden-Nederland and Pluimveeslachterij Van Miert* [1984] ECR 1721, at 1738, paras 22–23. See also, Case 804/79, *Commission v United Kingdom* [1981] ECR 1045, at 1072–1076, paras 17–32, and Case C-158/89, *Dietz-Matti* [1990] ECR I-2013 at I-2036–I-2037, paras 12–13.

[43] See paras 13 and 15.

[44] Whilst the concept of 'imperative reasons of general interest' is interpreted broadly, the application of the proportionality test is likely to limit the discretion enjoyed by Member States significantly. As shown by the *Tourist Guides* cases, this test may result in Member States being prevented from enforcing with respect to persons established in other Member States, national measures which pursue a legitimate objective where it appears that market forces can guarantee the achievement of this objective (see, judgments of 26 February 1991 in Case C-154/89, *Commission v France* at para 20, Case C-180/89, *Commission v Italy* at para 23, and Case C-198/89, *Commission v Greece* at para 24, not yet reported in ECR).

of facts in which these categories of persons pursue their activity in the host country and is therefore an application of the principle of non-discrimination.[45]

However of course, the fact that requirements which hinder the inter-state provision of services without any objective justification are unenforceable against foreign undertakings may place domestic providers of services – who remain bound to comply with these requirements – at a competitive disadvantage. The position in which domestic providers of services are placed may appear to them all the more unacceptable in cases in which the application of the requirements in question to foreign undertakings is held incompatible with Community law, not because the circumstances of the latter differ from those of domestic undertakings, but on the ground that these requirements are disproportionate to the objectives which they seek to achieve.

In such cases, domestic undertakings are indeed likely to request the repeal of the national measures in question which remain applicable to them. This means that the Court's decisions which establish that national measures hinder the inter-state provision of services without any objective justification may lead to a softening of the rules laying down the conditions under which nationals of the Member State concerned, as well as nationals of other Member States, may take up and pursue activities within that Member State. Thus, whilst freedom of establishment rests primarily on a prohibition of discrimination,[46] the development of the Court's case law concerning freedom to provide services might also lead to the suppression of national measures governing establishment which apply to nationals of any Member State but are not objectively justified by imperative reasons of general interest.

Conclusion

The Court has long been hesitant, if not reluctant, to hold expressly that non-discriminatory host country measures concerning services may amount to restrictions within Article 59 of the Treaty and to formulate in this field a rule similar to that laid down in *Cassis de Dijon*. The adoption of this rule in *Gouda* might be regarded as an example of 'judicial activism' by which the Court substitutes itself for the defaulting political actors. Whatever term is used, any suggestion that the Court exceeded its powers in adopting this approach must be rejected.

Whilst the Treaty entrusts the Council with a decisive role in the establishment of the common market, it does not provide for any effective remedy – whether legal or political – to the Council's failure to act. Furthermore, the objectives of the Community are not merely described in the recitals of the

[45] See, Case 427/85, *Commission v Germany* [1988] ECR 1123, at 1164–1165, paras 38–42 and judgment of 10 July 1991 in Case C-294/89, *Commission v France* at paras 27–28, not yet reported in ECR.

[46] See Case 6/64, *Costa v ENEL* [1964] ECR 585, at 596–597, and Case 2/74, *Reyners v Belgium* [1974] ECR 631, at 650, para 18. See, however, opinion delivered by Advocate General Van Gerven on 28 November 1990 in Case C-340/89, *Vlassopoulou v Ministerium für Justiz, Bundes- und Europaangelegenheiten Baden-Württemberg* at paras 6–10 (not yet published in ECR). In this case, after a thorough examination of the Court's case-law, Advocate General Van Gerven concludes that Article 52 of the Treaty is interpreted as prohibiting not only discrimination on grounds of nationality but also measures which hinder freedom of establishment in several Member States without any objective justification.

Treaty, but are laid down in its first provisions. Accordingly, they rank among the rules of law, observance of which must be ensured by the Court.[47] There- fore, in fostering the process of negative integration, the Court simply fulfils the duties with which it is entrusted by the Treaty. It ensures that Community citizens obtain the minimum benefits guaranteed by the Treaty. Moreover the prudence shown by the Court in this process has enabled it to avoid exceeding the limits traditionally assigned to the judiciary and indulging in policy- making.

---

[47] See Cappelletti *Is the European Court of Justice 'Running Wild'?* 12 ELRev 3, at 8–9.

Part 2

Irish Law

12 The Constitution of Ireland in a Changing Society

Thomas A. Finlay

The Constitution of Ireland was enacted by the people on 1 July 1937, and came into operation as from 29 December 1937. The first Constitution of Ireland as an independent State in modern times had been enacted a mere fifteen years earlier, pursuant to the Constitution of the Irish Free State (*Saorstat Éireann*) Act 1922, on 6 December 1922. In the intervening period between 1922 and 1937 there had tragically occurred in Ireland a civil war which was the cause of deeply felt and bitter division between the people, the wounds of which were but slowly healing in 1937.

The international scene in 1937 was, of course, one in which recovery from one of the greatest of modern depressions in worldwide economy was only just about being achieved, and it was one in which the threat of war, certainly in Europe and, as subsequent events were to prove, in the world at large, was great, real and increasing.

Two separate provisions for the amendment of the Constitution were contained in it as enacted. One of those was transitory and was contained in Article 51 of the Constitution. That was for the amendment of this Constitution, whether by way of variation, addition or repeal, by legislation alone unless the President after consultation with the Council of State should have signified in a message to the Chairman of each of the Houses of the *Oireachtas*, or Parliament, that the proposal was in his opinion one to affect an amendment of such a character and importance that the will of the people thereon ought to be ascertained by referendum. This right of amendment by Act of Parliament existed for a period only of three years after the date on which the first President should have entered upon his office. The first President of Ireland, Dr Douglas Hyde, entered upon his office on 25 June 1938, and, therefore, the power of amendment by simple statutory enactment expired on 25 June 1941.

The other and permanent provision for the amendment of the Constitution is contained in Article 46 thereof. The provision of that article is for the amendment of the Constitution, whether by way of variation, addition or repeal, in the following way. If a Bill proposing an amendment of the Constitution and containing no other proposal is passed by both Houses of the *Oireachtas*, that is to say, the *Dail* and the *Seanad*, the proposal contained in it is then submitted to the people by way of referendum. If such a referendum results in the acceptance of the proposed amendment by a simple majority, then the Bill is signed by the President upon his or her being satisfied of that fact, and duly promulgated as an amendment of the Constitution by the President.

In the period of almost fifty-four years since the coming into operation of the Irish Constitution in December 1937, there have been two statutes enacted pursuant to the transitory provisions of Article 51 containing amendments of the Constitution, and there have been eight proposals accepted upon sub-mission by referendum to the people, and enacted as amendments of the Constitution.

For the purpose of the subject matter of this essay it is necessary, I think, to consider in very summarized form the contents of these various amendments and the dates upon which they were enacted.

The amendments concerned are as follows. The First Amendment Act 1939, enacted on 2 September 1939, extended the definition of 'a time of war' (which was contained in the original Constitution for the purpose of enabling what might be broadly described as emergency legislation in such time) so as to include in it an armed conflict in which the State was not involved. The timing of this Act clearly indicates that it was a measure deemed necessary to deal with the position of Ireland taking up a stance of neutrality at the commence-ment of the Second World War.

The Second Amendment Act of 1941, enacted on 30 May 1941, within the three year period, was a major Act dealing very largely with a series of textual amendments and procedural amendments obviously required as the result of a period of three years' experience of the Constitution in operation. In relation to the question of fundamental rights or of the general structure of the Consti-tution, probably only two of the numerous amendments contained in the Act of 1941 would deserve a special mention. It was this Act which brought into operation a requirement that in the event of the Supreme Court reaching a decision on a question as to the validity of a post-constitutional statute, having regard to the provisions of the Constitution, that decision shall be pronounced by one judge, and no other opinion on such question, whether assenting or dissenting, shall be pronounced nor shall the existence of any such other opinion be disclosed. This provision undoubtedly creates an interesting and, at times, by no means facile, judicial problem but does not appear significantly to alter the structure of the constitutional rights created in the entire Consti-tution. The other provision which in the period subsequent to the termination of the Second World War created at least a political controversy, and some-times was the subject matter of legal controversy as well, was an addition contained in the 1941 Act to the provisions of Article 28(3) of the Constitution, providing that a national emergency declared by each House of the *Oireachtas* as affecting the vital interests of the State in time of war or armed rebellion, should include such time after the termination of any war, armed conflict or rebellion, as might elapse until each House of the *Oireachtas* shall have resolved that the national emergency had ceased to exist. The existence of a national emergency as declared under Article 28 enabled, of course, an immunity for legislation from constitutional challenge if it had been expressed to be for the purpose of securing the public safety and the preservation of the State during such time.

The resolution passed by both Houses of the *Oireachtas* on 4 September 1939 was not rescinded until 1976. It was then replaced by further resolution of September 1976 referable to the armed conflict then taking place in Northern Ireland pursuant to which an Emergency Powers Act 1976 was enacted expressed to be for the purpose of serving the public safety and preservation of the State. This Act was in force for twelve months only and no 'emergency legislation' has been in force since 1977 though the resolution of September 1976 has not been rescinded.

The amendments to the Constitution which have been made since 1941, each one of which required approval by referendum are as follows. The Third Amendment Act, enacted on 8 June 1972, permitted the adherence of the State to the EEC Treaties and gave to the enactments and directions of the European Community immunity from constitutional challenge and, in effect, a dominance over constitutional and domestic law. The Fourth Amendment Act, enacted on 5 January 1973 reduced the minimum age of persons entitled to vote at parliamentary and presidential elections from twenty-one to eighteen years of age.

The Fifth Amendment Act, also enacted on 5 January 1973, removed from the Constitution what had been subsections 1 and 2 of section 1 of Article 44 of the Constitution which had recognised the special position of the Catholic Church in Ireland and which also acknowledged the existence of a number of other specified religious denominations. The Sixth Amendment Act, enacted on 3 August 1979, made immune from constitutional challenge adoptions ordered by an adoption board which had been set up under statute. The challenge which had been apprehended and from which the immunity was in effect being granted was a challenge on the basis that the board, though not a judge, was inconsistently with the provisions of the Constitution exercising a judicial function.

The Seventh Amendment Act, also enacted on 3 August 1979, dealt with Article 18 and, in particular, with the provision for the election to the *Seanad* of members by universities. The Constitution, as originally enacted, provided for the election of three members of the *Seanad* by the National University of Ireland, and of three members by the University of Dublin. The amendment in an expanding university and higher education situation makes it constitutionally possible for legislation to provide for the election of *Seanad* members by any other institutions of higher education, in addition to the two universities specified in the original Constitution. The Eighth Amendment Act, enacted on 7 October 1983, constituted an acknowledgment by the State of the right to life of the unborn, and with due regard to the equal right to live of the mother, a guarantee by the State in its laws to respect and as far as practicable by its laws to defend and vindicate that right.

The Ninth Amendment Act, enacted on 2 August 1984, made it constitutionally permissible to legislate giving to persons other than citizens a right to vote at election for members of *Dail Éireann*. The purpose of that amendment was to permit of a right to vote at elections to *Dail Éireann* to be given to persons resident in Ireland who are citizens of other Member States of the European Community. The Tenth Amendment Act, enacted on 22 June 1987, gave constitutional permission for Ireland to ratify the Single European Act.

It will be seen from this list that in the half-century between 1941 and the present the eight amendments to the Constitution enacted by the people on referendum, fall into a limited number of categories. The Third, Ninth and Tenth Amendments are all associated with the membership by Ireland of the European Community. The Fourth Amendment constituted a political recognition of the increased responsibilities and powers of youth in Irish society. The Fifth Amendment was a conscious movement to emphasize the pluralist nature of Irish society. The Sixth and Seventh Amendments would appear to fall into the category of removing doubts as to a logical development, in one instance in regard to the whole concept of adoption which had come into force for the first time in the mid-1950s in Ireland and, in the other instance, to the expansion of higher education and university institutions. The Eighth Amendment represents a decision by the people to insert into the Constitution a specific guarantee and protection for a fundamental right perceived to be threatened by developments in the societies of countries outside Ireland.

These amendments to the Constitution, made since 1941, can, I think, when related to the massive changes in Irish society over that period, both of internal and external origin, be fairly described as minimal. To the extent that the Constitution now affords a broadly satisfactory fundamental law for Irish society, as I strongly believe it does, the reason for that cannot lie in the enacted amendments, but is, in my view, very largely to be found in two major principles affecting the interpretation of the Constitution which have been developed by the courts in Ireland.

These are, firstly, the principle originally laid down by Kenny J in the High Court in the case of *Ryan v The Attorney General*[1] and subsequently confirmed by the decision of the Supreme Court in that case that 'the personal rights which may be invoked to invalidate legislation are not confined to those specified in Article 40, but include all those rights which result from the christian and democratic nature of the State.' The right identified in that case was a right to bodily integrity relative to the plaintiff's claim that the provisions of the Health (Flouridation of Water Supplies) Act 1960 was invalid, having regard to the Constitution, on the ground (*inter alia*) that fluoride which was to be contained in the water was dangerous to health.

In the course of his judgment in that case Kenny J gave a limited number of examples of what could be considered as being such personal rights not mentioned in Article 40 or in other articles of the Constitution. These examples were: the right to free movement within the State and the right to marry.

In the course of its decision, the Supreme Court in that case stated as follows:

> 'The court agrees with Mr Justice Kenny that the "personal rights" mentioned in section 3(1) are not exhausted by the enumeration of "life, person, good name and property rights" in section 3(2), as is shown by the use of the words "in particular", nor by the more detailed treatment of specified rights in subsequent sections of the Article. To attempt to make a list of all the rights which may properly fall within the category of "personal rights" would be difficult and, fortunately, is unnecessary in this present case.'

The specific article of the Constutition with which these judgments deal was Article 40.3 which, in full, reads as follows:

> '3.1.   The State guarantees in its laws to respect, and, as far as practicable, by its laws to defend and vindicate the personal rights of the citizen.
> 3.2.   The State shall, in particular, by its laws protect as best it may from unjust attack and, in the case of injustice done, vindicate the life, person, good name, and property rights of every citizen.'

Since the decision in *Ryan v The Attorney General* a number of such unspecified or, as they are sometimes described, unenumerated personal rights, have been

[1] [1965] IR 294.

identified. In *The State (C) v Frawley*[2] I, sitting in the High Court, came to the following conclusion:

> 'If the unspecified personal rights guaranteed by Article 40 follow in part or in whole from the Christian and democratic nature of the State, it is surely beyond argument that they include freedom from torture and from inhuman or degrading treatment and punishment. Such a conclusion would appear to me to be inescapable, even if there had never been a European Convention of Human Rights or if Ireland had never been a party to it.'

The right to litigate was dealt with by Kenny J in *Macauley v The Minister for Posts and Telegraphs*[3] in the following terms:

> 'That there is a right to have recourse to the High Court to defend and vindicate a legal right, that is one of the personal rights of the citizen included in the general guarantee of Article 40.3, seems to me to be a necessary inference from Article 34.3.1. . .'

Whilst in some succeeding cases doubt was cast not on the existence of the right to litigate but on the question as to whether it should or could not properly be defined as a right of property expressly protected in the Constitution, it would appear not unlikely that it is properly identified as an unspecified right.

Further rights were identified in *Murtagh Properties v Cleary*.[4] The right to work and to earn a livelihood was identified as a protected, though not specified, personal right. This was confirmed and emphasised in the decision in *Murphy v Stewart*.[5] A qualified right to travel outside the state and for that purpose to obtain a passport was identified in *KM v The Minister for Foreign Affairs*.[6] In *The State (Healy) v Donoghue*,[7] the right to justice and fair procedures was identified as an unspecified right protected by Article 40.3 of the Constitution, and in particular, in certain circumstances, the absence of legal aid was recognised as a violation of that right. In *McGee v The Attorney General*,[8] the right of privacy within the marriage was identified as an unenumerated right.

The second general principle which is necessarily connected to the concept of identifying unspecified or unenumerated personal rights protected by the provisions of Article 40 of the Constitution has been the method of and the time and the standards of the time at which constitutional tests should be applied to legislation.

Two of the major judgments dealing with these topics are to be found in the judgment of Walsh J in *McGee v The Attorney General*,[9] and of O'Higgins CJ in *The State (Healy) v Donoghue*.[10] Both these statements of principle appear to me to be of sufficient importance to warrant a full quotation.

[2] [1976] IR 365.
[3] [1966] IR 345.
[4] [1972] IR 330.
[5] [1973] IR 97.
[6] Unreported, High Court, 29 May 1978.
[7] [1976] IR 325.
[8] [1974] IR 284.
[9] *Ibid.*
[10] *Supra.* note 7.

Walsh J, in *McGee v The Attorney General*,[11] states as follows:

'In this country it falls finally upon the judges to interpret the Constitution, and in doing so to determine, where necessary, the rights which are superior or antecedent to positive law, or which are imprescriptible or inalienable. In the performance of this difficult duty there are certain guidelines laid down in the Constitution for the judge. The very structure and content of the articles dealing with fundamental rights clearly indicate that justice is not subordinate to the law. In particular, the terms of section 3 of Article 40 expressly subordinate the law to justice. Both Aristotle and the Christian philosophers have regarded justice as the highest human virtue. The virtue of prudence was also esteemed by Aristotle, as by the philosophers of the Christian world. But the great additional virtue introduced by Christianity was that of charity – not the charity which consists of giving to the deserving for that is justice, but the charity which is also called mercy. According to the Preamble the people gave themselves the Constitution to promote the common good with due observance of prudence, justice and charity, so that the dignity and freedom of the individual might be assured. The judges must, therefore, as best they can from their training and their experience interpret these rights in accordance with their ideas of prudence, justice and charity. It is but natural that from time to time the prevailing ideas of these virtues may be conditioned by the passage of time; no interpretation of the Constitution is intended to be final for all time. It is given in the light of prevailing ideas and concepts.'

O'Higgins CJ, in *The State (Healy) v Donoghue*,[12] states as follows:

'The preamble to the Constitution records that the people "seeking to promote the common good, with due observance of prudence, justice and charity, so that the dignity and freedom of the individual may be assured, true social order attained, the unity of our country restored, and concord established with other nations, do hereby adopt, enact, and give to ourselves this Constitution." In my view, this preamble makes it clear that rights given by the Constitution must be considered in accordance with concepts of prudence, justice and charity which may gradually change or develop as society changes and develops and which fall to be interpreted from time to time in accordance with prevailing ideas. The Preamble envisages a Constitution which can absorb or be adapted to such changes. In other words, the Constitution did not seek to impose for all time the ideas prevalent or accepted with regard to these virtues at the time of its enactment. Mr Justice Walsh expressed this view very clearly in *McGee v The Attorney General* when he said at p. 319 of the report:'

The learned Chief Justice then quoted extensively from the passage in the judgment of Walsh J which I have just set out.

I have no doubt that under these two interrelated doctrines of interpretation of the Constitution that the courts can continue, as I feel confident that they have done already, to adapt and make appropriate the Irish Constitution to the changing needs of Irish society. It may be that some structural changes will necessarily have to be made in the Constitution by the method of amendment by referendum. Examples of such definitive changes in unambiguously expressed standards or limits are to be found in the amendments to which I have referred in such questions as the minimum age for voting; the right of non-citizens to vote; ratification and joining of international organizations,

[11] *Supra.* note 8 at 318.
[12] *Supra.* note 7 at 347.

such as the European Community; and a particular concern with regard to a relatively modern legal concept in Ireland of adoption.

In broad terms, however, it would appear to me that the experience of the last fifty years would strongly support the contention that interpretation necessarily and properly confined to interpretation and not used as a mask for amendment or variation, carried out in accordance with the principles which I have sought to describe in short terms in this essay, probably provides the most ready manner by which the fundamental laws of this State can be made reasonably fit to provide for the changes of Irish society as it develops into the future.

13 The Judicial Power, Justice and the Constitution of Ireland

Brian Walsh

Article 6, section 1 of the Constitution states (in the English language text)

> 'All powers of government, legislative, executive and judicial, derive under God, from the people, whose right it is to designate the rulers of the State and, in final appeal, to decide all questions of national policy, according to the requirements of the common good'.

Section 2 prescribes that

> 'These powers of government are exercisable only by or on the authority of the organs of State established by this Constitution'.

This division of powers does not give paramountcy in all circumstances to any one of the organs exercising the powers of government over the others'.

It was not until 1961 (twenty-four years after the enactment of the Constitution) that the courts, the judicial organs of the State as envisaged by Article 6, section 2, were established. Whether the delay was due simply to official inertia or, as some people thought, to the desire to hold over the heads of the existing courts and judiciary the continuing threat of disestablishment without any right of appointment to the new courts is impossible to say. The 'old courts' did not enjoy any of the powers conferred on the proposed 'new courts' save to the extent provided by Article 58, one of the transitory provisions of the Constitution which continued to have the 'force of law' notwithstanding that it had to be omitted from every official text of the Constitution published after the date on which the first President should have entered upon his office.[1]

It is interesting to note that Article 2 of the Constitution of the Irish Free State stated that

> 'All powers of government and all authority, legislative, executive and judicial in Ireland, are derived from the people of Ireland, and the same shall be exercised in the Irish Free State through the organisations established by or under, and in accord with, this Constitution.'

In view of the current debate concerning Articles 2 and 3 of the Constitution it is of particular interest to note the reference in Article 2 of the Constitution of

[1] *The Constitution of Ireland*: Art. 52 (no longer printed).

the Irish Free State to 'the people of Ireland'[2] rather than 'the people of the Irish Free State'. The significance of this phraseology is to be gleaned from the fact that while in British jurisprudence the Constitution of the Irish Free State was regarded as an Act of the British Parliament the Irish view was that it was to be regarded as the Act of a constituent assembly in Ireland. Neither is it to be overlooked that the 'Treaty' which was scheduled to that Constitution was entitled 'Articles of Agreement for a Treaty between Great Britain and Ireland'. It is also of interest to note that while the phrase 'the people of Ireland' also appeared in the 1916 Proclamation, it does not appear in Article 6 of the present Constitution. Nevertheless, it may be deduced from the provisions of the Preamble and of Articles 1 and 2 of the Constitution that 'the people' referred to in Article 6 as the grantors of the judicial power of government, as of the other powers of government, are the people of Ireland. Similarly, Article 30 of the Constitution, dealing with the powers of the Attorney General, the reference to offences being prosecuted 'in the name of the People' must necessarily refer to the same people.

Therefore, the judges under the present Constitution, as did the judges under the former Constitution, derive their judicial power, as a co-ordinate of government, from the people of Ireland. Article 34 of the Constitution provides that justice shall be administered in courts established by law by judges appointed in the manner provided by the Constitution and, save in such special and limited cases as may be prescribed by law, shall be administered in public.[3] There is nothing more precise laid down by the Constitution as to the boundaries of the area of the judicial power of government. But it is an essential characteristic of this power of government that it is one which cannot be delegated.

Article 34 of the Constitution provides that every judge appointed under the Constitution shall make a declaration that he will uphold the Constitution and the laws. Significantly this declaration mentions the Constitution before mentioning the laws. Naturally it follows that it is not laws generally which have that rank but only those which are not inconsistent with the Constitution or are not invalid having regard to the provisions of the Constitution. The supremacy of the Constitution is more specifically declared in Articles 15, 26 and 34. All judges shall be independent in the exercise of their judicial functions and are subject only to the Constitution and the law.

Nevertheless, as is apparent from the Constitution itself, and underlined in judgments of the Supreme Court, the emphasis is on the administration of justice and where the law and justice do not coincide the courts will administer justice. That does not mean that judges have a complete unfettered freedom. They are not at large to decide according to their personal predilections. The limitations upon their freedom may be found in the Constitution itself, in the laws, in precedent, in tradition and even in judicial technique itself. Many of these limitations may themselves change from time to time but so long as they exist they act as limitations for the time being. One might ask, is there not some contradiction between a limitation imposed by the Constitution and limita-

---

[2] '. . . the great principle . . . that all legislative, administrative and judicial power had its source and was derived from the sovereign people of Ireland'. Hugh Kennedy KC Attorney General, August 5 1922. Brian Farrell *The Drafting of the Irish Free State Constitution* (1975) 10 Ir Jur 112.
[3] See the decision of the Supreme Court *In re R Limited* [1989] IR 126 which superimposed 'denial of justice between the parties' as a necessary precondition to the discretionary judicial power to hear cases other than in public.

tions imposed by law. The answer, I believe, is in the negative. The Constitution itself places the emphasis upon justice, not merely in relation to the judges' functions but in relation to the administration of the State itself, as is evidenced in Article 40. Therefore if there is a conflict between the law and justice the law must yield place to justice. This is clearly illustrated by the decisions of the Supreme Court in relation to the Rent Restrictions Act cases.[4]

But the concept of justice itself may vary from time to time or may be different in one community from that in another. What justice is may depend upon the acceptance of certain ethical standards. Discussion of such issues has always been the concern of ethical, social and political philosophers, as well as of jurists. Justice is a moral value and one which the law ought to try to attain. It may be distinguished as social, political, economic, legal and probably other kinds of justice. Therefore, the standard for judging whether some act or course of conduct is just from the social, political and economic standpoints is its inconsistency or otherwise with the social, political or economic philosophy of the person judging. Thus the justice or otherwise of the expropriation of property or even the interference with property without adequate or any compensation could be judged differently by persons holding different philosophies. Thus a law enacted to give effect to such a purpose might in some jurisdictions have to be implemented and applied strictly according to its terms. But if by reason of constitutional provisions, such as those found in the Irish Constitution, which permit the courts to condemn such a law it is because the courts are permitted to and have the duty under the Constitution to judge and condemn by extra-legal standards of justice. Thus each of our judges must work from a philosophical conviction which does not differ from the philosophy underlying and informing the Constitution.

It is unnecessary to trace the development of the different concepts of justice beyond noting the fact that the Mosaic law evolved the idea of justice according to law more so than did any other philosophy. This was based on the belief or acceptance that law and justice were the same because both proceeded from God and the Hebrew tradition emphasized the importance of law for the doing of justice. However, so far as Ireland is concerned, the most important influence is that which originated in Greek philosophy where amidst the tangled notions of justice there appeared the concept of natural law. That in its turn offered the intellectual basis for the development of the same concept in Roman law. St Thomas Aquinas (the 'angelic doctor') saw eternal law, divine law and natural law as unalterable, all based on divine reason and as setting the standards for human law and justice. *Duns Scotus* (the 'subtle doctor') who exalted free will above reason, considered that justice was not to be willed as a means to an end but solely as an end in itself and that law proceeded from the divine will itself and not from the divine reason. It is not necessary to deal here with the utilitarianism of *Bentham* or the Marxist thesis that concepts of law and justice are but reflexes of the economic and class structure of society.

Theoretically law is not essential to the administration of justice. In disputes justice could be achieved by judges and courts deciding individual issues on their merits and in accordance with the perceived dictates of justice. But in practice the merits of deciding most issues in accordance with generally applicable known and published rules are probably greater even though the

---

[4] *Blake v Attorney General* [1982] IR 117. *Article 26 and the Housing (Private Rented Dwellings) Bill 1981* [1983] IR 181; see also *Brennan v Attorney General* [1984] ILRM 94.

general rules may not be suitable or fair in every individual case. However, the judicial power of interpretation and the application of judicial discretion and equity can do much to mitigate injustice.

Justice in the broad sense is not exclusively reserved to the courts as both the executive and the legislative organs of government are also expected to act in accordance with the dictates of justice. But in the last analysis, under the provisions of the Constitution particularly Article 40, section 3, the ultimate decision as to whether or not there has been an injustice rests with the judicial power and therefore that supremacy must be guaranteed, as it is, by a basic law. Article 43 also requires the application of a concept of justice. If some intervention in property rights is just for the purposes of Article 43 it cannot at the same time be unjust for the purposes of Article 40 section 3.[5]

In the field of property rights the most delicate questions of justice can arise. The starting point must be a philosophical concept of what are property rights. The natural right to the private ownership of property is very different from a right to retain all the property one has legally acquired. Article 43 imposes upon the owner of property the obligation to recognize that his ownership is not absolute and may be regulated by the principles of social justice. Nobody is given the right to accumulate property and retain it and to assert that right against the requirements of social justice. The nature of the property does not effect this principle. Strictly speaking one cannot claim as of right more property than one requires for one's own support. While the right of private property exists in the interest of the common good it is subordinate to the common good. Thus the judicial power is called upon to decide whether in particular individual cases a property right must yield to the claims of justice and whether, in such cases, just compensation must be available. But in some cases justice may not require any compensation as when property is taken to satisfy taxes the lawful tax demands the penalties incurred for wrong-doing or indeed in cases of unjust or unconscionable enrichment. This is an aspect of justice which the courts must determine when the matter is presented to them for decision and is one where the decision must be conditioned by the underlying philosophy of the Constitution. Article 43 (and its philosophy), attracted much confused and ill-informed comment varying from claims that it is a provision which could quite properly find its place in the Constitution of any communist State, to claims that it makes property rights absolute and untouchable. Neither of these is correct as should be plain to anyone taking the trouble to understand the philosophy which informs Article 43. The reference in Article 43 Section 1, to '*maoin tsaoghalta*' or 'external goods', in contrast to 'goods of the body' and 'goods of the soul', provides the clue to the philosophy in question. These were the ideas of St Thomas Aquinas.[6] This philosophy is in sharp contrast, for example, with the provisions of the French Civil Code (Articles 544 et 545) which accepts the definition of property as being the right to enjoy and dispose of 'things' in the most absolute manner provided that it is not prescribed by law. It also contrasts with the common law's orientation in

---

[5] *Dreher v Irish Land Commission* [1984] ILRM 94.

[6] It is submitted that Kenny J was not correct in thinking that, in the context, 'external goods' was not the same as 'maoin tsoaghalta' (worldly goods). *Central Dublin Development Association & Ors. v Attorney General* [1975] 109 ILTR 69 at 83; *Committee on the Price of Building Land* (1973) 'The Kenny Report' (P.R.L 3632) Stationery Office, Dublin, at p. 46.

favour of property rights also reflected in traditional harshness of punishments for offences against property.

Lord Coke's statement that the common law could 'control Acts of Parliament, and adjudge them to be utterly void' for being 'against common right and reason'[7] has been described by Professor Pollock as a 'typical example of the sweeping nature and the inaccuracy of Coke's statements'.[8]

In many countries there exist formal structures for administrative law and the administration of justice within that sphere. In Ireland such tribunals are few and decisions on many matters are made by officials or boards or by Ministers. The advantages claimed are speed, secrecy, expert knowledge, detailed knowledge of the relevant rules, freedom from rules of evidence or procedure and the need to avoid overwhelming the courts. But cases come to court occasionally which show that such forms of administrative adjudication may fail to observe the basic requirements of constitutional justice and may confuse policy with fairness or are motivated by administrative convenience at the expense of justice.

It has been pointed out in a number of cases that the rights guaranteed by the Constitution do not spring from the Constitution itself. Many are rights which are correctly described as being natural rights, rights superior to and antecedent to all positive law. These are guaranteed by the Constitution. Rights which are specifically granted by the Constitution do not come into the classification of natural rights. Such rights derive from positive law. It has also been decided, that rights, which are specified in the Constitution do not exhaust the list of those which are protected or guaranteed by the Constitution. The Constitution appears to reflect an acceptance of the philosophy of St Thomas Aquinas. He was in complete agreement with the Greek tradition, both in its Aristotelian and Platonic modes, that the law must be concerned with seeing things whole and that it is but part of the whole human situation and draws its validity from its position in the entire scheme of things. The law, like religion and education, must serve ends defined by other disciplines rather than serve only its own symmetry. Thus it cannot isolate itself in abstract technicalities and legal forms looking for answers to human problems in an aggregation of already existing rules or else finding no answers at all. The law must be concerned with extra-legal values.

The framers of the Constitution, and the people who enacted it, designed and adopted a system where there was a separation or division of the powers of government. The Constitution seeks to design a political system which would make it unnecessary to exercise the right of revolution. As the authority of the *Oireachtas* and of the executive depend upon the consent of the governed, a dissatisfied majority need never go beyond the ballot box to work its will. One of the functions of the judicial power is to preserve and maintain the constitutional allocation of power between the executive, the legislative and the judicial branches of government. Yet the separation of power exists not to avoid friction between the different departments of government but rather to ensure that by that very friction the country be governed as a democracy and not as an autocracy. This phraseology derives from Mr Justice Brandeis.[9]

Yet it is important to stress that, unlike the executive and the legislative

---

[7] *Dr Bonham's* case: 77 Eng Rep 646 & Coke 114a (CP 1610).
[8] F Pollock *A First Book of Jurisprudence* 250 (1896).
[9] *Myers v United States*, 272 US 52, 293 (1926) Brandeis J dissenting.

organs of government, the judicial power is required to furnish reasons for its decisions. There must be reasoned opinions, usually in writing, to support the decisions. These reasons are addressed not only to the parties, and the legal profession but also to all of the people of the State. The practice of supporting decisions with reasoned opinions presupposes a mature people who will in the end judge their judges rationally.

The judicial power is the authorative interpreter of the Constitution and is also the authoritative interpreter of the law. But it is not the exclusive interpreter because in the performance of their assigned constitutional and legal duties each branch of government, whether it be executive, legislative or judicial, must initially interpret the Constitution and the laws. But other governmental institutions do not feel a primary responsibility for the resolution of constitutional problems. This increases the primacy of the judicial power in this area. Because the judiciary is the prime institution for the protection of constitutional and legal rights it is essential to ensure that the judiciary provides an effective remedy against infringement of such rights. Some legal philosophers have debated whether there can be a right without a remedy. For the person deprived of his constitutional rights, however, there can be no debate. His rights are meaningless unless there are fair and effective remedies by which he can enforce them. In Ireland the courts have answered this question in the affirmative to the effect that wherever there is a constitutionally protected right there is a remedy. Procedural deficiencies will not leave a constitutional right without protection and enforcement where necessary. *Ubi jus ibi remedium*[10]

A primary function of the judicial power is to prevent the people of the country, as well as the executive and the legislature of the country, from doing what they would like to do when what they would like to do runs counter to the law or to the Constitution, or to both. Included in this duty is a duty to keep the courts from doing what they would like to do if what they would like to do runs counter to the Constitution and the law. The fact that judges are sometimes called upon to face and decide some of the important social, political and economic and even philosophical issues thrown up by their times does not mean that the judicial power is charged with making social, political, economic or philosophical decisions. To the extent that that function is an executive or legislative function it is the function of the people's elected representatives. The judges are charged with the task of deciding issues according to the Constitution and the law. In most cases the issues arise in the framework of concrete litigation and therefore the issues must be decided on facts and, so far as the Supreme Court is concerned, in a binding finding of facts made by some lower court or perhaps even some administrative agency.

The Constitution does not take the form of a list of specifics. On the contrary. It has been expressly decided that it also guarantees unspecified rights.[11] There are therefore very few cases where the constitutional answers are clear all one way or the other. Conflicts are inescapable whether they relate to freedom of speech and threats to public order or to public morality, fair procedures, society's rights to protection against depravity, and religious freedom against administrative convenience or political expediency. Perhaps

---

[10] *Meskell v C.I.E.* [1973] IR 121; *Educational Co of Ireland Ltd v Fitzpatrick* (402) [1961] IR 345; *Society for the Protection of Unborn Children (Ireland) Limited v Grogan & Ors* [1990] ILRM 350.

[11] *Ryan v Attorney General* [1965] IR 294.

most difficult of all is the case which is not one which arises in a framework of concrete issues, such as a reference by the President to the Supreme Court pursuant to Article 26 of the Constitution. Such a reference may raise questions of social policy, economic policy, ethics and virtually any other matter. Yet it has to be treated in relation to hypothetical situations rather than actual events. This procedure is not one which has aroused any enthusiasm in the Supreme Court.[12]

Important aspects of the most fundamental issues confronting Society can arrive for judicial determination. Their resolution one way or the other may influence and even determine future history. In the last thirty years the chief subject of cases coming to the Supreme Court has been the relationship of the individual to the organs of government in all of these fields. The judges are not, by virtue of their training, experts in the field of economics or public policy. But they are the special guardians of just and legal procedures and of the standards of ethics and fair play that should be the counterpoints of the extensive affirmative powers of the other organs of government. Thus, as the case law has determined, in criminal prosecutions juries are to be fairly and representatively selected, evidence is to be obtained without violating the Constitution and the persons detained or in respect of offences are to have the benefit of legal assistance, access to medical assistance and freedom of communication.

Enquiries and investigations, whether conducted by judicial officers or by committees, or by other bodies, are to be conducted with due regard for the constitutional right of the witness to know the pertinency of the questions and to be free from public inquisition which is not related to a legitimate purpose and to be free to defend himself.

Many decisions of the last fifty years have dealt with questions of whether a person's liberty or property may be curtailed or taken without fair legal procedures. Similar considerations protect persons' membership of a trade union, or dismissal from employment effected for reasons not to be disclosed when the accusers are not known. So also is to be found the right to be heard before being condemned to suffer grevious loss of any kind even though it may not involve the stigma and hardship of a criminal conviction. And to avoid internal contradictions, the question of a person's right to be told the reason for his dismissal is a necessary adjunct to the right not to suffer such a loss in an arbitrary manner, or to defend innocence, or in order to show that perhaps the true reason for the deprivation was one forbidden by the Constitution. It is also to be noted that the judicial power has exploded the once popular fallacy that a declaration of a state of emergency under Article 28 of the Constitution is sufficient in itself to set at naught the protections and rights guaranteed by the Constitution.[13]

One of the results of the division of the organs of government has been to cast social, economic, philosophical and political questions in the form of law suits. In this way important aspects of the most fundamental issues confronting democracy end up ultimately in court for judicial determination. They may be issues upon which society, consciously or unconsciously, is deeply divided. They may arouse the deepest emotions. The fact that some plaintiff in a suit seeks the protection of a political right does not mean that it presents a political

---

[12] *Re-Housing (Private Rental Dwellings) Bill supra* at p. 186.
[13] *State (Lynch) v Cooney* [1982] IR 337.

question to the courts. The case of *O'Donovan v The Attorney General*[14] was a successful challenge to the apportionment which had been made by the *Oireachtas* in relation to *Dáil* constituencies. That particular decision resulted in fresh apportionment, the Bill for which was sent directly to the Supreme Court as a reference under Article 26 and found not to be repugnant in any way to the Constitution.[15] It is of course self-evident that responsible and legitimate government demands fairness of representation. Therefore decisions on voting rights and the apportionment of constituencies are of central importance and, within the limits imposed by the Constitution, must accord with justice. Yet the decisions in such cases could have had a profound effect on political results in elections and could determine who would govern the country. The Constitution itself requires a distribution based on numerical criteria allowing for reasonable variations, though what particular variation might be regarded as reasonable is a matter which could only be decided empirically. The tolerance of variations remains yet to be fully tested but one may take as a guideline what was acceptable in the reference case and proceed either upwards or downwards, always bearing in mind that in the last analysis the differences may be mathematically reasonable rather than mathematically exact. To that extent the judicial power of government in any given case must arrive at its own decision based on its own ideas of what is reasonable and fair. Thus considerations such as weighting the rural vote more favourably than the urban vote and various other considerations which might appear to be reasonable to politicians are not permissible, even if all political parties might, in the political arena, agree that some such weighting was justified. The fact that constituency commissions make recommendations which are acceptable to the *Oireachtas* does not render them immune from being tested by the judical power. However very few cases coming before the courts have such a direct relationship to political matters. There are many areas where the subject matters of cases before the courts are the subject of political debate not so much in the sense of the debate reflecting or impinging upon party political considerations as upon matters in respect of which existing legislation is thought to be deficient or, where no legislation exists, there ought to be some. Indeed many of the matters may not be regarded as political ones in the strict sense, even though they are frequently referred to in political speeches. There are other matters which have a political content but whose political content as such is not easily discernible by the public in general. The decision in *Byrne v Ireland*[16] swept aside what might be called the executive immunity, or the State immunity, for the wrongful acts of its executive members and the servants and agents of the executive. Legislation had been urged for many years by various groups in favour of such a situation but had always been stoutly resisted by the executive on the grounds of the cost to the taxpayer. Thus justice was being subordinated to considerations of administative expediency or economy. Eventually the matter was tested and cured by the simple accident of Mrs Byrne falling into a hole left in the road by the Post Office. The political effect of this decision was such that it would have been an extremely unpopular move for the *Oireachtas* to attempt by legislation in any way to attempt to reduce this field of liability on any such grounds. Yet, before the decision, there had been

---

[14] *O'Donovan v Attorney General* [1961] IR 114.
[15] *Article 26 and the Electoral (Amendment) Bill* [1984] IR 268.
[16] *Byrne v Ireland* [1972] IR 241.

no apparent prospect of the law ever being amended by the *Oireachtas* to conform to what the ordinary citizen would have regarded as fair and reasonable. The decision in the *McGee* case[17] was also in an area with a very high political content at that time as the question in issue was one which had in effect produced a Parliamentary stalemate. Again by invoking the Constitution, the matter was disposed of by the judicial power.

In police matters the legislative organ of government took no positive steps to ensure that the detection and investigation of crime was conducted along methods which did not offend against the basic law of the State. Eventually the judicial power stepped in and dealt with the question of inadmissability of evidence obtained in violation of the Constitution both as to search and seizure and confessions. These decisions are based upon the simple conclusion that justice does not permit the ends to justify the means and, also, the important consideration that if the police are engaged in breaking the law who is to protect the citizen.[18]

In our modern complex society every person can properly be regarded as a consumer of justice because what had once looked trivial has now become important and what had previously dominated the stage had now shifted to the deep background. The new factor is the power and the responsibility of the citizen entitled to a free vote in a representative democracy. One becomes a consumer of justice, and of law, firstly by having one's daily life regulated by official rules or becoming involved in the legal mechanism, as for example being charged with a crime or engaging in a civil lawsuit. The second way in a democratic system is that it is possible for citizens to influence the shape and the form of the law and the quality of justice by voting and by advocating reforms and asserting group interests. The third way is that the people must shoulder the responsibility for those acts which their representatives do in their name and by the force of their authority. That includes the evil and foolish and unjust acts as well as the good ones. This frequently presents one of the most difficult matters for the judicial organ of government. After some particularly dastardly event there is often a great clamour for action both from the public and from the media. There is thus a temptation to act in a precipitate manner which may result in having an innocent person convicted. As far back as the 16th century this was perceived by the famous French essayist, *Michel de Montaigne*, who himself had been an experienced lawyer and judge. He said:

'How many innocent people we have known to be punished, I mean without the fault of the judges, and how many are there that we have not known of . . . How many condemnations I have witnessed more criminal than the crime'.[19]

The truth of this has recently been amply demonstrated in England by the cases of the *Guildford Four*, the *Birmingham Six* and the *Maguire family*.

What the judicial power must resist above all else is falling into the trap of accepting that 'it may be expedient that one man should die for the people'. The so-called democratic control of justice, if left completely untrammelled, could have such results. Security forces and police forces are subject to far

[17] *McGee v Attorney General* [1974] IR 284.
[18] *People v O'Brien* [1965] IR 142; *People v Madden* [1977] IR 336; *People v Quilligan* [1986] IR 495; *DPP v Healy* [1990] ILRM 313.
[19] Montaigne *Essays Bk*. III No 13 (Penguin Classics) (1958) p. 351.

more direct public pressure than are judges. They may be pressured into acting hastily or illegally. Many people take the view that injustices are inevitable and thus it may be expedient that somebody 'should die for the people', if the effect would be to deter wrongdoers and to reassure the people. The best answer to that attitude is the one contained in the words of my late and distinguished colleague in the Supreme Court, Mr Justice Kingsmill Moore, when he said that 'the plea that "it is expedient that one man should die for the multitude" must always be met uncompromisingly by a judge with the words "I find no fault in this just man", and he must not falter in his determination'.[20] The consumers of injustice must always be rescued when they have been identified.

It is therefore absolutely essential, bearing in mind the mandate of the Constitution, that judges and courts must never allow questions of procedure, rules, or judicial or administrative convenience to hamper proper investigation and review of cases, even where many years have passed after the time which the rules prescribe for appeal. Unfortunately there have been convictions of innocent persons. Where these have been detected, they have been set right by the courts on appeal, and in other cases by the executive power without resort to the courts, although the latter procedure cannot erase the conviction. Pardon does not equal acquittal.

The administration of justice is one area where the citizens in a democratic society cannot afford to trust the averages or to be beguiled by averages. In a representative democracy the citizens find themselves identified with the prosecution. This is one of the results of representative government. Therefore, every citizen is a participator, one could say an accomplice, in the deeds that are done in his name and by his authority. In matters of political or legislative discretion it may be reasonable to evaluate the whole record and set off failures against success and trust the averages. No such option is permissible to the judicial organ of government. No judge may in good conscience say that efficiency in detecting and punishing crime is a more important consideration than the protection of citizens from lawlessness whether it proceeds from criminals or from the agents of the State.

Not unexpectedly these are matters which are often the subject of some controversy in which politicians join. To that extent the courts' decisions on these matters have an impact on politics. However, as the courts have often stressed, the Constitution is a guarantee of fair procedures. It could not be seriously suggested that there should be a constitutional amendment to permit unfair procedures.

These are but a few illustrations of the situations in which the judicial power was called upon to decide some of the dominant social, political and philosophical issues thrown up by the age, yet in no case was it indicated that the judicial organ was either charged with, or indulged in, making social, political or philosophical decisions.

The judicial power cannot initiate actions on its own account and must wait the arrival of a case. In view of the dominant position of the legal profession in our legal system it is clear that it plays a crucial role. Even if lawyers do not always inaugurate all thought upon a particular matter, at least they can be sufficiently alert to detect the nuances of various judicial dicta and to seek to put them to the test. This process may sometimes take many years. For

---

[20] *Attorney General v Ryan's Car Hire Ltd* [1965] IR 642. Per Kingsmill Moore J at 654.

example, the issue of the income tax of working married couples[21] was one which was awaiting a sponsor for at least twenty years before it eventually arrived in court. Yet the executive and legislative authorities were well acquainted with the issue and yet took no action. By the time it did eventually come to court there had already been significant social changes in the country which cast in a very concrete form the question which a generation earlier might have been considered almost abstract.

The most important function of the judicial power is the power of judicial review of legislation. While one almost always associates this type of judicial activity with the United States, historically speaking it is important to point out that there is one very clear difference between the Irish and the American situation. The Constitution of the United States, unlike the Constitution of Ireland, did not expressly grant the powers of judicial review. In the great case of *Marbury v Madison*[22] Chief Justice Marshall pointed out that it was 'emphatically the problem and duty of the judicial department to say what the law is'. He emphasised the supremacy of the Constitution and that the validity of any law passed under the legislative power granted by the Constitution must, of necessity, not be contrary to that very Constitution. Yet, the legitimacy of judicial review in the United States has frequently been challenged because of the absence of any explicit reference to it in the Constitution of the United States. No such challenge to legitimacy can be raised in respect of the Constitution of Ireland which expressly recognises the power of the courts to pass upon the validity of Acts of the *Oireachtas*.

There is however one aspect of it which is worth noting. It is the constitutional requirement of the single opinion in cases referred under Article 26 and required by Article 34 for cases dealing with the validity of Acts of the *Oireachtas* passed since the enactment of the Constitution.[23] It is no secret that judges, and indeed many lawyers and students of law, do not like the single judgment rule because it prohibits the revelation of the existence of any other opinion, whether dissenting or assenting, which might in itself be of considerable importance and interest and which might indeed serve as a base for future legal development in some particular field as has been the experience in the United States. On the other hand, perhaps from the public point of view and the State point of view, for a judicial tribunal to speak with certainty in deciding an important case, such as the validity of an Act of the *Oireachtas*, it might be considered desirable, if not essential, that it should speak with a single voice. A diversity of opinion expressed among the judges might tend to destroy much of the force of their holding that an enactment was invalid or not invalid as the case might be. Yet no decision is possible unless at least a majority of the court are agreed upon it and no reasons can be given unless at least the majority of the court can agree upon those reasons.[24]

In the United States efforts to require more than a bare majority have failed. It has also been proposed that the members of the United States Supreme Court should give their opinions seriatim rather than is the custom, since the days of Chief Justice Marshall, of giving a judgment of the Court in addition to

---

[21] *Murphy v Attorney General* [1982] IR 241.
[22] *Maybury v Madison* (1803) 5 US (1 Cranch) 137.
[23] *State (Sheerin) v Kennedy* [1966] IR 379.
[24] *State (Hunt) v O'Donovan* [1975] IR 90.

which the other judges might or might not append assents or dissents.[25] If there is a criticism of the Irish system in the breasts of the members of the Supreme Court of Ireland it is that those who are not in the majority, if it be a majority decision, or those who although part of the majority would like to add something else, are being forced into sides against their will. In the High Court when such a case is heard by a bench of more than one judge, the single opinion rules do not apply. If there is any future consideration of this matter in any proposal to amend the Constitution the matter will have to be carefully balanced between considerations of the apparently united front approach and the approach which would give the members of the court perhaps somewhat more latitude and which might even benefit the future development of law at the possible expense of weakening the impact of the decision.

It is the business of the *Oireachtas* and of the executive organ of government as the elected representatives of the people to propound social policies. The judicial function is to apply the Constitution and the laws enacted by the *Oireachtas* in the particular controversies which reach the courts. But to determine whether a law applies to a particular factual situation involves a determination of what the law means. Where the *Oireachtas* intends a legal rule to govern certain facts there is little scope for interpretation and the judicial function would be neither difficult nor very important so far as the interpretation of law if that is all it was concerned with. But when the court has an added power, namely the power to determine whether the law enacted by the *Oireachtas* goes beyond the authority vested in the *Oireachtas* by the Constitution the situation is radically different because the courts also have the authority to declare what the Constitution means. A judicial power which can deny the validity of programmes undertaken by other organs of government might, within the effective ambit of that judicial power of denial, be thought of as being more effectively the law giver rather than those who wrote or enacted it.

This concept of judicial power might suggest that elected representatives of the people are subordinate to judges who are not elected by the people and who sit for life. At first sight such an imbalance would seem inconsistent with the democratic postulates underlying a representative democratic State which, according to the Preamble of the Constitution, derives its powers from the consent of the People. But this dilemma springs from the tension between the principle of majority rule and the purposes to be served by enacting into the fundamental law limits beyond which the majority, acting through the power of the legislature or executive, may not go.

Those whose devotion to representative government is uncompromising, or who are profoundly sceptical of the omniscience of judges, tend to feel that judicial review of the co-ordinate branches of government is hazardous and that the *Oireachtas* – like the British Parliament, whose laws are not subject to judicial invalidation – should be trusted to recognize constitutional limitations and not to overstep them.

But while in the long run faith in the wisdom and integrity of popular majorities and of the legislature and executive, and their agents, is a vital element in democratic institutions, yet in the short run, popular majorities can be, and have been, indifferent and even hostile to other crucial democratic values – especially the rights of minorities to dissent, or merely to survive with

---

[25] This is the procedure followed in the European Court of Human Rights.

dignity and respect. Guarantees of fundamental human rights are intended to give these rights a vitality which can permanently withstand the assaults tolerated or even initiated by occasional despotic majorities. Yet these declarations of rights are likely to prove inadequate in times of stress when they may be needed unless they also contemplate effective mechanisms for the enforcement of the rights declared. It is this which has given lasting and fundamental importance to the guarantees extended in and contemplated by the Constitution of Ireland. This carries with it the assurance that the judicial power is in a peculiar manner the guardian of these rights because the guarantees are self executing.

The decisions of the judicial power are not to be relieved of criticism. But it must be informed and responsible criticism, and in a representative democracy, where the people are ultimately responsible for all that happens in their name, the people are entitled as of right to require that all criticism be both informed and responsible.

The Constitution gives the judicial power a very special position. It is not a position of special privilege but a position of special responsibility as the ultimate interpreters of the law and of the Constitution itself. As the people gave themselves the Constitution it is obviously in the interests of the people that they should follow and understand the interpretation of it. If the interpretation of the Constitution is such that responsible citizens who form their own conclusions think the time has come to alter the Constitution then the machinery for doing so is available. But until that is done the courts and the judges must interpret it as it is.

Some persons seem to be content to interpret the Constitution for themselves and then wish to rush to the polls to amend that interpretation. It is undoubtedly true that for the last thirty years there has been an ever-growing awareness of the Constitution and its provisions. The ordinary person in the street is indeed very conscious of the fact that his rights are protected in the Constitution and he looks to the judicial power to see that these rights are given effect. Interpretation of the Constitution is not a matter on which private judgment is permissible. Rather must people look to those to whom the Constitution has committed the function of interpreting the Constitution and follow carefully and understand these interpretations.

The following extract appeared in *The Economist* of May 10 1952 on the occasion of the constitutional case which followed President Truman's seizure of the steel mills.

'At the first sound of a new argument over the United States Constitution and its interpretation, the hearts of Americans leap with fearful joy. The blood stirs powerfully in their veins and a new lustre brightens their eyes. Like King Harry's men before Harfleur, they stand like greyhounds in the slips, straining upon the start. Last week, the old bugle note rang out, clear and thrilling, calling Americans to a fresh debate on the Constitution . . .'.

In the Irish context, can the same be said? Or, perhaps more pertinently, ought we be able to say it?

14 The Irish Judge as Law-Maker

Declan Costello

The question whether judges make law in the course of their adjudication on controversial issues of law, has itself been a controversial issue of law. Reflecting on the nature of the judicial process seventy years ago from an American perspective (which included over a century's experience of adjudication involving the construction of a written Constitution) Judge Cardoza said: 'I take judge-made laws as one of the existing realities of life'.[1]

At that time English judges were much slower to question the received wisdom that judges merely declare the law and do not make it and most would then have agreed, with Bacon, that: 'Their office is *jus dicere* and not *jus dare*'. But judicial attitudes have been changing and there is now a considerable body of evidence to suggest that most English judges would, with perhaps varying degrees of enthusiasm and subject to differing qualifications, now agree with Judge Cardoza. Trenchantly, Lord Radcliffe has written:

> 'Of course, judges make law. How can they help it? The legislature and the judicial process respectively are two complementary sources of law and in a well ordered state each has to undertake its functions and limitations'.[2]

Less enthusiastically, Lord Reid wrote:

> 'We must accept the fact that for better or for worse, judges do make law, and tackle the question how they approach this task and how they should approach it'.[3]

Lord Denning had no doubts:

> 'The judges do every day make law, although it is almost heresy to say so. If the truth is recognised, then we may escape from the dead hand of the past and conscientiously mould new principles to meet the needs of the present day'.[4]

Lord Devlin has been more circumspect; for him judges adjudicating on common law issues make law, but when construing a statute they are merely applying the law established by parliament.[5]

[1] *The Nature of the Judicial Process* (Yale University Press 1921).
[2] Quoted in Stevens 'Judicial Legislation and the Law Lords: Four Interpretations' *Irish Jurist* vol X (NS) p. 3.
[3] *Ibid.* p. 217.
[4] *Ibid.* p. 239.
[5] Patrick Devlin *The Judge* (Oxford University Press 1981) p. 14.

Like judges elsewhere, Irish judges spend most of their time resolving disputed questions of fact and applying settled law to their conclusions. But exceptionally, in the High Court, in the Court of Criminal Appeal and above all in the Supreme Court, judges in adjudicating on disputed issues of law, make law. This happens both in respect of common law issues (recently the Irish courts have ruled that in certain circumstances a common law duty of care may be imposed on local authorities when carrying out certain statutory functions) and in statutory construction (for example in the field of extradition law and the procedures to be followed on the issuing of search warrants) but most spectacularly they have done so when adjudicating on constitutional issues.

The breadth and scope of the issues upon which the Irish courts are required to adjudicate in constitutional cases is quite remarkable. Writing with considerable insight in the early part of the last century on the American constitution, de Tocqueville pointed out that 'scarcely any political question that arises in the United States is not resolved sooner or later into a judicial question'. A similar comment could now be made on the Irish Constitution. Many of the important political questions of modern times have been transformed into justiciable constitutional issues on which the courts have had to reach legal conclusions. Two Anglo–Irish Agreements relating to Northern Ireland, Ireland's ratification of the Single European Act, the visit of President Reagan to this country, the legal propriety of holding the 1989 general election, afford examples of the production of constitutional from political issues. Controversial issues of sexual morality have also been transformed into legal issues by plaintiffs, impatient with parliamentary failure to repeal laws of which they disapprove, seeking their condemnation by means of declaratory judgments of their constitutional invalidity. And fundamental jurisprudential issues such as the relationship of law and morality, and the power of parliament to enforce a community's moral ethos have been presented for determination by the courts. There are over 650 cases cited in the second edition of Professor Kelly's authoritative text book on the *Irish Constitution*[6] and a supplement published three years later cited 200 more. Inevitably, in the course of adjudicating on a wide range of issues, the courts have established a wide range of new law. As a result, and by way of example, the courts, and not parliament, have determined the criteria on which an accused will be admitted to bail, on which evidence illegally obtained will be admitted in a criminal trial, the circumstances in which the rules of natural justice are to be applied in the sphere of administrative law. In addition, they have created new causes of action for damages for breach of constitutional rights, and have greatly expanded the circumstances in which landlords may recover possession of their property and increase rents, notwithstanding parliamentary views to the contrary. Most importantly, they have decided that the Constitution protects all fundamental personal rights and not just those specified in the constitutional text and that the courts will, if necessary, specify what those unspecified rights are and determine their content and scope. By accepting jurisdiction in such a wide range of constitutional issues the Irish courts now exercise a law-making power which, it can plausibly be argued, is as comprehensive as that exercised by any judiciary in the world.

Judge Cardoza had asked the question: 'What is it that I do when I decide a

---

[6] *The Irish Constitution* (Dublin 1984).

case', and eloquently answered it in four lectures delivered at Yale University. The scope of this essay is much more modest – it seeks to examine some of the legal problems which arise in the course of the judicial process in those constitutional cases in which judges may make law.

There are of course well known theoretical objections to judge-made law – that it is undemocratic, being made by appointed officials instead of elected representatives, and that it acts retroactively. In the Irish context, further objection can be raised; is it constitutional for judges to make law? The Constitution provides that 'The sole and exclusive power of making laws for the State is . . . vested in the *Oireachtas*; no other legislative authority has power to make laws for the State'. How then, constitutionally, can the Irish courts 'make law'? The Constitution makes a clear distinction between the legislative and judicial powers of government; the *Oireachtas* enacts laws, and the courts administer justice. But if the judicial process in the administration of justice is examined it will be seen that it is inherent in it (and particularly in disputes which involve the broad concepts which are to be found in the Constitution) that the courts may be required from time to time to establish rules of conduct which have the force of law in that they are enforced as law and, in the case of judgments of the Supreme Court, are followed by other courts. If this power to establish enforceable rules of conduct is inherent in the judicial power of government, then it obtains constitutional recognition by virtue of the specific recognition of the judicial power. References to the rules established by the courts as 'judicial legislation' and to judges who establish them as 'legislators' is a convenient metaphorical extension of the terms 'legislation' and 'legislator'. Understood as such, no wrongful arrogation by the judiciary of the exclusive legislative powers of the *Oireachtas* takes place.

How do they go about this task in constitutional cases? At first sight, it may seem trite to say that in most cases in which constitutional issues fall for determination judges are primarily concerned with the construction of the constitutional text. But this statement contains a number of important consequences which need to be appreciated. Firstly, judges are required to uphold the Constitution (they take an oath to do so) so that in the many contentious moral and political issues which arise, there can be no question that their own views can be applied. A judge may be a legal positivist and have no use for natural law concepts, but if the Constitution (as it does) explicitly recognises the existence of rights anterior to positive law these jurisprudential views must yield to the clear conclusions which are to be drawn from the construction of the constitutional text. Again, judges will have settled views of their own on the moral issues which may arise in the context of constitutional disputes. The courts' task, depending on the submissions made, may well be to decide (*a*) whether the constitution permits the enactment of laws to preserve the moral ethos of society, (*b*) whether the plaintiff has a personal right which has been infringed; (*c*) whether the admitted restriction on the exercise of a protected right is constitutionally permissible. The judge may be required to make value judgments and to prefer one moral value to another. In all these controversies, they must be guided by the constitutional text. It would of course be idle to pretend that judges are not subject, like others, to subconscious influences and prejudices. But they are required to give reasons for their conclusions – a discipline which not only assists in self-critical examination, but which also, by exposing them to the critical examination of others, helps towards judicial objectivity.

Secondly, the requirement to construe the relevant provisions of the Constitution may considerably reduce the persuasive force of the case-law from other jurisdictions such as that of the US Supreme Court and the Court of Human Rights. The US Constitution and the European Convention on Human Rights and Fundamental Freedoms contain many of the concepts which are to be found in the Irish Constitution and the views of distinguished courts from other jurisdictions on common concepts are obviously of considerable value. But these concepts have been differently formulated in basic documents recognising and entrenching fundamental rights and when the Irish courts come to specify the nature and scope of these concepts in the factual situation with which the court is faced these textual differences may be of critical significance. For example, the US Supreme Court has construed the Fourteenth Amendment of the US Constitution as containing a protected right to privacy and has held that this right was infringed by laws which prohibited the sale of contraceptives to married couples. The Irish Supreme Court followed this decision and held that one of the unspecified personal rights protected by the Irish Constitution was a right to privacy and that it was infringed by a law which prohibited the sale of contraceptives to married couples. But later the US Supreme Court developed the right of privacy and held that the Fourteenth Amendment embraced a qualified right for a woman to determine whether to bear a child. There are cogent arguments (which are now academic because of the passing of a constitutional amendment which prohibits the enactment of an abortion law) to suggest that the text of the Irish Constitution would never permit such a construction. The Constitution's Preamble in the light of which the later fundamental rights fall to be construed contains a specific recognition (not to be found in the US Constitution) that the Irish people are not only a religious people but a specifically Christian people. The human person which is acknowledged by the Constitution as being endowed with rights anterior to positive law must properly be regarded as a being endowed by God with an immortal soul and created for a supernatural end. As so construed, it would follow that the sanctity of human life is inherent in the concept of the human person which is to be found in the Irish Constitution and indeed basic to all the fundamental rights therein protected. It would logically follow that a constitutionally protected right to privacy could not be construed so as to permit a law which allowed abortion at any period of pregnancy as the rights contained in the Constitution should properly be extended to the unborn.

Unlike the Irish Constitution, the European Convention expressly protects the right to privacy and expressly provides for the circumstances in which the exercise of the right may be legislatively limited (Article 8) – legislation may impose restrictions which are 'necessary in a democratic society' . . . 'for the protection of morals'. This provision (not to be found in the Irish Constitution) has been construed by the Court of Human Rights as meaning that a State must establish a 'pressing social need' in order to justify legislative restrictions for the protection of morals. Although both the Irish Supreme Court and the Court of Human Rights have concluded that legislation to protect society's moral ethos is constitutionally permissible the textual difference between the Irish Constitution and the Convention was one reason which resulted in different conclusions between the two Courts on an Irish law relating to homosexual behaviour.

In controversies on the construction of statutes, it is sometimes urged that the court should resolve ambiguities by ascertaining the 'intention of parliament'. This is a concept which needs to be treated with considerable reserve. It is largely based on the fiction that there is such a thing as a corporate entity, 'the parliament' which had an ascertainable 'intention' when it enacted a statute. This is a fiction because (*a*) legislation may frequently be enacted by majority votes comprising legislators holding widely different intentions when voting for the measure and (*b*) many who comprise the majority vote to enact a law without any considered views on it. The 'intention of parliament' is also an ambiguous concept. Does it mean that the court should endeavour (*a*) to ascertain the meaning which parliament intended to convey by the words employed in the statute or (*b*) the purpose which parliament intended to achieve by the use of the words employed in the statute. When considering this concept, in the context of a dispute as to the meaning of words used in the Irish Constitution, further difficulties present themselves. The Irish Constitution was not enacted by a constitutional convention (as the American Constitution was) or by a parliamentary assembly – it was enacted by a majority of voters in a plebiscite held in 1937. Obviously, therefore, the court cannot attempt to resolve a controversial issue of construction by attempting to ascertain what the 685,105 voters who voted in its favour intended the words in the text to mean.

There is another aspect of the historical approach to constitutional construction which requires to be considered. Constitutions deal in broad generalities leaving to the courts the task of specifying their scope and extent on a case-by-case basis. A question of construction presents itself; should judges consider these concepts as historically they were generally understood when the Constitution was enacted in 1937 or by generally-accepted current attitudes? The point can be illustrated by the right to privacy. It is an historical fact that the right to privacy would not in 1937 have been regarded by the general public as a fundamental right to be constitutionally protected. By present day attitudes, it would be so regarded. If, therefore, a plaintiff claims that a right to privacy is a right which though unspecified in the Constitution is nonetheless protected by it, should this claim fail because the concept of personal rights should be considered by reference to 1937 rather than to contemporary attitudes? This question has been decisively answered by the Irish Supreme Court. In a case relating to privacy in marital relations, the High Court had accepted a submission that the right claimed was not constitutionally protected because public attitudes at the time of the enactment of the impugned law (the mid-1930s) did not recognise such a right. This judgment was overruled in the Supreme Court which, *sub silentio*, rejected this submission.[7] Later the Supreme Court explicitly established that the Constitution's basic concepts are to be construed in the light of contemporary ideas, holding that the Constitution did not impose those ideas which were prevalent at the time of its enactment. Thus, the Supreme Court has decisively rejected the views of some commentators on the American Constitution to the effect that constitutions should be construed according to the original intent of their framers and has accepted the approach adopted to the construction of the EC Treaty favoured by the European Court of Justice which prefers a dynamic and evolutionary interpretation to that of a static interpretation of the text of the Treaty.

[7] *McGee v Attorney General* [1974] IR 284.

Constitutional adjudication may pose other problems of constitutional construction. Should the text be construed literally or is a purposive approach to be preferred? The answer to this question may be of crucial importance. The right to personal liberty is protected in the Constitution by the laconic sentence 'No citizen shall be deprived of his personal liberty save in accordance with law'. If construed literally this could mean that the *Oireachtas* may constitutionally enact whatever laws it deems appropriate depriving a citizen of his liberty. For many years, this is how the Supreme Court in fact construed the constitutional text so that in effect the right to liberty was not an entrenched right and its exercise could be limited in any way the *Oireachtas* thought fit. But if the Article is construed by reference to the Preamble, if it is borne in mind that the Constitution acknowledges that other rights are natural rights which antecede positive law, then it is reasonable to conclude that the purpose of the Constitution was to entrench all the basic rights it was enacted to protect and that the exercise of the right to liberty could only be limited by laws which did not infringe the basic norms of the democratic society envisaged by the Constitution. This is how the Supreme Court subsequently construed the article. The anomalous results which would flow from a literal construction of the text can be illustrated by other examples. Some of the protective clauses protect the rights of 'citizens' ('all citizens' are held to be equal before the law, and the State is required to vindicate the personal rights of the 'citizen'). But the rights guaranteed in other articles are guaranteed to 'persons' (no 'person' can be charged with a criminal offence save in due course of law). A literal construction of the text could result in protecting those rights of non-citizens which are to be found in articles referring to 'persons' and withhold protection of those rights specified in articles which refer to 'citizens'. If, however, all the fundamental rights' articles are construed in the light of the Preamble, if the Constitution is regarded as a basic law, whose purpose is to create a society in which justice is to be observed for all, and the dignity and freedom of every individual is to be assured, then the Constitution could reasonably be construed as protecting the rights of all members of society, citizens and noncitizens alike.

Only some of the protected rights are referred to as 'natural rights' and a literal construction of the text would lead to the conclusion that only the right to private property and the rights of the family are 'natural rights' and that the other fundamental personal rights referred to in the Constitution cannot be so regarded. Again, problems can arise when limitations on the exercise of rights fall to be considered. Some articles provide that the rights which are acknowledged may be restricted 'in accordance with law' without providing any indication of the laws which may be validly enacted, whilst the exercise of other rights are said to be 'subject to public order and morality' or to limitations reconciling their exercise with the exigencies of the common good. If a statute is impugned on the grounds that it unconstitutionally interferes with a guaranteed right, quite extraordinary results might flow from a literal construction and some basic rights might well obtain a much higher degree of protection than others.

In suggesting that judges, having to choose a rule of construction in constitutional cases, should frequently prefer a purposive to a literal approach the reason for doing this should be clearly understood. It should be remembered that the Court is not construing a badly drafted statute – it is construing the Constitution which is both a political as well as a legal document. That means that it is designed to be inspirational as well as normative and that its language approaches rhetoric which would be out of place in a modern statute. This means that a minute textual analysis of the constitutional text is not the correct approach and that it would be wrong to infer a legal significance in every drafting difference which may be found.

Experience has shown that if a disputed text is objectively considered in the context of the whole Constitution with a view to ascertaining its purpose, then a great many apparent anomalies will disappear. Furthermore, in construing the broad generalities which are to be found in the constitutional text, a consideration and examination of the purpose for which rights have been entrenched as well as the purpose for which their exercise may be constitutionally limited, will help towards a rational resolution of many constitutional disputes.

In many cases, of course, no problem of constitutional construction arises. The issues for adjudication in constitutional cases take many different forms each providing its own particular problem for resolution. The dispute may require the balancing by the judge of the claims of conflicting rights. To take an example: it may be argued as a recent report from the Law Reform Commission has argued,[8] that there is no place for the offence of blasphemous libel in a society which respects freedom of speech and that injury to the feeling of others is a tenuous and anomalous basis for restricting freedom of speech. On the other hand, it can be argued that the hurt occasioned by blasphemy can be very considerable and that, as religious beliefs are for many sacred and precious, to affront them by blasphemy should not be tolerated. From this point of view, a law which restricted freedom of speech by prohibiting blasphemy could be justified by the need to protect believers against offence. The resolution of the dispute as to the validity of a law which prohibited with penal sanctions blasphemous utterances, would require the judge to determine whether the right to be protected against offence should be preferred to the right of freedom of expression.

The justiciable dispute may involve a claim that the exercise of a protected right should be limited in the interests of the common good – a common form of controversy which judges are called on to resolve. The exercise of personal rights may be limited, and limited with constitutional propriety, in many different ways. For example, the exercise of property rights are restricted by planning laws which may impose severe financial loss to landowners, their justification being the public interest in the protection of the environment. The court would then be required to consider and balance two different requirements of the common good, (i) the need to protect guaranteed basic rights (in the example given, the right to property) and (ii) the need to protect the environment in the public interest if such a law is challenged. Again, the exercise of the right to privacy may be restricted by laws enacted to preserve society's moral ethos and the court may be required to balance the claims of the common good which is furthered by the preservation of its moral ethos against the claims of those whose enjoyment of the right to privacy has been curtailed. Or the dispute may be about conflicting claims of justice. An absolute rule that evidence which has been obtained by illegal and/or unconstitutional means should never be admissible in a criminal trial may result in injustice in that an offender may be acquitted. On the other hand, a law which

---

[8] Consultation paper on *The Crime of Libel* para 231.

always permitted such evidence to be adduced could result in many cases in injustice to accused persons. The correct formulation of the rule requires the court to balance conflicting claims of justice – a task which has resulted in a good deal of conflicting judicial opinion.

Many constitutional controversies are ones of mixed law and fact. The judicial process may require (*a*) a factual assessment of the detriment to the plaintiff of the impugned legislation; (*b*) a factual assessment of the need, in the interest of the common good, for the impugned legislation; (*c*) a decision as to whether the object of the impugned legislation is one which the *Oireachtas* can constitutionally seek to further; (*d*) a decision as to whether the detriment to the plaintiff is out of proportion to the object which the legislation is designed to achieve; (*e*) a decision as to whether the legislation so limits the exercise of a protected right as to amount to a deprivation of its substance. In many instances, the issues which arise can be resolved without the aid of evidence and the courts will draw inferences of fact from the legislation itself. If, for example, a law was enacted which permitted the detention of suspects for questioning for, say, ten days, the court could reach a decision on its constitutional validity without any evidence either to establish that the law seriously infringed the citizen's right to liberty (which would be assumed) or that Parliament considered it necessary to enact it in the interests of the effective administration of justice.

There may however be cases in which one or other of the parties call evidence. The plaintiff may adduce evidence to establish that a law in fact restricts the exercise of a constitutionally protected right or to prove the extent of the detriment he suffers from the restriction of which he complains. There may be cases in which the State considers it necessary to establish by evidence the factual situation which it claims justified the impugned measure. When cases relate to laws dealing with complex social and economic issues which require, perhaps, decisions on the redistribution of wealth, or the determination of social priorities, the ability of the legislative organ of government to ascertain the factual situation and assess social needs and priorities is obviously superior to the judicial organ of government. For the judge to accept this fact is to accept a constitutional reality. But its acceptance does not mean that the courts abdicate their judicial function. The legislature may conclude that the exigencies of the common good require the enactment of certain measures. Whilst accepting the legislature's conclusions, the court may still be required to consider whether the extent of the restriction imposed on the enjoyment of constitutionally protected rights can be justified or whether the measure amounts to a negation of the right.

If it is accepted that the courts cannot abdicate their constitutional responsibilities by leaving consideration of the requirement of the common good to be decided exclusively by the legislature the nature of the considerations which the courts give to the question needs to be understood. The *Oireachtas* has the exclusive power of making laws for the common good; the courts are required by the Constitution to administer justice. The two functions are fundamentally distinct. It would clearly be a usurpation of the legislator's function for the courts to decide what laws are needed for the common good – they have neither the constitutional power nor the practical ability to do so. The Swiss Civil Code (Article 1) enjoins a Swiss judge to decide cases where no existing laws or customary rules apply 'according to the rule which he would lay down if he had himself to act as legislator'. The Irish judge approaches his judicial function in constitutional cases in a different way. When an issue arises as to whether the exercise of a protected right has been unconstitutionally restricted by legislation the judge does not consider what laws he would pass if he had been called upon to legislate on the subject-matter of the impugned legislation. His consideration of the problem is entirely different. He must decide firstly whether the object of the legislation is one which could reasonably be said to further the common good and secondly, the nature and extent of the detriment which it causes the plaintiff. He may then be required to consider whether the detriment to the plaintiff is out of proportion to the object which the legislation is designed to achieve, or to decide whether the legislation is so restrictive as to amount to a denial of a protected right. A decision adverse to the legislation amounts to a conclusion that the legislature has failed to reconcile properly two different objectives. It is not, however, an assessment of how the judge himself would have legislated had he been called upon to do so.

The exigencies of the common good may be relevant in the adjudication of constitutional issues in another way. When deciding such issues the court may be required to establish rules of conduct which have the force of laws of general application but a decision which establishes a rule of conduct which is detrimental to the common good cannot be a just one and so a party to a dispute is not entitled to benefit from such a rule. In considering however, the effect that a possible conclusion may have on the common good, the judge will not be required to consider what laws would further the common good as a legislator does. He will be required to test the rule which his conclusions may establish to see whether or not it is one detrimental to or beneficial to the common good. The consideration which he gives is distinct from and different to that which the legislator brings to bear in exercising his legislative functions.

The judicial process which produces judge-made law may require the judge to make a number of different decisions both of fact and law in the course of judicial adjudication. Disagreements between the courts and the legislature are inherent in the constitutional structures established for the protection of fundamental rights. An appreciation that both the courts and the legislature may make laws in the exercise of their constitutional functions but that they do so in entirely different ways and for different purposes will not eliminate such disagreements. But it should help to identify the differences that may arise and by so doing perhaps also help to minimise them.

15 Some Problems of Constitutional Interpretation

Donal Barrington

Traditionally lawyers used the term 'repugnant' to the Constitution to describe any measure which, in their opinion, violated the Constitution. But ever since the classic judgment of Walsh J in the *State (Sheerin) v Kennedy*,[1] it has been clear that the Constitution employs the adjectives 'repugnant' 'invalid' and 'inconsistent' as technical terms and that, in the Constitution, they have different meanings. The term 'repugnant', is used in relation to Bills which the President may, under Article 26 of the Constitution, refer to the Supreme Court. The purpose of the reference is to ascertain whether the Bill or any part of it is 'repugnant' to the Constitution. If the Supreme Court finds that the Bill or any part of it is repugnant to the Constitution the President must refuse to sign it. The Bill therefore remains a proposal which, because of its repugnancy to the Constitution, can never become law.

The term 'invalid' is used to describe something different. It refers to a measure which has formally been enacted but which never becomes law because it is an unconstitutional exercise of power under the form of legislation. Thus Article 15, section 4, of the Constitution forbids the *Oireachtas* to enact any law which is in any respect repugnant to the Constitution. It then goes on to provide –

'Every law enacted by the *Oireachtas* which is in any respect repugnant to this Constitution or to any provision thereof, shall, but to the extent only of such repugnancy, be invalid.'

If therefore the Bill which the *Oireachtas* purportedly enacted into law was in whole or in part repugnant to the Constitution the *Oireachtas* violated its constitutional duty in purporting to enact it and the Act, or the offending provision, never in fact became law but was invalid from the date of its purported enactment. This, I think, is important when one comes to the question of interpretation.

The Constitution uses the term 'inconsistent' in a totally different context. Article 50 of the Constitution refers to laws which were 'in force' in *Saorstát Éireann* immediately prior to the date of the coming into operation of the Constitution. The fact that these laws are referred to as being 'in force' on the date immediately prior to the date of the coming into operation of the Consti-

[1] [1966] IR 379.

tution implies that they were valid laws on that date. Such laws are carried forward by the Constitution, subject to the provisions of the Constitution itself and the extent to which they are not 'inconsistent' therewith. The laws referred to would include the Common law, statutes of the old Irish Parliament, statutes of the Parliament of the United Kingdom and statutes of the *Oireachtas* of *Saorstát Éireann*. Of these, the most important from the practical point of view are statutes of the Parliament of the United Kingdom and statutes of *Saorstát Éireann* in force immediately before the coming into operation of our present Constitution.

Reference of Bills to the Supreme Court – repugnancy

As previously stated the President may, in certain circumstances, refer a Bill to the Supreme Court for an opinion as to whether the Bill, or any part of it, is repugnant to the Constitution. The procedure is, in certain respects, useful. For one thing it can enable the President (and through him the Government) to clear in advance the constitutionality of the Bill. In this way it may satisfy constitutional critics of the Bill or may avoid the danger of an unconstitutional measure being enacted into Law and, perhaps after many years, falling to a constitutional challenge brought by a private citizen.

On the other hand it has the defect of this virtue. Once a provision of a Bill has been referred by the President to the Supreme Court, and found by the Supreme Court not to be repugnant to the Constitution, the corresponding provision of the Act becomes, as it were, clothed in constitutional immunity. No court whatsoever may question the validity of the relevant provision.[2]

This is all the more disturbing because the procedure for testing the constitutionality of the Bill leaves much to be desired. In the case of a reference under Article 26 of the Constitution the Supreme Court acts as both a court of first instance and a court of final appeal. It has not the benefit of an earlier debate in the High Court nor the opportunity to consider the judgment of a High Court judge on the issue in question. There is no counsel for an allegedly injured party present and no concrete facts in the light of which the matters at issue can be discussed. As a result the proceedings have a certain air of unreality.

The Attorney General (or his counsel) appears before the court to defend the constitutionality of the Bill. But there is no plaintiff. The court accordingly assigns solicitor and counsel to argue the case against the Bill. But counsel challenging the Bill has no client whose predicament he can draw to the attention of the court. One senior counsel who had been assigned to argue the case against a particular Bill complained that his brief consisted merely of a copy of the relevant Bill and a copy of the Constitution! For the rest counsel has to rely upon his own imagination. He has to invent hypothetical cases which might arise under the Bill with a view to testing its scope and meaning. But such hypothetical cases may appear unreal to lawyers and judges trained in the common law and accustomed to discuss legal problems in the light of concrete facts.

If the Bill expressly violates some provision of the Constitution counsel's job will be very easy. It will only be necessary to compare the text of the Bill with

[2] See Article 36, section 3, subsection 3.

the text of the Constitution for the disparity to appear. But such cases are rare because, presumably, no Government would knowingly violate the express provisions of the Constitution. Presumably, also, the Attorney General can be relied upon to warn the Government against any proposed measure which he considers unconstitutional. The real problem arises in cases of 'implied' repugnancy – that is to say where there is no express conflict between the Bill and the Constitution but where it is claimed that once the scope of the Bill and the scope of the Constitution are fully understood a conflict emerges.

In such cases the court presumes that the Bill is not repugnant to the Constitution. This presumption arises from the respect which one of the great organs of state owes to the others. The court presumes that the *Oireachtas* is not in violation of the Constitution until the contrary is clearly established.

Possibly, counsel attacking the Bill could adduce evidence[3] to rebut the presumption of constitutionality. But this has never been done. In its judgment on the reference of the Housing (Private Rented Dwellings) Bill 1981,[4] the Supreme Court complained that the matters at issue had, in the absence of evidence, to be dealt with as abstract problems as there was an absence or shortage of concrete facts. It added –

'The court, therefore, in a case such as this, has to act on abstract materials in order to cope with the social, economic, fiscal and other features that may be crucial to an understanding of the working and consequences of the referred Bill'.

As previously stated, counsel could possibly adduce evidence to show the practical scope of the Bill. But the time constraints are very tight. When the President refers a Bill to the Supreme Court for its opinion the court must give its decision 'as soon as may be, and in any case not later than sixty days'[5] after the date of the reference. This is not much time in which to assign solicitor and counsel to argue the case, to allow them to master their briefs, to permit them to collect and adduce expert evidence, to allow for the hearing and the arguing of the case in open court and to permit the court to consider, write and pronounce its judgment.

There is another problem. Suppose the constitutionality of the Bill does turn upon expert scientific evidence. Suppose for instance the Bill provides for the addition of a certain substance to the public water supply. Scientists may tell the court that the substance is beneficial to human health and, certainly, quite harmless in the quantities permitted by the Bill. In such circumstances the court has hardly any choice but to act in accordance with what it considers to be the best scientific evidence adduced before it. It may accordingly rely upon such evidence to uphold the constitutionality of the Bill. But suppose the passage of time shows the scientific evidence adduced before the court to be outdated or to have been false from the beginning. The citizens then would be stuck with a piece of legislation which permitted dangerous interference with the public water supply but the validity of which 'No court whatever' would have jurisdiction to question.[6]

---

[3] Article 26, section 2, of the Constitution refers only to 'arguments'.
[4] [1983] ILRM 246.
[5] See Article 26, section 2 of the Constitution.
[6] See Article 34, section 3, subsection 3, of the Constitution.

Acts of the *Oireachtas* – validity

Acts of the *Oireachtas*, like Bills passed by the two Houses, are presumed to be constitutional until the contrary is clearly established. In this case the challenge will usually come from a private citizen or association which claims to be aggrieved by the Act immediately or prospectively. There have been cases where the court has permitted challenges to legislation by citizens whose personal grievance against a particular piece of legislation was no greater than that of the citizens at large. But such cases have been the exception rather than the rule. At any rate since the decision in *Cahill v Sutton*[7] the policy of the courts has been to confine a plaintiff attempting to challenge the constitutionality of a piece of legislation to the facts of his own case. This contrasts strikingly with the procedure on the reference of a Bill discussed, and criticized, above. But it may be possible to ask whether the courts have not in their policy in relation to the validity of legislation swung to the other extreme. The reference procedure in relation to Bills appears to disclose a constitutional policy that unconstitutional Bills should not be enacted into law. A corollary would appear to be that legislation invalid for unconstitutionality should be detected and declared invalid as soon as possible. It is hard to see what public good is achieved by allowing legislation, suspected of being unconstitutional, to remain on the statute book.

The Supreme Court was unanimous on the result in *Cahill v Sutton*. The plaintiff it would appear, had very little merits. She was late in bringing her proceedings. Section 11, subsection 2(*b*) of the Statute of Limitations Act 1957 was invoked against her. She claimed that the subsection was unconstitutional because it did not provide for certain hard cases of which hers was not one. The court appears however to have accepted that her criticisms of the subsection were not without merit. She had pointed out that the corresponding section of the British Statute of Limitations contained savers of the kind which she alleged should be in the Irish Act. Mr Justice Henchy, in the course of his judgment (at page 88) said that while the court was unable to rule on the validity of her claim on the constitutional issue that it was proper to point out that 'the justice and fairness' of attaching to the Irish subsection a saver such as that which had been inserted in the corresponding English legislation 'are so obvious that the enactment by our Parliament of a similar provision would merit urgent consideration'.

The Supreme Court decision in *Cahill v Sutton* turned not so much on the plaintiff's status to attack the section as on her right to advance certain arguments in support of her attack. After all the section challenged was invoked against her. In the event it was invoked successfully and it barred her claim. It is hard therefore to accept that she was not aggrieved by the section. The court held however that she had no status to attack the section except by reference to the facts of her own case.[8]

The issue is put in the following passage from the judgment of Mr Justice Henchy which appears at page 280 of the Report.

---

[7] [1980] IR 269.

[8] On the plaintiff's status to sue in this case see the dissenting judgment of McCarthy J, in *Norris v Attorney General* [1984] IR 36; also the article by Whyte in *Solicitor's Gazette* December 1980, p. 229.

'Therefore, the plaintiff is seeking to be allowed to conjure up, invoke and champion the putative constitutional rights of a hypothetical third party, so that the provisions of s 11, sub-s 2(*b*), may be declared unconstitutional on the basis of that constitutional *jus tertii* – thus allowing the plaintiff to march through the resulting gap in the statute'.

The reference to the 'resulting gap' in the statute is significant. If there is a 'gap' resulting from the constitutional invalidity of the statute it is there and has been there from the date of the enactment of the statute. It does not result from the constitutional challenge. The question then becomes whether one will allow the plaintiff, by legal argument, to show the existence of the gap.

Take the cases of three plaintiffs all of whom attempt to challenge the constitutionality of a particular section. The facts of the first plaintiff's case do not precisely indicate the infirmity of the statute. She is held to have no status to advance the arguments which would show the statute to be invalid. She accordingly loses her case. Some time later the second plaintiff's case comes on for hearing. The facts of her case show the statute to be unconstitutional and she succeeds in her claim. Next the case of the third plaintiff comes on for hearing. The facts of her case are precisely the same as those of the first plaintiff's but she marches successfully through the 'gap'. Under these circumstances one might enquire whether the court has upheld the constitutional rights of the first plaintiff in allowing to be invoked against her a statute which was invalid and which she might have been able to show to be invalid had the court been prepared to listen to her submissions.

The presumption

It is permissible to ask what is the practical significance of an Act of the *Oireachtas* being presumed to be constitutional until the contrary is clearly established. Clearly it means that the onus of proof is on the plaintiff. But then the onus of proof is always on the plaintiff whether he is attacking a post-constitutional statute or a pre-constitutional statute which enjoys no presumption of constitutionality. The general principle is that he who asserts must prove and no court will lightly set aside a statute honestly passed by an elected Parliament – be it Irish or British – for the peace and good government of the country. For that reason Mr Thomas Conolly SC used to say that the presumption of constitutionality was not really of much practical importance in the conduct of a constitutional challenge to a statute before our courts. The onus of proof was always on the plaintiff and the case turned upon the strength of the evidence and arguments adduced on the plaintiff's behalf. If the court found these convincing the plaintiff succeeded; if it did not he failed.

There is one field, however, in which the presumption of constitutionality is of overwhelming importance and that is in the field of administrative law. The clear implication of the presumption of constitutionality is that when the *Oireachtas* grants a discretion to any administrative or subordinate body it intends that that discretion should be exercised in accordance with the Constitution and not otherwise. This doctrine – first propounded in *McDonald v Bord na a Con*[9] and expanded in *East Donegal Co-operative v Attorney General*[10] – is clearly

[9] [1965] IR 217.
[10] [1970] IR 317.

based on the presumption of constitutionality and brings all subordinate bodies exercising powers delegated by the *Oireachtas* under constitutional control.

It may also be possible to argue that there is a relationship between the presumption of constitutionality and the doctrine of judicial restraint. Clearly a statute which, in terms, violates the Constitution can not be presumed to be valid. On the other hand, the further one gets away from the text of the Constitution and the further one advances into complex areas of social policy, taxation or foreign affairs the more careful the court should be to exercise self-restraint and to defer to the decision of the *Oireachtas*. Likewise the vaguer and more general the principle upon which the plaintiff relies the more difficult it will be for him to defeat the presumption of constitutionality. Between these extreme cases lies the vast field within which the courts usually exercise their powers and within which the presumption will apply with varying degrees of force depending upon the nature of the statute in question, the constitutional provisions invoked and the general complexity of the case.

Pre-constitutional statutes – consistency

Article 50 of the Constitution carries forward statutes in force in *Saorstát Éireann* immediately prior to the coming into operation of the Constitution 'Subject to this Constitution and the extent to which they are not inconsistent therewith'. It is probably true to say that it was the intention of the framers of the Constitution to carry forward the general body of law existing in *Saorstát Éireann* prior to the coming into operation of the Constitution. It was clear however that this body of law might contain certain statutes which were in whole or in part inconsistent with the new Constitution and these were not to be carried forward.

Of the statutes referred to the most important were the statutes of the United Kingdom and statutes of the *Oireachtas* of *Saorstát Éireann*. Clearly it would be nonsense to presume that British parliamentarians in enacting legislation for Ireland had complied with the provisions of a constitution which did not exist at the relevant time. Likewise it would be absurd to suggest that they had accepted limitations on their legislative powers which would have violated their own principle of parliamentary sovereignty. The position of legislation passed by the *Oireachtas* of *Saorstát Éireann* may be more complex. But here again it would be absurd to presume that the *Oireachtas* of *Saorstát Éireann* in enacting legislation had complied with the provisions of a constitution which did not exist at the time the legislation was passed.

No special problem arises if the pre-constitutional legislation is, or is shown to be, inconsistent with the 1937 Constitution. Clearly such legislation was not carried forward by Article 50 and no longer forms part of the law of the State. Likewise if part of a pre-constitutional act is, or is shown to be, inconsistent with the Constitution that part cannot have been carried forward. In this case however one must be careful that what remains of the statute makes sense and is not in conflict with what the framers of the statute intended. The real problem arises in relation to pre-constitutional statutes which conferred wide discretions on administrative bodies or on private citizens. One could apply the so called '*intra vires* test' and ask oneself if the statute, or the section, on the date of its enactment allowed the body or person in question to do something which, if done now, would violate the Constitution. If so, one would conclude that the statute or section in question is inconsistent with the Constitution and was not carried by Article 50. This approach to the problem has the advantage of logic but it is a radical approach and could result in many pre-constitutional statutes failing to meet the test of consistency demanded by Article 50 of the Constitution. On the other hand one could argue that such statutes are to be carried forward subject to the Constitution 'and to the extent to which they are not inconsistent therewith'. In other words one could argue that the statute survives but that the discretions granted by it are now cut down and limited by the Constitution. This solution is less radical but also perhaps less logical. After all these statutes do not enjoy any presumption of constitutionality. One can hardly therefore cut down discretions granted by them by reference to the Constitution. They are statutes which were in force in *Saorstát Éireann* immediately prior to the date of the coming into operation of the Constitution. Logically it would appear that one should enquire what they meant on that date before deciding whether they are or are not consistent with the Constitution. However what is certain is that one cannot logically operate both these tests at the same time. If one chooses one test, one cannot choose the other. Yet the Supreme Court appears to have wavered between the two.

The first important case in which this matter came up for consideration was the case of *Educational Company of Ireland Ltd v Fitzpatrick*.[11] In that case the defendants placed a picket on their employer's premises with a view to compelling some of their fellow employees to join a trade union. The picket was clearly in breach of the constitutional right of association (or non-association) of the fellow employees. Yet the dispute appeared to be a trade dispute within the meaning of the Trade Disputes Act 1906 and the picketing appeared to be legal under that Act. If one were to apply the *intra vires* test one would conclude that the Trade Disputes Act 1906 was inconsistent with the Constitution and no longer formed part of the law of the State. That indeed was the conclusion which Mr Justice Budd drew in the High Court. The Supreme Court upheld his decision that the picketing was unlawful and unconstitutional but on different grounds. Mr Justice Kingsmill Moore, who delivered the principal majority judgment in the Supreme Court appears to have admitted that *prima facie* the picketing in question was covered by the Trade Disputes Act 1906 but added that that Act could no longer be relied upon to justify picketing in aid of a trade dispute where the dispute was concerned with an attempt to deprive persons of the right of free association or free dissociation guaranteed by the Constitution. He continued[12] –

'The definition of trade dispute must be read as if there were attached thereto the words, "Provided that a dispute between employers and workmen or between workmen and workmen as to whether a person shall or shall not become or remain a member of a trade union or having as its object a frustration of the right of any person to choose with whom he will or will not be associated in any form of union or association shall not be deemed to be a trade dispute for the purposes of this Act" '.

No doubt the Supreme Court, in taking this approach, was sensitive to the fact that both employers and trade unionists had come to accept the Trade Disputes

---

[11] [1961] IR 345.
[12] At p. 398 of the Report.

Act of 1906 as setting the ground rules for industrial disputes. To have ruled the entire Act unconstitutional might have led to serious industrial problems. The legal problem is that the adding of provisos to Acts of Parliament – and particularly to definition sections of Acts of Parliament – is part of the legislative process and is a function of the *Oireachtas* not of the courts.

In stark contrast to the Court's decision in *The Educational Company* case is its decision in *The State (Quinn) v Ryan*.[13] In that case the Supreme Court held that the provisions of section 27 of the Petty Sessions (Ireland) Act 1851 which authorized the backing of British warrants in Ireland and the immediate removal from the jurisdiction of the Irish courts of a person who had been arrested and detained under such a warrant was inconsistent with the Constitution and no longer formed part of the law of the State because it could be operated in such a way as to defeat the detainee's constitutional right to apply for habeas corpus. Mr Justice Walsh, in the course of his judgment (at page 130), laid down what he said was the proper test to be applied in such a case –

> 'The true test is to discover what is *intra vires* the statute. At the time the statute was passed and at all times up to the enactment and coming into force of the Constitution of *Saorstát Éireann* a prisoner could under these sections be instantly removed from this jurisdiction to the jurisdiction from whence the warrant came. If an act is *intra vires* a statute but at the same time inconsistent with the Constitution it is clear that the statute cannot stand'.

Of the two methods of approach to dealing with the problem of the consistency of pre-constitutional statutes with the Constitution that contained in the *intra vires* test would appear to be the more logical. However the scope for using the *intra vires* test will be severely restricted if a plaintiff challenging a pre-constitutional statute is bound by the rule in *Cahill v Sutton*.

The presumption again

Some people date the origin of the presumption of constitutionality from the judgment of Mr Justice Hanna in *Pigs Marketing Board v Donnelly*.[14] Indeed Mr Justice Hanna does in that case use words which are very similar to those in which the constitutional presumption is now formulated. At page 417 of the Report he writes –

> 'When the court has to consider the constitutionality of a law it must, in the first place, be accepted as an axiom that a law passed by the *Oireachtas*, the elected representatives of the people, is presumed to be constitutional unless and until the contrary is clearly established'.

But, in that case, Mr Justice Hanna was considering two Acts – The Pigs and Bacon Act 1935 and The Pigs and Bacon Act 1937 – both of which had been passed before the coming into operation of the Constitution. As we would put it nowadays he was considering the validity of these Acts having regard to the Constitution of 1922 and the consistency of these Acts with the Constitution of 1937.

[13] [1965] IR 70.
[14] [1939] IR 413.

The matter is not made easier by the fact that Mr Justice Hanna does not, in the passage quoted, distinguish between the *Oireachtas* of *Saorstát Éireann* and the *Oireachtas* established by the present Constitution. Clearly it would be quite absurd to presume that the *Oireachtas* of *Saorstát Éireann* had, in enacting laws, complied with the provisions of a constitution which did not yet exist. On the other hand it would be quite proper to presume that they had observed the provisions of the Constitution of 1922.

Mr Justice Hanna advances another important reason why laws, once enacted, are entitled to respect – they were enacted by the elected representatives of the people. But this reason applies to all laws in force in Ireland whether passed by the present *Oireachtas*, the former *Oireachtas* or the British Parliament. It is the reason why the onus of proof always rests on a plaintiff challenging the constitutionality of legislation and why it is sometimes difficult to distinguish between the onus which rests on a plaintiff when he is attacking legislation which does enjoy the presumption of constitutionality and that which rests on him when he is attacking legislation which enjoys no such presumption.

There is however one type of case where the distinction between the two kinds of legislation is vital. If the legislation under attack is post-constitutional legislation and enjoys the presumption of constitutionality the courts may safely assume that any discretions granted by it were intended by the *Oireachtas* to be exercised in accordance with the Constitution and not otherwise. But if the legislation was enacted prior to the coming into operation of the Constitution and either by the British Parliament or the *Oireachtas* of *Saorstát Éireann* the court may not safely draw any inference that the discretion was intended by the legislator to be exercised in accordance with the Constitution. Nor, I suggest, may it logically cut down the discretion by expressly, or impliedly, adding a proviso to it. That is a function of the legislator not of the judge.

To this suggested rule, however, there may be one exception. In many cases the wording of the present Constitution is identical with the wording of the Constitution of *Saorstát Éireann*. In such cases a presumption that legislation passed by the *Oireachtas* of *Saorstát Éireann* did not violate the Constitution of *Saorstát Éireann* may carry with it a presumption that it did not violate the corresponding provisions of the present Constitution either.

Amendment

A further complication arises if the present *Oireachtas* amends a pre-constitutional statute. No problem arises if the *Oireachtas* amends and re-enacts the pre-constitutional statute. The statute is then in the same position as a statute enacted by the present *Oireachtas* and enjoys the same presumption of constitutionality.[15] But the position of simple amendments to pre-constitutional statutes is more difficult.

There is a great deal of common sense in the opinion expressed by Mr Justice Pringle[16] –

---

[15] See *The People (Attorney General) v Conmey* [1975] IR 341.
[16] See *O'Brien v Manufacturing Engineering Co Ltd* [1973] IR 334 at 340.

'I would have thought that the Oireachtas should be presumed to have regarded the section which it purported to amend as not being repugnant to the Constitution in force at the time when the amending Act was passed.'

Similar opinions have been expressed by other High Court judges. But there are problems with this approach to the matter. For one thing the question of whether a pre-constitutional piece of legislation was or was not carried forward falls to be considered as of the date of the enactment of the Constitution. If, as of that date, the legislation was not consistent with the Constitution it was not carried forward and there was nothing for the *Oireachtas* to amend. Moreover the fact that the members of the *Oireachtas* may have thought that the pre-constitutional legislation was consistent with the Constitution is not conclusive. The question of whether a piece of pre-constitutional legislation is or is not consistent with the Constitution is a matter for the judge rather than for the legislator.

16 Observations on the Protection of Fundamental Rights in the Irish Constitution

Niall McCarthy

Tom Paine was born in Chetford, in England, in 1737. He is described as the son of a staymaker and small farmer. His great work *'The Rights of Man'* is published in two parts, the first in 1791, a reply to Burke's *'Reflections on the Revolution in France'*. There he said: 'Every generation must be free to act for itself, in all cases, as the agents of generations which preceded it. The vanity and presumption of governing beyond the grave is the most ridiculous and insolent of all tyrannies.' In context, Paine's prescription related to the form of government, not to so limited a field as the principle of *stare decisis*, but it is highly relevant both to the narrow area of unenumerated rights and the wide area of constitutional interpretation. The controversy in 1987 concerning the nomination of Judge Bork for appointment to the Supreme Court of the United States brought into sharp focus in that country at least the recurring debate between the fundamentalist and the interpretative schools of jurisprudence. 'If it's not in the book, then it isn't so' contrasts with 'the Constitution means what the judges say it means'. Portia vies with Humpty Dumpty. Let me explain. In *'The Merchant of Venice'* in her ruling on the meaning of the bond, Portia held Shylock to the letter; in 'Through the Looking Glass' Humpty Dumpty said, in a passage quoted by Lord Atkin in *Liversidge v Anderson*[1] 'Words mean what I say they mean, nothing more and nothing less.' In constitutional interpretation the argument has been between those who uphold the construction appropriate to the time of enactment of the Constitution – 1937, and those who uphold the construction of today. In *Norris v The Attorney General*[2], Chief Justice Thomas F O'Higgins, in approaching a question of the constitutionality of legislation passed by the British Parliament in 1861, said

> 'If on examination of such legislation now, in the light of the Constitution as it has been interpretated and understood since its enactment, inconsistencies are established, such legislation, to the extent thereof, must be held not to have been so continued. To achieve this result, however, the plaintiff must show that such inconsistencies exist. It is not sufficient to show that the legislation is out of date, is lacking in public support or approval, is out of tune with the mood or requirements of the times or is of a kind impossible to contemplate now being enacted by *Oireachtas Éireann*.'

[1] [1942] AC 206.
[2] [1984] IR 36 at 54.

It is a feature and a failing, common to theological, legal, and political debate that spontaneity, if not originality, of thought and felicity of expression are sacrificed to quotation from precedent, whether it be from the apostle Paul, the judgments of our judicial predecessors, or the appeals to history beloved of the politician. In our legal world – judicial, academic or practising – too often we seek to justify a conclusion by precedent rather than by principle. In all departments of life people see what they want to see. Judges are not exempt from this trait; judgments tend to be result orientated. Personal preference so promoted is most readily excused by quotation from the past, by blaming earlier judges and their judgments, not in so many words, but by careful attribution. We seldom want to be seen to recalibrate the scales of justice; we flinch from the bold confrontation with the past; we distinguish apparent error rather than bluntly say that previous decisions were wrong. Most people profess to be liberal; at heart, however, they are traditionalists. These are not necessarily opposing views – if liberalism is a tradition to the individual. We seek support for our domestic, financial, and legal decisions by calling upon the past. In the field of constitutional law, however, there is more scope for originality of thought – that spontaneity and felicity of expression which is most desirable: 'Lawyers are so much dominated by the ideas of the system which they administer, that it is difficult to enter into the atmosphere of a code of law alien to that to which they are accustomed.'[3]

With a dual system of government, the role of the judiciary becomes even more important – it acts as a brake, as a monitor, as an activist, and as a positive influence (securing that the Constitution keeps in step with the times rather than the times keep in step with the Constitution) becomes of great significance. The statement: 'The Constitution means what the judges say it means', is no blinding flash of jurisprudence. No one other than its guardians can be permitted to interpret the Constitution. Judges are, however, human beings with all the failings, prejudices, and misconceptions that attend upon that condition. It is in the nature of things that the judiciary are chosen from the middle classes; that is not to say, however, that individuals from other than the middle classes may not become leading lawyers. The point is, that when they do become leading lawyers they become members of the middle class with all the prejudices and traditions attached to them.

Despite the occasional evidence to the contrary, judges do not live in ivory towers; they read newspapers and watch television and listen to the radio as well as to their friends and colleagues. They are susceptible to changes in the mores, opinions, and values, of the nation. Oliver Wendell Holmes said:

'The life of the law has not been logic; it has been experience. The felt necessities of the time, the prevalent political theories, intuitions of public policy avowed or unconscious, even the prejudices which judges share with their fellowmen have had a good deal more to do than syllogism in determining the rule by which men should be governed.'

Are there no external restrictions on judicial creativity; is the construction of the Constitution to be papalist rather than populist, in religious terms, Catholic rather than Protestant?

Populism demands responsibility, or answerability – the right of the people

---

[3] Kennedy CJ in *Moore v Attorney General* [1934] IR 68.

to review the acts of their representatives at fairly regular electoral intervals. Papalism accepts no such restriction – the *Curia* is not elected but appointed by those then holding electoral favour; in ordinary circumstances and, empirically in Ireland, they are subject to no effective sanction – they can neither be removed nor questioned although they may be and are criticized. Populism, however, demands the rule of the majority; it is often called democracy, or more properly, representative democracy. The rule of the majority would ordinarily result in some form of oppression of the minority; here the argument for papalism assumes a new force. The true test of government by a majority may well be the manner in which it treats its minorities; if it treats them badly, they have no remedy save by recourse to the courts. Populist construction of the Constitution, if that means fundamentalism or originalism, will deny them anything, save within the narrow construction of rights: 'Constitutional rights are declared not alone because of bitter memories of the past but no less because of the improbable, but not-to-be-overlooked, perils of the future', (O'Dalaigh CJ)[4].

Whilst I have offended against the principle of eschewing quotation I have sought to demonstrate that the power of judicial review, where it is extended to the condemnation of legislative as well as executive action deriving from a written and consequently rigid constitution, emphasizes the great importance of the judicial role. The control exercised by the judiciary against the abuse of executive power contains within itself a very real danger – the abuse of judicial power. In the field of unenumerated rights the judicial power can only be self-restrained. It enjoins upon the judicial power to be alert not to substitute personal preference and, consequently, personal prejudice for the perceived legitimate needs of the people and of the nation. The judiciary must not err by adopting either extreme, that of refusal to go outside the expressed terms of the Constitution at one end or an excessive role of judicial law-making at the other. The former becomes entrenched by over reliance on precedent, the latter becomes uncontrolled unless supported by identifiable principle.

In the *Irish Times* of 27 July 1991, Dr Garret Fitzgerald, former *Taoiseach*, reviewed '*The Politics of the Irish Constitution*' by Basil Chubb[5] (Institute of Public Administration – 1991).

'He (Chubb) was right to draw attention to de Valera's explicit statement that under this Constitution it was the *Oireachtas* – and by clear implication only the *Oireachtas* – that had the right and duty to balance and co-ordinate personal and community rights through legislation, subject only to the right of the people to change the Constitution. De Valera clearly never envisaged the process by which, for example, the courts from 1965 onwards were to proclaim as inherent in the Constitution some dozen personal rights concerning which that document is actually silent – limiting substantially by this process the legislative powers of the *Oireachtas* upon which de Valera had placed such emphasis.

'Many are ambivalent about the extent to which the courts, exercising this interpretative function, intervene in the legislative process. Dr Chubb refers to the uncertainty thus created which makes it difficult for lawyers to give reliable advice to their clients in respect of some rights issues. But the legal inconvenience and the occasion and frustration of politicians at the striking down of legislation they have enacted have always seemed to me to be a reasonable price to pay for the assurance

---

[4] *McMahon v Attorney General* [1972] IR at 111.
[5] (Institute of Public Administration – 1991).

provided by this judicial control of legislation that personal rights will be vigilantly protected against even the most unintentional intrusion by the executive or legislature'

'The contrast between our position in relation to human rights and that in Britain is striking. In conversation with a member of the British Cabinet last year I was asked how our system of protection of human rights by the courts could possibly be accepted by politicians. If the British courts had possessed such a power in the immediate post-war period and had chosen to strike down some nationalisation measures introduced by the Labour Government, he wondered what the reaction would have been against such a judicial interference in the democratic political process.'

From 1965, the courts in Ireland proclaimed a series of unenumerated rights derived from man's rational being and the Christian and democratic nature of the State, recorded as first expressed by Mr Justice John Kenny in *Ryan v The Attorney General*[6] and iterated in the unanimous judgment of the Supreme Court delivered by O'Dalaigh CJ, where he said

'The court agrees with Mr Justice Kenny that the personal rights mentioned in Article 40.3.1 are not exhausted by the enumeration of life, person, good name and property rights in section 3.2 as is shown by the use of the words 'in particular'; nor by the more detached treatment of specific rights in the subsequent sections of the Article. To attempt to make a list of all the rights which may properly fall within the category of personal rights would be difficult and, fortunately, is unnecessary in this present case.'[7]

There is now a penumbra of unenumerated rights derived from man's rational being and from time to time discerned by the courts – e.g. the right to marital privacy; the right to travel; the right to marry or not to marry; the right not to be discriminated against at work; the right of access to the courts; the right to fair procedures; the right not to be forced into a union or association; the right to dispose of one's labour; the right to bodily integrity; the right of a child to be fed, to be reared and educated, to have the opportunity of working and of realising his or her full personality and dignity as a human being; the right to beget children. The catalogue remains open.

---

[6] [1965] IR 294 at 313.
[7] ID, at 344.

17 The Irish Constitution and Freedom of Expression

Nial Fennelly

Freedom of expression is the premise upon which all other civil rights are based. Without it, democratic freedom of choice of public representatives and governments would not exist and religious and other freedoms such as assembly would be meaningless. 'People cannot adequately influence the decisions which affect their lives unless they can be adequately informed on facts and arguments relevant to the decisions.'[1] Less obviously, rights of property and individual liberty would be very much curtailed in their exercise if only for the reason that access to justice also implies freedom of expression. In short, it is a liberty that we take for granted.

It remains true, however, that the principal Article of the Irish Constitution which guarantees this freedom has never been subjected to detailed judicial scrutiny[2]. Such case-law as exists tends to emphasize the qualifications or restrictions on the constitutional guarantee, of which there are many.

Freed from the bitter political and religious divisions of the 16th and 17th centuries and influenced, no doubt, by the emergence of a more stable democratic Constitution the common law judges of the 19th century were capable of giving a generous formulation of the concept of freedom of expression. It is true that this commenced in a negative way with the abolition of press licensing in the 17th century and was still being formulated in the early 19th century by Lord Ellenborough as follows:

'The law of England is a law of liberty, and consistently with this liberty we have not what is called an imprimatur; there is no such preliminary license necessary; but if a man publish a paper, he is exposed to the penal consequences, as he is in every other act, if it be illegal'[3].

In his celebrated work on the *Law of the Constitution*, Dicey was concerned to demonstrate the superiority of the rights of Englishmen over those formal declarations contained in the Constitutions of Continental States[4]. Having acknowledged that, *'the phrases "freedom of discussion" or "liberty of the press" are rarely found in any part of the Statute Book nor among the maxims of the common law'*, the

---

[1] Lord Simon of Glaisdale in *Attorney General v Times Newspapers Ltd* [1973] AC 2273.
[2] Kelly, *The Irish Constitution* 2nd ed. p. 563.
[3] *R v Cobbett* [1804] 29 *State Trials*.1.
[4] A V Dicey, *Law of the Constitution*, 9th Edition, 1945, Chapter VI.

author went on to identify the essentially negative or pragmatic form of liberty under English law by stating that:

> 'The so-called liberty of the press is a mere application of the general principle, that no man is punishable except for a distinct breach of the law'.

Nonetheless, throughout the 19th century, judges expressed views about liberty of expression which were often based on declared public policy grounds but which were very probably influenced by the philosophical ideas of antecedent rights as declared in the written Constitutions of France, Belgium and the United States of America.

For example, Crompton J in 1863 thought that:

> 'Nothing is more important than that fair and full latitude of discussion should be allowed to writers upon any public matter, whether it be the conduct of public men or the proceedings in Courts of Justice, or in Parliament, or the publication of a scheme or literary work'[5].

The concept of latitude also appealed to Lord Esher MR in *Merivale v Carson*[6] where he thought that 'every latitude must be given to opinion and to prejudice, and then an ordinary judgment must say whether any fair man would make such a comment on the work'. Both these cases were, of course, dealing with the issue of fair comment in the law of defamation. When dealing with the restraint on free expression necessarily involved in the concept of contempt of court, the Privy Council, in the elegant language of Lord Atkin[7] said:

> 'No wrong is committed by any member of the public who exercises the ordinary right of criticising, in good faith, in private or public, the public act done in the seat of justice. The path of criticism is a public way: the wrong-headed are permitted to err therein: provided that members of the public abstain from imputing improper motives to those taking part in the administration of justice, and are genuinely exercising a right of criticism, and not acting in malice or attempting to impair the administration of justice, they are immune. Justice is not a cloistered virtue: she must be allowed to suffer the scrutiny and respectful, even though outspoken, comments of ordinary men'.

It is interesting to note that Lord O'Brien, in 1901, spoke to similar effect:

> 'In his private personal character a judge receives no more protection from the law than any other member of the community at large; and, even in his judicial character, he should always welcome fair, decent, candid, and, I would add, vigorous criticism of his judicial conduct . . .'[8]

It is right to note also, of course, that the Irish courts, in modern times, have had to deal with a number of cases of contempt of court, mostly taking the form of 'scandalising the court'. In each of these cases, and notably in the judgments of Mr Justice O'Higgins as Chief Justice, express importance has been attributed to the need to respect the constitutional right of freedom of

---

[5] *Campbell v Spottiswoode* (1863) 3 B&S 769.
[6] (1887) 20 QBD 275.
[7] *Ambard v Attorney General for Trinidad and Tobago* [1936] AC 322.
[8] *R v McHugh* [1901] 2 IR 569.

expression while protecting also the authority of the courts and the integrity of the administration of justice. In *Cullen v Toibin*[9], O'Higgins CJ said that 'the freedom of the press and of communication which is guaranteed by the Constitution . . . cannot be lightly curtailed'. In an earlier case of *In Re Kennedy and McCann*[10] he said:

> 'The right of free speech and the free expression of opinion are valued rights. Their preservation, however, depends on the observance of the acceptable limit that they must not be used to undermine public order or morality or the authority of the State.'

In the same year, in *Hibernia National Review Ltd*[11], Kenny J delivered the judgment of the Supreme Court, with which O'Higgins CJ agreed and expressly adopted Lord Atkins' view that justice was 'not a cloistered virtue'.

This multiplicity of references arises from the fact that there has been so little explicit consideration, in Irish Constitutional Law, of that guaranteed right of freedom of expression which is contained in Article 40.6.1(*i*) of the Constitution. This 'valued right' finds itself in the company of two other named but very similar rights namely:
– right of the citizens to assemble peaceably and without arms;
– the right of the citizens to form associations and unions.

Each of these rights is heavily qualified by the prefatory statement that:

> 'The State guarantees liberty for the exercise of the following rights, subject to *public order and morality* . . .'

The Constitution nonetheless guarantees:

> 'i. The right of the citizens to express freely their convictions and opinions.
>   The education of public opinion being, however, a matter of such grave import to the common good, the State shall endeavour to ensure that organs of public opinion, such as the radio, the press, the cinema, while serving their rightful liberty of expression, including criticism of Government policy, shall not be used to undermine public order or morality or the authority of the State.
>   The publication or utterance of blasphemous, seditious, or indecent matter is an offence which shall be punishable in accordance with law.'

The foregoing declaration, with all its qualifications, stands starkly in contrast to the first amendment to the Constitution of the United States of America, which has just attained the age of 200 years:

> 'Congress *shall make no law* respecting an establishment of religion, or prohibiting the free exercise thereof; or abridging the freedom of speech, or of the press, or the right of people peaceably to assemble, and to petition the Government for a redress of grievances'. (My emphasis).

The Irish formulation of the guarantee has given rise to a surprising problem of construction. On the language of the American First Amendment, there is

[9] [1984] ILRM 577.
[10] [1976] IR 386.
[11] [1976] IR 388.

no room for a distinction between the communication of facts and of opinions. It speaks only of 'freedom of speech'. Article 10 of the European Convention on Human Rights is more explicit:

> 'Everyone has the right to freedom of expression. This right shall include freedom to hold opinions and to receive and impart information and ideas . . . '.

Even Halsbury[12] seeks to express the unexpressed concept of an unwritten constitution and says: 'Freedom of expression incorporates both the right to receive and to express ideas and information . . .'. The language used in Article 40, however, appears to guarantee the freedom of expression only in relation to 'convictions and opinions' without, at any rate expressly, referring to the right to communicate information. For this reason, Mr Justice Costello in two reported cases has taken the view that Article 40.6.1(*i*) does not contain any guarantee of the right to communicate information. He has held this to be a separate unenumerated right guaranteed by Article 40(3).

In *Attorney General v Paperlink*,[13] Costello J distinguished between 'the right to express freely convictions and opinions (which) is expressly provided for in Article 40.6.1(*i*)'. He thought also, however, that 'the act of communication is the exercise of such a basic human faculty that a right to communicate must inhere in the citizen by virtue of his human personality and must be guaranteed by the Constitution'. Having asked himself, in what Article that guarantee was contained, he thought that it must be 'one of those personal unspecified rights of the citizen protected by Article 40.3.1'. He followed this view in *Kearney v Minister for Justice*.[14] He there held that the plaintiff, a prisoner, had been subjected to an unjustified infringement of his constitutional right to communicate when certain letters were not delivered to him in prison. Again he found the origin of this right to communicate not in the citizens' right 'to express freely their convictions and opinions' (Article 40.6) but in the unspecified right to communicate information (Article 40.3). This problem of interpretation has not yet been considered by the Supreme Court and it may give rise to a number of problems and anomalies.

Firstly, the second and third paragraphs of the constitutional provision appear to qualify the first. The obligation on the State to make it an offence to publish 'blasphemous, seditious or indecent matter' would not appear to be restricted to matters of opinion; it must apply also to factual material. Why, therefore, is it found in a provision whose introductory words are said to concern only 'convictions and opinions'?

Secondly, the distinction between fact and opinion, which frequently has to be made in the law of defamation, is notoriously difficult and calls for fine judgment in many cases. Much published material includes a mixture. Can it really have been intended that different parts of the same publication would be covered by differently worded constitutional guarantees?

Thirdly, the second paragraph of the provision recognizes a 'rightful liberty of expression' as residing in the organs of public opinion. This liberty does not appear, for once, to be restricted to *citizens*. Many of those organs are owned by corporate bodies. Is a corporately owned newspaper to be entitled, under this

---

[12] Halsbury's *Laws of England*, 4th Edition Volume 8, para 834.
[13] [1984] ILRM 373.
[14] [1986] IR 116.

provision, to a free expression of opinions but not, because of the terms of Article 40.3, to enjoy freedom of communication of information? The idea of reserving enjoyment of personal and human rights only to Irish citizens and not extending their benefit to bodies corporate or to foreign (including EC) citizens within our shores is, in spite of the explicit language of the Constitution regarded as unacceptable and inconvenient and the courts have succeeded in avoiding such an uncomfortable result. The devices used have so far failed to confront the issue of principle.

A further curious feature of the provision is the company in which one finds the guaranteed right of free expression. It is one of three rights stated to be guaranteed only 'subject to public order and morality'. The other two rights are, as stated above, the rights of peaceable assembly and freedom of association. Each of these rights is, in turn, subjected by the Constitution to an express reservation, in favour of the *Oireachtas*, to pass laws regulating or controlling their exercise. Freedom of expression is not subjected, at least expressly, to any such reservation. Surprisingly, there is a much greater body of case-law relating to the regulation of the right of association, especially in the area of industrial relations law, than there is regarding freedom of expression. The Supreme Court has not been slow to uphold the constitutional right of freedom of association in the face of legislation seeking to regulate trade unions[15] or of political parties[16]. The willingness of the Supreme Court to vindicate the right of freedom of association even in the face of an express right of statutory regulation should give useful support to rights of freedom of expression.

The State (Lynch) v Cooney[17] stands out, however, as the only case in which the Supreme Court has had to consider a serious attack on the constitutionality of an Act of the *Oireachtas* founded upon the right of free expression contained in Article 40.6. It concerned the power of the Minister for Posts & Telegraphs (now the Minister for Communications) to direct *Radio Telefís Éireann*, the national broadcasting Authority, to refrain from 'the broadcasting of a particular matter or any matter of a particular class (which) would be likely to promote, or incite to, crime or would tend to undermine the authority of the State . . . '. This power was contained in section 31 of the Broadcasting Authority Act 1960, as amended. In February 1982, the Minister made an order preventing RTE from broadcasting a party political broadcast from 'the organisation styling itself Provisional *Sinn Féin*'. RTE had invited *Sinn Féin* to make a party political broadcast and the applicant, a member of the Party, applied to the High Court for an order of *certiorari* quashing the Minister's direction or, alternatively, for a declaration that section 31 of the Act of 1960 was unconstitutional.

In defending the case, counsel on behalf of the Minister appears to have made a submission in the High Court which was the direct opposite to that which was made in the Supreme Court. In the High Court, the Minister submitted, through his counsel, that his order, being a purely administrative Order, was not subject to review by the court either on the grounds of unreasonableness or otherwise. The High Court judge accepted this submission and held, as a consequence, that it conferred on the Minister 'a far-reaching power of veto over material for broadcasting, which power is not,

---

[15] *National Union of Railway Men v Sullivan* [1947] IR 77
[16] *Loftus v Attorney General* [1979] IR 221.
[17] [1982] IR 337.

prima facie, susceptible of control by the courts (or by any other body, save the House of the *Oireachtas*) once it appears that the Minister has formed an opinion of the nature mentioned in the sub-section'. He went on to say that:

> 'It would seem to follow from this conclusion that the Minister might form an opinion on wholly unreasonable grounds and prohibit access to broadcasting time by some person or persons, or the broadcasting of certain matters or matters of a particular class, and the court would be powerless to relieve against the exercise of such power'.

Based on this reasoning, the learned High Court judge, Mr Justice O'Hanlon, not unreasonably concluded that the Act did not contain sufficient safeguards 'for the constitutionally guaranteed rights of freedom for expression of convictions and opinions – with particular reference to the protection of freedom of the press and the radio, and now of television, from the control of the Executive'.

On appeal, the Supreme Court held that Mr Justice O'Hanlon was wrong in concluding that the 'Section empowered the Minister to act in an unfettered and unreviewable manner', although it does not reveal the circumstances in which the State was allowed to resile from the submission it had made in the High Court. The judgment of the Supreme Court, on the issue of constitutionality, delivered by O'Higgins CJ, expressly recognized the power of the State, by legislation, to control the freedom of expression and free speech conferred by Article 40.6.1(*i*). The nature of this power is described:

> 'The basis for any attempt at control must be, according to the Constitution, the overriding considerations of public order and public morality. The constitutional provision in question refers to organs of public opinion and these must be held to include television as well as radio. It places upon the State the obligation to ensure that these organs of public opinion shall not be used to undermine public order or public morality or the authority of the State. It follows that the use of such organs of public opinion for the purpose of securing or advocating support for organisations which seek by violence to overthrow the State or its institutions is a use which is prohibited by the Constitution. Therefore, it is clearly the duty of the State to intervene to prevent broadcasts on radio or television which are aimed at such a result or which in any way would be likely to have the effect of promoting or inciting crime or endangering the authority of the State. These, however, are objective determinations and obviously the fundamental rights of citizens to express freely their convictions and opinions cannot be curtailed or prevented on *any irrational or capricious ground*. It must be presumed that when the *Oireachtas* conferred these powers on the Minister it intended that they be exercised only in conformity with the Constitution'[18].

I have quoted this passage in full and I have italicized certain words for reasons which shall shortly appear. In short, however, the Supreme Court held that the delegated power, being exercised by the Minister, had to be exercised reasonably in the light of the Constitution, that the presumption of constitutionality in favour of the legislation involved such an assumption and that therefore, on the assumption of such reasonable behaviour by the Minister, the Act could not be unconstitutional.

The Court went on, in separate judgments, to review the reasonableness of

---

[18] *State (Lynch) v Cooney* [1982] IR 33–7.

the actual exercise of the ministerial power. The State had placed before the court evidence of the paramilitary involvements of the political party called *Sinn Féin* and its support for the objectives of the IRA. Each of the judges thought that the material placed before the court was sufficient to enable the Minister reasonably to form the opinion required by the section and more specifically that it showed that the organisation in question was involved in the advancement of a cause and the use of methods which were contrary to the legitimate authority of the State.

This case presents interesting problems for analysis in connection, more generally, with the protection of constitutional rights but, specifically, the protection of the right of freedom of expression. It seems to this writer that an unusual result has been achieved by delegating to a Minister the actual power of control over freedom of expression.

A study of the case-law cited both in the High Court and the Supreme Court identifies the very notable omission of any reference to the crucial decision in *Associated Provincial Picture Houses Ltd v Wednesbury Corporation*[19] where Lord Greene MR adopted the famous dictum that:

> 'It is true to say that, if a decision on a competent matter is so unreasonable that no reasonable authority could ever have come to it, then the Courts can interfere . . .; but to prove a case of that kind would require something overwhelming'.

The *Wednesbury* test of unreasonableness or irrationality had by then passed into the language of administrative lawyers. It was not, however, adverted to in the Supreme Court. Both O'Higgins CJ and Henchy J thought that the evidence before the Minister was so overwhelming that any decision to the contrary would have been perverse. Walsh J came nearest to posing the *Wednesbury* test when he asked himself 'whether any grounds existed for making such an order'. He thought that the evidence was sufficient 'to enable a Minister reasonably to form the opinion that any broadcast made on behalf of that party . . . could itself amount to an advancement of a cause and of methods which are inimical to the legitimate authority of the State'. It is clear, therefore, that the court was not asked to consider the matter in the light that the reasonableness of the Minister's decision could be reviewed only if it could be shown to be so unreasonable as to meet the *Wednesbury* criteria.

The extent and nature of those criteria has by now, of course, been extensively considered by the Supreme Court. In *The State (Keegan) v Stardust Victims Compensation Tribunal*[20] Mr Justice Henchy delivered what has become the leading judgment on the topic and considered that 'the test of unreasonableness or irrationality in judicial review lies in considering whether the impugned decision plainly and unambiguously flies in the face of fundamental reason and common sense'.

More recently, the Supreme Court in *O'Keeffe v An Bord Pleanala*[21] adopted a particularly strong and far-reaching formulation of the original *Wednesbury* test. Finlay CJ states:

> 'The circumstances under which the court can intervene on the basis of irrationality with the decision maker involved in an administrative function are limited and rare.

[19] (1948) 1 KB 223.
[20] [1986] IR 642.
[21] Unreported, February 1991.

The court cannot intervene with the decision of an administrative decision-making authority merely on the grounds that:

(*a*) it is satisfied that on the facts as found it would have raised different inferences and conclusions, or

(*b*) it is satisfied that the case against the decision made by the authority was much stronger than the case for it . . .

I am satisfied that in order for an appellant for judicial review to satisfy a court that the decision-making authority has acted irrationally in the sense which I have outlined above so that the court can intervene and quash its decision, it is necessary that the applicant should establish to the satisfaction of the court that the decision-making authority had before it no relevant material which would support its decision'.

This formulation has been described as significantly narrowing the grounds for judicial review[22]. What are its implications for the decision in *Lynch*? In view of the strong views for O'Higgins CJ and Henchy J, it is unlikely that *Lynch* would have been decided differently if the *Keegan* and *O'Keeffe* decisions had then been made and been cited to the court. A more general problem arises. It arises from the dual effect of these cases with their re-statement of the *Wednesbury* test and the well-known principle deriving from *East Donegal Cooperative Livestock Marts Ltd v Attorney General*[23], that, by reason of the presumption of constitutionality, all administrative powers contained in statutes must be assumed in advance and for the purpose of assessing constitutionality, to be exercisable only in a reasonable fashion.

In these circumstances, is adequate protection given to the exercise of the guaranteed right? The right of freedom of expression, apart from being guaranteed by Article 40.6.1(*i*) is, presumably, also one of the personal rights of a citizen and Article 40.3.1 provides:

'The State guarantees in its Laws to respect, and, as far as practicable, by its Laws to defend and vindicate the personal rights of the citizen'.

In considering the adequacy of such a defence or vindication, one would normally look to such protective mechanisms by way of adequate notice and fair hearing as have frequently been implied into legislation with the effect of rescuing them from constitutional challenge. In *Lynch* each of the separate judgments upheld the validity of the Minister's decision to exercise his power without any form of hearing on the ground of urgency combined with the involvement of the issue of security of the State. There is, with respect, room for argument about this. It should be noted that RTE proposed, in view of their small number of candidates at the election, to allow *Sinn Féin* one two-minute broadcast on each of its five outlets (two television and three radio). It appears that the actual material to be broadcast was not itself directed to undermining the security of the State at all and the Minister could have ascertained this by means of enquiry prior to the making of his order. In the result, there are two very substantial hurdles placed before the attempted exercise of the right of free expression in this case. Firstly, there was, in the circumstances, no obligation on the Minister to give any hearing to the persons affected. Secondly, it appears that the court could review his decision only on the basis of *Wednesbury* criteria of irrationality.

---

[22] Hogan and Morgan *Administrative Law in Ireland*, 2nd ed., 526.
[23] [1970] IR 317.

It is interesting to compare *Lynch* with *Irish Family Planning Association Ltd v Ryan*[24]. The Censorship Board, established under the Censorship of Publications Act 1929, made an order prohibiting the sale and distribution of a booklet on Family Planning published by the plaintiff. Section 6 of the Act provided that:

> 'When examining a book under this section the Censorship Board may communicate with the author, editor or publisher of the book and may take into account any representation made by him in relation thereto'.

The Board did not, in fact, communicate at all with the publishers. On this ground, Hamilton J (as he then was) held the decision of the Board to be null and void because the plaintiff had been given no opportunity to state its case. The Supreme Court upheld this view, basing its conclusion on the particular nature of the publication. Having reviewed it, O'Higgins CJ considered that: 'Far from being pornographic or lewdly commercial or pandering to prurient curiosity, it simply aimed at giving basic factual information on a delicate topic as to which there is genuine concern'. In expressing this opinion, with which all other members of the court agreed, the Chief Justice was not, of course, substituting his own view for that of the Censorship Board. He was, however, making the point that the *audi alteram partem* rule was not obligatory on the Board in all circumstances and, for that purpose, the court looked at the nature of the material. Most notably of all, however, a study of the report shows that the plaintiffs challenged the constitutionality of the Censorship of Publications Act 1946 on the ground *iner alia* that it infringed the constitutional right of freedom of expression. Both the High Court and the Supreme Court, however, decided the case without reference at all to the constitutional provisions.

The constitutional right of freedom of expression remains, therefore, somewhat of an enigma. *Lynch* and *Irish Family Planning* provided particular invitations to explore it which were not accepted. There remain anomalies in the interpretation of the provision. Is the right to free expression confined to citizens? Do the organs of public opinion have a special position? Obviously, we must await the appropriate case.

[24] [1979] IR 295.

18 Criminal Justice and the Constitution in Ireland

James Casey

In the last twenty-five years, since the seminal decision in *Ryan v Attorney General*[1] the judicial development of the Irish Constitution has been both remarkable and rapid. Though this has affected many areas of the law, its impact has been particularly noticeable in the sphere of criminal law and procedure. Founding upon broad and vague textual provisions – such as the guarantee of individual liberty[2] and of trial in due course of law[3] – the courts have placed limits on executive and legislative power in this field. Virtually all aspects of the criminal process – pre-trial and post-trial – have been affected. Many of these developments took place during O'Higgins J's period as Chief Justice, and it thus seems particularly appropriate to survey them in a book of essays in his honour.

The Pre-Trial Stage

Nulla poena sine lege

The principle *nulla poena sine lege* finds partial expression in Article 15.5 of *Bunreacht na hÉireann*, prohibiting retroactive legislation, criminal or otherwise. But the principle is not exhausted by this provision, for it is also apt to embrace the notion that a penal law must distinguish with reasonable clarity between prohibited and permissible acts. This aspect won acceptance from the Supreme Court in *King v Attorney General*[4] where one of the grounds for condeming as unconstitutional part of section 4 of the Vagrancy Act 1824 was its lack of precision. Henchy J (Griffin and Parke JJ concurring) spoke of:

> '. . . the basic concept inherent in our legal system that a man may walk abroad in the secure knowledge that he will not be singled out from his fellow-citizens and branded and punished as a criminal unless it has been established beyond reasonable doubt that he has deviated from a clearly prescribed standard of conduct . . .'[5]

---

[1] [1965] IR 249.
[2] Article 40.4.1.
[3] Article 38.1.
[4] [1981] IR 233.
[5] At 257.

And Kenny J said:

> 'It is a fundamental feature of our system of government by law (and not by decree or diktat) that citizens may be convicted only of offences which have been specified with precision by the judges who made the common law, or of offences which, created by statute, are expressed without ambiguity.'[6]

The judges in *King's* case cite almost no authority in support of their conclusions,[7] and the report shows that those referred to by counsel came purely from the common-law world.[8] But the principle involved finds much wider acceptance, for it features in the UN's Universal Declaration of Human Rights (1948), the International Covenant on Civil and Political Rights (1966) and the European Convention on Human Rights (1950).[9] An important consequence of the *King* case, therefore, is to reinforce by constitutional precept the international obligations of the State.

The case also brings Irish constitutional law into line with that of certain other European states. The principle it enshrines has been applied by the French Constitutional Council and the Spanish Constitutional Court. And its significance has been stressed by one French scholar who, using a phrase familiar in the jurisprudence of the European Court of Justice, has called it:

> '. . . certainly the most important criminal law principle in guaranteeing the legal security of the citizen before the penal apparatus of the state.'[10]

For its part, the Spanish Constitutional Court has derived the same principle from a constitutional ban on retroactive criminal legislation[11] and has likewise linked it to the concept of legal security (*segurided juridica*).[12]

Arrest and questioning

What is the purpose of an arrest? When O'Higgins J departed to Luxembourg the answer seemed – curiously[13] – unsettled. O'Higgins CJ and Walsh J were clearly of opinion that, special statutory provisions apart, no one could be arrested or detained in order to be questioned or so that evidence against

---

[6] At 263.

[7] Though Kenny J found support for his conclusion in the Supreme Court decision in *People (Attorney General) v Edge* [1943] IR 115.

[8] The authorities cited were principally Irish constitutional cases, but they included also US decisions – e.g. *Papachristiou v City of Jacksonville* (1972) 405 US 156 – and a Privy Council case, *Hinds v The Queen* [1977] AC 195.

[9] Universal Declaration, Article 11.2: International Covenant, Article 15.1: European Convention, Article 7(2).

[10] Poullain *La Practique Française de la Justice Constitutionelle* (Paris, 1990). p. 254: '. . . certainement le principe le plus important du droit des peines pour assurer la securité juridique du citoyen devant l'appareil repressif de l'État.'

[11] Spanish Constitution, Article 25.1.

[12] See its judgment 62/1982 (15 October), *Boletín de Jurisprudencia Constitucional* – 19, p. 919. The *Tribunal Constitucional* also said that '. . . the legislator . . . must make the maximum effort possible to ensure that legal security is safeguarded in the definition of standards.' ('. . . el legislador . . . debe hacer el máximo esfuerzo posible para que la seguridad jurídica quede salvaguardada en la definición de los tipos.')

[13] In the light of the Supreme Court decision in *Dunne v Clinton* 1 Frewen 563.

him/her might be obtained. But it is not certain that this view was supported by their colleagues; the majority judgment in *Shaw's* case[14] seemed to leave the issue open. Now, however, the O'Higgins/Walsh doctrine has plainly prevailed; see *People (DPP) v Higgins*.[15] So where the *Gardaí* know – or should have known – that an arrest or detention was unlawful, evidence obtained as a consequence thereof will be inadmissible as having been secured by a conscious and deliberate violation of the accused's constitutional rights.

Also unsettled until recently was the answer to a connected question – when does a violation of constitutional rights attract the epithets 'conscious and deliberate'? Again, the majority judgment in *Shaw's* case seemed to adopt a subjective test – that there must be an element of *mala fides* or wilfulness on the part of those perpetrating the violation.[16] But the recent case of *Kenny*[17] plainly overrules *Shaw* and affirms that (in the words of McCarthy J in *Healy's* case[18]):

'. . . the only test is whether or not the act or omission that constituted such violation was itself a conscious and deliberate act; the fact that the violator did not realise it was in breach of a constitutional right is irrelevant.'

For, as the same learned judge observed, if it were otherwise there would be a premium upon ignorance.

Bail

In the 1965 case of *O'Callaghan*[19] the Supreme Court – as is well known – created a very strong presumption in favour of bail for persons accused of crime. The court emphasized that innocence was to be presumed until conviction and denounced the idea that a person could be denied bail on the ground that he/she might commit further offences while at liberty. During O'Higgins CJ's tenure the court had no clear opportunity to reconsider these matters; but one may perhaps infer from Henchy J's judgment in *Gilliland's* case[20] a desire to see such an opportunity arise.

It subsequently did arise in *DPP v Ryan*[21], but the court – unanimously – reaffirmed the principles laid down in *O'Callaghan's* case. In particular it rejected a novel argument – that an accused's constitutional right to liberty must be balanced against possible injury to the constitutional rights of others. Finlay CJ, for the court, laid heavy emphasis on the difficulties this would involve – such as how an intention to commit further offences would be proved and what standards of proof would apply. And McCarthy J concurring separately, summarized the objections in two lapidary sentences:

---

[14] *People (DPP) v Shaw* [1982] IR 1 at 55, where Griffin J (with whom Henchy, Kenny and Parke JJ agreed) said: '. . . I do not think it is correct to state without qualification that no person may be arrested with or without a warrant for the purpose of interrogation or the securing of evidence from that person.'

[15] Unreported, Supreme Court, 22 November 1985.

[16] [1982] IR 1, 55–56.

[17] *People (DPP) v Kenny* [1990] ILRM 569.

[18] *DPP v Healy* [1990] ILRM 313, 328.

[19] *People (Attorney General) v O'Callaghan* [1966] IR 501.

[20] *People (Attorney General) v Gilliland* [1986] ILRM 357.

[21] [1989] IR 399.

'The pointing finger of accusation, not of crime done, but of crime feared, would become the test. Such appears to me to be far from a balancing of constitutional rights; it is a recalibration of the scales of justice.'[22]

Delay

The right of a person accused of a criminal offence to be tried with reasonable expedition is recognized by international human rights instruments – such as the International Covenant on Civil and Political Rights[23] and the European Convention on Human Rights.[24] It features also in West European constitutions of recent vintage – e.g. Article 24.2 of the Spanish Constitution of 1978[25] and Article 32.2 of the Portuguese Constitution of 1976 (as revised in 1982).[26] Unsurprisingly, given its date, it finds no mention in the text of *Bunreacht na hÉireann*, but judicial exegesis has supplied this omission. In *State (O'Connell) v Fawsitt*[27] the Supreme Court held, in Finlay CJ's words:

'. . . a person charged with a criminal offence is entitled, as part of his right to be tried in due course of law, to a trial with reasonable expedition.[28]

Commentary

In three of the areas discussed above – legal certainty, bail and delay – the Supreme Court has displayed an impressive unanimity of view. This will doubtless insulate the relevant decisions against possible subsequent revisionist views, and the fact – noted above – that the *King* and *O'Connell* decisions give constitutional force to the State's international obligations should further protect them.

No such unanimity is found on the issue of admissibility of unconstitutionally obtained evidence; in *Kenny's* case – the latest Supreme Court decision on the matter – two judges, Griffin and Lynch JJ, dissented. For the moment, however, what Finlay CJ has called 'the absolute protection rule' holds the field. This contrasts with the US position, where the exclusionary rule's purpose is now seen as deterring unlawful police conduct, and where a number of exceptions has been grafted on to it. Thus in *US v Leon*[29] the Supreme Court held admissible evidence obtained in the reasonable – though erroneous – good-faith, belief that a search was lawful. It is noteworthy that the *Leon* decision was cited to the Irish Supreme Court in *Kenny's* case, and that the majority expressly declined to adopt its reasoning.

A similar rejection of current US Supreme Court doctrine occurred in the

---

[22] At 410.
[23] Article 9(3).
[24] Article 6(1). On the interpretation of this provision by the European Court of Human Rights, see *Milasi v Italy* (1988) 10 EHRR 333; *Baggetta v Italy* (1988) 10 EHRR 325; *B v Austria* (1991) 13 EHRR 20.
[25] '. . . all persons have the right . . . to a public trial without undue delays . . .'
[26] 'Everyone charged with an offence . . . shall be tried in the shortest space of time compatible with defence safeguards.'
[27] [1986] IR 362.
[28] At 378.
[29] (1984) 468 US 897.

bail case of *DPP v Ryan*.[30] There counsel cited *US v Salerno*[31], which upheld the constitutionality of certain pre-trial detention provisions of the Bail Reform Act of 1984. Rehnquist CJ, delivering the majority opinion, said that the government's interest in community safety could, in appropriate cases, outweigh an individual's liberty interest. This was particularly so where the government mustered convincing proof that the arrested person, already indicted or held to answer for a serious crime, presented a demonstrable danger to the community. But *Ryan's* case declined to admit any such balancing exercise as a guide for judicial discretion in granting bail.

It can thus be seen that the constitutionalizing of aspects of criminal procedure – a phenemenon familiar in the US – is emphatically not the product of uncritical acceptance of American ideas.[32] The Irish Supreme Court has hewn its own distinctive path, taking guidance from any source it deems appropriate. So far these sources have been found mainly in the common-law world,[33] but closer acquaintance with European constitutional systems may alter this.[34] Nor, usually, has inspiration explicitly been drawn from international instruments, but in *State (Healy) v Donoghue*[35] O'Higgins CJ made specific reference to the European Convention on Human Rights.[36] And, more recently, in *O'Leary v Attorney General*.[37] Costello J quoted from a variety of international human rights conventions.[38]

The Trial Stage

Legal representation

Article 6(3) of the European Convention on Human Rights provides:

> 'Everyone charged with a criminal offence has the following minimum rights:
> (c) to defend himself in person or through legal assistance of his own choosing or, if he has not sufficient means to pay for legal assistance, to be given it free when the interests of justice so require.'

---

[30] [1989] IR 399.

[31] (1987) 481 US 739.

[32] In *DPP v Healy* [1990] ILRM 313 the Supreme Court majority held that a person arrested or detained has a constitutional right of access to a solicitor whose attendance he/she, or others *bona fide* acting on his/her behalf, has requested. The court, *per* Finlay CJ (at 317), left open the questions whether the Gardaí were obliged to inform the detained person about that right of access, and whether a detained person had a right to have a solicitor present during questioning. Cf. *Miranda v Arizona* (1966) 384 US 436.

[33] Thus in *State (O'Connell) v Fawsitt* [1988] IR 362 the authorities cited, apart from Irish and English decisions, included three US Supreme Court decisions, a Privy Council decision in a Jamaican appeal and one of the Alberta Queen's Bench; see [1988] IR 362 at 363.

[34] It is interesting to note that the Spanish Constitutional Court has established a distinction, similar to that in Irish law, between unconstitutionally and illegally obtained evidence. The former has been ruled inadmissible where fundamental rights or liberties are violated, whereas the question of the latter has been left open: STC 114/1984, de 29 de Noviembre, BJC–44, p. 1446.

[35] [1976] IR 325.

[36] At 351, citing Article 6(3)(c) of the Convention on the provision of free legal aid in criminal cases.

[37] [1991] ILRM 454.

[38] At 458. Costello J refers to Article 11 of the UN Universal Declaration of Human Rights: Article 6(2) of the European Convention on Human Rights: Article 8(2) of the American Convention on Human Rights: and Article 7 of the African Charter on Human and Peoples' Rights.

The Criminal Justice (Legal Aid) Act 1962 enshrines the system for implementing the State's obligations in this regard. It conditions entitlement to legal aid on (*a*) the insufficiency of the accused's means, and (*b*) such aid being essential in the interests of justice.

The effect of the Supreme Court decision in *State (Healy) v Donoghue*[39] is again to give the international obligation a constitutional underpinning. The court there quashed the convictions of persons who had been granted legal aid, but had subsequently been convicted without legal representation. The *ratio* would seem to be that Articles 38.1, 40.3 and 4 provide constitutional safeguards for impecunious persons facing criminal charges. So when, under the 1962 Act, legal aid for an accused has been found essential in the interests of justice his/her rights will be violated by a conviction in its absence.

The special interest of *Healy's* case lies in an unusual kind of teamwork between the legislature and the courts. The Supreme Court was not required to hold legislation unconstitutional, or to indicate by implication that legislation to implement constitutional rights was essential. Instead it saw the 1962 Act as implementing constitutional guarantees and insisted upon strict compliance with the terms. But it went beyond this, by requiring that those facing possible prison sentences and without means to obtain legal representation be *specifically* informed of their right to legal aid. If I may quote what I have written elsewhere:

'The case has a twofold importance. It obliges District Justices to be on the *qui vive* in such circumstances, and thus affects the daily operation of the criminal law. But its constitutional underpinnings seem to involve the additional result that public funds for criminal legal aid cannot be the victim of a Finance Department axe in any future expenditure crisis.'[40]

A properly constituted court

The constitutional guarantee of trial in due course of law requires that the court of trial be properly constituted. This was established in *Shelly v District Justice Mahon*.[41] On 28 May 1987 the respondent had convicted the applicant of a road traffic offence. Before that date the respondent had attained the age of sixty-five – the statutory retirement age for District Justices. He could have been continued in office on a year to year basis but, because of an oversight, the conditions governing this had not been fulfilled. Following the discovery of this omission, the Courts (No. 2) Act 1988 was enacted to allow the retrospective extension of such terms of office. A saver (section 1(3)) provided, in effect, that any such retroactive validation should be limited so as not to conflict with a constitutional right of any person. In the High Court Blayney J had no doubt that the general validation must necessarily be limited so as not to apply to criminal convictions. On appeal, the Supreme Court, in a majority decision,[42] agreed. Walsh J put the matter thus:

[39] [1976] IR 325.
[40] Casey, 'The Development of Constitutional Law under Chief Justice O'Higgins' (1986) XXI *Irish Jurist* (n.s.) 7, 22.
[41] [1990] 1 IR 36.
[42] Walsh, Griffin, Hederman and McCarthy JJ; Costello J dissenting.

'. . . the applicant, like all persons accused of criminal offences, had a constitutional right to have his case decided in a court set up under the Constitution and presided over by a judge appointed in accordance with the Constitution. He was not afforded that right. His case was not heard by a judge appointed under the Constitution.'[43]

The same error, in regard to the same District Justice, gave rise to a more difficult question in *Glavin v Governor, Training Unit, Mountjoy Prison*.[44] Here the applicant had been returned for trial on indictment by District Justice Mahon, again on a date subsequent to the justice's sixty-fifth birthday. In the Circuit Court he pleaded guilty to the charge and was sentenced to a term of imprisonent. He now sought *habeas corpus*, claiming that his return for trial was invalid and that in consequence the Circuit Court lacked jurisdiction to convict and sentence him. The Supreme Court unanimously accepted this argument. As O'Flaherty J expressed it:

'The single question for resolution is whether the entitlement to a proper, valid preliminary examination is so inexorably bound up with the trial that it should be held that a failure to hold a proper preliminary examination means that there has been a failure to afford the due process that is required by Article 38.1 of the Constitution. I believe that the two are so connected . . . The argument put by the appellants is that the entitlement to a preliminary examination is a legal right and that no constitutional right has been infringed. That would appear to be super-ficially correct but once it is realised that the holding of the preliminary examination and the trial are inextricably bound together then it must follow that if there has been a failure to hold a proper preliminary examination the trial or anything that happens after a purported return for trial is not in accordance with the Constitution; there is a failure of due process.'[45]

The same constitutional principle would obviously apply to the Special Criminal Court, but thus far the attempts so to apply it have been unsuccessful. In *Eccles v Ireland*[46] it was contended that section 39(2) of the Offences Against the State Act 1939, making Special Criminal Court members removable at will by the Government, deprived those members of judicial independence; consequently those tried before such a court were deprived of a trial in due course of law. But the Supreme Court held that the power conferred by section 39(2) must be exercised in a constitutional manner. Any use of that power to interfere with the Special Criminal Court's judicial independence would infringe the constitutional rights of those accused before it; and the ordinary courts would prevent and correct any attempt to do this. In *McGlinchey v Governor Portlaoise Prison*[47] the applicant claimed that the Special Criminal Court which convicted him was improperly constituted, since two of its members were retired – not serving – judges. This argument was rejected on two grounds: (*a*) that section 39(3) of the 1939 Act was directed only to the qualifications required for initial appointment – e.g. that one be a High Court judge. It did not require that such qualifications

[43] [1990] 1 IR 36, 42.
[44] [1991] ILRM 478.
[45] At 492.
[46] [1985] IR 545. Lynch J implicitly adopted the reasoning in the *Eccles* case in *Sloan v Culligan and Windle* (unreported, 1990 No. 104 JR, 25 January 1991) when repelling a challenge to the constitutionality of Section 51, Courts of Justice Act 1936, which permits the appointment of temporary District Justices.
[47] [1988] IR 671.

be held thereafter; (*b*) that in any event the retired judges who sat remained qualified for appointment under section 39(3) as barristers or solicitors of seven years' standing.

The presumption of innocence

The presumption of innocence has long been part of Irish law, but it was not certain until recently that it had achieved constitutional status. Now, however, *O'Leary v Attorney General*[48] confirms that it has. Costello J there said:

> 'I have little difficulty . . . in construing the Constitution as conferring on every accused in every criminal trial a constitutionally protected right to the presumption of innocence.'[49]

Costello J based his conclusions on two grounds. Firstly, the Constitution was to be construed in the light of contemporary concepts of fundamental rights, and as international human rights instruments showed, the right to the presumption of innocence now enjoyed universal recognition.[50] Secondly, the presumption had for so long been a fundamental postulate in Irish criminal trials that a trial held otherwise than in accordance with it would *prima facie* be one not held in due course of law.

But Costello J was of opinion that the right in question was not an absolute right whose enjoyment could never be abridged. Thus the *Oireachtas* could in certain circumstances restrict the exercise of the right;[51] in particular it could shift the *evidential* burden of proof. If, however, statute shifted the *legal* burden of proof – as where its effect would be that the court *must* convict the accused should he/she fail to adduce exculpatory evidence – then the Constitution might be infringed. But all would depend on the way in which the statute was drafted. A provision requiring an inference to be drawn once certain facts were established would therefore not necessarily be unconstitutional.

The Post-Trial Stage

The rule against double jeopardy

Article 14(7) of the International Covenant on Civil and Political Rights (1966) provides:

> 'No one shall be liable to be tried or punished again for an offence for which he has already been finally convicted or acquitted in accordance with the law and penal procedure in each country.'

The principle thus stated is a familiar one in both common and civil law systems – in the former as the rule against double jeopardy, in the latter as the

---

[48] [1991] ILRM 454.
[49] At 458.
[50] Costello J cites, *inter alia*, Article 11 of the UN Universal Declaration of Human Rights and Article 6(2) of the European Convention on Human Rights.
[51] Costello J refers to the European Human Rights Commission's decision in *X v UK*. Application No. 5124/71, *Collection of Decisions ECHR* 135. See, too, the decision of the European Court of Human Rights in *Salabiaku v France* (1991) 13 EHRR 379.

principle of *non bis in idem*. Curiously, however, it does not find explicit mention in the European Convention on Human Rights.[52]

Like the presumption of innocence, the rule against double jeopardy has long been recognized in Irish criminal procedure. And like that presumption it may now have attained constitutional status, though we lack clear authority to this effect. But there would seem to be little difficulty in holding the rule to be included in the constitutional concepts of trial in due course of law and of fairness in criminal procedures. Indeed the Spanish *Tribunal Constitucional* has held the *non bis in idem* principle to be *implicitly* enshrined in the 1978 Constitution.[53]

If now constitutionally enshrined the rule would certainly place restrictions on the power of the *Oireachtas* to regulate criminal procedure. These restrictions, however, would probably not include a bar on prosecution appeals against acquittals. The Supreme Court has held that an appeal lies to it from a Central Criminal Court acquittal,[54] and it could presumably order a retrial if it found the verdict flawed.[55] Of course, this appellate jurisdiction is derived from the specific constitutional provisions defining the competences of the Supreme Court.[56] But it has not been suggested that there is any constitutional impediment to the *Oireachtas* legislating for other appeals against acquittals. Certainly the rule against double jeopardy – even if constitutionalized – would not prevent this being done.[57]

The Constitution's separation of powers doctrine also provides some protection against double jeopardy.[58] In *Costello v DPP and Attorney General*[59] the Supreme Court struck down section 62 of the Courts of Justice Act 1936, which allowed the DPP, on a District Justice's refusing to send an accused forward for trial, himself to direct a return for trial. The court, *per* O'Higgins CJ, held that in conducting the preliminary examination of an indictable offence a District Judge was exercising the judicial power of the State. When, in the exercise of such judicial power, there was a determination of the relevant justiciable issues, that determination could not be set aside or reversed by any

---

[52] See further, Fawcett *The Application of the European Convention on Human Rights* (Oxford, 1987), p. 201.

[53] See STC 2/1981, de 30 de enero, BJC–2, p. 119; STC 94/1986, de 8 de julio, BJC 1986–63, p. 870.

[54] *People (Attorney General) v Conmey* [1975] IR 341: *People (DPP) v O'Shea* [1982] IR 384.

[55] This issue, oddly, still awaits resolution: see *People (DPP) v Quilligan (No. 2)* [1989] IR 46.

[56] In particular Article 34.4.3.

[57] Certainly so far as *directed* acquittals are concerned, for then the accused has not been in jeopardy: see *O'Shea's* case [1982] IR 384, *per* O'Higgins CJ at 406–407.

[58] And not only in respect of fresh criminal proceedings. In *McGrath v Commissioner, Garda Síochána* [1990] ILRM 5 the applicant – a *Garda* – had been acquitted in the Circuit Court on three counts of embezzlement. Subsequently, disciplinary proceedings were commenced against him under the *Garda Síochána* (Discipline) Regulations 1971 (SI No. 316 of 1971), alleging three instances of corrupt or improper practice. These related to the same sums of money as were involved in the embezzlement charges. Lynch J prohibited the disciplinary inquiry from examining these charges, on the ground that in attributing corruption or dishonesty to the applicant they contradicted the jury's verdict at the trial. These issues had been determined by the courts appointed under the Constitution for the determination of such matters and it was not now open to the inquiry to investigate them.

[59] [1984] IR 436.

other authority. Since section 62 authorized an executive interference in the judicial domain it was inconsistent with the Constitution.[60]

Punishment

Prima facie it is for the legislature to prescribe the penalties that will attach to criminal offences, and it will clearly enjoy a large measure of discretion in this regard. But that its power is not without limit is demonstrated by the recent Supreme Court decision in *Cox v Ireland and Attorney General*.[61] In this case the plaintiff, a community school teacher, had in February 1988 been convicted by the Special Criminal Court of a scheduled offence under the Offences against the State Act 1939. He was sentenced to two years' imprisonment which, with remission, he duly served. The school board was prepared to re-employ him from September 1989 but was informed that section 34 of the 1939 Act prevented this. This provision applied only to persons convicted in the Special Criminal Court of scheduled offences under the 1939 Act and stipulated that, in addition to any punishment imposed by that court, they should suffer certain forfeitures and disqualifications. Thus they would immediately forfeit any post remunerated from public funds and any pension payable out of such funds. They would also be disqualified for seven years from holding any post remunerated out of public funds, and – in perpetuity – from receiving any pension or gratuity payable therefrom. The Supreme Court held section 34 unconstitutional, effectively recognizing a principle of proportionality in the fixing of criminal punishments. To protect public peace and order and maintain its own authority, said the court, the State was entitled to impose onerous penalties as a deterrent to the commission of crimes. But in pursuing these objectives it must, as far as practicable, continue to protect citizens' constitutional rights. On analysis, section 34 constituted a failure of such protection not warranted by the objectives sought to be achieved.[62]

It seems unlikely that many statutory provisions will fall victim to the proportionality principle implicit in *Cox's* case. But the recognition of that principle may provide constitutional security against the legislature's being stampeded by public opinion into prescribing absurdly tough penalties for relatively innocuous offences.[63]

---

[60] This does not invalidate section 18 of the Criminal Procedure Act 1967, under which the DPP may substitute or add charges founded upon the material considered by the District Court: *O'Shea v DPP and Attorney General* [1989] ILRM 309 and *Walsh v President of the Circuit Court* [1989] ILRM 325.

[61] Unreported, Supreme Court (No. 361/90), 11 July 1991.

[62] The court reached this conclusion on a combination of grounds: (*a*) that section 34 *prima facie* constituted an attack on the constitutional right to earn a livelihood, and on constitutionally protected property rights such as those to a pension, gratuity, etc already earned: (*b*) it applied only to scheduled offences – but these varied in seriousness, some carrying only a maximum fine of £IR25: (*c*) the mandatory nature of its forfeiture provisions took no account of individual motive: (*d*) they applied *only* to a conviction in the Special Criminal Court, and whether or not the accused appeared in that court depended upon an executive decision by the Director of Public Prosecutions.

[63] The French *Conseil Constitutionnel* has given constitutional status to the principle that sanctions should be proportionate to the offences to which they are attached. See Poullain, *op cit*. note 10, p. 253.

19 Administrative Law Remedies under Chief Justice O'Higgins

Anthony M. Collins

The rule of law requires that every person injured by the actions of the State or its servants has access to an effective remedy. This article highlights Chief Justice O'Higgins' contribution to the development of this process during his judicial career in Ireland. It will be contended that, whilst he may at times have failed to convince a majority of his Supreme Court colleagues, his views on Irish administrative remedies have generally come to be accepted as the law.

The Constitution and administrative law remedies

We may begin with *State (Healy) v Donoghue*.[1] On 15 January 1975 the applicant, then 18 years of age, was convicted on charges of breaking and entering and stealing certain property without being informed of his right to apply for legal aid under the Criminal Justice (Legal Aid) Act 1962.[2] On 29 January 1975 he was also tried and convicted on a separate charge of larceny. Whilst on the latter occasion he had been assigned a solicitor under the 1962 Act, at the date of his trial the solicitors who had operated the scheme had withdrawn their services. The applicant sought to have conditional orders of *certiorari* and *habeas corpus* in respect of both convictions made absolute.

Although the scope of the courts' powers of review on an application for *habeas corpus* had been laid down some two years earlier in *State (Royle) v Kelly*,[3] the position was considerably less certain as concerned applications for *certiorari*. Here counsel for the respondents submitted, *inter alia*, that in making his second order, the District Justice had acted within jurisdiction and accordingly his order could not be quashed on an application for *certiorari*.[4]

In the High Court Gannon J had pointed out that:

'the determination of the question of whether or not a court of local and limited jurisdiction is acting within its jurisdiction is not confined to an examination of the statutory limits or jurisdiction imposed on the court . . . this question involves also

[1] [1976] IR 325; 110 ILTR 9; 112 ILTR 37.
[2] No 12 of 1962.
[3] [1974] IR 259 at 267–8 per Walsh J.
[4] [1976] IR 325 at 359 per Griffin J. It would appear that this argument was also made in the High Court: see *dicta* of Gannon J at 333.

203

an examination of whether or not the court is performing the basic function for which it is established – the administration of justice. Even if all the formalities of the statutory limitation of the court be complied with and if the court procedures are formally satisfied, it is my opinion that the court in such instance is not acting within its jurisdiction if, at the same time, the person accused is deprived of any of his basic rights of justice at a criminal trial'[5]

Gannon J was thus prepared to accede to the application to quash the second conviction on the basis that the respondent District Justice had entered upon the trial of the applicant after it had been considered in the interests of justice that he should have had access to professional assistance and, in so doing had exceeded his jurisdiction.[6] However he refused the first application on the ground that neither the 1962 Act nor the Constitution created a right in an accused person to be informed of the availability of criminal legal aid.[7]

The Supreme Court unanimously upheld the first but reversed the second finding. Chief Justice O'Higgins noted that the Constitution did not seek to impose for all time the interpretation favoured in 1937 of the ideas of charity, prudence and justice set out in the preamble. In considering how these ideas would be applied in the second half of the twentieth century, he held that,

'[i]t is justice which is to be administered in the Courts and this concept of justice must import not only fairness, and fair procedures, but also regard to the dignity of the individual. No court under the Constitution has jurisdiction to act contrary to justice',

before going on to concur with the above cited passage from the judgment of Gannon J.[8] In so finding Chief Justice O'Higgins placed the concept of justice, as protected by the Constitution, in a position superior to statute or the common law. Where a court or tribunal, in the course of acting within its jurisdiction, offends against this principle, it will be deemed to have exceeded its remit and its orders become amenable to be quashed by way of *certiorari*.[9]

It may be said that this decision merely restates the well-established principle that *certiorari* will issue where the High Court is satisfied that the essentials of justice have been disregarded.[10] But apart altogether from setting this principle in a modern context, which is evidenced by both the frequency with which this decision is cited in court and the variety of circumstances in which it has been applied: where an applicant's solicitor was denied the opportunity of properly cross-examining the arresting guard;[11] to prevent the Director of

---

[5] [1976] IR 325 at 333.
[6] [1976] IR 325 at 340–1.
[7] [1974] IR 325 at 339–40.
[8] [1976] IR 325 at 348–9.
[9] See also Kenny J at 364, where he held that:
  'If the High Court comes to the conclusion that the trial was not fair, it should grant *certiorari*. The cases in which this state-side order may be granted cannot, and should not, be limited by reference to any formula or final statement of principle. The strength of this great remedy is its flexibility'.
[10] See O'Connor *The Irish Justice of the Peace* 2nd edn, (Dublin, 1915), vol. I, at pp. 330–1.
[11] *Gill v Connellan*, [1988] ILRM 448 at 454–5 per Lynch J, where *State (Healy) v Donoghue* was expressly followed.

Public Prosecutions from proceeding with charges where the prosecuting authorities innocently disposed of evidence before a criminal trial;[12] where a District Justice refused to grant an accused person an adjournment to permit him to obtain legal representation;[13] where a District Justice permitted the prosecution to adduce aditional evidence the day after he had informed counsel that he would only announce his judgment;[14] the seminal contribution of *State (Healy) v Donoghue* was to put administrative law remedies at the service of those wishing to vindicate their rights under the Constitution.

For a remedy to be effective, access thereto should not be denied by the operation of technical rules. Albeit indirectly, *State (Healy) v Donoghue* provided the rationale for the decision in *State (Holland) v Kennedy* which appears to mark the end of the distinction between errors of law falling within jurisdiction and errors of law going to the jurisdiction of the court at Irish administrative law.[15] Here a 15 year old applicant pleaded guilty to occasioning an unprovoked assault upon a bystander. On the strength of the evidence of the assault, the respondent certified that the applicant was of so unruly a character that he could not be detained in a place of detention under Part V of the Children Act 1908,[16] and proceeded to sentence him to one month's imprisonment. The applicant sought to quash the respondent's order. Counsel for the respondent argued that since the order was good on its face and any error made fell within the jurisdiction of the courts, the applicant's remedy was by way of appeal and not by way of *certiorari*. As Henchy J, with whom Chief Justice O'Higgins agreed, held,

'. . . it does not necessarily follow that a court or a tribunal, vested with powers of a judicial nature, which commenced a hearing within jurisdiction will be treated as continuing to act within jurisdiction. For any one of a number of reasons it may exceed jurisdiction and thereby make its decisions liable to be quashed on *certiorari*. For instance, it may fall into an unconstitutinality, or it may breach the bounds of natural justice, or it may fail to stay within the bounds of the jurisdiction conferred on it by statute. It is an error of the latter kind that prevents the impugned order in this case from being held to have been made within jurisdiction.'[17]

The use of administrative law remedies to uphold rights protected by the Constitution was taken a step further in *State (Lynch) v Cooney*.[18] There the applicant sought to have quashed an order[19] made by the respondent under section 31(1) of the Broadcasting Authority Act 1960,[20] *inter alia*, on the

---

[12] *Murphy v Director of Public Prosecutions* [1989] ILRM 71.

[13] *Flynn v Ruane* [1989] ILRM 690.

[14] *Dawson v Hamill* [1990] ILRM 257.

[15] [1977] IR 193. It should be noted that since neither *Anisminic Ltd v Foreign Compensation Commission* [1969] 2 AC 147, [1969] 2 WLR 163; [1969] 1 All ER 208, nor *State (Healy) v Donoghue* appear to have been cited either in the High or the Supreme Courts. See *State (Cork County Council) v Fawcitt* (High Court, 13 March 1981, McMahon J; Hogan & Morgan *Administrative Law in Ireland* (London, 1991), at pp. 345–54; Collins & O'Reilly *Civil Proceedings and the State in Ireland: a Practitioner's Guide* (Dublin, 1990), at para. 4.3.

[16] 8 Ed VIII, c. 67.

[17] [1977] IR 193 at 201.

[18] [1982] IR 337.

[19] Broadcasting Authority Act 1960 (Section 31) (No 2) Order 1982 (SI No 21).

[20] No 10 of 1960. Section 31(1) was itself inserted by section 16 of the Broadcasting Authority (Amendment) Act 1976 (No 37 of 1976).

grounds of its incompatibility with the Constitution. The respondents contended that an application for *certiorari* was not an appropriate procedure by which to challenge the constitutional validity of an Act of the *Oireachtas*.[21] In his judgment Chief Justice O'Higgins held as follows,

> '. . . the prosecutor . . . sought to challenge the validity of the order of which he complains both on the basis of the Minister's power to make it and, alternatively, on the alleged invalidity of the section under which the Minister purported to act. In so doing the prosecutor has used to the utmost limit the quick and effective remedy of *certiorari* in the face of an illegality. . . . While it might be preferable to have questions concerning the constitutionality of legislation dealt with by declaratory action in which the High Court, and this Court on appeal, could have the benefit of pleadings and, where necessary, submissions, I can see no real objection to the course adopted by the prosecutor. From his point of view the securing of the relief was of the utmost urgency and he could not, justly, be restricted to seeking it on grounds which did not contemplate the invalidity of the enabling section. It was on the basis of similar claims for State Side relief that questions of validity of legislation have been decided by the High Court and this Court in the past: see *State (Burke) v Lennon* and *State (Nicolaou) v An Bord Uchtála*. In my view, therefore, the procedure adopted by the prosecutor in these circumstanes is correct and entitles him to question the validity not only of the order of which he complains but also of the section under which it is made.'[22]

State (Burke) v Lennon[23] was an application for an order of *habeas corpus* and no point was taken as to whether the constitutionality of the applicant's detention could be challenged by way of *certiorari*. Not only has a court hearing an application for *habes corpus* a wider scope for review than upon the hearing of an application for *certiorari*,[24] but since *State (Burke) v Lennon* a specific procedure was provided for where an applicant wishes to challenge the constitutionality of post-1937 legislation in the course of the hearing of an application for *habeas corpus*.[25]

In *State (Nicolaou) v An Bord Uchtála*[26] Murnaghan J expressly refused to make a conditional order of *certiorari* on the ground that the order challenged in the proceedings had been made on the basis of an allegedly unconstitutional act. In his view, the constitutional question could be more conveniently decided in a substantive action on notice to the necessary parties.[27] On appeal the Supreme Court reversed this decision, without giving reasons.[28]

State (Lynch) v Cooney thus definitively settled this point. In contrast with the position in plenary proceedings, in applications for judicial review evidence is

---

[21] This is expressed very clearly by Walsh J at [1982] IR 373.
[22] [1982] IR 337 at 363. Griffin & Hederman JJ concurred in the whole of the Chief Justice's judgment, as did Walsh J at 373–4.
[23] [1940] IR 136.
[24] See Collins & O'Reilly op. cit., at para. 3.2.
[25] Constitution of Ireland, Art. 40.4.3. See Collins & O'Reilly op. cit., at para.3.18.
[26] [1966] IR 567.
[27] [1966] IR 567 at 572.
[28] [1966] IR 567 at 574.

heard on affidavit,[29] and time limits adhered to more strictly.[30] It is instructive to contrast the flexible approach adopted by the Supreme Court in *State (Lynch) v Cooney*, with that followed by the House of Lords in *O'Reilly v Mackman*.[31] In the latter case it was held that since all the remedies for the infringement of rights protected by public law could be obtained on an application for judicial review, it would be contrary to public policy and an abuse of process to allow a person to proceed by way of plenary proceedings in order to establish that a decision of a public authority infringed rights protected at public law. If followed in Ireland, *O'Reilly v Mackman* would require all persons wishing to uphold their constitutional rights in circumstances governed by public or administrative law to commence proceedings by way of judicial review. It was always unlikely that *O'Reilly v Mackman* would find favour with the Irish courts[32] and this was confirmed by Costello J in *O'Donnell v Corporation of Dún Laoghaire*.[33]

Thus the boundaries of the remedy of *certiorari*, and by extension that of prohibition,[34] were expanded to permit the courts to scrutinise all decisions of bodies subject to judicial review where such decisions were founded wholly or partially upon an error of law, including a failure to uphold constitutionally protected rights.[35] The process which culminated in *State (Lynch) v Cooney*, coupled with the amendments to the Rules of the Superior Courts introduced in 1986,[36] ensure that administrative remedies constitute a well oiled rifle in the arsenal of the constitutional lawyer.

Availability of administrative law remedies

This is not to say that the reach of administrative law remedies has been expanded to the point that they are available in every circumstance where a party apprehends an infringement of his or her constitutional rights. In *State (Abenglen Properties Ltd) v Dublin Corporation*, after tracing the development of and basis for the remedy of *certiorari*, Chief Justice O'Higgins defined its scope as follows:

> 'it is the great remedy available to citizens, on application to the High Court, when any body or tribunal (be it a court or otherwise), having legal authority to affect

---

[29] Contrast Lord Diplock's comment in *O'Reilly v Mackman* [1983] 2 AC 237 at 282–3, where he stated that 'The facts . . . can seldom be a matter of relevant dispute upon an application for judicial review' with the difficulties which arose in finding the facts in *State (Nicolaou) v An Bord Uchtála* [1966] IR 567.

[30] During the hearing in the High Court in *State (Nicolaou) v An Bord Uchtála* a difficulty arose as to the absence of a statement of the grounds upon which it was alleged the order was unconstitutional (see [1966] IR 567 at 589 per Murnaghan J). The report does not indicate why reliance was not placed upon Order 60 of the Rules of the Superior Courts 1962.

[31] [1983] 2 AC 237; [1983] 3 WLR 1096; [1982] 3 All ER 1124.

[32] See *Collins & O'Reilly* op. cit., at para. 4.14.

[33] [1991] ILRM 301 at 311–5.

[34] Hogan & Morgan op. cit., observe at p. 568 that 'There is no real difference in principle between the two remedies, save that prohibition may be invoked at an earlier stage. The difference is thus almost exclusively one of tense.'

[35] Whilst an infringement of the constitutional right to fair procedures may appear at first sight to be a violation of a procedural right, viewed from a constitutional perspective it must be regarded as a violation of a substantive right.

[36] See in particular Order 84, rules 18(2) & 19, permitting applications for declaratory and injunctive relief to be made and combined with applications for state side orders by way of judicial review.

their rights and having a duty to act judicially in accordance with the law and the Constitution, acts in excess of legal authority or contrary to its duty. Despite this development and extension, however, *certiorari* still retains its essential features. Its purpose is to supervise the exercise of jurisdiction by such bodies or tribunals and to control any usurpation or action in excess of jurisdiction. It is not available to correct errors or to review decisions or to make the High Court a court of appeal from the decisions complained of. In addition it remains a discretionary remedy.'[37]

In a system governed by precedent, authoritative statements of the law are always welcome. The courts have, in general, remained faithful to this definition, although not without some deviations. In *Murphy v Turf Club*[38] the High Court refused an application by way of judicial review which sought to challenge the respondent's determination to revoke the applicant's licence as a racehorse trainer on the ground that the matter was governed by a private contract between the parties. Whilst in both *Quirke v Bord Luthchleas na hÉireann*[39] and *O'Neill v Beaumont Hospital Board*[40] judicial review was granted in analogous circumstances, the point was not argued in the first case and was expressly conceded by the respondent in the second.[41] In *O'Neill v Iarnród Éireann*,[42] the Supreme Court has indicated that such doubts as may exist will soon be dissipated. In allowing the appliant's appeal against the refusal of the High Court to grant leave to apply for judicial review on the ground that the issue should only be decided after full argument, the weight of opinion expressed clearly seemed to favour the proposition that relief by way of judicial review,

'. . . lies only against public authorities in respect of the duties conferred upon them by law. It does not apply in matters between private persons whose relationship arises from contract.'[43]

The scope of judicial discretion

The exercise of the jurisdiction to make an order of *certiorari* demanded the attention of the Supreme Court in *State (Abenglen Properties Ltd) v Dublin Corporation*.[44] On 6 October 1980 the applicants,[45] a firm of property developers, applied to obtain outline planning permission for a site at Percy Place, Dublin under section 26 of the Local Government (Planning & Development) Act 1963,[46] as amended by the Local Government (Planning &

---

[37] [1984] IR 381 at 392.
[38] [1989] IR 172.
[39] [1988] IR 83.
[40] [1990] ILRM 419.
[41] [1990] ILRM 419 at 437 per Finlay CJ. See also *Ryan v VIP Taxi Co-Operative Ltd* Irish Times Law Report, 10 April 1989.
[42] [1991] ILRM 129.
[43] [1991] ILRM 129 at 133 per Hederman J. Although he dissented from the decision to grant leave to apply, his views on this issue reflected the views of the majority of the court.
[44] [1984] IR 381.
[45] Although Abenglen Properties Ltd are described in the text of the judgments as the prosecutors, the word applicants is used in compliance with the changes introduced by Order 84 of the Rules of the Superior Courts 1986 (SI No 15).
[46] No 28 of 1963.

Development) Act 1976.[47] Section 26(4) of the 1963 Act provided that where an application is properly made under this section the planning authority must give notice of its decision within a period of two months, beginning on the day on which it receives the application. If it fails to do so, the planning authority is regarded as having granted the permission sought on the last day of the expiry of the two month period.

On 5 December 1980 the respondents granted outline planning permission to the applicants, subject to conditions which had the effect of radically modifying the terms of the original application. On 3 February 1981, the applicants sought to have this decision quashed by way of an order of *certiorari*. The choice of date was not entirely fortuitous. Under section 26(5) of the 1963 Act, the applicants had the right to appeal the respondent's decision to *An Bord Pleanála* provided they did so within one month of its receipt. Section 82(3a) of the 1963 Act laid down a time limit of two months from the date upon which a decision is given in which *certiorari* proceedings challenging the validity of a decision of a planning authority must be commenced.[48]

By acting as they did, the applicants had forfeited their statutory right of appeal. They argued that were they to be successful in their application for *certiorari*, this would entail the nullity of the respondents' decision. In the absence of a decision on the original application, the respondents would be deemed to have decided to grant permission. In the High Court, D'Arcy J held that, notwithstanding the prior existence of an alternative remedy, *certiorari* would issue.

On the hearing of the appeal and cross-appeal, it was argued that an applicant does not become entitled to relief by way of *certiorari* merely by showing that he has been adversely affected by a determination of a body against which such relief may be available. He must also show that his personal or property rights have been effected by the impugned order and that no other equally effective and convenient legal remedy is available to him. The applicants claimed that the mere fact that they had been aggrieved by the respondents' decision entitled them to relief *ex debito justitiae* and that the existence of an alternative remedy had no bearing upon the exercise of the court's discretion.

The kernel of the problem before the Supreme Court was whether, in the circumstances of the case, *certiorari* was available *ex debito justitiae*.[49]

In his judgment Henchy J emphasised that the determination of the planning authority did not exhibit an error of law on its face. In the absence of a failure by the respondents to act in disregard of the requirements of natural justice, *certiorari* would not lie. Griffin J, who was in the majority, did not concur in this aspect of Henchy J's judgment.[50]

---

[47] No 20 of 1976.

[48] The High Court declared this provision to be unconstitutional in *Brady v Donegal County Council* [1989] ILRM 282, which was reversed on appeal to the Supreme Court.

[49] 'That merely means this, in my judgment, that the court in such circumstances will exercise its discretion in granting the relief. In all discretionary remedies it is well known and settled that in certain circumstances – I will not say in all of them, but in a great many of them – the court, although nominally it has a discretion, if it is to act according to the ordinary principles upon which judicial discretion is exercised, must exercise that discretion in a particular way. . .', *R Stafford JJ* [1940] 2 KB 33 at 43 per Sir Wilfrid Greene MR.

[50] [1984] IR 381 at 406. Hederman J concurred with the entirety of Henchy J's judgment.

The majority appear to have distinguished *Abenglen* from *State (Vossa) v Ó Floinn,*[51] upon which the applicants had based their case. In *Vozza,* the applicant, who spoke imperfect English and an Italian *patois,* was charged with attempted larceny. During the course of the hearing in the District Court the respondent amended the charge without either asking the applicant whether he admitted same nor informing him of his right to jury trial. This omission was contrary to the provisions of section 2(2)(*a*)(ii) of the Criminal Justice Act 1951.[52] After his release by order of the Minister for Justice, the applicant sought to have his conviction quashed. The High Court refused to grant relief on the ground that he had disentitled himself by his conduct.[53] The former Supreme Court unanimously reversed the determination of the High Court, holding that the applicant was, in the circumstances of the case entitled to relief *ex debito justitiae.*[54]

In *Abenglen* Henchy J held that the *ratio decidendi* of *Vozza* depended upon the fact that the purpose of the application had been to quash a conviction for a criminal offence. Accordingly,

'. . . the reasoning in the relevant judgments has no bearing on the present case where the decision questioned is that of a planning authority purporting to exercise a civil jurisdiction of an administrative nature relating to the grant or refusal of a development permission. In a case such as the present, the aggrieved person is entitled to *certiorari* only on a discretionary basis.'[55]

Thus a court could always take into account the applicant's conduct and the existence of an alternative remedy in deciding whether to exercise its discretion to grant an order of *certiorari.*[56] Reliance was also placed upon the idea that where the Oireachtas has provided for a given scheme, *certiorari* should not issue when the use of that procedure would have been adequate to dispose of the application.[57]

In a concurring opinion, Walsh J held that the default provisions of the Irish planning legislation had been enacted for the sole purpose of compelling a planning authority to direct its mind to an application. Thus any decision by a planning authority, *ultra vires* or otherwise, would constitute a decision for the purposes of the Planning Acts. Since the making of an order of *certiorari* quashing the responents' decision would be thus of no benefit to the applicants, the court could and should refuse to grant the relief sought. Such views as were expressed by Walsh J on the nature of *certiorari* were therefore *obiter.*[58]

In his judgment, Chief Justice O'Higgins described the nature of the discretion vested in the court as follows:

'This discretion remains unfettered where the applicant for the relief has no real interest in the proceedings and is not a person aggrieved by the decision: . . . Where, however, such applicant has been affected or penalised and is an aggrieved person, it is commonly said that *certiorari* issues *ex debito justitiae*. This should not be taken as

[51] [1957] IR 227.
[52] No 2 of 1951.
[53] [1957] IR 227 at 233 per Davitt P.; at 238–9 per Dixon J.
[54] [1957] IR 227 at 243–4 per Maguire CJ; at 245 per Lavery J; at 250 per Kingsmill Moore J.
[55] [1984] IR 381 at 403.
[56] [1984] IR 381 at 403.
[57] [1984] IR 381 at 403–4.
[58] [1984] IR 381 at 397–8. For criticism of Walsh J's approach, see Hogan, 'Remoulding Certiorari', 17 *Irish Jurist* (n.s.) (1982), 32–58 at pp. 42–44.

meaning that a discretion does not remain in the High Court as to whether to give the relief or to refuse it. There may be exceptional and rare cases where a criminal conviction has been recorded otherwise than in due course of law and the matter cannot be set right except by *certiorari*. In such circumstances the discretion may be exercisable only in favour of quashing: . . . In the vast majority of cases, however, a person whose legal rights have been infringed may be awarded *certiorari ex debito justitiae* if he can establish any of the recognised grounds for quashing: but the court retains a discretion to refuse his application if his conduct has been such as to disentitle him to relief or, I may add, if the relief is not necessary for the protection of those rights.[59] For the court to act otherwise, almost as of course, once an irregularity or defect has been established in the impugned proceedings, would be to debase this great remedy.'[60]

In deciding whether to exercise this discretion, he pointed out that a court should bear in mind,

'. . . all of the circumstances of the case, including the purpose for which *certiorari* has been sought, the adequacy of the alternative remedy and, of course, the conduct of the applicant. If the decision impugned is made without jurisdiction or in breach of natural justice then, normally, the existence of a right of appeal or of a failure to avail of such, should be immaterial. Again, if an appeal can only deal with the merits and not with the question of the jurisdiction involved, the existence of such ought not to be a ground for refusing relief. Other than these, there may be cases where the decision exhibits an error of law and a perfectly simple appeal can rectify the complaint, or where administrative legislation provides adequate appeal machinery which is particularly suitable for dealing with errors in the application of the code in question.[61] In such cases, while retaining always the power to quash, a court should be slow to do so unless satisfied that, for some particular reason, the appeal or alternative remedy is not adequate.'[62]

The view expressed by the majority in *Abenglen* might appear to free the courts from any limits upon the exercise of the jurisdiction to grant relief by way of *certiorari*. It may be argued that a court has such a wide discretion in three specific situations.

(a) Lack of interest

There can be little doubt that the courts retain an unfettered discretion to grant relief where the applicant has no real interest in, and is not a person aggrieved by, the decision challenged in the proceedings. In *State (Toft) v Galway Corporation* two persons outbid the applicant at a public auction and succeeded in purchasing premises at Salthill, Galway. The successful pur-

---

[59] Hogan has described this passage as 'a lucid statement of sound principle.' (see 'Remoulding Certiorari', *Irish Jurist* (n.s.) (1982), at p. 42).

[60] [1984] IR 381 at 393–4.

[61] In drafting Order 84, rule 26(4) of the Rules of the Superior Courts 1986 it was specifically provided that:

'Where the relief sought is an order of *certiorari* and the Court is satisfied that there are grounds for quashing the decision to which the application relates, the Court may, in addition to quashing it, remit the matter to the Court, tribunal or authority concerned with a direction to reconsider it and reach a decision in accordance with the findings of the Court.'

The use of this procedure has become increasingly common: see *Singh v Ruane* [1990] ILRM 62; *Dawson v Hamill* [1990] ILRM 257.

[62] [1984] IR 381 at 393.

chasers established a limited company in whose name the property was to be held. Planning permission was sought, and granted, for the premises, but the company was misdescribed on the face of the planning permission. The applicant sought to have the grant of planning permission quashed on the basis that the company in whose favour it purported to have been made did not exist. Chief Justice O'Higgins held that

> '[i]t is said with justification that *certiorari* issues *ex debito justitiae* where an aggrieved or complaining person can point to his legal rights being affected by the order or decision sought to be annulled. In such circumstances a court will be more concerned with dealing with the irregularity than with the conduct of the prosecutor. In this case, however, the appellant can only point to the inconvenience or disadvantage to him of a similar business to his own being opened in adjoining premises. He can point to no right of his being infringed by the order made by the Galway Corporation.'[63]

(b) Lack of benefit

It would also appear that the courts retain a wide discretion as to whether to grant *certiorari* where the making of such an order would be of no real benefit to the applicant.[64] This line of reasoning could lead to relief being refused where an applicant was charged with an indictable offence, on the grounds that it would always be open to the prosecuting authorities to recommence proceedings against him. There would seem to be two safeguards against such an eventuality. In *State (O'Connell) v Fawsitt* a unanimous Supreme Court held that prohibition would issue to prevent a criminal trial where it had been excessively delayed so as to prejudice the chances of a fair trial.[65] Furthermore, in *Glavin v Governor of the Training Unit, Mountjoy Prison*, where the applicant succeeded in having quashed an order returning him for trial on other grounds, the Supreme Court left open the question as to whether the Director of Public Prosecutions was empowered to take any further steps in the matter.[66]

(c) Availability of an alternative remedy

In *State (Roche) v Delap*[67] Henchy J, speaking for the majority of the Supreme Court, followed *R (Miller) v Monaghan JJ*[68] where he held that it was not open to an applicant to apply for an order of *certiorari* in circumstances where his appeal had already been opened in the Circuit Court. This decision was subsequently applied by O'Hanlon J in *State (Butler) v Ruane*[69] where the appeal had not yet come on for hearing.

Apart from its unusual facts, it may in any case be argued that *State (Roche) v Delap* was decided contrary to persuasive authority. In *State (Cunningham) v Ó Floinn*[70] the former Supreme Court adopted a different approach in circum-

---

[63] [1981] ILRM 439 at 442.
[64] *State (Walsh) v Maguire* [1979] IR 372 at 385–6 per Henchy J. O'Higgins CJ agreed with this part of the judgment (at 378).
[65] [1986] IR 362 at 379.
[66] [1991] ILRM 478 at 496 per Keane J.
[67] [1980] IR 170.
[68] (1906) 40 ILTR 51.
[69] High Court, 5 May 1986.
[70] [1960] IR 198; 95 ILTR 24.

stances where an applicant had taken an appeal from conviction to the Circuit Court. In *State (Glover) v McCarthy* counsel for the respondent relied upon *State (Roche) v Delap* in support of the proposition that where an appeal is pursued simultaneously with an application for *certiorari* the latter remedy would not lie. In granting the relief sought, Gannon J held that

'. . . the principal factor which would guide the court in the exercise of its discretion in a case where the alternatives of *certiorari* and appeal lie in the objective of achieving the just resolution of the matters at issue with nominal inconvenience consistent with regularity of judicial procedures.'[71]

A further distinction was drawn by Carroll J in *State (Wilson) v Neilan*[72] where it was held that an applicant would not be obliged to elect between proceeding by way of appeal or judicial review where the grounds on which the impugned order was challenged went to the jurisdiction of, or want of natural justice in, the proceedings before the trial court. Such a criterion would at least in theory, encompass all cases in which *certiorari* could be granted.[73]

Is *Abenglen* still the law?

In so far as a case does not fall under any one of these three instances it may be asked whether the majority view in *Abenglen* can be taken to represent the law.

The leak in the *Abenglen* dyke first appeared in *State (Furey) v Minister for Defence*.[74] The applicant had been discharged from the Army in August 1985. He sought to challenge this decision by way of *certiorari* in proceedings commenced in October 1979. By a two to one majority, consisting of Chief Justice O'Higgins and McCarthy J,[75] the Supreme Court expressly followed and applied *State (Vozza) v Ó Floinn*, in effect holding that *certiorari* should issue *ex debito justitiae*. In reaching the decision of the majority of the Court, McCarthy J drew an analogy between the applicant and a person convicted of a minor criminal offence.[76] *Furey* has since been applied in *O'Donnell v Dun Laoghaire Corporation*, where notwithstanding his delay, the applicant was permitted to challenge the validity of managerial orders which purported to impose water rates within the Borough of Dún Laoghaire.[77] On these facts no analogy lay with criminal proceedings. *O'Donnell* casts grave doubts over the continued viability of the majority view in *Abenglen*.

Furthermore, it may also be asked whether any court has a discretion to refuse an order of *certiorari* where the order challenged was adopted on the basis of a measure subsequently found to be unconstitutional. In *State (Nicolaou) v An Bord Uchtála* Teevan J conceded that were the constitutional challenge to have succeeded in the High Court, delay would not have been a bar to the grant of

---

[71] [1981] ILRM 47.
[72] [1985] IR 89.
[73] See, for instance, *State (Daly) v Ruane* [1988] ILRM 117 at 124 per O'Hanlon J.
[74] For comment on this decision see Hogan, 'Natural and Constitutional Justice – Adieu to Laissez-Faire', 19 *Irish Jurist* (n.s.) (1984), 309–321 at pp. 309–315.
[75] Griffin J dissented.
[76] [1988] ILRM 88 at 99–100.
[77] [1991] ILRM 301 at 317–8 per Costello J.

relief.[78] If it is true that powers granted under the Constitution cannot be exercised unjustly or unfairly, and that every citizen whose rights may be affected by decisions taken by others has the right to fair and just procedures,[79] it might be argued that a court has no discretion in the matter but rather a positive duty to grant the relief sought in such circumstances.[80]

Further evidence of a judicial slide away from *Abenglen* may also be found in *P & F Sharpe Ltd v Dublin City and County Manager*[81] where *Abenglen* was distinguished, and in *Mythen v Employment Appeals Tribunal*[82] where it was not followed. In the latter case the Employment Appeals tribunal was deemed to have erred as to the extent of its jurisdiction in failing to entertain the applicant's claim. *Certiorari* lay, notwithstanding the existence of an alternative remedy by way of a full re-hearing on appeal to the Circuit Court, with the possibility of a further re-hearing on appeal.[83] It should also be pointed out that in *White v Hussey*[84] and *Connors v Delap*,[85] where the High Court refused to grant relief in circumstances similar to those which arose in *Vozza*, neither *Vozza* nor *Furey* appear to have been cited in argument.[86]

Even assuming that *Furey* and *O'Donnell* represent the law,[87] they do not provide a complete answer to all of the questions raised by *Abenglen*. Particular difficulties arise as regards the temporal effect of a declaration by a court annulling an administrative or judicial decision. If that declaration has the effect of vitiating the decision for all time, are all persons who were affected thereby entitled to seek orders for relief in their individual circumstances? *Furey* appears to open the door to that possibility. On what basis, then, may the courts decide to withhold relief?

The issue arose, but was not conclusively resolved, in *Byrne v Frawley*.[88] The applicants had been tried in the Dublin Circuit Court before a judge and a jury selected in accordance with the provisions of the Juries Act 1927[89] on 10 and 11 November 1975. On 12 November the Supreme Court handed down judgment in *de Burca & Anderson v Attorney General*,[90] which invalidated certain provisions of the 1927 Act. On the resumption of the trial five days later, no application was made by the defence to have the jury discharged, although one of the counsel who appeared for Byrne had also acted for one of the plaintiffs in *de*

---

[78] [1966] IR 567 at 597. Henchy J (at 609) appears to have reserved his position, merely noting that counsel for the Attorney General and the respondent had both conceded the point.

[79] See, for instance, *Garvey v Ireland* [1981] IR 75 at 96–7 per O'Higgins CJ.

[80] It appears that where constitutionally protected rights are at stake, the discretion to grant injunctive relief can only be exercised in favour of upholding the right at issue: see *Society for the Protection of Unborn Children Ireland Ltd v Grogan* [1990] 1 CMLR 689 at 699 per Finlay CJ, 702 per Walsh J; *Attorney-General v X* (High Court, 17 February 1992, Costello J).

[81] [1989] ILRM 565 at 572 per O'Hanlon J (High Court); at 581 per Finlay CJ.

[82] [1989] ILRM 844 at 833 per Barrington J.

[83] By failing to qualify the right to appeal from the Circuit Court, section 10(4) of the Unfair Dismissals Act 1977 (No 10) provides for what must be the most generous, if not extravagant, appeal procedure in Ireland. It is possible to have three full hearings in any given case, apart from the prospect of an appeal to the Supreme Court on disputed issues of law.

[84] [1989] ILRM 109.

[85] [1989] ILRM 93.

[86] For criticism of these cases, see Collins '*Ex Debito justitiae?*', 10 *Dublin University Law Journal* (n.s.) (1988), 130–146.

[87] In the absence of a decision of a full Supreme Court on this point. See the views of McCarthy J in *Doyle v Hearne* [1987] IR 601 at 617.

[88] [1978] IR 326.

[89] No 23 of 1927.

[90] [1976] IR 38.

Burca. The applicant was convicted on a charge of receiving stolen goods[91] and sentenced to seven years penal servitude. In two subsequent applications to the Court of Criminal Appeal no reference was made to the unconstitutional composition of the jury before which he had been tried. However, on 24 May 1976, the applicant sought and obtained a conditional order of *certiorari* on this very ground.

As the 1927 Act came into force prior to the adoption of the 1937 Constitution, any declaration by the courts as to its inconsistency therewith had the consequence of vitiating it as of and from 29 December 1937. Article 50.1 of the Constitution provides as follows,

> 'Subject to this Constitution and to the extent to which they are not inconsistent therewith, the laws in force in *Saorstát Éireann* immediately prior to the date of the coming into operation of this constitution shall continue to be of full force and effect. . . .'

Notwithstanding differences as to the retrospective effect of declarations of nullity upon legislation adopted after 1937, in *Murphy v Attorney General*, the Supreme Court considered that as a consequence of Article 50,

> '[i]n pronouncing the provision of any such law to be inconsistent with the Constitution, a court makes a declaration which can only be a declaration that the law in question was never in force once the Constitution came into operation.'[92]

Whilst in agreement as to the result, in *Byrne* the Supreme Court divided 3 to 2 as to the reasoning behind its decision. Since the 1927 Act had excluded approximately 80% of adult citizens from jury service, Henchy J was of the view that such juries were but a 'simulacrum of the jury postulated by Article 38.5 of the Constitution'.[93] Although the applicant had been the first person entitled to successfully rely upon the unconstitutionality of such a jury in the Circuit Court, notwithstanding the publicity surrounding *de Burca* decision, he had failed to do so. According to Henchy J:

> '[s]uch retrospective acquiescence in the mode of trial and in conviction and its legal consequences would appear to raise an insuperable barrier against a successful challenge at this stage to the validity of such a conviction or sentence.'[94]

In relying upon the views put forward by both himself and Walsh J in *de Burca*, Chief Justice O'Higgins found that as none of the juries constituted under the provisions of the 1927 Act had included persons who were not entitled to be members, the acts and verdicts of those juries could not be subsequently upset. He argued that were this not so,

> '. . . it would seem to me to follow with inexorable logic that each trial held with such a jury would have been a nullity and that sentences imposed and carried out, including sentences of death, would have been a nullity and that sentences imposed

---

[91] Under section 33(1) of the Larceny Act 1916 (6 & 7 Geo. V, c. 60).

[92] [1982] 241 at 297 per O'Higgins CJ. See also Henchy J at 307, Griffin J at 328. Kenny J expressed no view on this issue and Parke J concurred with Henchy & Griffin JJ.

[93] [1978] IR 326 at 348.

[94] [1978] IR 326 at 349. See Casey, 'The Development of Constitutional Law under Chief Justice O'Higgins', 21 *Irish Jurist* (n.s.) (1986) 7 at p. 19.

and carried out, including sentences of death, would have been imposed and carried out without legal authority. . . . Could organised society accept such a conclusion? There being a supposed unconstitutinality in the trial jury itself, neither consent or lack of objection or passage of time could remedy the situation. As a further consequence, this would seem to mean that all those who have been convicted by such juries and are serving sentences would be entitled to orders similar to the order sought by the prosecutor in the present case. It does not seem to me that it could be urged as an answer to such proceedings that the person convicted had acquiesced in his trial by the jury selected. Acquiescence depends on knowledge; if the person convicted did not know of the suggested invalidity, he cannot be said to have acquiesced. In any event acquiesence cannot confer validity, just as consent cannot confer jurisdiction.'[95]

If *Furey* had represented the state of the law at that time, Mr Byrne might have been able to overcome this obstacle. In his judgment, Chief Justice O'Higgins clearly implies that had he reached the same conclusion as his colleagues, Mr Byrne might well have been entitled to his order *ex debito justitiae*.[96]

Conclusion

Irish administrative law is rooted in jurisprudential concepts which often sit uneasily beside those derived from the Constitution. Perhaps understandably, the responsibility of applying these rules to the ever changing conditions of modern life has been entrusted to the judiciary. Thus the administrative law remedies available to the citizen in Ireland are exclusively the product of judicial creativity. From this brief excursus, it is obvious that Chief Justice O'Higgins has made a lasting contribution to this process. It is a particular tribute to both his foresight and his ability to express what the law is that his judgments continue to light the way for Irish lawyers and judges. On the basis of recent developments, it may even come to pass that a future Supreme Court may find Chief Justice O'Higgins's reasoning in *Abenglen* more persuasive than that then supported by the majority of his colleagues.

---

[95] [1978] IR 326 at 341–2.
[96] [1978] IR 326 at 342. See also *Glavin v Governor of the Training Unit, Mountjoy Prison* [1991] ILRM 478, where the grounds on which relief was obtained were raised for the first time over three years after the date of the applicant's trial.

Part 3

The Impact of European Community Law on National Law

20 The Interface between Community Law and National Law: the United Kingdom Experience

David Vaughan and Fergus Randolph

Incorporation of Community law into the United Kingdom national legal order

There was good reason for the founding fathers of the European Community *not* to lay down specific measures for the incorporation of the Treaty provisions into the national legal orders of the different Member States; they would not have been workable. Even in the early days of six Member States, different traditions regarding incorporation of international law into national legal orders existed. When the United Kingdom joined the European Community in 1973, the first of many problems was that under UK legal principles, international treaty provisions formed a different legal order to the provisions in domestic law. In order for those provisions to be effective in the national legal order, domestic legislation had to be enacted. Thus it was that Lord Denning MR stated in *McWhirter v Attorney-General*[1] – a case decided before the *European Communities Act 1972* had been passed by Parliament – that '[e]ven though the Treaty of Rome has been signed, it has no effect, so far as these Courts are concerned, until it is made an Act of Parliament. Once it is implemented by an Act of Parliament, these Courts must go by the Act of Parliament.'

The Act of Parliament which incorporated the Community treaties into UK domestic law was the *European Communities Act 1972* and it came into force on 1 January 1973. By coming into force on that date, the United Kingdom complied with its obligations under the Treaty of Accession and the Act annexed to it. Article 2 of the Accession Treaty provided that the Treaty should enter into force on 1 January 1973, whilst Article 2 of the Act of Accession provided that '[f]rom the date of accession, the provisions of the original Treaties and the acts adopted by the institutions of the Communities shall be binding on the new Member States and shall apply in those States under the conditions laid down in those Treaties and in this Act.' – the so-called '*acquis communautaire*' provision.

---

[1] [1972] CMLR 882 at 886.

European Communities Act 1972

The European Communities Act 1972 ('The 1972 Act') is by and large a statute replete with technical matters[2] which need not interest us here. However, two sections of the 1972 Act are extremely critical to the incorporation and development of Community law within the United Kingdom.

Section 2 of the 1972 Act is entitled 'General Implementation of Treaties'. Section 2(1) makes provision for enforceable Community rights which are to be given legal effect in the United Kingdom without further enactment. Section 2(1) provides that '[a]ll such rights, powers, liabilities, obligations and restrictions from time to time created or arising by or under the Treaties, and all such remedies and procedures from time to time provided for by or under the Treaties, as in accordance with the Treaties are *without further enactment* to be given legal effect or used in the United Kingdom shall be recognised and available in law, and be enforced, allowed and followed accordingly; and the expression 'enforceable Community right' and similar expressions shall be read as referring to one to which this sub-section applies.' (emphasis added).

Through this provision, the courts in the United Kingdom have been able and indeed willing to apply directly effective provisions of Community law to the exclusion of conflicting national provisions. The problems confronting the courts have tended to relate to what constitutes an enforceable Community right; once this has been decided, there has been little difficulty in applying that enforceable right.

Section 2(4) of the 1972 Act requires the courts in the United Kingdom to give full effect, in their interpretation of present and future statutes, to the provisions of section 2, including those in section 2(1). Section 2(4) provides that '. . . any such provision (of any such extent) as might be made by Act of Parliament, *and any enactment passed or to be passed*, other than one contained in this Part of this Act, shall be construed and have effect subject to the foregoing provisions of this section . . .' [emphasis added].[3]

Section 3 of the 1972 Act is entitled 'Decisions on, and proof of, Treaties and Community instruments etc.' This section provides for the treatment and proof of the Treaties and Community instruments in legal proceedings within the United Kingdom. Questions as to their validity, meaning and effect are to be determined in accordance with the jurisprudence of the European Court of Justice thus.

Section 3(1) provides that

'[f]or the purposes of all legal proceedings any question as to the meaning or effect of any of the Treaties, or as to the validity, meaning or effect of any Community instrument, shall be treated as a question of law (and, if not referred to the European Court, be for determination as such in accordance with the principles laid down by and any relevant decision of the European Court).'

---

[2] They include amendments to the existing law on such diverse matters as customs duties (s 5), agriculture (s 6), sugar (s 7), cinematograph films (s 8), companies (s 9) and provisions relating to Community offences (s 11).

[3] As Lord Bridge stated in *R v Secretary of State for Transport, ex parte Factortame Limited* [1990] 2 AC 85 (HL No. 1), this has exactly the same effect as if a section were to be incorporated in all Acts of Parliament, which in terms enacted that the provisions of the Act are to be without prejudice to the directly enforceable Community rights of nationals of any Member State of the EEC (at page 140).

Section 3(2) provides that

'[j]udicial notice shall be taken of the Treaties, of the Official Journal of the Communities and of any decision of, or expression of opinion by the European Court on any such question as aforesaid; and the Official Journal shall be admissible as evidence of any instrument or other act thereby communicated of any of the Communities or of any Community institution.'

Direct effect of directives

As mentioned above, the main problem confronting the national courts in the context of the relationship between Community law and national law has been identifying the enforceable Community rights upon which individuals in a national forum can rely. Many Articles of the EEC Treaty, for example, provide for rights and obligations which must be capable of enforcement at the national level by the local judiciary. But the most startling progress has come from a direction which 30 or even 25 years ago would have been entirely unthinkable – the implementation of directives into national law. It could be thought from the wording of the EEC Treaty that directives were not intended to have direct effect; they were clearly differentiated from their then more powerful cousins, regulations. Directives were, and still are, only binding as to the results to be achieved; the Member States have the choice of form and methods by which the measure is to enter into the national law. From the start, the directive was clearly conceived as a compromise legislative form, useful when there was not sufficient consensus at the Community level for a regulation to be adopted, with all the powers inherent therein. For this reason, the directive was a useful tool which became increasingly important as time went by. Think of Value Added Tax law without the Sixth Directive, the financial service sector without its relevant directives and the whole Single Market initiative without the plethora of harmonising measures, all contained in directives.

The growing use of the directive as an instrument for important legislative change led the European Court of Justice to take into account this increasingly important legislative form in a radical, but entirely rational way. If directives were being used to a greater extent to alter the legislative landscape, it would be inequitable to deny rights to those affected by the directives. This is but one of the examples of the European Court of Justice using its inherent rights as a 'supreme court' to mould Community law according to present-day reality. Given the fact that direct effect is an extremely powerful tool, it is not surprising that the Court moved slowly at first. However, the important point to note at the start is that the impetus towards direct effect for directives came from individuals in the Member States seeking to rely upon certain measures contained in directives. The Court was thus reacting to a growing conviction in the Community that individuals should be entitled to rely upon measures encapsulated in a legislative form which was increasingly being used.

The Court first held that an individual could rely on a right contained in a Directive in 1974: Case 41/74, *Van Duyn v Home Office*.[4] However, the issue was first specifically raised in a judgment of the Court in Case 33/70, *Spa SACE v*

[4] [1974] ECR 1337.

Ministry for Finance of the Italian Republic,[5] which was summarised in the headnote to the case as follows:

> 'A directive, the object of which is to impose on a Member State a final date for the performance of a Community obligation does not concern solely the relations between the Commission and that State, but also entails legal consequences of which both the other Member States concerned in its performance and individuals may avail themselves when, by its very nature, the provision establishing this obligation is directly applicable.'

It is interesting to note that within a year of its accession to the Community, the United Kingdom, albeit unwillingly on the facts, led the Court of Justice to decide on a preliminary reference that measures in directives could be directly effective. The Court has progressed steadily from that date laying down various principles which should apply to the question. For example, directives are not capable of being directly effective until after the date they should be applied by the Member States;[6] individual provisions of a directive may have direct effect, even where other provisions may not;[7] individuals may rely on a directive as against the State, whether acting as employer or public authority,[8] but not as against other individuals.

However, the European Court of Justice has gone further. Where the question of direct effect does not arise, the national court must still interpret the national law implementing the directive in question in conformity with the terms of that directive.[9] This has recently been given added piquancy by a decision of the European Court, in which it was expressly stated that all legislation, including legislation adopted prior to the directive in question, must be interpreted so as to be in conformity with the directive.[10] This will have interesting repercussions in the United Kingdom, where the courts have to date accepted the principle of interpretation (even interpretation contrary to the specific words) of national law so as to be in conformity with a directive but only insofar as those national measures which implemented the particular directive in question are concerned.[11] The House of Lords has refused to carry out this process of interpretation with regard to national legislation enacted before the adoption of a particular directive.[12] This refusal was based on the fact that a British statute would be distorted if it were to be interpreted to be in conformity with the terms of a directive, which directive the statute was not passed to implement. It will be interesting to see how far the United Kingdom

---

[5] [1970] ECR 1213.
[6] Case 148/78, *Publico Ministero v Ratti* [1979] ECR 1629.
[7] Case 8/81, *Becker v Finanzamt Munster Innenstadt* [1982] ECR 53.
[8] Case 152/84, *Marshall v Southampton and South West Hampshire Area Health Authority* [1986] ECR 723; Case 22/84, *Johnston v Chief Constable of the Royal Ulster Constabulary* [1986] ECR 1651; Case 188/89, *Foster and Others v British Gas plc* of 12 July 1990.
[9] Case 14/83, *Von Colson and Kamann v Land Nordrhein-Westfalen* [1984] ECR 1891.
[10] Case 106/89, *Marleasing SA v La Commercial Internacional de Alimentacion SA* judgment of 13 November 1990. See now Joined Cases 6/90 and 9/90, *Francovich and Bonifaci and Others v Italy* judgment of 19 November 1991, on the responsibility of a Member State in damages for failure to implement a directive into national law.
[11] *Pickstone v Freemans* [1989] 3 CMLR 221; *Lister v Forth Dry Dock & Engineering Co Ltd* [1989] 2 CMLR 194.
[12] *Duke v GEC Reliance* [1988] 1 All ER 626; it is now almost certainly inconsistent with *Marleasing* (*supra*).

courts are prepared to use the tool of interpretation to ensure national law complies with Community law.

A very recent decision of the European Court has taken the role of the directive one step further. In Joined Cases 6/90 and 9/90, *Francovich and Bonifaci and Others v Italy*,[13] the European Court of Justice held that even where the provisions of a directive were found not to be directly effective, if a Member State had failed to implement the directive in time pursuant to Article 189 of the EC Treaty, an individual affected by this lack of implementation could bring an action for damages against the Member State in question. The Court found that this liability of the Member States was dependant on three criteria:

(a) the implementation of the provisions of the directive had to have the effect of granting rights to individuals; and

(b) these rights had to be capable of being identified from the provisions of the directive; and that

(c) there was a causal link between the breach of the Member State's obligation and the damage caused to the individual in question.

This decision clearly strengthens the hand of the Community and its institutions as against Member States with respect to the latter's Treaty obligations, in particular the implementation of the provisions of directives into domestic law. However, it also avoids all the problems of horizontal direct effect, whereby the provisions of directives were not deemed to be capable of direct effect as between individuals. This decision offers a neat solution to individuals who are unable to rely on the provisions of a directive for one reason or another and where the relevant Member State has failed to implement those provisions. Where the Member State has implemented the provisions of a directive, the individual can of course then rely on them *qua* domestic provisions.

Application of Community law within the United Kingdom

Thus far, we have examined the tools which are at the disposal of the national courts, and with regard to the 1972 Act, at the disposal of the English courts necessary for the implementation of Community law into the national legal systems. The following section looks at the progress achieved by the English courts in different areas using the tools described above. One point above all becomes clear in this section – the adaptability and versatility of the English courts in their application of Community law.

Substantive law

Two cases, which have recently been making headlines, not only in the legal press, are good illustrations of how versatile and adaptable the English courts have become in their dealings with Community law.

The first case is that of *R v Secretary of State for Transport, ex parte Factortame Limited and Others*.[14] After the European Court of Justice ruled on the preliminary reference from the House of Lords, it was declared that 'EC rewrites

---

[13] Judgment of 19 November 1991.

[14] Case 213/89, judgment of the Court of 19 June 1990; judgment of 25 July 1991; [1990] 2 AC 85 and [1990] 3 WLR 818.

British constitution'.[15] Needless to say, the judgment had not done that – it had simply brought out into the open certain basic principles of Community law which had been established over a long period of time.[16] It was the fact that supremacy of Community law over domestic law was so clearly demonstrated by the overturning of a domestic rule relating to interim relief, which shocked the establishment. This 'procedural' aspect was rightly seized upon as being the most interesting part of the case, leading as it did to the doing away of the presumption that legislation was *intra vires* until otherwise proven and the immunity of the Crown from interim relief.

The substantive issue in the case concerned UK measures designed to avoid so-called quota hopping by fishing vessels, contained in the Merchant Shipping Act 1988 and the Merchant Shipping (Registration of Fishing Vessels) *Regulations* 1988. The Court held that although Member States were entitled to determine the criteria by which shipping vessels could be registered and flagged within their jurisdiction, those criteria had to be compatible with Community law.

The second case, or rather series of cases, concerns section 47 of the Shops Act 1950, the effect of which is to restrict shop trading on Sundays. There is considerable confusion over the law as it stands at present. However, in one case,[17] the European Court of Justice decided, on reference from the Cwmbran Magistrates' Court, that, in order to be compatible with Community law, any national rules prohibiting retailers from opening their premises on a Sunday had to be proportionate to the aim of those rules. Even without the subsequent cases of *Union Departmentale des Syndicats CGT de l'Aisne v SIDEF Conforama and Others*[18] and *Ministere Public v Marchandise, Chapuis and Trafitex SA,*[19] the application of the principle of proportionality has given rise to considerable difficulties. In particular, Mr Justice Hoffman in *Stoke-on-Trent City Council v B & Q plc*[20] based his decision on the proposition that in performing the proportionality test, the role of the court was limited to asking whether there was any rational basis for the legislation.[21]

Procedural law

The application of Community law in the national courts has not only had an effect on substantive domestic law but also on its procedural aspects as well. Thus from *R v Secretary of State, ex parte Factortame,*[22] it is clear that the presumption of legality at the interim stage and the rules against injunctions against the Crown can have no effect in Community law cases. The immunity of the Crown from giving cross-undertakings when obtaining interlocutory injunctions, where Community law issues are involved, must almost certainly no

---

[15] *The Independent,* 20 June 1990; or more provocatively, 'Spanish Fishermen 1, British Sovereignty 0': *The European,* 26–28 July 1991.

[16] See Lord Bridge in *Factortame* [1990] 3 WLR 818, where he sets out the correct position (see pages 857–858).

[17] Case 145/88: *Torfaen Borough Council v B & Q plc* [1989] ECR 3851.

[18] Case 312/89; judgment of 28 February 1991, not yet reported.

[19] Case 332/89; judgment of 28 February 1991, not yet reported.

[20] [1991] 2 WLR 42.

[21] This, and the problems created by *Conforama* and *Marchandise,* has now given rise to two further references: Case 304/90, *Reading Borough Council v Payless DIY Ltd and Others* (reference by the Stipendiary Magistrate) and Case 164/91, *Stoke-on-Trent v B & Q plc* (reference by the House of Lords).

[22] [1990] 2 AC 85 and [1990] 3 WLR 818.

longer be sustainable. Another example is the preparedness of the courts to give leave to appeal from an arbitration in order to enable a reference to be made to the European Court of Justice.[23]

Moreover, the principle of administrative reasonableness in the *Wednesbury*[24] rules is not applicable in Community law cases: the question is whether the decision under review is correct or not: see *R v Ministry for Agriculture, Fisheries and Food, ex parte Bell Lines*.[25]

Remedies

The subject of remedies in the national courts for breaches of Community law has known a marked expansion over the years, and it will continue to be in this area that progress is made as more Community regulation affects more and different areas of activity, previously regulated by purely 'domestic' provisions, and as the effects of *Factortame* and *Zuckerfabrik Süderdithmarschen AG v Haupzollamt Itzehoe*[26] make themselves felt.

In terms of private law claims, it has been decided that damages will be available against a party who breaches a directly effective provision of Community law, the cause of action being breach of statutory duty; see *Garden Cottage Foods Ltd v Milk Marketing Board*.[27]

The English courts have distinguished the position of remedies existing in private law with that existing in public law. In *Bourgoin SA v Ministry of Agriculture, Fisheries and Food*,[28] the Court of Appeal found by a majority that a breach simpliciter of a public law right, *in casu* Article 30 of the EC Treaty, would not give rise to damages, and that the only rights available to the aggrieved party would be pursuant to judicial review.[29] In other words, the breach of Article 30 did not, in the eyes of the Court, constitute a breach of statutory duty, for which an action for damages would be permissible. However, the Court did make it clear that where a breach of Articles 30, 85 and 86 of the EC Treaty constitutes a tort, damages will be available to the plaintiff, whether the defendant is a private or public person. Even if a private law claim is based on a public law decision, the two elements may be inextricably mixed and the public law issues cannot be severed from the private law issues. Thus, such a claim, although based on an *ultra vires* act, could be a private law claim,

---

[23] *Bulk Oil (Zug) AG v Sun International Ltd* [1984] 1 WLR 147.
[24] *Wednesbury Corporation v Ministry of Housing and Local Government* [1965] 1 WLR 261.
[25] [1984] 2 CMLR 502.
[26] Joined Cases 143/88 and 92/89; judgment of 21 February 1991, relating to interim measures by a national court in respect of Community legislation.
[27] [1983] 2 All ER 770 (HL).
[28] [1985] 3 All ER 585 (HL), (CA). Leave was given to appeal to the House of Lords, but it was settled as a result of a substantial payment by the British government to the plaintiffs. The issue of damages is at present before the divisional court in *Factortame* on a claim by the relevant fishermen and shareholders. The case of *Bourgoin* is almost certainly overruled or of no effect in the light of Joined Cases 6/90 and 9/90, *Francovich and Boniface and Others v Italy*, judgment of 19 November 1991.
[29] See *R v Ministry of Agriculture, Fisheries and Food, ex parte Bostock* Court of Appeal 7 December 1990 [1991] 1 CMLR 687, where it was held that it was reasonable to grant leave for judicial review out of time where a judgment of the European Court had thrown doubt on the compatibility of the national legislation with the relevant Community provisions, such compatibility not having been in doubt prior to the judgment; this is another example of the flexibility of domestic procedural rules in the application of Community law.

with the plaintiff proceeding by writ or originating summons; see *An Bord Bainne Cooperative Ltd v Milk Marketing Board.*[30]

Preliminary references to the European Court of Justice

Any examination of the interface between Community law and national law would not be complete without some discussion on the subject of preliminary references, the mechanism by which a harmonious and harmonised growth of Community law throughout the different Member States is achieved. When an EC issue is raised before the courts, the question will arise as to whether or not it should be referred to the European Court of Justice, and if it should, at which stage.

Discretionary references

The English courts have laid down various guidelines to deal with the question of discretionary references. These were first stated in *Bulmer v Bollinger,*[31] and further developed in *Samex*[32] and in *R v Pharmaceutical Society of Great Britain, ex parte Association of Pharmaceutical Importers (API).*[33] It should be noted that these guidelines, whilst clearly influential, are not binding.

In order to decide whether a reference is necessary to enable the court to give judgment, per Article 177(2) of the Treaty of Rome:

   (i) the point must be conclusive or reasonably conclusive (or possibly potentially decisive);
  (ii) the issue has not already been decided or is otherwise '*acte clair*';
 (iii) the court should decide the facts first; but that does not exclude a reference if some of the facts are undecided.[34] Indeed there may be some cases where the reference may be necessary to decide which facts need to be decided or where the facts are not relevant to the legal issue, that is to say where the answer will be the same whatever version of the facts is accepted.

With regard to the exercise of discretion itself, the guidelines referred to above cover such matters as:

  (i) the time to get a ruling;[35]
 (ii) the undesirability of overloading the Court, which would only seem relevant today in the context of a case where other courts have asked the same question and where the decision of the European Court of Justice is awaited, which

---

[30] [1984] 2 CMLR 584 (CA). There was a subsequent settlement of this action for a very substantial sum of damages, the precise figures not having been made public.

[31] [1974] Ch 401.

[32] [1983] 1 All ER 1042.

[33] [1987] 3 CMLR 951.

[34] See *R v Pharmaceutical Society of Great Britain, ex parte Association of Pharmaceutical Importers (API)* [1987] 3 CMLR 951. See also *R v Ministry for Agriculture, Fisheries and Food, ex parte Agegate* [1987] 3 CMLR 939, and compare the ECJ's judgment in *Irish Creamery Milk Suppliers v An Taoiseach* [1981] ECR 735.

[35] The present length of time required for obtaining a reference is about 18 months on average (already too long) and much longer in complicated cases.

would then suggest an adjournment to await the answer of the Court;
(iii) the need to formulate the question clearly;
(iv) the difficulty and importance of the case, suggesting in some cases that it is better for the judge at first instance to decide the case himself;[36]
(v) expense;
(vi) wishes of the parties.[37]

The English courts, like the European Court of Justice in *CILFIT*,[38] have always warned against the national judge assuming he knows what Community law is on a particular point. Indeed, the Court's wording in *CILFIT* itself reflects closely the warnings in previous English cases with their warnings about language, texts and methods of interpretation[39] and the advantage of the panoramic view of the Court in Luxembourg.[40]

Mandatory references

In the ordinary event, the only court under a mandatory duty to refer in the English system will be the House of Lords, but there are some cases where the Court of Appeal is the final court, for it is not possible to appeal to the House of Lords in all cases. The fact that the Court of Appeal has decided not to refer the question and has refused leave to appeal to the House of Lords does not convert the Court of Appeal into a court bound to refer, for the House of Lords can still in the course of events give leave.[41] Indeed the fact that an EC point has to be decided may well be a reason for the House of Lords to give leave in a case where they might not otherwise do so. Equally the fact that a case is bound to go to the House of Lords is a reason for the Court of Appeal, or indeed a Court of first instance, to refer a case to avoid the expense and delay of an appeal to the House of Lords and a reference from that court.

In *CILFIT*, it was stated that the only exception to the need for a court of final resort to make a reference under Article 177(3) of a necessary question of Community law is if it is '*acte clair*' by reason of a previous decision of the European Court of Justice or if the answer is so obvious that there is no scope for any reasonable doubt as to the answer to the question raised.

A recent case, however, would seem to have moved away from the rigid attitude, maybe in the face of a growing confidence by individual judges and courts in dealing with Community law matters. The case, *R v London Boroughs Transport Committee, ex parte Freight Transport Association Ltd*,[42] was decided by the House of Lords in July 1991. The case concerned noisy vehicle restrictions

---

[36] See *R v Ministry for Agriculture, Fisheries and Food, ex parte Bell Lines* [1984] 2 CMLR 502, where the relevant tribunal was the Divisional Court.
[37] Recent cases have rejected the suggestion that the Court should hesitate before making a reference against the wishes of one of the parties: see *R v Pharmaceutical Society of Great Britain, ex parte Association of Pharmaceutical Importers (API)* [1987] 3 CMLR 951. However, it is thought that the Court would, in the ordinary event, be reluctant not to refer if both parties agreed it was necessary and appropriate, or vice-versa.
[38] Case 283/81, *CILFIT Srl et al v Ministry of Health* [1982] ECR 3415.
[39] *R v Henn and Darby* [1981] AC 850.
[40] *SAMEX (supra)*.
[41] See *R v Pharmaceutical Society of Great Britain, ex parte Association of Pharmaceutical Importers (API)* [1987] 3 CMLR 951.
[42] [1991] 1 WLR 828.

relating to air brakes in London. It was argued by those seeking to have the restrictions removed that they were contrary to Community law, in particular Council Directive 70/157 and Council Directive 71/320. The applicants sought a reference to the European Court of Justice from the House of Lords. It was argued that a reference was necessary because the Court of Appeal had held, in the same case, that the relevant restriction was contrary to Community law in the form of the two directives mentioned above. The House of Lords refused the application for a reference, deciding the matters to be referred on the basis of *acte clair*. The Court held that the directives in question had nothing to do with the specific question of air brake noise, that thus Community law had not been infringed in this regard or generally, and that there was therefore nothing for the Court of Justice to decide.

This somewhat creative use of the '*acte clair*' doctrine in a case where it would be difficult to say that the issue of Community law was 'obvious', would seem to indicate some restiveness on the part of the House of Lords with the strict application of the *CILFIT* rule, and a preparedness to interpret the judgment progressively. Indeed, now all Supreme Courts accept the primacy of Community law unequivocally, it may well be the time for the Court of Justice to loosen the shackles of *CILFIT* to accord with present legal enforcement of Community law. What might have been appropriate when the delays occasioned by a reference were a matter of months, can scarcely be acceptable when the delay can be measured in years. There can scarcely be any justification for converting Supreme Courts into judicial post-boxes.

Conclusion

From the above, it can be seen that from the start, the United Kingdom courts have been loyally carrying out their tasks of applying and interpreting the law brought before them, adapting national laws and procedures where appropriate. The fact that Community law was based on a system not familiar to many would not appear to have caused undue problems. Indeed, it would seem that most national courts actually rather relish the intricacies of Community law and the intellectual challenge of the interrelated legal systems. Indeed despite their initial unfamiliarity with the Community legal system, United Kingdom judges are possibly more at home than some of their continental colleagues in dealing with such a precedent-based legal system. They are probably more prepared, at least at first instance, to decide questions of Community law themselves rather than automatically referring them to the Court of Justice. In a fully developed system, this surely should be the norm with the Community legal system giving effect to the principles of subsidiarity in the same way as the political system. Unless this happens to a greater extent, the present Community legal order will soon be overwhelmed by references from national courts, to add to the growing number of cases involving failure by Member States to fulfil their Community obligations, in neither of which fields can the Court of First Instance, even with its extended jurisdiction, provide any relief.

21 The Widening Scope of Constitutional Law

John Temple Lang

This is a plea for Irish lawyers to adopt, in particular in published writings, a much wider view of what is covered by constitutional law than they have usually done in the past. This is necessary for a variety of reasons, and in several areas. The fact that not all the developments mentioned here will necessarily be welcome to all Irish lawyers is no reason to ignore them. Irish lawyers can make substantial contributions in these areas if they can apply some of the sound legal knowledge and good sense which Judge O'Higgins has always shown.

European Community Law

The essence of a written constitution is a document setting out, in an authoritative and relatively inflexible form, the powers of governmental institutions in a given territory. Ireland therefore has two constitutions now: the Constitution of 1937, and the Constitution which it shares with the other Member States of the European Community.[1] This second Constitution governs the powers of the Community Institutions in Ireland and elsewhere. The relationships between those institutions and the institutions set up by the 1937 Constitution are themselves governed by what is essentially constitutional law. So it is no longer satisfactory merely to discuss the 1937 Constitution and to explain why Article 29 includes provisions enabling the powers of EC institutions to be exercised, and to leave it at that. As has been said by an English writer, 'Constitutional lawyers should develop the habit, if they have not yet done so, of considering Community law where it is relevant as part and parcel of English law: to put the whole treatment of Community matters into one place would not be conducive to that habit'.[2]

The first reason why it is not satisfactory to regard the scope of Irish constitutional law as ending, as it were, with Article 29.4.3 is that the two bodies of constitutional law which now apply in Ireland are not separate or

---

[1] B. Chubb, *The Politics of the Irish Constitution* (1991) chap 8; J. Temple Lang, '*European Community Law, Irish Law and the Irish Legal Profession – Protection of the Individual and co-operation between Member States and the Community*' (1983) DULJ; J. Casey *Constitutional Law in Ireland* (1987) 176; B., McMahon & F. Murphy *European Community Law in Ireland* (1989) chaps 14 and 15.

[2] De Smith *Constitutional and Administrative Law* (4th ed) pp. 105–106.

self-contained. They overlap and inter-relate. The Government set up under the 1937 Constitution votes in the Community legislative Institution. Community regulations take effect without any action of the *Oireachtas*: in the EC sphere Ireland is no longer a dualist State. Even EC directives, which are intended to be implemented by whatever national measures are appropriate, must be used by the Irish courts to interpret the measures giving effect to them[3], and create rights which the Irish courts must enforce against State bodies.[4] Irish authorities have a duty to apply Community law, and have wide and far-reaching duties to cooperate with the Community Institutions in achieving Community objectives.[5] In Ireland Community law is largely applied by Irish governmental bodies: the relationship between Irish Governmental Institutions and the Community Institutions is a symbiotic one.[6]

The second reason why the traditional approach to the limits of Irish constititian law is now unsatisfactory is that it ignores the fact that Community law has reduced the scope for the exercise of the powers set out in the 1937 Constitution. Irish governmental institutions no longer have power to adopt measures which are incompatible with Community law or which interfere with its operation[7], or where Community legislation is exhaustive. Even more important, in certain spheres Irish Institutions, like those of all other EC Member States, no longer have any powers at all except insofar as they may have been delegated back to them. One of these areas of exclusive Community power is external trade and all other aspects of 'commercial policy' under Article 113 EEC.[8] Another important area of exclusive EC power concerns conservation of the biological resources of the sea.[9] The fact that the Constitution no longer in practice enables an Irish government to make a treaty on visible trade, or a fisheries agreement, with a non-Member State, without EC authorisation is surely something which should now be

---

[3] Case 14/83, *Von Colson* [1984] ECR 1891; Case 79/83, *Harz* [1984] ECR 1921; Case 125/88 *Nijman* [1989] ECR 3533; Case 222/84, *Johnston v RUC* [1986] ECR 1651; Case 80/86 *Kolpinghuis Nijmegen* [1987] ECR 3969; Case C-106/89, *Marleasing* judgment of 13 November 1990. In Case C 87/90–89/90. *Verhooen*, Advocate General Darmon in his Opinion of 29 May 1991 said: 'A national court . . . is required to interpret, of its own motion, and to the fullest possible extent, provisions of national law in the light of the wording and of the objective of the Community law measure, even if that measure is not directly effective'. See *Organon Laboratories v Department of Health* [1990] CMLR 49.

[4] E.g. case 148/78, *Ratti* [1979] ECR 1629; Case 196/80, *Anglo Irish Meat v Minister for Agriculture* [1981] ECR 2263; Case 190/87, *Moorman* [1988] ECR 4689 at paras 22–24.

[5] Article 5 EEC Treaty: J. Temple Lang *Community Constitutional Law: Article 5 EEC Treaty* 27 CML Rev 645–681 (1990); H. G. Schermers and P. Pearson, 'Some comments on Article 5 of the EEC Treaty,' in Baur, Hopt and Mailänder, *Festschrift für Ernst Steindorff* (1990, de Gruyther, Berlin) 1359–1378; O. Due 'Article 5 du traité CEE – une disposition de caractère fédéral? Schuman Lecture, Florence, 17th June 1991.

[6] Due, op. cit. supra f.n.5 says 'Member States constitute, in a sense, organs of the Community'; Temple Lang. 'European Community Constitutional Law: The division of powers between the Community and Member States' 39 NILQ 209 at p. 219 (1988).

[7] E.g. Case 83/78 *Pigs Marketing Board v Redmond* [1978] ECR 2347; Case 177/78, *Pigs and Bacon Commission v McCarren* [1979] ECR 2162; Case 281/87, *Commission v Greece* [1989] ECR 4015.

[8] Case 174/84, *Bulk Oil v Sun Oil*, [1986] ECR 559; Opinion 1/76 (*Natural Rubber*) [1979] ECR 2871; Case 41/76, *Donckerwolcke* [1976] ECR 1921.

[9] Case 804/79, *Commission v UK* [1981] ECR 1045; Case 348/88, *Hakvoort* [1990] ECR I–1647; other areas of exclusive EC competence concern treaties on the supply of nuclear materials; Ruling 1/78, (*Physical Protection of Nuclear Materials*), [1978] ECR 2151; and ECSC competition cases; Case 30/59, *Steenkolenmijnen* [1961] ECR at pp 22, 41.

mentioned in a book on Irish Constitutional Law. A third reason is that Community law has *increased* the powers of the Irish authorities in certain respects. Under the 1937 Constitution only the High Court and Supreme Court can decide whether Irish legislation is compatible with the Constitution. However, under Community law any Irish court may, if appropriate, decide that Irish legislative or other measures are incompatible with Community law.[10] Both the Court of Justice[11] and the Irish Courts[12] may suspend the operation of Irish legislation as an interlocutory remedy if it appears to be incompatible with Community law.

The juxtaposition of Community law and Irish law has also created a situation in which the interpretation of the Irish Consitution may be a matter of Community law, and not purely of Irish law. Article 29.4.3 authorises Irish measures which would otherwise be unconstitutional if they are 'necessitated by the obligations of membership of the Communities'.[13] This must mean (and was certainly intended to mean) 'necessitated objectively by the obligations of membership as determined by Community law'. In other words, it enabled the Irish authorities to do everything which Community law, correctly interpreted, might oblige them to do, but did not otherwise exempt them from the duty to respect the 1937 Consitution. It cannot be interpreted as meaning 'necessitated by the obligations of membership of the Communities as ultimately judged subjectively by the Irish courts'. It should not be misinterpreted in this way merely because of a fear that some day the two legal systems will conflict, and the Irish courts want to have the last word if that happens. In other words, Article 29.4.3 is a renvoi from the Constitution of Ireland to the constitutional law of the Community, and in particular to Article 5. To interpret Article 29.4.3, a reference to Luxembourg under Article 177 might be necessary.

Yet another reason why Irish constitutional law needs to be looked at in a wider context concerns the fact that in recent years purely Irish constitutional issues have involved questions to which principles of Community law offered answers. In the Rent Acts case[14] the Irish Supreme Court applied what was in essence the principle of proportionality which is found, inter alia, in EC law, that a measure must not impose hardship or inconvenience which is clearly unnecessary or disproportionate to the objective to be achieved. In the Spouses tax case[15] the Supreme Court applied the principle that a constitutional right may sometimes be declared effectively *ex nunc* and need not necessarily be given its full effects retroactively *erga omnes* if this would create great inconvenience. This principle is also found in Community law[16] (and of course also in the national constitutional laws of various States). It is not argued here that the Irish Supreme Court got its ideas from Community law,

[10] Case 106/77, *Simmenthal* [1978] ECR 629; Case C-348/89, *Mecanarte-Metalurgica*, judgment of 27 June 1991.
[11] Case 61/77R, *Commission v Ireland* [1977] ECR 1411.
[12] Case C-213/89, *Factortame* judgment of 19 June 1990.
[13] Mr Justice Walsh of the Supreme Court, as he then was, writing extra-judicially in Capotorti and others (eds.), *Du Droit International au Droit de l'Intégration: Liber Amicorum Pierre Pescatore* (1987) 805 at pp. 811–814; Curtin *Some Reflections on European Community Law in Ireland* 11 DULJ (1989) 207, at pp. 209–213.
[14] *Blake and Madigan v Attorney General* [1982] IR 177. The principle of proportionality was referred to expressly by the Supreme Court in *Hand v Dublin Corporation and Attorney General* 7 March 1991.
[15] *Murphy v Attorney General* [1982] IR 241.
[16] Case 43/75, *Defrenne* [1976] ECR 455.

although that may well have been so: the Supreme Court referred expressly to it. The point being made is that similar problems have arisen in Community constitutional law and that Community law offered similar solutions. Convergent evolution, if nothing more, did the rest.

Irish measures in the EC law sphere may be reviewed for compatibility with Community law both by the Irish Courts and by the Court in Luxembourg. Community law has created what are, in effect, two procedures for judicial review by the Community Court of the compatibility of national legislation with EC law, under Articles 169–170 and 177 EEC Treaty respectively.

Perhaps the most important reason for a wider vision of constitutional law concerns the fact that the grounds on which Community and national measures may be set aside are determined by Community law, and are (naturally) the same throughout the Community. These grounds include principles of fundamental rights, drawn from the European Convention on Human Rights and from the fundamental rights rules of the national constitutional laws of all the Member States,[17] and a range of general principles of administrative law.[18] Throughout much of Europe, in the EC law sphere, the rights of individuals and companies are protected by a common body of safeguards which are directly applicable in national courts. This is a development of great legal, psychological and political significance:[19] we are establishing an ethically-based common law of Europe. Community law fundamental rights rules bind Member States when they apply Community law.[20] The list of human rights and general principles of administrative law is open-ended, just as the list of fundamental rights is under the 1937 Constitution.[21] Cross-fertilisation should be reciprocal: Irish constitutional law can draw inspiration from the European Convention on Human Rights, Irish constitutional law can contribute to the development of the Community's list of fundamental rights, and in the EC law sphere the European Convention on Human Rights is, in effect, already part of Irish law. That being so, the definition of the 'EC law sphere' becomes extremely important: it is discussed below.

This is important for other reasons: all the Member States of the Council of Europe are parties to the European Convention on Human rights, and the fact that the Community law looks to the Convention as a source of human rights principles creates a link between Community law and European States which are not yet members of the European Community. In addition, the fact that there are now two European Courts applying fundamental rights principles

---

[17] On fundamental rights see M. Reid, *The Impact of Community Law on the Irish Constitution* (1990) pp. 81–101 (which however does not deal with all the issues which arise); J. Temple Lang, 'The Development of European Community Constitutional Law' 25 *The International Lawyer* 455–470 (1991).

[18] The 'general principles of law' include proportionality and legal certainty: see the *Reports for the 12th Congress of FIDE*. The Federation Internationale pour le Droit Européen (Paris 1986), Vol. 1.

[19] J. Temple Lang, *'The Direct Effects of European Community law on Individuals and Companies,'* The *Lord Fletcher Lecture 1984* (Law Society, London); J. Temple Lang, *'The Duties of National Courts under the Constitutional Law of the European Community,'* The *Dominik Lasok Lecture (1987 Exeter)* at pp. 27–28,

[20] Case 5/88, *Wachauf* [1989] ECR 2609; Case C-260/89, *Elliniki Radiophonia Tiléorassi*, judgment of 18 June, 1991. J. Temple Lang *Community Constitutional Law: Article 5 EEC Treaty* 27 Common Market L. Rev. 645 at p. 655 (1990).

[21] *Ryan v Attorney General* [1965] IR 294.

may create some risk of conflicting interpretations. However, this risk is probably minimal: the Court of Justice has always stressed that it is applying Community fundamental rights principles *derived from* the constitutional laws of Member States as well as from the Convention on Human Rights. It is not interpreting or applying the Convention as such.

Article 29.6 of the Constitution states the 'dualist' principle that treaties become part of domestic Irish law only as may be determined by the Oireachtas. That principle has also been significantly modified by Community law. Under Article 228 of the EEC Treaty, international agreements made by the Community, if appropriately drafted, will be part of the domestic law of Member States,[22] even if the States in question have not ratified them. Any breach by a Member State of its obligations under EC law to comply with such a treaty would be subject to the jurisdiction of the Court.

Unlike almost all federations, the European Community has no list of the powers of either the Community or its Member States. Almost all of the powers of the Community are concurrent powers, and Community law is administered to a far greater extent by the States than in other federal-type systems. The result is great flexibility, a moving boundary between EC and national law and, as stated above, a symbiotic relationship which demands – and has given rise to – an elaborate range of specific legal duties, elaborated in over 120 judgments, binding both States and Community institutions to cooperate with one another. These duties apply to all State authorities, legislative, executive and judicial, and to local authorities and State enterprises. They include the duty to enforce and give full effect to EC law: the duty to implement EC objectives: the duty not to interfere with the operation of EC rules and of EC institutions: the duty not to encourage breaches of EC law or to defeat its objectives: the duty to clarify the national law position in relation to EC law: the legal duty to obey certain EC acts which would not otherwise be legally binding: the duty to consult the Commission, to provide information to it, and to carry out promises made to it, and certain duties in the sphere of external relations.[23]

In addition, the Community institutions have obligations (which have so far been much less fully worked out) to cooperate with Member States and to provide them with information and advice.[24]

All these duties, which are legally enforceable and not merely conventions of the EC constitution, are far more elaborate than those arising in normal federations, and the case-law of the Court is still developing. They have considerable effects on the exercise of the powers of Irish governmental institutions. They should be kept directly in mind by all Irish constitutional lawyers.

Revision of the European Community Treaties

During 1991 negotiations have been going on for the revision of the European Community Treaties. Irish politicians have contributed little to the discussion

---

[22] Case 104/81, *Kupferberg* [1982] ECR 3641; Case C-18/90, *Kziber*, judgment dated 31 January 1991; Case 181/73, *Haegeman* [1974] ECR 449.

[23] *Temple Lang* op cit *supra* fn. 5.

[24] Article 155 EEC Treaty; Case 230/81, *Luxembourg v Parliament* [1983] ECR 255; Case 52/84, *Commission v Belgium* [1986] ECR 89; Case 44/84, *Hurd v Jones* [1986] ECR 29; Case C-2/88, *Imm Zwartfeld* [1990] 3 CMLR 455.

of this revision. Irish constitutional lawyers might have done more to analyse the issues from an Irish viewpoint. For example, it has been suggested that the Commission should be more democratically chosen. But one of the roles of the Commission is to make proposals in the interests of the Community as a whole, including the interests of the smaller Member States such as Ireland. A more democratically chosen or controlled Commission would be less independent, and would be likely to give more weight to the interests of the larger Member States. How could more democracy be reconciled with the interest of the smaller States? The Commission itself has perhaps not sufficiently explained why its hitherto exclusive right to propose EC measures is an important safeguard for the interests of smaller Member States, and why therefore it is important to make qualified majority voting more readily acceptable than it would otherwise be.

I do not suggest that Irish lawyers should consider these issues only for the purpose of protecting Irish interests. They should also be seeking to make a contribution to thinking throughout the Community on these issues. An argument is more likely to be generally accepted if it is clearly not made merely in the interests of one Member State. There is no reason why Ireland's attitude on neutrality should prevent Irish lawyers from making a useful contribution on other issues. Intelligent arguments carry more weight than what are to be perceived to be expressions of self-interest. (Nor, in domestic constitutional controversies, should the undoubted inertia of conservative thinking continue to discourage serious discussion, or make our collective thinking defensive, rather than making a positive contribution to the designing of a Community which is still under construction).

In particular it is not in the interests of Ireland that Irish thinking should come to be regarded as largely obstructive and intended to prevent any increase in the powers of the Community institutions. A State which was believed, rightly or wrongly, to be opposed to any improvement or strengthening of the Community would rapidly lose influence. On the other hand, by intelligent arguments Irish lawyers, who combine the experience of a written constitution with a common law background, might be able to solve some of the problems created by attitudes in the UK towards European integration. The fact that Ireland has no experience of federalism does not mean that Irish lawyers have nothing useful to say about the future constitution of the Community. And the fact that in Ireland there is little discussion of foreign policy makes it all the more important that lawyers should contribute to discussion of constitutional issues concerning the EC.

In fact, small Member States with open economies such as Ireland would gain more than they would lose by the strengthening of the powers of the Community institutions.

For example, it has been agreed in Maastricht that the Court should have power to fine Member States for failure to comply with EC law. (In fact this may be unnecessary as if Member States are already obliged to pay compensation to companies and individuals for losses caused by breach of directly applicable EC rules.[25] This would help to ensure that the markets in the larger

---

[25] See e.g. Case 33/76, *Rewe* [1976] ECR 1989 and a long series of cases concerned with refunds of taxes collected contrary to EC law: see also Cases C-6/90 and C-9/90, *Francovich*, Opinion of Advocate General Mischo of 28 May 1991, judgment of 19 November 1991; *J. Temple Lang* op. cit supra f.n. 5 at pp. 652–654: Commission's answer to written Questions Nos. 886–87 and 887/87, OJ No. C. 303/3, 28 November 1988.

Member States are open to Irish exports, and would more than outweigh the risk that Ireland might be fined from time to time.

Intelligent discussion of these issues is also needed because it seems clear that a further referendum will be needed to enable Ireland to ratify the revisions of the Community Treaties which result from the 1991 Intergovernmental Conferences.

It would be unsatisfactory if the reasons for the Irish positions, and the arguments for ratification in due course, were not explained until the referendum campaign. The *Crotty* case[26] shows that lack of preparation and planning can cause serious inconvenience.

Discussion is also needed of the terms and scope of the constitutional change needed. Should it be limited, like the change brought about by the *Crotty* judgement, to the new treaties, or should it be broad enough to allow for the next conference on political integration, visualised in 1996? In particular, should it deal with the issue of ratification by Ireland of treaties such as the European Community Patent Convention, which have been negotiated under EC auspices but which the Treaties do not expressly contemplate and ratifaction of which may therefore not be 'necessitated by the obligations of membership'? It would be odd if this problem, which has been seen and left unresolved for many years, was left unsolved in a second referendum, in particular as the need for the next referendum is clearly foreseeable in advance. It would be still worse if the broad uncertainty, created by the *Crotty* judgment, as to the extent of the State's freedom to bind itself in its external relations was left unresolved a second time.

There is no reason why Irish constitutional lawyers should leave discussion of all such issues largely to politicians or to people in other Member States. By doing so they not only impoverish debate in Ireland: they increase the tendency for Irish companies to go to non-Irish lawyers for legal advice on EC issues.

Fundamental rights, moral principles and the permissible scope of legislation

In recent years in Ireland there has been controversy over issues such as contraceptives and homosexuality. These controversies have concerned primarily moral and social questions, but have been too little concerned with the questions of the desirable and permissible scope for legislative intervention in citizens' lives in a democratic society. The European Court of Human Rights has held that the Convention prevents homosexual acts in private between consenting adult males being treated as crimes.[27] Several entirely different rationales for its conclusion would be possible. One is that it is discriminatory and unjustifiable to treat men in this respect differently from women.

Another is that it is not permissible for a State to prohibit private acts

---

[26] *Crotty v An Taoiseach* [1987] ILRM 400; G. Hogan *The Supreme Court and the Single European Act* XXII Ir Jur N.S. (1987) 55; J. Temple Lang, '*The Irish Court case which delayed the Single European Act*' 24 CML Rev. 709 (1987); Gwynn Morgan *Constitutional Law of Ireland* (2nd ed., 1990) 264–265: McMahon and Murphy *European Community Law in Ireland* (1989) 296–299.

[27] See Eur. Court H.R., *Dudgeon* case (Series A No. 45), (1982) 4 ECHR, *Norris* judgment of 26 October, 1988, Series A, No. 142; Connelly *Irish Law and the judgment of the European Court of Human Rights in the Dudgeon Case* 4 DULJ (1982) 25.

between adults without proof of more serious social ill-effects than have been shown to result: after all, adultery, and homosexual acts between females, are not criminal even though they are considered immoral, socially undesirable, damaging to family life, and grounds for divorce and separation. This second rationale could be based on a principle about the extent of State powers, or on a right of privacy (which may come to the same thing in this context):[28] this is the basis for the judgment of the Court of Human Rights.

A third possible rationale would be to say that homosexual activity should be regarded as just as 'normal' as heterosexual activity: this is the argument of homosexual people themselves, but one on which the Court of Human Rights has not pronounced (and could not pronounce).

The first two arguments might logically be acceptable without in any way accepting the third, and the first two arguments provide a less controversial and broader basis for solving other controversies in a pluralistic society such as that in Western Europe. As the Court of Human Rights decided in the way suggested, Ireland is not obliged to choose between the third argument and ceasing to adhere to the Convention: there are at least two independent and intellectually respectable arguments for arriving at the same conclusion *on legal grounds.* Irish lawyers would perform a useful service by pointing this out, and by discussing publicly how far it is permissible and appropriate to use State powers to impose specific moral principles in citizens' lives. Permissible *and* appropriate: even if legislation is permissible under human rights principles, there may be reasons of legal policy why it is unwise. The American experience with Prohibition was a disaster on legal grounds, quite apart from the question of its moral justification. Once again discussion of such issues should not be left to non-Irish participants, or to people who display a limited knowledge of constitutional principles, and little objectivity.

The failure to think clearly about such subjects may have been the explanation for the curious criticism by the *Oireachtas* Joint Committee of the fundamental rights clause in the now-superseded draft Treaty on European Union.[29] The Committee said that it feared conflict between the clause and the fundamental rights provisions of the Constitution of Ireland, although the clause went no further than existing EC law, and was clearly less likely to give rise to conflict than the European Convention on Human Rights itself. The Convention is an important influence for liberty and justice throughout Europe, and one of the best statements of fundamental rights in the world. It would be very unfortunate if it became a cause of confused thinking to Irish lawyers and a source of concern, apparently only because of a single issue, however important.[30] If this happened, it would certainly interfere with Irish lawyers making the contribution to European Human Rights law of which they are capable. If Irish lawyers fear that some day the Human Rights Courts in Strasbourg will decide that a woman has a fundamental right to have an abortion, they should have the confidence to argue that such a conclusion

---

[28] J. Casey *Constitutional Law in Ireland* (1987) 310 on a 'zone of autonomy'.

[29] Fourth Joint Committee on the Secondary Legislation of the EC, Report No. 14, European Parliament – *Draft Treaty establishing the European Union* (PL. 3063, March 1985); J. Temple Lang, 'The proposed Treaty setting up the European Union: Constitutional Implications for Ireland', 2 *Irish Studies in Int'l. Affairs* 143 at p. 151–153 (1985).

[30] Mr Justice Walsh in *Capotorti and others* (eds.), op. cit. footnote 13, 805 at p. 815 et seq. explains the position very clearly.

would be legally wrong, rather than distorting constitutional thinking on other issues, or causing them to be wholly neglected.

Any society dominated by a relatively homogenous viewpoint risks embodying too much of that viewpoint in legislation which unnecessarily restricts the freedom of minorities. It is the function of human rights provisions in constitutions and in the European Convention to limit this, and so to contribute to justice for minorities and to diminish friction between groups. The permissible scope for legislation, which is clearly indicated in the European Convention and which has been the subject of intelligent debate elsewhere, needs to be discussed seriously in Ireland.

Northern Ireland

The fundamental rights issues referred to above are important not only in themselves and because of Ireland's obligations under the European Convention on Human Rights, but also because of Northern Ireland. One way of reducing tensions caused by disagreements over ethical issues or fear of domination by one group or another is to reduce to a minimum legislative measures which regulate personal behaviour. Calls for a Bill of Rights in Northern Ireland would be more convincing if the fundamental rights provisions of the 1937 Constitution were more intelligently understood. Differences of opinion between any majority and any minority are less important insofar as agreement can be reached on the interpretation of constitutional provisions on fundamental rights, where they exist, and that a given moral issue need not necessarily (or should not) be the subject of legislation at all. Since the need or otherwise for legislation on a given question (whatever public opinion in Ireland may think) is not itself a moral issue, but a social, legal and policy one, some of the heat is removed from debate if discussion can be concentrated on this issue. Anything which Irish lawyers can do to ease tensions in Northern Ireland should be done.

This is not a plea for Irish lawyers to participate in negotiations on new structures in Northern Ireland: it is a plea for clarification and improvement of Irish constitutional law on issues which are controversial there, on which a satisfactory solution would be a useful precedent. It is often said that a Bill of Rights would be a good thing in Northern Ireland: there are many reasons why it would be desirable for the same fundamental rights rules to apply throughout the island. (In the EC law sphere, the same fundamental rights principles already apply). But it would be so only if they were not only satisfactory but accepted as satisfactory, and too little effect has been given to improving them either for this or for other purposes. In particular the question of permissible scope for legislative intervention needs to be carefully considered.

Fundamental Rights and Equality

Article 40.1 reads 'All citizens shall, as human persons, be held equal before the law . . .' But it was not until Community legislation made it necessary to do so that legislation was enacted requiring equal pay for men and women.

Even if Article 40.1 was thought not to apply to anyone except the State,[31] this in itself would not explain why no claim was ever brought under that Article against discrimination against women by the State itself in its salary and wage policies which, in retrospect, seem indefensible.[32] Of course the case-law did not encourage such claims. But it is surprising that so few analyses were published criticising the case-law in this respect, and developing in detail the arguments which would have shown that, at least in relation to the State's own pay policies, different treatment for men and women was unjustifiable. This is one of the most unfortunate failures of Irish constitutional lawyers, and the most important area in which the Community has brought about improvements in Irish law. There never was any doubt that equal pay for equal work was a principle of Community law: Article 119 EEC Treaty stated it without qualification. If therefore Article 40.1 is as limited in scope as has traditionally been believed, the rights of women and of some minorities are significantly better protected by Community law than by Irish law, and their lawyers have every reason to claim that Community fundamental rights principles apply whenever possible.

Constitutional Justice

It is now clear that the 1937 Constitution provides some guarantees of 'due process' and fair procedures.[33] The effect therefore must be that these guarantees override inconsistent legislation and require legislation to be interpreted

---

[31] Reid The *Impact of Community Law on the Irish Constitution* (1990) p. 44 says 'the extent to which equality is enforceable against bodies or individuals other than the State is unknown'. See Temple Lang *Private Law Aspects of the Irish Constitution* VI Ir Jur (1971) 237; Beytagh, *Equality under the Irish and American Constitutions* XVIII Ir Jur N.S. (1983) 56 and 219 at pp. 74–77, 230–232.

[32] Kenny J in *Murtagh Properties v Cleary* [1972] IR 330 at p. 336 said that 'what is or is not an adequate means of livelihood is a matter for the *Oireachtas*' and concluded from that statement that the remuneration in the public service (which paid women less than men, irrespective of their family circumstances) was consistent with Article 40.1 *Reid* op. cit. f.n. 31, p. 26 says of equal pay that 'to date no case-law suggests that any such right exists' but does not try to explain why the relevant arguments were never fully developed by commentators or by counsel. Part of the failure is perhaps due to the practice in published material on Irish law of merely summarising the caselaw without analysis. This was particularly unfortunate in connection with the Constitution. See for a useful analysis Forde *Equality and The Constitution* XVII I Jur N.S. (1982) 295, pp. 318–326.

[33] *The State (Quinn) v Ryan* [1965] IR 70 at p. 123; *McDonald v Bord na Con* [1965] IR 217 at p. 242 per Walsh J.; *Re Haughey* [1971] IR 217; *East Donegal Cooperative Society v Attorney General* [1970] IR 317 at p. 341 per Walsh J; *N v K* [1986] ILRM 75 at p. 88 per Henchy J; *Glover v BLN* [1973] IR 388 at p. 425, 427 per Walsh J; *Meskill v C.I.E.* [1973] IR 121. *The State (Gleeson) v Minister for Defence*, [1976] IR 280 at p. 295 per Henchy J; *Leary v National Union of Vehicle Builders* [1976] IR 400; *M v M* Supreme Court 8 October 1979; *Kiely v Minister for Social Welfare* (No. 2) [1977] IR 267; *O'Donoghue v Veterinary Council* [1975] IR 398 at p. 404; *The State (Healy) v Donoghue* [1976] IR 325; *Burke v Minister for Labour* [1979] IR 354; *Loftus v Attorney General* [1979] IR 221; *Garvey v Ireland* [1981] IR 75; *The State (McFadden) v Governor of Mountjoy* [1981] ILRM 113: *The People v Lynch* [1982] IR 64 at p. 84 per Walsh J; *O'Brien v Bord na Móna* [1983] IR 255 at pp. 270–271; *The State (Williams) v Army Pensions Board* [1983] IR 308; *S v S* [1983] IR 68.

    The State (McKeown) v Scully [1986] ILRM 133 at p. 135 per O'Hanlon J.; *The State (Irish Pharmaceutical Union) v Employment Appeals Tribunal*, Supreme Court, 14 March 1986 per McCarthy J. [1987] ILRM 36; *The People (DPP) v Conroy*, Supreme Court, 31 July 1986.

    Gunn v Bord an Cholaiste Naisiunta Ealaine is Deartha, Supreme Court 12 May 1988. In *Ellis v Assistant Commissioner O'Dea*, Supreme Court, 5 December 1989, Walsh J said: 'All persons

in a way consistent with those guarantees even if that is not the normal interpretation of the legislation in question.[34] It was therefore plainly incorrect to say that 'constitutional justice' added nothing to the existing common law rules of natural justice and is redundant.[35] On the contrary, it is important to be as clear as possible what procedural principles are constitutionally guaranteed. It is perhaps unfortunate that the distinction between what is constitutionally guaranteed and what is not is unclear, and that the issues have been regarded more as questions of administrative law rather than constitutional law.

Clear thinking about what principles of fair procedure should be regarded as having constitutional status, and in what situations they should apply, would be promoted by a study of the corresponding questions under the constitutional laws of other countries. In particular since the Constitution guarantees the jurisdiction of the courts and since the courts can hardly exercise jurisdiction satisfactorily if an administrative body has not given reasons for its final decision, the present uncertainty as to whether such bodies need given reasons needs to be clarified. If they are not obliged to give reasons, as a matter of Irish law,[36] there would be a clear difference in this respect between Irish law and EC law, and the latter, in its sphere (which, once again, requires precise definition) would provide much more effective protection for the citizen. Moreover, a study of comparative constitutional and administrative law would show that the overwhelming weight of judicial opinion is that for judicial review to be effective and efficient, administrative bodies must be obliged to give their reasons for their decisions. If indeed this is a question of Irish constitutional law, it would be appropriate to make arguments of policy and of principle, concerned with the effectiveness of the constitutional right to judicial review, which it might not be appropriate to make if the question was merely one of administrative law.

'Constitutional Justice' began as an entirely indigenous development. However, the principles of fundamental rights and general principles of law being elaborated by the Court in Luxembourg also include procedural safeguards and rules of due process, although these apply, of course, only in the Community law sphere. General principles of Community law give Treaty status to

---

appearing before the courts of Ireland are entitled to protection against unfair or unjust procedures or practices . . . no person may be removed . . . out of this jurisdiction . . . if to do so would expose him to practices or procedures which if exercised within this State would amount to infringements of his constitutional right to fair and just procedures: '*Glavin v Governor of Mountjoy*, Supreme Court, 21 December 1990. Most recently in *Ambiorix Ltd v Minister for the Environment* McCarthy J said 'The Constitution guarantees fair procedures in the administration of justice: discovery of documents is part of these procedures' (Supreme Court, 23 July 1991) and Finlay CJ referred to 'The fundamental constitutional origin of the decision of this court in *Murphy v Dublin Corporation*' [1972] IR 215). See also *International Fishing Vessels Ltd v Minister for the Marine* Supreme Court 22 February 1991 per McCarthy J.

[34] *East Donegal Cooperative Ltd v Attorney General* [1970] IR 317 at p 341 per Walsh J.

[35] Kelly *The Irish Constitution* (1980) at p. 190; Temple Lang op. cit supra footnote 1, at p. 8. See also Kelly, Hogan and Whyte *The Irish Constitution* (supplement to the 2nd edition 1987) at pp. 54–57; see Casey *Constitutional Law in Ireland* (1987) at pp. 335–340.

[36] *Kiely v Minister for Social Welfare* (No. 2) [1977] IR 267 at p. 274; cp. *Garvey v Ireland* [1981] IR 75 at p. 102 per Henchy J; *The State (Creedon) v Criminal Injuries Compensation Tribunal*, Supreme Court, 14 March 1988.

the citizen's right to be heard before a decision is taken affecting his rights,[37] the right to judicial review of administrative decisions,[38] the right to obtain legal advice,[39] and the right to know the reasons for decisions.[40] If these Community rules on due process are significantly different from Irish 'Constitutional Justice', it becomes important to determine whether a given situation is within the sphere governed by Community law, or is only subject to Irish law.

Misunderstandings of the 1937 Constitution

Another reason why more authoritative published analysis of the 1937 constitution would be desirable is that its implications are often misunderstood, even by civil servants. One example will be sufficient: for some time the Department of Social Welfare was refusing to grant the allowance for deserted wives to divorced women, on the grounds that the Constitution did not recognise divorce. This particular piece of nonsense was ultimately corrected by the Attorney General's Office, but not before much hardship and injustice had been caused. We should understand the Constitution better than that.

Ecclesiastical law and private clubs

Another area where some consideration of the relevant constitutional law principles may prove necessary concerns church law, and in particular the canon law of the Roman Catholic Church. It is conventional to say that this is entirely outside the sphere of civil (i.e. State) law, for two reasons: first that membership of the Church, and therefore submission to canon law, is voluntary, and secondly that canon law derives no part of its effect from the State, and has no civil law effects. A canon law court, it is said, is therefore not administering justice within the meaning of Article 34 of the 1937 Constitution. Even if this is correct, it does not entirely resolve the matter. Suppose that a priest holds a position in an Irish university as teacher of Catholic theology. His writings are criticised and he is investigated, as it seems that some priests in other countries have been, by a canon law tribunal which concludes in substance that his views are not sufficiently orthodox for it to be appropriate for him to teach official Catholic theology. He therefore loses his job. If he wishes to claim that that the canon law procedure did not adequately respect his right to be heard in his own defence (it seems that canon law practice is sometimes defective in this respect), can he ask the Irish courts to order his reinstatement, because the canon law determination has affected his

---

[37] Case 17/74, *Transocean Marine Paint* [1974] ECR 1063; Case 264/82, *Timex v Council* [1985] ECR 849; Case 141/84, *De Compte* [1985] ECR 1951; Case C-49/88, *Al-jubail Fertilizer*, judgment of 17 June 1991.
[38] Case 294/83, *Parti Ecologiste 'Les Verts' v European Parliament* [1986] ECR 1339 at para. 23; Case 222/86, *Heylens* [1987] ECR 4097; Case 222/84, *Johnston v RUC* [1986] ECR 1651.
[39] Case 155/79, *AM & S* [1982] ECR 1575.
[40] Article 190 EEC Treaty: Case 24/62, *Germany v Commission* [1963] ECR 63.

secular post? It is submitted that he could do so: the rule in *Glover v BLN*[41] applies to private posts.

It has been suggested that ecclesiastical annulments of marriage might be given effect in Irish law. For similar reasons, this could be done only if church court procedures in annulment cases fulfilled the requirements of constitutional due process: that is not clear.

How do these principles apply to clubs? Club membership, like church membership, is voluntary, and members of clubs cannot normally be obliged to accept any particular individual as members.[42] But if a club openly or systematically refuses membership to women, or to people of any particular religion or race, is that unconstitutional? In such circumstancess it might be unconstitutional for the club to receive funds from public sources, but that would not resolve the matter. A club membership which is in principle open to anyone who may be proposed, seconded and voted in is not a purely private club, and may not be free to discriminate in a way which would be plainly unjustifiable if a public authority did it.

Public international law

Article 29.1.3 reads 'Ireland accepts the generally recognised principles of international law as its rule of conduct in its relations with other States'. The case-law and other authorities do not make it clear whether this means that customary public international law rules are part of Irish domestic law and have constitutional status.[43] In extradition negotiations the view has been taken that they are. This was an unexpected position because it is not generally accepted that international law *forbids* the extradition of persons charged with political offences (thereby giving individuals rights) as distinct from merely *allowing* a State to refuse extradition in such circumstances.

It is surprising that so important a question in relation to Article 29.1.3 has gone unresolved for so long, and that there has been so little published analysis of the issues involved. Comparison with the situation under the constitutional laws of other States would be useful.

State prerogatives

Another situation in which comparative analysis of the case law would have clarified the law concerns the prerogatives of the State, which were considered in *Webb v Ireland* by the Supreme Court.[44] The late J M Kelly criticised this judgment on the ground that it involved '. . . the mysterious disappearance of the prerogative right of treasure trove, and its approximate – but only approxi-

---

[41] *Glover v BLN [1973] IR 388; Garvey v Ireland* [1981] IR 75; *Gunn v Bord an Cholaiste Naisiunta Ealaine is Deartha,* Supreme Court, 12 May 1988 per Walsh J; *Ryan v VIP Taxi Cooperative Society,* High Court, 20 January 1989.

[42] *Tierney v Amalgamated Society of Woodworkers* [1959] IR 254.

[43] Casey *Constitutional Law in Ireland* (1987) p. 169–171: Kelly *The Irish Constitution* (1980) pp. 147–150: Connelly '*Non-Extradition for Political Offences*' XVII Ir Jur N.S. (1982) 59 at p. 79–81; see in re *Criminal Law (Jurisdiction) Bill* 1975, [1977] IR 129.

[44] [1988] ILRM 565.

mate – reincarnation in a different shape'.[45] This criticism, it is suggested, fails to distinguish between the many rights which any State may have under its domestic law, including the residual right to an important res nullius, and rights which used to derive from the royal prerogative as such. The latter naturally have disappeared: there is no reason why the former cannot continue to exist. This distinction is essentially that which the Supreme Court has drawn. Chief Justice Finlay said:

> '. . . a necessary ingredient of sovereignty in a modern State, and certainly in this State, having regard to the terms of the Constitution, with an emphasis on its historical origins and a constant concern for the common good, is and should be an ownership by the State of objects which constitute antiquities of importance which are discovered and which have no known owner' (at p. 594).

This passage would not have received criticism if constitutional lawyers had previously drawn the distinction between uniquely royal prerogatives and other rights of a modern state, a distinction which was in fact first drawn in *Re Irish Employers' Mutual Insurance Association*[46] in 1955.

The sphere of Community law – national measures governed by Community principles

In this paper reference has been made repeatedly to 'the sphere of EC law' in which Member States must respect the basic principles of EC law on fundamental rights, including the 'general principles of law'. This sphere needs definition.

The sphere of Community law, in this sense, certainly includes:

- all measures by which Member States implement Community law;[47]
- all measures of Member States which affect rights protected by Community law, or which are in areas specifically regulated by Community law;[48]

---

[45] Kelly, *'Hidden Treasure and the Constitution'* (1988) DULJ 5.

[46] [1955] IR 176.

[47] Cases in which the Court or Advocates General have said that Member States must respect general principles of Community law when they are obliged to implement Community rules include: Case 52/76, *Benedetti v Munari* [1977] ECR 163 at pp. 187–188, per Advocate General Reischl; Joined cases 41, 121 and 796/79, *Testa* [1980] ECR 1979 paras. 18, 21; Case 230/78, *Eridania* [1979] ECR 2747 at p. 2771; Joined cases 213–215/81, *Norddeutsches Vieh – und Fleischkontor v Balm* [1982] ECR 3583 at paras. 9, 12, 13; Joined cases 205–215/82, *Deutsche Milchkontor* [1983] ECR 2633 at para. 17 and Advocate General VerLoren van Themaat at p. 2675; Joined cases 201 and 202/85, *Klensch* [1986] ECR 3477 at paras. 8 and 9 and Advocate General Slynn at p. 3500; Case 12/86, *Demirel* [1987] ECR 3719 at para. 28; Case 80/86, *Kolpinghuis Nijmegen* [1987] ECR 3969 at para. 13; Case 5/88, *Wachauf* [1989] 2609 at para. 17–22 and conclusions of Advocate General Jacobs at p. 2629.

[48] Cases of Member States exercising powers which affect rights protected by Community law or in situations regulated by Community law, and being obliged to respect general principles of Community law include: Case 36/75, *Rutili* [1975] ECR 1219, Case 43/75, *Defrenne v Sabena* [1976] ECR 455 at p. 490 per Advocate General Trabucchi, at page 490, Case 52/76, *Benedetti v Munari* [1977] ECR 163 at p. 188 per Advocate General Reischl at page 187, Case 52/79, *Debauve* [1980] ECR 833, paras. 18–19, Case 32/79, *Commission v UK* [1980] ECR 2403 at

– all measures adopted by Member States on behalf of the Community, or on the basis of powers delegated by the Community.

The Advocate General in *Jongeneel Kaas*[49] used wider language. He said that Community general principles and fundamental rights rules

'may come into operation only in cases where the application of substantive rules of Community law is involved . . . only in cases which display some connection with the legal order of the Community.'

However, this is not very precise, and it is not clear whether these phrases should apply to any situations not covered by the three principles suggested above. To clarify the issue, the word 'specifically' in the second principle requires explanation. In the economic and social fields covered by the Treaties, the duty not to discriminate on the grounds of nationality applies universally. In this sense the whole economic and social area is 'regulated' by at least one substantive principle of EC law. However, this does not necessarily mean that all EC fundamental rights rules and general principles of law apply so widely.

In one case[50] the Court was asked to consider if certain provisions of the French law on audiovisual communication was contrary to the European Convention on Human Rights. The Court refused, saying that it fell within the jurisdiction of the national legislator, although it also said that the legislation would comply with Article 30 only if it was non-discriminatory and did not exceed what is necessary to give priority to exploitation in cinemas. Article 36 certainly involves the principle of proportionality[51] and it must be strictly interpreted because it sets out exceptions to the right to free movement of goods given by Community law. The Court has now clarified this in the *Greek Television* case.[52] There the Court said that national laws in the area of application of Community law must comply with fundamental rights principles, and that this applies to national laws restricting freedom to provide services, even if for purposes expressly permitted by the Treaty.

The rules summarised above, if they are correctly formulated, constitute a reasonable result in practice. In any case, the sphere in which EC fundamental rights rules and general principles undoubtedly apply to national measures is already wide, and will widen as more EC legislation is adopted.

The third principle also requires comment. In certain circumstances Member States, even if they no longer have any powers of their own, may act on behalf of the Community, either because they have been authorised to do

---

para 46, Case 157/79, Pleck, [1980] ECR 2171 at para. 19; Case 222/84, *Johnston v RUC* [1986] ECR 1651 at paras. 18 and 38; Case 294/83, *Parti Écologiste Les Verts v European Parliament* [1986] ECR 1339 at para. 23; Case 222/86, *Heylens* [1987] ECR 4097 at pp. 4117–4119; Case 186/87, *Cowan* [1989] ECR 195, p. 220 and 222; Case C-260/89, *Elliniki Radiophonia Tiléorassia* judgment of 18 June 1991, paras 41–45.

[49] Case 237/82, *Jongeneel Kaas* [1984] ECR 483 at p. 520; see Case 118/75, *Watson and Belman* [1976] ECR 1185 at pp. 1206–1208 per Advocate General Trabucchi.

[50] Joined cases 60 and 61/84, *Cinéthèque v Fédération Nationale des Cinémas Français* [1985] ECR 2605 at para. 26.

[51] E.g. Case 272/80, *Biologische Produkten* [1981] ECR 3277; Oliver, *Free Movement of Goods in the EEC* (2nd. ed., 1988) pp. 168–176.

[52] Case C-260/89, *Elliniki Radiophonia Tiléorassi* judgment of 18 June, 1991, paras. 41–45.

so, or in effect as trustee or agent of necessity.[53] Since the Community institutions are themselves always bound by the principles being discussed, it follows (although the point has not yet arisen) that they would also apply to any national measures taken, in this strict sense, on behalf of the Community.

It is important to remember that in the EC law sphere discussed here, *all* governmental acts, legislative, executive, administrative and judicial must respect the basic principles of EC Law.

Comparative Constitutional Law

At this point it should be clear that to think adequately both about constitutional issues arising under the 1937 Constitution and about EC constitutional questions, a knowledge of comparative constitutional law is required. It is not enough to look at the precedents offered by US Constitutional law, useful though they have undoubtedly been in the past. It is essential for Irish constitutional lawyers to look to the case law of the European Court of Human Rights in Strasbourg, and to the national constitutional laws of other EC Member States. In a new legal system such as Community law, cases of first impression arise frequently. It is unsatisfactory that foreseeable issues of great importance should be seriously considered only when the accidents of litigation or the ingenuity of lawyers have raised them. It may be objected that, apart from the UK, all the other EC Member States are civil law countries. So they are, and EC law is in many respects closer to civil law than to common law. But that makes it all the more necessary for Irish lawyers to study comparative constitutional law if we are to make our full contribution to Community law, and if we are to understand fully the Community law context in which the Irish Constitution is now operating. Adequate knowledge will not come without effort, and it cannot be satisfactorily learned ad hoc to meet the needs of an individual case. Irish lawyers should not risk clients taking cases on Community constitutional issues to lawyers from other countries who may be regarded as having a wider knowledge of comparative constitutional law. In addition if, as seems increasingly likely, the UK ultimately gets some form of written constitution, Irish lawyers with their experience of a common law written constitution may be better placed than English lawyers to see its implications and to advise on it, if they are adequately informed about comparative constitutional law, and not merely specialists in Irish law.

Conclusion

Irish Constitutional law is a broader subject than has been conventionally understood, and needs more detailed and careful published analysis and discussion. When it is given this analysis, Irish lawyers will be contributing not only to Irish law but also to the development of European Community law. Both contributions need to be made. 'Ireland now has three Constitutions,

---

[53] para. 46, Case 157/79, *Pleck*, [1980] ECR 2171 at para. 19; Case 804/79, *Commission v UK* [1981] ECR 1045 at para. 30 '. . . Member States may henceforth act only as trustees of the common interest . . .'; Joined cases 47 and 48/83, *Van Miert* [1984] ECR 1721 at p. 1738; Case 174/84, *Bulk Oil v Sun Oil* [1986] ECR 559 at para. 31 and at p. 570 per Advocate General Slynn.

namely, the Constitution of Ireland, the European Community Treaties and Acts of the Community Institutions, and the European Convention of Human Rights'.[54] These are three of the main legal influences towards a more just society in Ireland. They should not now be seen as separate from one another, they are interlinked, and Irish lawyers need to think intelligently about all three. A new legal Europe is being built. It will be pluralistic but moral. It needs a constructive intelligent contribution from lawyers of all Member States, not a selfish, short-sighted, or obstructive attitude. In particular it needs constructive criticism from Ireland, a country with a strict rule of law in which ethical constitutional principles are taken seriously, even if they are not always calmly and analytically discussed. The development of Irish constitutional law has not been evenly spread: it has progressed further, and achieved better results, in some areas than in others. It is time that we took more seriously the need to analyse profoundly the many issues arising under our own Constitution and to criticise the imperfections in our traditional interpretations of it. Only when we have done that properly will we be in a position to make our full contribution to the development of Community constitutional law.

---

[54] Mr Justice Walsh op cit *supra* footnote 13 at p. 817 'Community law . . . has the paramount force and effect of constitutional provisions'; *Doyle v An Taoiseach*, Supreme Court 29 March 1985 per Henchy J. Gwynn Morgan *Constitutional Law of Ireland* (2nd ed., 1990) 32. Casey *Constitutional Law in Ireland* (1987) is much better than Kelly *The Irish Constitution* (1980) in the respects raised by this paper.

22 The Status of Non Implemented Directives before Irish Courts Post Marleasing

Mary Finlay Geoghegan

The Judgment of the Court of Justice in *Marleasing S.A. v La Comercial Internacional De Alimentation S.A.* on 13 November 1990[1] appears to re-open the question of the precise status in the national legal systems of directives not implemented by Member States by the prescribed date. The purpose of this short essay is to analyse the position in Ireland following *Marleasing*.

Pre-Marleasing

Prior to *Marleasing* the principles in relation to non-implemented or partially or incorrectly implemented directives appeared relatively clear and might be summarized as follows:

(i) Wherever the provisions of a directive appear, as far as their subject matter is concerned, to be unconditional and sufficiently precise, those provisions may be relied upon by an individual against the State where the State fails to implement the directive in national law by the end of the period prescribed or where it fails to implement the directive correctly.[2]

(ii) The underlying principle for the above conclusion was that it would be incompatible with the binding nature of a directive on Member States set out in Article 189 of the Treaty to permit a Member State to plead as against individuals its own failure to perform the obligations which the directive entails.[3]

(iii) A directive may not itself impose obligations on an individual and a provision of a Directive may not be relied upon as such against such a person. This follows from the fact that Article 189 of the Treaty only makes a directive binding upon each Member State.[4]

(vi) The notion of State for the purposes of the above principles has been extended to include any organization or body which is subject to the authority or control of the State or has special powers beyond those

---

[1] Case C-106/89, [1990] ECR I-4135.
[2] Case 8/81, *Becker v Finanzamt Munster-Innenstadt* [1982] ECR 53.
[3] Case 148/78, *Publico Ministero v Ratti* [1990] ECR 1629.
[4] Case 152/84, *Marshall v Southampton and Southwest Hampshire Area Health Authority* [1986] ECR 723.

which result from the normal rules applicable to relations between individuls ('Emanations of the State').[5]

(v)   The Member States' obligation under Article 189 arising from a directive and their duty under Article 5 of the Treaty is binding on all the authorities of the Member States including for matters within their jurisdiction, the Courts. Hence, in applying national law and in particular the provisions of a national law specifically introduced in order to implement a directive national courts are required to interpret their national law in the light of the wording and the purpose of the directive in order to achieve the result referred to in the third paragraph of Article 189.[6]

(vi)   The foregoing rule in relation to interpretation is not confined to those provisions of a directive which have direct effect.

(vii)   The rules of interpretation as explained in *Von Colson and Kamann* are limited by the general principles of law which form part of Community law and, in particular, the principles of legal certainty and non-rectro activity.[7]

(viii)   A Directive cannot of itself and independently of a national law adopted by a Member State for its implementation have the effect of determining or aggravating the liability in criminal law of persons who act in contravention of the provisions of that Directive.[8]

(ix)   Provisions of a directive which have direct effect may only be relied upon after the expiry of the prescribed date for its implemenation.

Whilst in *Becker v Finanzamt Munster-Innenstadt*[9] itself the Court of Justice did not fully face up to the issue as to whether provisions in a directive considered to have direct effect could have horizontal effect (i.e. affect rights between two individuals) or only vertical effect (i.e. affect rights between an individual and the State or an emanation of the State) the Court of Justice appeared to fully and clearly face up to the issue in *Marshall v Southampton and South West Hampshire Area Health Authority*[10] and exclude any horizontal effect. This exclusion was fully explained by reference to the fact that Article 189 of the Treaty only makes directives binding upon Member States.

The exclusion of horizontal effects for directly effective provisions in non-implemented Directives as decided in *Marshall* undoubtedly limits significantly the effectiveness of directives in Member States unwilling to implement directives and thus the effective application of EC law.

The Court of Justice has sought to lessen the impact of this exclusion by the development of the concept of the 'emanation of the State' as in *Johnston v Chief Constable of the RUC*[11] and *Foster v British Gas*[12]. Whilst one can appreciate the efforts and understand their purpose they may not be entirely consistent with the underlying estoppel principle which permits the enforcement of rights

---

[5] Case C-188/89, *Foster v British Gas* [1990] ECR I-3313.
[6] Case 14/83, *Von Colson and Kamann v Land Nordrhein-Westfalen* [1984] 1891 and Case 222/84, *Johnston v Chief Constable of the RUC* [1986] ECR 1651.
[7] Case 80/86, *Kolpinghuis Nijmegen BV* [1987] ECR 3969.
[8] Case 14/86, *Pretore di Salo v X* [1987] ECR 2545.
[9] *Supra*, note 2.
[10] *Supra*, note 4.
[11] Case 222/84, [1986] ECR 1651.
[12] Case C-188/89, *supra*, note 5.

granted in a non-implemented directive against the State. However this is a separate topic not the subject of this essay.

The Court of Justice is rightly concerned to secure the effective application of EC law. It recognizes the difficulty created for the effective application of non-implemented directives by the terms of Article 189 of the Treaty. In *Marleasing* it was sought to approach the problem through the role of national courts in securing the effective application of EC law. It was perhaps prompted by the trenchant views which it expressed on this subject, albeit in a slightly different context, *Regina v Secretary of State for Transport ex parte Factortame Limited*.[13] I wish to suggest that in *Marleasing* the Court has found a sound constitutional solution to the status of non-implemented directives in national legal systems but that in doing so it has to a certain extent derogated from the total exclusion of horizontal effects as expressed in *Marshall*.

The Marleasing judgment

The judgment of the Court in *Marleasing* was given in an Article 177 reference from the *Juziado De Primera Instancia E Instruccion Oviedo*. The facts as set out in the opinion of Mr Advocate General Van Gerven were that La Comercial Internacional De Alimenation S.A. ('La Comercial') was a public limited company incorporated by three persons. Marleasing was a significant creditor and in reliance upon certain articles of the Spanish Civil Code sought primarily to have La Commercial declared null and void. In its defence La Comercial relied inter alia on Article 11 of the first Company Law Directive[14] ('Directive 68/151') which lists exhaustively the cases in which nullity of a company may be declared. The grounds listed did not include any of the grounds upon which *Marleasing* sought to have the nullity declared in accordance with the Spanish Civil Code. Spain was under an obligation to implement Directive 68/151 as from the date of its accession but this had not been done. The Spanish Court referred the following question to the Court:

> 'Is Article 11 of Council Directive 68/151/EEC of 9 March 1968 which has not been implemented in national law directly applicable so as to preclude a declaration of nullity of a public limited company on a ground other than those set out in the said Article?'

The short and succinct judgment of the Court changes the question asked and states the essential opinion of the Court in four paragraphs:

> '6. With regard to the question whether an individual may rely on the directive against a national law, it should be observed that, as the Court has consistently held, a directive may not of itself impose obligations on an individual and, consequently, a provision of a directive may not be relied upon as such against such a person (judgment of 26 February 1986 in Case 152/84, *Marshall v Southampton and South-West Hampshire Area Health Authority*[1986] ECR 723).
> 7. However, it is apparent from the documents before the Court that the national court seeks in substance to ascertain whether a national court hearing a case which falls within the scope of Directive 68/151 is required to interpret its

---

13 Case C-213/89, [1990] ECR I-2433, paragraphs 20 and 21.
14 Council Directive 68/151 of 9 March 1968, OJ L 65/8.

national law in the light of the wording and the purpose of that directive in order to preclude a declaration of nullity of a public limited company on a ground other than those listed in Article 11 of the Directive.

8. In order to reply to that question, it should be observed that, as the Court pointed out in its judgment of 10 April 1984 in Case 14/83 (*Von Colson and Kamann v Land Nordrhein-Westfalen* [1984] ECR 1981, at paragraph 26), the Member States' obligation arising from a directive to achieve the result envisaged by the directive and their duty under Article 5 of the Treaty to take all appropriate measures whether general or particulr, to ensure the fulfilment of that obligation, is binding on all the authorities of Member States including, for matters within their jurisdiction, the Courts. It follows that, in applying national law, whether the provisions in question were adopted before or after the directive, the national court called upon to interpret it is required to do so, as far as possible, in the light of the wording and the purpose of the directive in order to achieve the result pursued by the latter and thereby comply with the third paragraph of Article 189 of the Treaty.

9. It follows that the requirement that national law must be interpreted in conformity with Article 11 of Directive 68/151 precludes the interpretation of provisions of national law relating to public limited companies in such a manner that the nullity of a public limited company may be ordered on grounds other than those exhaustively listed in Article 11 of the directive in question.'[15]

At first glance the use of the term 'national law' by the Court of Justice to mean the pre-existing provisions of the Spanish Civil Code in contradistinction to Directive 68/151 both in the rephrasing of the question and the dicta in paragraph 8 of the judgment presents some difficulty to an Irish lawyer. The direction by the Court in paragraph 8 to a national court is to interpret the national law 'as far as possible, in the light of the wording and the purpose of the directive in order to achieve the result pursued by the latter and thereby comply with the third paragraph of Article 189 of the Treaty'. In the ordinary use of the term it would simply not be possible to interpret the relevant provisions of the Spanish Civil Code in the light of the wording and purpose of Directive 68/151. The Spanish Judge was faced with two inconsistent laws relating to the granting of declarations of nullity of limited companies. The Spanish Civil Code appeared to permit the grant of a declaration of nullity on several grounds whereas Article 11 of Directive 68/151 limited exhaustively the grounds for the grant of a declaration of nullity and such grounds did not include those permitted by the Spanish Civil Code.

Further, if the Court of Justice intends by *Marleasing* to direct national courts to interpret pre-existing legislation of purely domestic origin 'in the light of the wording and purpose' of subsequent non implemented directives whilst at the same time taking the view that such non implemented directives do not form part of national law then it appears to be turning national courts into legislators which would be a dangerous constitutional principle.

However, in an Irish context, this difficulty is simply overcome if one regards both the pre-existing purely domestic law such as the provisions of the Spanish Civil Code and the non-implemented Directive 68/151 as forming the Irish national law. This would be correct having regard to section 2 of the European Communities Act 1972 which provides:

[15] *Supra*, note 1 at 4158–4159.

'2. From the 1st day of January 1973, the treaties governing the European Communities and the existing and future acts adopted by the institutions of those Communities shall be binding on the State and shall be part of the domestic law thereof under the conditions laid down in those treaties.'

Notwithstanding the limits placed on the effects of directives by Article 189 of the Treaty, non implemented directives appear from the above section to form part of Irish law. Thus if *Marleasing* had been before an Irish court with, let us assume hypothetically, pre-existing laws of purely Irish origin similar to the Spanish Civil Code relied upon and Directive 68/151 not implemented in Ireland, the 'national law' to be both interpreted and applied by the Irish court must be the corpus of laws consisting of the conflicting law of purely domestic origin and the non-implemented directive. The question which an Irish court would have needed answered by the Court of Justice would have been how to interpret the the relative supremacy of these conflicting provisions so as to know which law was to be applied in deciding the case before it. In the context of the questions which may be put in an Article 177 reference the question as originally put by the Spanish court and rephrased by the Court of Justice is sufficiently close to allow the answer be considered. The answer to such a hypothetical question from an Irish court would seem from *Marleasing* to be that the Irish court must interpret the entire Irish law in such a manner that the provisions of the non-implemented directive prevail; or to put the answer another way, the Irish court may no longer apply those provisions of the pre-existing law of purely domestic origin which are inconsistent with the provisions of the non-implemented directive.

Post *Marleasing*

The most important question which remains after *Marleasing* is precisely what the Court of Justice means by the statement in paragraph 8 that 'in applying national law . . . the national court called upon to interpret it is required to do as far as possible, in the light of the wording and the purpose of the directive in order to achieve the result pursued by the latter and thereby comply with the third paragraph of article 189 of the Treaty'. It is the phrase 'as far as possible' that causes the uncertainty. However, in the light of the answer given by the Court of Justice in the *Marleasing* case to the particular question put by the Spanish court, even as rephrased, two clear principles seem to have been decided or restated.

In the Irish context the first principle decided by the Court of Justice in *Marleasing* is that an Irish court hearing a claim between two private individuals in relation to a matter where there exists law of purely Irish legislative origin which is inconsistent with a directive, the prescribed dates for the implementation of which has passed but which has not been expressly implemented in Irish law, may no longer apply the inconsistent law of purely Irish origin.

This solution, certainly in the Irish context, appears a good constitutional solution to the difficult question of the status in national law of non-implemented directives after the prescribed date. The reason for which I say that is as follows.

If one accepts the principle of the supremacy of EC law and also that the obligations imposed on Member States by Article 5 and 189 of the Treaty include, for matters within their jurisdiction, the national courts of Member States as suggested in *Von Colson and Kamann*[16] then it seems to follow from the provisions of Article 189 in relation to directives that part of such an obligation on the national court must be to desist from applying inconsistent provisions of purely domestic origin after the prescribed date for the implementation of a directive.

Another way of looking at the problem is by analogy with constitutional principles. Accepting the supremacy of EC law and according to directives a higher constitutional status than purely domestic legislation then a directive after the prescribed date for implementation must at minimum prevent all authorities of Member States including national courts from applying any laws inconsistent with the directive. Not to so hold would be to deprive non-implemented directives of any effectiveness in erring Member States.

The constitutional solution of depriving existing laws inconsistent with a new law of higher constitutional status of any effect is of course the principle in Article 50 of the Irish Constitution (1937). As such it is a principle of constitutional law well known to Judge O'Higgins who was a member of the Court who decided *Marleasing*.

My analysis of the full effect of *Marleasing* goes no further in permitting individuals to rely on rights conferred by non-implemented directives than does the express terms of the judgment itself. However, I would suggest that *Marleasing* alters the principle as commonly understood to have been decided by *Marshall*, notwithstanding the recital in paragraph 6 of *Marleasing*. In this paragraph the Court recited with approval the earlier decision in *Marshall*, to the effect that 'a provision of a directive may not be relied upon against such a person [an individual]'. In my view that is precisely what the Court permitted La Comercial to do subsequently in the same judgment. La Comercial set up as its defence to the claim of Marleasing for a declaration of nullity its right pursuant to Article 11 of Directive 68/151 not to have a declaration of nullity made except upon the grounds listed in that Article. La Comercial thus set up the provisions of the non-implemented directive against the existing inconsistent Spanish law to defeat the claim of Marleasing. The Court decided that the Spanish court must decide that it was permitted to do so. To that extent the non-implemented directive does affect rights between individuals.

The second principle affirmed by the Court of Justice in *Marleasing* is that an Irish court is prohibited, in a claim made before it by any person in reliance upon the provisions of a non-implemented Directive, from granting a remedy against an individual (other than the State or an emanation of the State) where such remedy would impose either a civil or criminal obligation on such individual defendant. This is clear I think from the reference to the principles decided in *Marshall* contained in paragraph 6 of the judgment in *Marleasing* and is, I suggest, the limitation intended by the words 'as far as possible' in paragraph 8. In practice this means that if one takes, for example, Council Directive 85/374 of 25 July 1985 on the liability for defective products[17] which ought to have been implemented in Ireland by 30 July 1988 but which was only implemented by an Act which came into force on 16 December 1991. If a claim is brought before an Irish court in reliance upon the provisions of this directive in relation to a cause of action which arose in 1989 against a person

[16] *Supra*, note 6.
[17] OJ 1985 L 210/29.

other than the State or an emanation of the State then an Irish court clearly could not award damages against a person liable in accordance with the provisions of the directive.

If, as I suggest, national courts are now precluded from applying national laws inconsistent with non-implemented directives, but also precluded from applying, in claims between individuals, rights or obligations intended to be conferred by non-implemented directives then there may be a lacuna of applicable law. However this does not appear a dangerous or illogical consequence. It is already a situation well known in Irish law, as the courts declare null and void an Act of the *Oireachtas* as being repugnant to the Constitution but it is and remains a matter for the *Oireachtas* to enact replacement legislation and until such time as it does there may exist a lacuna.

The Court of Justice has minimised the effect of any such lacuna and made another significant advance in protecting individuals from the effect of Member States failing to implement directives which are intended to grant rights or benefits to individuals. In its judgment of 19 November 1991 in *Andrea Francovich and Danila Bonifaci v Italy*[18] it has decided that an individual may recover damages from a Member State who has failed to implement a directive where three conditions are met:

(i) the directive must include the creation of rights for individuals, and
(ii) the content of those rights must be ascertainable from the terms of the directive itself, and
(iii) there must exist a causal link between the damage suffered by the individual and the breach by the Member State of its obligation to implement the directive.

Such liability of Member States for damages to individuals would appear neatly to supplement the above suggested principles. If a national court remains precluded from granting relief to an individual who seeks to assert rights intended to be conferred on him by a directive against another individual in such a way as it would impose an obligation on that other individual then it would appear, where the above conditions are met, the national court may be able to grant relief to the plaintiff individual in the form of damages against the State for any loss or damage suffered by reason of the non-implementation. Taking again the example of the liability for defective products Directive 85/374/EEC in Ireland, the State may be liable for damages which would have been recoverable from persons liable under the Directive if it had been implemented by 30 July 1991 in respect of causes of action arising between 1 August 1988 and 16 December 1991.

There is one further judgment of the Court of Justice since *Marleasing* which will be of great benefit to individuals in relation to rights that were intended to be conferred by directives but where Member States have failed to fully implement directives. It is the judgment in *Theresa Emmott and The Minister for Social Welfare v the Attorney General*.[19] Judge O'Higgins acted as Judge Rapporteur. The judgment is a fine example of his practical approach which was manifest throughout his judicial career.

Mrs Emmott, a married woman, was a social welfare recipient in Ireland. Ireland ought to have implemented Directive 79/7 on the equal treatment for

[18] Joined Cases C-6/90 and C-9/90, not yet reported in ECR.
[19] Case C-208/90, judgment of 25 July 1991, not yet reported in ECR.

men and women in matters of social security[20] by 23 December 1984. It did not do so. It partially implemented the Directive in 1986. In its judgment in *Norah McDermott and Ann Cotter v The Minister for Social Welfare and the Attorney General*[21] the Court of Justice held that Article 4(1) of Directive 79/7 had direct effect from 23 December 1984. On 22 July 1988 Mrs Emmott was given leave to institute proceedings for Judicial Review by the High Court in Ireland for the purpose of recovering the benefits which she had not been paid since 23 December 1984, in breach of Article 4(1) of Directive 79/7. The State pleaded *inter alia* Mrs Emmott's delay in initiating proceedings and sought to rely on Order 84 rule 21(1) of the Rules of the Superior Courts 1986 to defeat her claim. The High Court referred a question as to whether it was contrary to the general principles of Community law for the relevant authorities of a Member State to rely upon national procedural rules, in particular rules relating to time limits in bringing claims in defence of a claim such as this so as to restrict or refuse such compensation.

The Court of Justice answered the question in the affirmative and stated in paragraph 23 of its judgment the essential principle as follows:

> 'It follows that, until such time as a directive has been properly transposed, a defaulting Member State may not rely on an individual's delay in initiating proceedings against it in order to protect rights conferred upon him by the provisions of the directive and that a period laid down by national law within which proceedings must be initiated cannot begin to run before that time.'

It is evident that this principle is of very significant benefit to individuals deprived of rights by reason of its State's failure to fully or properly implement a directive.

Conclusion

The *Marleasing* judgment requires the amendment of the principles relating to non-implemented or partially or incorrectly implemented directives by the deletion of the principle stated at paragraph (iii) above and its replacement by the following.'

(a) A national court may not after the prescribed date for the implementation of a directive apply any law inconsistent with the provisions of the directive.

(b) A directive may not of itself impose obligations on an individual.

Francovich and Bonifaci requires the addition of a principle to the effect that an individual may recover damages from a Member State which has failed to implement a directive where the three conditions referred to earlier in this essay are met.

Emmott requires the addition of a principle to the effect that until such time as a directive has been properly transposed, a defaulting Member State may not rely on an individuals' delay in initiating proceedings against it in order to

---

[20] OJ 1979, L 6/24.
[21] Case 286/85, [1987] ECR 1453.

protect rights conferred upon him by the provisions of the directive and that a period laid down by national law within which proceedings must be initiated cannot begin to run before the full implementation of the Directive.

The question which I have not addressed in this short essay is the position of an Irish court in relation to a claim before it where the conflicting laws are provisions of the Irish Constitution and a non-implemented directive. Hopefully, this is a purely theoretical question and, as such, not of particular interest to a practising lawyer!

23 Review by French Courts of the Conformity of National Provisions with Community Law

Pierre Roseren*

On 25 July 1991, the Court of Justice delivered a preliminary ruling in the *Stoeckel* case[1] in answer to a question referred to it by a French lower criminal court. In essence it ruled that France could not, under Community law, maintain a legislative provision prohibiting night work by women where night work for men was not subject to such a prohibition. The *Confédération Générale du Travail*, one of the major trades unions in France, considered this judgment to be unacceptable on the ground that the Court had imposed its own law on France in violation of all democratic law-making processes.[2]

Of its nature, Community law calls into question the powers of State authorities as laid down in the Constitutions of the Member States. By holding the legislative prohibition at issue to be incompatible with the Community principle of equality of men and women, the judgment has the effect of setting aside an Act of the French Parliament.

Community law not only challenges the constitutional powers of parliament but also the latter's position in relation to courts. The referring criminal court will be under a duty to disregard[3] the legislative provision declared to be contrary to Community law when it decides on the substance of the case.

Through the operation of Community law, the constitutional status of French courts has been considerably enhanced in relation to Parliament, the acts of which, as a sovereign body under French law, were considered to be immune from judicial review by both the judicial and administrative[4] courts of law.

Disregarding laws inconsistent with Community law has not proved an easy task for French courts. Such approach was the more surprising having regard to the monist approach of the French legal system to international law. French courts have readily ensured the precedence of Community law over inconsistent administrative provisions, but their status inherited from the 1789

---

* The views expressed in this Article are personal to the author. Thanks are due to Anthony Collins, Legal Secretary at the Court of Justice of the European Communities for his valuable suggestions regarding both substantial and linguistic aspects of this Article.
[1] Case C-345/89, not yet reported.
[2] *Le Monde* 7 August 1991, p. 13.
[3] See Cases 6/64, *Costa v ENEL*, [1964] ECR 585, at 594 per Advocate General Lagrange and 106/77; *Simmenthal*, [1978] ECR 629, at 644, para 21 per Advocate General Reischl, ruling that every national court must set aside any provision of national law which may conflict with the Community rule.
[4] Administrative courts have jurisdiction over all litigation in which one of the administrative organs of the French State is a party.

suggestions regarding both substantial and linguistic aspects of this Article. Revolution, has for a long time prevented them from disregarding legislative provisions contrary to Community law.

Review by French Courts of the Conformity of Administrative Acts with Community Law

The precedence of rules of international and Community law over administrative acts has never been questioned by French courts. As early as 1901, the *Conseil d'Etat*, the highest administrative court, annulled an administrative act taxing a foreign diplomat in France which had been adopted in violation of an international convention binding France.[5]

In the field of Community law, the same court declared void an importer's notice which had the object and effect of delaying and restricting imports of shoes originating in and imported from other Member States of the Community, thereby infringing Articles 30 and 31 of the EEC Treaty.[6]

The *Conseil d'Etat* has also ensured the precedence of Community secondary legislation, i.e. acts taken by the Community institutions, over national administrative acts. It thus annulled a decree inconsistent with the provisions of a Council Directive.[7] Administrative courts have even raised *ex officio* the violation of a Community Regulation by an administrative act.[8]

On the contrary, French courts have, for historical and constitutional reasons, been far more hesitant to ensure the precedence of Community law over legislative provisions.

Review by French Courts of the Conformity of Legislative Provisions with Community Law

Lack of jurisdiction in ordinary courts to review the constitutionality of laws

Since the French Revolution of 1789, judicial and administrative courts have declined to review the constitutionality of laws. Disregarding such an act on the ground that it violates the Constitution boils down, it is held, to delivering a negative judgment on the operation of Parliament, which an ordinary court is not empowered to do.

Mr Foyer[9] recalls that the Fathers of the Revolution did not want the courts to impose the same treatment on the representatives of the people as was inflicted on the Kings of France by the pre-revolutionary local parliaments. A power to review laws, reminiscent of these former courts' right to refuse to register the King's ordinances, and to deliver admonishments to the Crown, was all the more outrageous to the Fathers of the Revolution as laws were henceforth to be considered as the expression of the will of the People. The Constitution of 3 September 1791 thus provided that 'there is no authority superior to that of the law'. Article 3(1) of the 1958 Constitution underlines the principle that, 'National sovereignty belongs to the people, which shall exercise this sovereignty through its representatives and by means of referendum'.

[5] C.E. 12 June 1901, *Ducaud*, Rec. Lebon p. 524.
[6] C.E. 18 December 1981, *Syndicat National du Commerce de la Chaussure et Autres* Rec. p. 475.
[7] C.E. 28 September 1984, *Confédération nationale des sociétés de protection des animaux de France et des pays d'expression française*, Rec. p. 513.
[8] C.E. 10 July 1970, *Synacomex*, Rec. p. 477.
[9] '*Le mépris de la loi par le juge*', [1990], *La vie judiciaire*, nos 2286, 2288 and 2289.

Specific provisions[10] were adopted to remind the courts of their lack of jurisdiction to question the constitutionality of laws.

Ever since, French courts have scrupulously observed this French approach to the separation of powers. The *Conseil d'Etat* dismissed an action[11] for annulment brought against an administrative act, which alleged the unconstitutionality of the enabling statute. The *Conseil d'Etat* considered that, under French public law, such a submission may not, of its nature, be made before it.

This approach of French courts still obtains today.[12] It is underpinned by the establishment in 1958 of the Constitutional Council, a judicial body entrusted with the power of review of the constitutionality of Acts of Parliament before they come into force.

The initial refusal of ordinary courts to review the conformity of laws with treaties

The cautious stand taken by ordinary courts in relation to laws spilled over to their approach to the relationship between laws and international treaties. Mr Matter, *Procureur Général at the Cour de Cassation*, very aptly summed up the general opinion formerly prevailing.[13] Replying to the question as to the duty of a judge in case of a conflict between a treaty and a subsequent law inconsistent therewith, the *Procureur Général* peremptorily declared that there was no room for any doubt. Courts did not recognize, and were not empowered to recognize, any will other than that of the Law. In his view, this was the very principle on which the French legal system was based.

Since then, the gradual opening up of the French legal order to conventional international law led the drafters of the Constitutions of 1946 and 1958[14] to ensure the prevalence of treaties over laws. The question then arose as to whether the new constitutional provisions empowered the courts to review the conformity of laws adopted subsequent[15] to the entry into force of treaties and to set aside laws inconsistent therewith.

Two opposing opinions were asserted. It was argued that, faced with a contradiction between a treaty and a law, the courts had to apply the higher rule, in pursuance of the express provision in the Constitution to that effect. The opposite view was that courts would in reality, by ensuring the prevalence of treaties over Laws, review the constitutionality of the latter, which was beyond their jurisdiction. In Mr Foyer's[16] opinion, Article 55 of the Consti-

[10] Article 127 of the French Penal Code provides that 'Any judge . . . who interferes with the exercise of the legislative powers either by making rules involving legislative dispositions, or by preventing or impeding the enforcement of one or several laws, or by questioning whether a law should be promulgated or executed . . . shall be deemed guilty of breach of duty and sentenced to loss of civil rights'.

[11] C.E. 6 November 1936, *Sieur Arrighi* Rec. p. 966.

[12] C.E. 22 October 1989, *Roujansky* (1989) La Semaine Juridique II no 21371 and 21 December 1990, *Confédération Nationale des Associations Familiales Catholiques et autres*, (1991) Dalloz *Jurisprudence*, p. 283 ruling that 'the Conseil d'Etat is not empowered to decide on the conformity of laws with the principles laid down in the Preamble to the Constitution'.

[13] Opinion in Cass. Civ. 22 December 1931, (1932) Sirey 1, p. 257.

[14] Article 55 of the 1958 Constitution is worded as follows: 'Treaties or agreements duly ratified or approved shall, upon their publication, have an authority superior to that of laws, subject to each agreement or treaty, to its application by the other party'.

[15] Both administrative and judicial courts readily ensure the precedence of treaties over inconsistent previous laws which are deemed to be repealed or set aside by such treaties. C.E. 15 March 1972 *Dame Veuve Sadok Ali*, Rec. p. 213 and 15 February 1980 *Gabor Winter*, Rec. p. 87.

[16] See note 9 above.

tution binds Parliament and the Government but does not empower the judges to set aside a law contrary to that provision in that it infringes a treaty.

This latter opinion was endorsed by the *Conseil d'Etat*.[17] On the basis of legislative provisions adopted after the ratification of the EEC treaty, the government authorized the import into France of semolina of Algerian origin in exemption of a levy required by a Community Regulation. The *Conseil d'Etat* dismissed the action for annulment brought against the government's decisions by French semolina producers who alleged that the Community Regulation had been violated by the contested decisions.

The *Conseil d'Etat* held that the national legislative provisions prohibited the levy envisaged by the Community Regulations from being imposed. The reasoned submissions made on the case by Mrs Questiaux,[18] the *Commissaire du gouvernement*, shed some light on the reasoning implicit in the judgment. She took the view that ultimately, courts are not empowered to criticize or to disregard laws. On the contrary, their role is the subordinate function of applying laws.

This judgment ran obviously counter to previous judgments of the Court of Justice ruling that Community law prevails over any national provision.[19] Nevertheless, until the *Nicolo* judgment,[20] the *Conseil d'Etat* would not depart from the opinion that courts lack jurisdiction to ensure the precedence over subsequent inconsistent laws or treaties,[21] among which Community treaties and acts of secondary Community legislation.

In *Union démocratique du travail* the *Conseil d'Etat* found[22] that a decree governing the organization of the election of representatives to the Assembly of the European Communities limited itself to implementing the provisions of a law. The allegation that the decree could infringe the EEC Treaty inevitably required the administrative court to review the conformity of the provisions of the law with the Treaty. The *Conseil d'Etat* could not, therefore, examine this argument. Likewise, the *Conseil d'Etat* ruled[23] that it could not entertain the submission that a decree was illegal since such submission implied a decision on the conformity of the Law of 24 May 1976 implemented by the decree with a Council Directive.

The gradual development of the judicial review of the conformity of laws with treaties

(a) *The Constitutional Council*
The preventive review of the constitutionality of laws entrusted by the drafters of the Constitution of 1958 to the Constitutional Council brought to an end the dogma of the immunity of laws from judicial review. French ordinary courts were further encouraged to give up their former cautious approach regarding the conformity of laws with treaties by the very bold decisions delivered by the Constitutional Council from 1971 onwards.

---

[17] C.E. 1 March 1968, *Syndicat général des fabricants de semoules de France*, Rec. p. 149.
[18] (1968) *Revue Trimestrielle de Droit européen*, 388–395.
[19] See Case 6/64, reported in note 3 above.
[20] C.E. 20 October 1989, (1989) *Revue français de droit administratif*, p. 823.
[21] C.E. 31 October 1980, *L. . .*, Rec. p. 403, declining to examine the alleged violation of the European Convention on Human Rights by the law concerning voluntary interruption of pregnancy.
[22] C.E. 22 October 1979 *Union démocratique du travail*, Rec. p. 384.
[23] C.E. 13 December 1985 *Société International Sales and Import Corporation*, Rec. p. 377.

That year the Constitutional Council extended its scope of review of the conformity of laws to the Preamble of the Constitution and no longer confined itself to appraising the conformity of laws solely in relation to the provisions of the Constitution.[24] As the Preamble lays down the list of the major principles governing the operation of a democratic and modern State, this extension was to bring about a much more thorough review of constitutionality of legislation.

Moreover, the Constitutional Council was called upon, under Article 61(2)[25] of the Constitution, to decide on the conformity of an Act relating to voluntary interruption of pregnancy with Article 2 of the European Convention on Human Rights. The Constitutional Council held[26] that under Article 61, it had no jurisdiction to review the conformity of laws with treaties. The supremacy of treaties over laws, as laid down in Article 55 of the Constitution could not, in the Constitutional Council's view, be ensured through the review of constitutionality of laws provided for by Article 61, since these two provisions established two kinds of judicial review of a different nature. Since then, the Constitutional Council has declined several times to examine the conformity of laws with treaties.

It followed that ordinary courts were implicitly empowered by Article 55 of the Constitution to review the conformity of laws to treaties, otherwise denial of justice would have occurred. The Constitutional Council thus established the jurisdiction of ordinary courts to ensure the precedence of treaties over laws and refused to follow the *Algerian Semolina* ruling. The latter had indeed created a judicial vacuum in that it had left no legal remedy against possible infringements of Article 55 by Parliament.

These decisions of the Constitutional Council carried all the more weight as, under Article 62(2) of the Constitution, they must be recognized by all courts. Moreover, in its decision of 3 September 1986[27] concerning the law relating to entry and residence of aliens in France, it held that the prevalence of treaties over laws as enshrined in Article 55 of the Constitution is mandatory and that all State authorities are under a duty to ensure the application of international conventions.

(b) Judicial courts

A short while after the Constitutional Council had delivered its decision on voluntary interruption of pregnancy, the Court of Cassation resorted to the implied powers of ordinary courts to review the conformity of laws to treaties which had been adduced from Article 55 of the Constitution.

In the *Jacques Vabre* judgment[28] the Court of Cassation set aside a legislative provision of the French Customs Code which it held to be contrary to Article 95 of the EEC Treaty, on the ground that under Article 55 of the Constitution this Treaty prevails over legislation inconsistent therewith. The EEC Treaty has

---

[24] Decision of 16 July 1971, Favoreu and Philip *Les grandes décisions du Conseil constitutionnel*, (1984), 3rd ed., p. 222.

[25] Under Article 61(2), the President of the Republic, the Prime Minister, the President of the National Assembly, the President of the Senate, 60 Deputies or 60 Senators may, before their promulgation, submit laws to the Constitutional Council, which shall rule on their constitutionality.

[26] Decision of 15 January 1975 reported in *Favoreu and Philip, ibid*, p. 295.

[27] (1987) *Revenue française de droit administratif*, p. 120.

[28] Cass. Ch. mixte 24 May 1975, *Administration des Douanes v Société Café Jacques Vabre e.a.* (1975) Dalloz *Jurisprudence*, p. 505.

established an autonomous legal order which is integrated into the legal order of Member States. By reason of its special nature, this legal order is directly applicable to the nationals of Member States and thus binds their courts.

This judgment is based both on Article 55 of the Constitution and on the specific nature of Community law. To that extent, the Court of Cassation did not entirely follow the opinion of its *Procureur Général* who had suggested that it base the precedence of the EEC Treaty exclusively on the specific nature of Community law.[29]

The Court of Cassation followed this approach a few months later in the *Van Kempis* judgment[30] where no mention is made of Article 55 of the Constitution. Since then judicial courts have consistently ensured the precedence of Community law over laws, including the Act of 10 August 1981 on the price of books.[31] Likewise, judicial courts are even prepared to examine *ex officio* the conformity of laws with the European Convention on Human Rights.[32]

(c) Administrative courts

Under the cumulative pressure of Community law[33] and of the judgments delivered both by the Constitutional Council and judicial courts, the *Conseil d'Etat* was led first to qualify, then to reverse, its *Algerian Semolina* judgment of 1 March 1968.

(i) The judicial 'immunity' from Community law for administrative acts adopted on the basis of laws subsequent and contrary to France's international undertakings placed the French legal order in complete contradiction with Community law and with the case-law of the Court of Justice.

For instance, a Law of 24 May 1976, amended the State monopoly of manufactured tobacco in order to implement the relevant provisions of the EEC Treaty as specified by a Directive of 1972. Article 6 of this Law provided that the retail price of each product was the same throughout the country and that it was fixed under conditions laid down by decree. In conformity with Article 10 of Decree No 76–1324, retail selling prices of tobacco had been fixed by order of the Minister for Economic Affairs and Finance.

In a judgment of 21 June 1983,[34] the Court of Justice held that France, by fixing the retail selling prices of manufactured tobacco at a different level from that determined by manufacturers or importers had failed to fulfil its obligations under Community law in that compulsory price fixing had been unlawfully extended to imported manufactured tobacco. In spite of this judgment, the *Conseil d'Etat* subsequently dismissed an action for annulment brought by an importer against an administrative decision refusing the

---

[29] (1975) Dalloz *Jurisprudence*, p. 504.

[30] Cass. 3rd civ. Ch. 15 December 1975, Bulletin Civ. III No 373 p. 282. See also Cass. Crim 16 June 1983, *Rossi di Montalera*, (1983) *La Semaine Juridique* II No 20044.

[31] Cass. Com. 15 May 1985, *Association des centres distributeurs Edouard Leclerc e.a.* Bull. Civ. IV, No 156, pp. 133–134.

[32] Cass. Crim. 5 May 1978, *Coulon*, Bull. crim. no 139, p. 352 and 5 December 1978 *Baroum Chérif*, Bull. crim. no 346, p. 906.

[33] See in that respect the opinion of the Commissaire du gouvernement in the *Nicolo* case in (1989) *La Semaine Juridique*, Jurisprudence, no 21371: 'Nowadays, wide areas of our law consist to a large extent in truly international legal provisions. If we cannot ensure the supremacy of treaties over laws, such developments will be hampered. France cannot at the same time consent to limitations of sovereignty and uphold the supremacy of its laws before French courts. Your judgment of 1968 seems to have underestimated the inconsistency of such approach'.

[34] Case 90/82, [1983] ECR 2011 at 2032, para. 30 per Advocate General Mancini.

authorisation to raise the price of certain products.[35] The *Conseil d'Etat* considered that the government had limited itself to applying the single price principle laid down by the law and that challenging the legality of the decree boiled down to a challenge to the conformity of the law with Community law.

Since France did not amend the law to bring it into conformity with the judgment of the Court of Justice that Court delivered a second judgment against France for failure to fulfil its Community obligations.[36]

Furthermore, the position of the *Conseil d'Etat* placed the two branches of the French court system – judicial and administrative courts – in contradiction with each other. Depending on the judicial remedy available – action before an administrative court or before a judicial court – the plaintiff could lose or win his case. These inconsistencies between both branches of the judiciary led in fact to preposterous and unjustifiable practical consequences.[37]

Lastly, the position of the *Conseil d'Etat* was likely to lead to incongruities within the administrative branch itself. Depending whether the government had implemented Community law upon reliance on the independent regulatory powers conferred directly by Article 37(1) of the Constitution[38] or on the basis of a law, the administrative courts found they enjoyed or did not enjoy jurisdiction to adjudicate on the conformity of administrative provisions with Community law.[39]

(ii) The *Conseil d'Etat* was therefore led to mitigate the consequences of its case-law by interpreting laws in such a way as require them to be consistent with treaties. To that extent, laws were deemed to have implicitly reserved the operation of such treaties.[40]

On the other hand the *Conseil d'Etat* made the distinction between laws enabling the Executive to take executive provisions and laws establishing substantial provisions.

When administrative provisions had been taken not to implement the substantive provisions of a law but were merely based on an enabling law, the administrative court considered it had jurisdiction to review the conformity of the administrative provisions with Community law. Thus, the *Conseil d'Etat* agreed to examine the allegation that the EEC treaty had been infringed by a decree adopted on the basis of an enabling law of 1978 to prohibit the marketing of deep-frozen yogurts as yogurt.[41]

On the contrary, when a law had laid down substantial provisions which the government had confined itself to implementing, the *Conseil d'Etat* declined to examine the submission alleging the illegality of the administrative act in relation to Community law. The *Conseil d'Etat* held that an action for annulment brought against a decree punishing infringements to the Act of 10 August 1981 on the price of books could not be entertained as it necessarily implied a review of the conformity of the Act with the Treaty.[42]

---

[35] C.E. 13 December 1985, quoted in note 23 above.

[36] Case 169/87, *Commission v France* [1988] p. 4093 at 4118, para. 15 per Advocate General Cruz Vilaça.

[37] Compare e.g. the judgments concerning the same Law quoted in notes 31 and 42.

[38] 'Matters other than those that fall within the domain of law shall be of a regulatory character.'

[39] See the *Synacomex* judgment reported in note 8 above.

[40] See judgment of 13 December 1985 quoted in note 35 specifying alternatively that the Minister had not acted in violation of the relevant Community provisions.

[41] C.E. 19 November 1986, *Société SMANOR et Syndicat national des produits surgelés*, Rec. p. 260.

[42] C.E. 8 February 1985, *Association des Centres distributeurs Edouard Leclerc*, Rec. p. 25.

(iii) Ultimately, the *Conseil d'Etat* was led to reverse the *Algerian Semolina* case in the *Nicolo* judgment.[43] Such a reversal was bound to constitute a judicial event of considerable importance, after the *Conseil d'Etat* had refused for more than 20 years to review the conformity of laws with treaties.

Mr Nicolo claimed that Article 227–1 of the EEC Treaty had been infringed by the law of 7 July 1977 relating to the election of the French representatives to the European Parliament, insofar as it included the French overseas Départements and Territories into the national constituency. The *Conseil d'Etat* agreed to review the conformity of the law with Article 227–1 which defines the territorial scope of application of the EEC Treaty. The *Conseil d'Etat* tersely found that the provisions laid down by the law were not incompatible with the clear provisions of Article 227–1. By implication the *Conseil d'Etat* considered that it had jurisdiction under Article 55 of the Constitution to review the conformity of the law at issue with the EEC Treaty.

The court later confirmed this solution in its judgment of 21 December 1990[44] where it held that having regard to the requirements laid down in Article 1 of the Law No 75–17, concerning voluntary interruption of pregnancy, the combined provisions of Laws of 17 January 1975 and 31 December 1979 were not incompatible with Article 2(4) of the European Convention on Human Rights and Article 6 of the International Covenant on Civil and Political Rights.

Other administrative courts have also reviewed the validity of legislative provisions in relation to Community secondary legislation. The *Conseil d'Etat* held that a law cannot prevent the application of a Community Regulation even if the law is subsequent to the adoption of the Regulation.[45] Furthermore, the Nantes Administrative Court of Appeal has found that a provision of the General Tax Code laid down by a Law of 1978 was not incompatible with the objectives of a Community Directive.[46]

The Legal Basis of the Primacy of Community Law

Some of the judgments quoted above entertain certain doubts as from which legal order – national or Community law – the legal basis of the primacy of Community law is drawn. In his opinion in *Nicolo*, the Commissaire du gouvernement advocated an exclusive reliance upon national law, and ruled out any reliance upon Community law in that respect. Having regard to the flaws affecting a national law basis, this opinion is debatable.

The inappropriateness of a basis in national law for the primacy of Community law

Article 55 of the Constitution appears insufficient in several respects to establish the undisputed precedence of Community law over any rule of national law.

(a) Nothing in theory would prevent Parliament from repealing Article 55,

---

[43] See note 20 above.
[44] See note 12 above.
[45] C.E. 24 September 1990, *Boisdet*, (1990) *Actualité juridique – Droit administratif, Doctrine*, p. 863.
[46] 4 April 1990, (1990) *Revue de jurisprudence Française* no 931. See also Paris Administrative Court of Appeal, 20 March 1990, *ibid.* no 678.

thus unilaterally bringing to an end the supremacy of Community law in the French legal system. Such an occurrence may seem remote and unreal but it may be useful to recall past attempts – fortunately ill-fated – aimed at preventing courts from ensuring the precedence of treaties over laws 'for whatever reason'.[47] If such an amendment were adopted according to the rules governing the amendments[48] to the Constitution, Article 55 would be replaced by a prohibition on Courts from ensuring the precedence of Community law over national legislation.

(b) Article 55 of the Constitution only covers 'treaties or regularly ratified or approved international agreements'. Therefore this provision is not appropriate to ensure the prevalence over national law of Community secondary legislation such as Regulations of the Council or of the Commission.

It emerges from *Simmenthal*[49] that not only the provisions of the Treaties but also the acts of Community institutions prevail over national law. On the other hand, these acts are, under Community law, automatically integrated into French law without any national measure incorporating same. As early as 1973[50] the Court of Justice condemned the practice whereby Community Regulations were reenacted into domestic law:

> 'According to the terms of Article 189 and 191 of the Treaty, Regulations are, as such, directly applicable in all Member States and come into force solely by virtue of their publication in the Official Journal of the Communities, as from the date specified in them, or in the absence thereof, as from the date provided in the Treaty.
> Consequently, all methods of implementation are contrary to the Treaty which would have the result of creating an obstacle to the direct effect of Community Regulations and of jeopardizing their simultaneous and uniform application in the whole of the Community.'

As every conversion into national law of directly applicable provisions of secondary Community legislation is prohibited, and as such provisions prevail over national provisions, it appears that Article 55 of the Constitution cannot constitute a valid legal basis for the supremacy of secondary Community law.

(c) Lastly, Article 55 makes the supremacy of the Treaties dependent on their reciprocal application by the other contracting parties. Apart from the fact that this provision seems to have been drafted for the purpose of bilateral conventions, such a reciprocity clause is incompatible with the objectives pursued by the Community. Indeed the Community constitutes a new legal order the subjects of which comprise not only Member States but also their nationals.[51]

---

[47] G. Isaac, 'A propos de l'"amendement Aurillac": vers une obligation pour les juges d'appliquer les lois contraires aux traités,' (1980) *Gazette du Palais 2*, Doctrine, p. 583.
[48] Under Article 89 of the Constitution
'. . .
(2) The Government or Parliamentary bill for amendment must be passed by the two Assemblies in identical terms. The amendment shall become definitive after approval by a referendum.
(3) Nevertheless, the proposed amendment shall not be submitted to a referendum when the President of the Republic decides to submit it to Parliament convened in Congress; in this case, the proposed amendment shall be approved only if it is accepted by a three-fifths majority of the votes cast. . .'.
[49] See note 3 above.
[50] Case 39/72, *Commission v Italy* [1973] p. 101, at 114, para. 17 per Advocate General Mayras.
[51] Case 26/62, *Van Gend & Loos* [1963] ECR, p. 3, at 12, per Advocate General Roemer.

The Court of Justice has definitely ruled out that a Member State could withhold performance of its own obligations on the ground that another party had failed to perform its own:

'In fact, the Treaty is not limited to creating reciprocal obligations between the different natural and legal persons to whom it is applicable, but establishes a new legal order which governs the powers, rights and obligations of the said persons, as well as the necessary procedures for taking cognizance of and penalizing any breach of it. Therefore, except where otherwise expressly provided, the basic concept of the Treaty requires that the Member States shall not take the law into their own hands. Therefore the fact that the Council failed to carry out its obligations cannot relieve the defendant States from carrying out theirs.'[52]

Likewise the French Court of Cassation[53] had also found that no plea adduced from the failure of another party to perform its obligations may be put forward by a State before national courts since failure by a Member State to fulfil its obligations under the Treaty is amenable to the Court of Justice under Article 169 of the Treaty.

The specific nature of Community law as the basis of its primacy

The Court of Justice bases the primacy of Community law on its specific nature, stemming from a transfer of real powers from the Member States to the Community and from its direct applicability both to nationals of Member States and to themselves.

'. . . the law stemming from the Treaty, an independent source of law, could not, because of its special and original nature, be overridden by domestic legal provisions, however framed, without being deprived of its character as Community law and without the legal basis of the Community itself being called into question.'[54]

The Court later specified that:

'Indeed any recognition that national legislative measures which encroach upon the field within which the Community exercises its legislative power or which are otherwise incompatible with the provisions of Community law had any legal effect would amount to a corresponding denial of the effectiveness of obligations undertaken unconditionally and irrevocably by Member States pursuant to the treaty and would thus imperil the very foundations of the Community.'[55]

Since the supremacy of Community law over national law results from the very nature of the Community it could not be made dependent on requirements obtaining in national law. The primacy of Community law is an 'existential requirement':[56] since this law is common to all Member States it

---

[52] Joined cases 90 & 91/63, *Commission v Luxembourg and Belgium* [1964] ECR, p. 625, at 631, per Advocate General Roemer.
[53] See note 28 above.
[54] Case 6/64 quoted in note 3 above.
[55] Case 106/77 quoted in note 3 above.
[56] P. Pescatore, *L'ordre juridique des Communautés européennes* (Presses Universitaires de Liège, 1973), p. 227.

must necessarily prevail over any conflicting national rule of whatever nature, constitutional, legislative or administrative.[57]

Therefore Article 55 of the Constitution is ruled out as the appropriate basis for the supremacy of Community law, including secondary legislation. It may be recalled in that connection that in the aforementioned *Boisdet* judgment[58] the *Conseil d'Etat* itself has ensured the prevalence of a Community Regulation over an inconsistent law without relying on Article 55 of the Constitution.

The Liberation of Courts from National Procedural Fetters

Once the supremacy of Community law rests on its special nature, national courts are empowered and obliged by such law to set aside any procedural rule of whatever nature, insofar as such a rule impairs the full effectiveness of Community law. This considerably increases the powers of courts within the national legal systems by exempting them from undue procedural hindrances, as will emerge from the following examples.

(1) The Court of Justice ruled[59] that a provision of national law whereby a court is bound on points of law by the rulings of a superior court could not deprive the inferior courts of their power to refer to the Court questions of interpretation of Community law involving such rulings. The inferior court must be free, if it considers that the ruling on law made by the superior court could lead it to give a judgment contrary to Community law, to refer to the Court questions which concern it.

This decision was justified on the ground that if inferior courts were to be bound without being able to refer matters to the Court, the jurisdiction of the latter to give preliminary rulings and the application of Community law at all levels of the judicial systems of the Member States would be compromised.

(2) The Court further found[60] that, even if a national legal order prohibits courts, in accordance with the constitutional principle of the separation of powers, from applying a law inconsistent with Community law on the ground that such law thereby being unconstitutional must first be repealed or declared to be unconstitutional by the competent constitutional authority of the Member State, national courts are nevertheless under a duty to give full effect to the relevant Community provisions, refusing of their own motion to apply the conflicting law, and it is not necessary for those courts to request or await the prior setting aside of such law by Parliament or by a constitutional court.

Such decision invalidates proposals floated in the wake of the *Nicolo* ruling in order to neutralize the 'new' administrative courts' power to review the conformity of Laws to international treaties. For instance it was suggested[61] to grant the Constitutional Council the exclusive power to review the conformity of laws with treaties. If such a proposal had been acted upon, the issue of conformity would have been a preliminary question to be referred beforehand to the Constitutional Council. It was also suggested to maintain the power of the Minister for Foreign Affairs to interpret international conventions but to

---

[57] See Case 6/64 cited in note 3 above.
[58] See note 45 above.
[59] Case 166/73, *Rheinmühlen* [1974] ECR 33, at 38, para. 4 per Advocate General Warner.
[60] See Case 106/77 mentioned in note 3 above.
[61] See Foyer quoted in note 9 above.

make his interpretation binding both on the Constitutional Council and on ordinary courts.

But there cannot be, under Community law, any other procedure to be observed by a national court called upon to apply Community law than the one laid down in Article 177 of the EEC Treaty. The prevalence of the Treaty implies the prevalence of both its provisions and its system of legal remedies. Article 177 gives the Court of Justice the final say in the interpretation and the review of validity of Community law in accordance with Article 164 of the Treaty. Indeed, that provision entrusts the Court of Justice with the duty of ensuring the observance of the law in the interpretation and application of the EEC Treaty.

(3) In its judgment of 19 June 1990[62] the Court of Justice ruled that no rule of national law should prevent a court seised of a dispute governed by Community law from granting interim relief in order to ensure the full effectiveness of the judgment to be given. In such a case the national court must accordingly under Community law set aside such national provision.

(4) Lastly, Community law precludes the authorities of a Member State from relying, in proceedings brought against them by an individual before the national courts in order to protect rights directly conferred upon him by the provisions of a Directive, on national procedural rules relating to time-limits for bringing proceedings so long as that Member State has not properly transposed that Directive into its domestic legal system.[63] In such an occurrence national courts may not, under Community law, declare the individual's action time-barred and they must therefore disregard the national time-limitation rule.

Conclusion

French courts no longer challenge the principle of the supremacy of Community law over national law as such. Community law has amplified the relative 'decline' of laws initiated by the review of the constitutionality of laws set up in 1958. The absolute democratic principle and its corollary, the sovereignty of laws, have now been replaced by the duty of Parliament to observe international and Community rules. Community law has promoted French Courts from their former subordinate role of applying laws to the task of reviewing their validity in relation to France's international commitments. Community law has also conferred the necessary powers to that effect on French courts. The judicial co-operation under Article 177 of the EEC Treaty between French courts and the Court of Justice has proved instrumental in such a process.

However, there still remain sizeable divergencies between the case-law of the Court of Justice and decisions of French administrative courts concerning the effect of Community law in French law.

For instance, the *Conseil d'Etat* ruled that the validity of an individual administrative act may not be reviewed in direct relation to a Community

---

[62] Case C-213/89, *Factortame* [1990] ECR I-2433, at I-2474, para. 23 per Advocate General Tesauro.

[63] Judgment of 25 July 1991, case C-208/90, *Emmott*, not yet reported.

Directive.[64] This runs directly counter to numerous judgments of the Court of Justice declaring that provisions of Directives may produce direct effects in the legal order of Member States.[65] This ruling of the *Conseil d'Etat* still holds good to-day although the Administrative Court has qualified it to a certain extent by finding[66] that state authorities may not lawfully, once the deadline set for implementing a Directive has expired, maintain administrative provisions incompatible with the obectives set by the Directive.

On the other hand, the *Conseil d'Etat* failed to take into consideration a ruling of the Court of Justice[67] declaring that France had failed to fulfil its Community obligations by rendering exports to the other Member States conditional upon submission of an export declaration previously endorsed by the competent state authority. In the ensuing action for damages brought by an aggrieved exporter against the French State[68] the *Conseil d'Etat* did not find the export declaration as illegal under French law on the ground that such measure had been taken in the general interest. Instead, the Administrative Court held that the State was liable to the plaintiff not in tort but on the basis of absolute liability such as is incurred by the State when it breaches the principle of the citizens' equality of duties in relation to common good.

Having regard to those decisions, it is interesting to point out that the Court of Justice has ruled lately[69] that individuals must be allowed before national courts to claim compensation of damages resulting from a Member State's failure to implement a Directive. Now French courts are faced with the formidable new challenge of finding the State not only liable in tort for breach of its Community obligations but also for failing to implement a Directive creating rights to individuals. It may safely be said that Community law sets new challenges to Parliament and Courts alike. A new challenge is looming up for them: the notification of the Maastricht Treaty in relation to national sovereignty. It may well be that ratification of the Treaty, to the extent that it implies giving up some of their sovereignty by Member States, will only be constitutionally feasible in France after prior amendment of the Constitution.[70]

---

[64] C.E. 28 December 1978, *Cohn-Bendit* Rec. p. 524 ruling that Directives cannot be relied upon by nationals of Member States in actions for annulment brought against individual administrative decisions failing general implementing provisions by the Government.

[65] See Case 8/81, *Becker* [1981] ECR 53, at 71, para. 25 per Advocate General Slynn.

[66] C.E. 3 February 1989, *Compagnie Alitalia* (1989) Revue française de droit administratif, p. 415.

[67] Case 68/76, *Commission v France* [1977] 515, at 531, para. 24 per Advocate General Capotorti.

[68] C.E. 23 March 1984, *Société Alivar* Rec. p. 128.

[69] Judgment of 19 November 1991, Cases C-6/90 and 9/90, *Francovich e.a. v Italian Republic*, not yet reported.

[70] Under Article 54 of the Constitution 'if the Constitutional Council, the matter having been referred to it by the President of the Republic, by the Premier, or by the President of one or the other Assembly, shall declare that an international commitment contains a clause contrary to the Constitution, the authorisation to ratify or approve this commitment may be given only after amendment of the Constitution'.

Part 4

Judicial Review in Other European Jurisdictions

24 Judicial Review of Legislation in the Netherlands

T Koopmans

A system of national legislation was unknown in the United Dutch Republics; probably, the lawyers of the period had only a hazy idea as to what 'national' legislation might mean. There were some union institutions, like the fleet and the army, and also a representative body called the 'States General' of the provinces; its powers were, however, extremely limited, and they did not include what we would now call law-giving powers. It is only after the collapse of the Republics, in 1795, that a real 'central government' was established at The Hague, previously the capital of Holland (admittedly the most important, economically and politically, of the seven Republics). Under growing French influence, national taxes were introduced, a rudimentary system of education was organized, and a Dutch version of the French codes entered into force.

When the country became again independent after the fall of Napoleon, in 1813, there was no restoration in the true sense of the word: the Netherlands became a unitary State, and a Kingdom at that, initially together with the Southern Netherlands, which had been under Spanish and Austrian rule in republican times. The experience was short-lived, as Belgium seceded already in 1830. The Northern part continued its walk through history as a unitary state, under the title 'Kingdom of the Netherlands', which it had assumed before the secession. The new Kingdom had a national Parliament called 'States General', but unlike its republican predecessor this body did not represent cities, or regions, or provinces, it was considered to represent the population directly (although universal suffrage was only introduced in 1918).[1]

In its early years, the Kingdom was very much influenced by the British constitutional model. Britain, the old enemy on the Seven Seas, was now hailed as the great friend who had helped to re-establish independence; it was also, and very properly, taken to be the new leading power in Europe. Whatever the motives, the influence was strong, not only in the Netherlands but also in Belgium, which had to construct, in a way, a new constitutional system. Both countries adopted a written constitution, and both constitutions gave a prominent place to the legislative power. Parliament was not sovereign, in the *Diceyan* sense of the term, as it had to observe the provisions of the

---

[1] See, about the birth and the early years of the unitary state: EF Kossmann, *The Low Countries* (Oxford 1978) ch. I–IV.

constitution;[2] but the whole constitutional fabric seemed to be devised in such a way that the legislative power was only limited by its own assessment as to what kind of laws might possibly be contrary to the Constitution. The prevailing impression in the Netherlands was that a decent government and a decent Parliament would, of course, never act in violation of the Constitution.

In 1848, when revolutions broke out in the main capitals of the European continent, the Netherlands quietly modernized their Constitution. In accordance with the spirit of the times, provisions were introduced to reduce royal prerogatives and to emphasize ministerial responsibility. More or less accidentally, a sentence was added declaring that 'statutes are inviolable'. It was to remain the basis of much constitutional thinking for about one century, although one of the leading politicians of the 19th century expressed already his misgivings at an early stage: he thought the new provision was a 'slogan' that would 'act as a shield against the Constitution', making everybody feel 'outside a closed door'.[3] Knocking at that door only started after World War II. In the first part of the 20th century, the rule of inviolability had become one of the main assumptions underlying the case law of the courts, and it had also become accepted wisdom among the constitutional lawyers.

The rule was thought to mean that judicial review of legislation was excluded. The theory behind it was that the government and the States General, which constitute the legislative power and which act on the advice of the Council of State (a very dignified body consisting of deserving administrative lawyers and of elder statesmen), will be sufficiently aware of the constitutional implications of what they are doing. As they will not have any inclination to violate the Constitution, because of the very position they occupy in the constitutional system, judicial supervision of constitutionality of legislation is superfluous. And as it is superfluous it is dangerous, because the search for hidden violations of the Constitution might entice the courts into the area of politics. Some spice was added to this opinion by the generally accepted view that constitutional questions have predominantly a political character. When, for example, the Constitution provides that the electoral system shall be based on proportional representation, it was for the legislative bodies to decide whether a certain threshold – a minimum number of votes required to share in the allocation of seats – is compatible with the notion of proportionality or not. Such a problem was, in the view then prevailing, a matter to be settled by political debate, and not by the courts.[4]

As a result, the case-law of the *Hoge Raad* – Supreme Court in matters of private law, criminal law and tax – shows some degree of similarity with British cases where courts refuse to enter into problems of validity of statutes adopted by Parliament. Like the British courts, the *Hoge Raad* did not inquire 'whether an act of the legislature was *ultra vires*'; neither did it 'go behind what has been enacted . . . and . . . inquire how the enactment came to be made, whether it arose out of incorrect information' or not etc.[5]

---

[2] See, on the notion of sovereignty of Parliament, AW Bradley, in: Jowell and Oliver (eds.), *The Changing Constitution* (Oxford 1985) ch. 2.

[3] He was Jan Rudolf Thorbecke, 1798–1872, still considered as the most important Dutch liberal politician and constitutionalist.

[4] See, on the Dutch electoral system, Hans Daalder, in: SE Finer (ed.), *Adversary Politics and Electoral Reform* (London 1975) p. 223.

[5] Quotations from *Mortensen v Peters* (1906) 8 F (Just Cas) 93; *Hoani Te Heuheu Tukino v Aotea District Maori Land Board* [1941] AC (PC) 322.

The first breach in the system was made in 1953. During a revision of constitutional provisions which concerned the end of constitutional links with Indonesia, Parliament adopted an amendment intended to adjust the Constitution to the coming evolution of international law, and in particular to the requirements of European integration as they were then in the air. Technically, the amendment was so badly drafted that it had to be redone in 1956; it was only then that observers started to discover the scope of the modification. In the 1956 version, the Constitution paves the way for far reaching forms of international integration, by providing that legislative, administrative and judicial powers can be transferred to institutions of international organizations, and that provisions of international treaties 'which, according to their nature, are capable of binding the citizens', shall have this binding force after publication; they will then prevail over earlier or later provisions of national law in case of incompatibility.[6]

There is little doubt that the purpose of the constitutional amendment was to 'open' the Constitution for the consequences of the integration process: in 1953, the European Coal and Steel Community began its activities; in 1956, the establishment of a European Defence Community was hotly debated. From this point of view, the amendment had the effect which was intended. Priority of treaty rules over national legislation facilitated the transition from a purely national legal system to a more pluralistic situation where Community rules are to be applied by the national courts.[7] Accordingly, the *Hoge Raad* found no problems where courts in other Member States did. Unlike French courts, it had no difficulty in admitting that treaty rules and provisions adopted by EEC institutions also prevail over later statutes, as the *lex posterior* maxim does not apply to this conflict according to the constitutional amendment. And unlike Italian and German courts, the *Hoge Raad* can set aside national legislation it considers contrary to EEC rules without feeling obliged to scrutinize the constitutionality of EEC provisions, for example as far as observance of human rights is concerned. International rules simply come first, as soon as they can be considered as being 'capable of binding the citizens'.

The meaning of the latter expression was gradually developed by the *Hoge Raad* in a number of cases starting in the early sixties. In one of the first judgments, in 1960, a lower court had made a distinction between 'provisions which, by their very nature, can be directly applied by the courts' and 'provisions which have no other purpose than to give instructions to legislative or administrative bodies'. The *Hoge Raad* affirmed; it held that international treaty provisions obliging contracting States to modify their legislation do not create any right a citizen can rely upon before a national court.[8] This view presents an interesting parallelism with the art and manner in which the Court of Justice defines such notions as direct effect and direct applicability under Community law. In later years, the *Hoge Raad* seemed more and more inclined

---

[6] See, on the 1953 and 1956 revisions, HF van Panhuys, *The Netherlands Constitution and International Law*, 47 AJIL 537 (1953) and 58 AJIL 88 (1964).

[7] See also my article 'Receptivity and its limits, the Dutch case', in: St. John Bates and others (eds.), *In memoriam J.D.B. Mitchell* (London 1983) p. 91.

[8] This was the *AOW I* case (Ned. Jurispr. 1960 no. 483). It concerned conscientious objections to social security schemes for old age pensions; a vicar considered such schemes contrary to the European Convention on Human Rights.

to interpret the Dutch constitutional expression in the light of the case law of the Court of Justice.[9]

The most important blow to the principle of inviolability of statutes was not delivered by Community law, but by the implementation of the European Convention on Human Rights.

Initially, this seemed most unlikely. The Convention had been ratified, and the right of individual complaints had been recognized, for the very reason that the Convention was generally presumed to be a fairly harmless instrument. It was taken for granted that the Dutch legal order was in complete harmony with the human rights provisions. Confidential government papers which have recently been made accessible leave no doubt on this point.[10] The first cases on the impact of the Convention on Dutch legislation did not look very promising for human rights activists: Dutch courts followed a restrictive line when interpreting the rights conferred by the Convention, but they gave a broad scope to the exceptions admitted by it. In a famous judgment of 1962, the *Hoge Raad* held that legislation limiting the right of organizing religious processions to places where such processions were customary before 1848 (i.e. to the then Catholic regions of the country) was not contrary to the freedom of religion as embodied in Article 9 of the Convention. The court examined the reasons the legislative bodies had adduced when the 1848 rule was elevated to law, and it found that the main reason had been the protection of public order (one of the grounds justifying an exception under Article 9, paragraph 2, of the Convention). In verifying if such a reason could still be considered as valid in 1962, the court simply stated that the question to be resolved was whether a reasonable legislator could still think that the rule was necessary for the protection of public order, and it said that it was 'not unimaginable' that a reasonable legislator would think so.[11] Although this judgment has been much criticized, it was generally considered as typically representing the court's view on judicial attitudes to the Convention. However, after somewhat more than twenty years, it turned out to have been the thin end of the wedge.

The first signs of a slow change occurred in the late sixties and the early seventies, when Article 10 of the Convention, on freedom of expression, began to be quoted more often than the corresponding Article 7 of the Constitution. New problems arose on the relationship between public order and freedom to express opinions in new and different forms (it was the time of the great Vietnam demonstrations and, more generally, of student and youth rebellions); the constitutional provision was not very helpful as it protected only freedom of the press, and not manifestations of opinion by wearing sandwichboards, waving flags or shouting slogans. But once started, the movement towards a less restrictive interpretation of the Convention soon gathered speed. Courts began to take the Convention's provisions on human rights more seriously, to the point of treating them as a kind of European Bill of Rights. This development was greatly helped by case law of the European Court of Human Rights. Judgments condemning the Netherlands for not complying with the Convention first met with dismay; however, after some

---

[9] See, on the notion of direct effect in Community law, TC Hartley, *The foundations of European Community Law* (2nd ed., Oxford 1988) ch 7.

[10] Extracts have been published in a monthly law review (*Rechtsgeleerd Magazijn Themis* 1991 p. 220).

[11] This was the *Geertruidenberg II* case (Ned. Jurispr. 1962 no. 107). It concerned a small town in the catholic south of the country where it appeared impossible to establish that processions had taken place before 1848.

time a puzzled search began for the reasons why Dutch legislation on such matters as disciplinary measures for conscripts and rights of appeal for psychiatric patients could possibly violate human rights provisions.[12] As Dutch courts had themselves power to strike down national rules which are not in conformity with the Convention under the Constitution as it stands since 1953–1956, a new line of investigative case law developed.

Nowadays, the *Hoge Raad* considers that most of the Convention's provisions defining human rights can be directly applied, and are thus capable of overruling national legislation, statutes included. In that way, many concepts originating in the Convention gradually found their way into the case-law of the Dutch courts. The protection of 'family life', according to Article 8 of the Convention, had, for example, a profound influence. The courts held in particular that rules on expulsion of non-nationals had to respect this principle. Recently, the *Hoge Raad* began to take a fresh look at different provisions of the Civil Code on family law; it ruled, amongst others, that the legal situation of children of divorced couples should be settled on the basis of Article 8 of the Convention.[13] This was especially interesting because the Civil Code provisions on such matters as parental authority and guardianship of minors were not old-fashioned or traditional rules, as they had been thoroughly revised in recent years. Similarly, the *Hoge Raad* held that a mother of an illegitimate child could not block recognition of the child by the biological father – as the Code said – when the man in question could justify having lived together with mother and child, his 'family life' then being protected by the Convention.

As a result, statutes seem a lot less 'inviolable' than twenty or thirty years ago.

As case law on the European Convention developed, it seemed more and more odd, and for some observers even absurd, that Dutch courts could rely on the Convention but not on the Constitution when the compatibility of statutes with human rights standards was challenged. There seemed to be some lack of harmony in the Dutch legal system, as it allowed courts to refashion family law on the basis of human rights defined by an international treaty, but not on the basis of the Netherlands Constitution. Some authors admonished the Dutch constitutionalists 'to find the tone in which this discord can be resolved'. In other terms: the debate on judicial review of legislation was reopened.

The debate became more intense when criticism of legislative performance increased. Was the idea that important political decisions were to be taken by a body representing the population not a hollow slogan, when important statutes were in fact concocted by civil servants and subsequently adopted by the States General without any real debate; or when government decisions on financial margins rather than policy considerations determined the scope of the citizens' rights under social security schemes? Confidence in the wisdom of representative bodies, which had characterized Dutch political culture for a considerable period of time, seemed to erode. A statute limiting students' rights under a 'study financing system' (which amounted to a generalized scholarship scheme) was adopted in great haste by the two chambers of Parliament in order to meet a financial deadline; it was discovered only

---

[12] An example is the European Court's judgment in *Engel* (June 8, 1976, CEDH series A vol. 22).
[13] Interesting reports on the impact of Article 8 on Dutch case-law have been prepared for the 1990 meeting of the Netherlands Lawyers Association: *Handelingen Ned. Juristenvereniging* 120-I.

afterwards that university students already enrolled for certain courses, in the expectation that the system would apply to them, were retroactively deprived of that benefit. The argument that such legislation violates legal certainty was accepted by the *Hoge Raad*; but the court emphasized once again its powerlessness when holding that it could not strike down a statute for other reasons than those permitted by the constitutional amendments of 1953–1956.[14] Nevertheless, the judgment acted as a signal that the legislative power can not always be trusted.

At the same time, people are getting more litigious. Unpopular government decisions are often challenged in actions for interim injunctions; and this even happens in cases where the government decision is of a highly political nature. Thus, the government decided in 1985, after years of public debate accompanied by mass demonstrations, that American cruise missiles were to be stationed in the south of the country, unless some political conditions were met before a certain date. The Dutch peace movement, particularly strong at the time, immediately brought an action for interim relief, alleging that the decision had been taken in violation of obligations existing under public international law. The judge of first instance and the court of appeal refused to take the case because of lack of jurisdiction; the *Hoge Raad*, however, considered courts were competent to examine the issue, but it found that, in the present state of public international law, no rule or principle had been disregarded by the government decision.[15] It would be very hard indeed to imagine a comparable decision in the fifties or the sixties. The case has, of course, no direct bearing on problems of judicial review of legislation, but it illustrates how, even without judicial review, political decisions tend to be attacked before the courts.

A new chapter was added to the debate by the appearance upon the scene of a new generation of lawyers. Generally speaking, they see law much more as value-oriented than their predecessors used to do. Protection of human rights is a creed to them, rather than just an element, among others, of the constitutional system. They established prospering associations and successful reviews on human rights, on penal reform, on protection of minorities and on emancipation of women. They took the lessons of the European Court of Human Rights to heart and advocated full implementation in the Netherlands of legal principles such as fair trial and equality of arms which, in that form, had previously been unknown in criminal justice. They studied American constitutional law and were impressed by the contribution the US Supreme Court had made to the evolution of society. And, most importantly, they pinned their faith in the activities of judges, not in politics.

One of the central concepts in the change of the ideological climate is the necessity of 'legal protection'. The State, once considered to be the fountain of justice and the guarantee for the rule of law, is more and more seen as the main menace to individual liberties. Consequently, acts of public authorities ought to be reviewable, whatever their legal status. Those who propound this doctrine find some support in the case law of both European courts. The

---

[14] *Harmonisatiewet* case (Ned. Jurispr. 1989 no. 469). There was an interesting side-debate on the question whether the inviolability rule was not only enshrined in the Netherlands Constitution, but also in the Charter of the Kingdom, a constitutional document on links between the Netherlands and the Dutch Antilles.

[15] The *Cruise missile* case was only decided in 1989 (Ned. Jurispr. 1991 no. 248).

European Court of Human Rights held indeed that Article 6 of the European Convention, by providing that everyone is entitled to a fair hearing by an independent tribunal if his civil rights and obligations are in issue, implies that everybody has the right to have his claims on civil rights settled by a court; and the European Court further found that the notion of civil rights includes any pecuniary claim against public authorities.[16] The Court of Justice of the European Community came to comparable solutions when it examined national legislation preventing persons who felt themselves wronged by discrimination to pursue their claims by litigation before the courts; such legislation, said the Court, could not be validly invoked in order to deprive an individual of the possibility of asserting by judicial process the rights conferred to him by Community law (in the case at issue: the equal treatment directive).[17]

Looked at from this perspective, the constitutional rule on inviolability of statutes obviously constitutes an obstruction to justice. If there is a fundamental right for everybody to have his or her conflicts with public authorities on the extent and scope of his or her rights settled by the judiciary, there can be no possible justification for the only exception Dutch constitutional law permits, in forbidding courts to look into the constitutionality of statutes.

Some followers of this school of thought admit that the inviolability rule may have been justified in the past. They maintain, however, that post-war legal evolutions, culminating in effective human rights protection and in European integration, have gradually eliminated any justification that may have existed previously. In their view, comparative research points in the same direction: in the pre-war world, judicial review of legislation may have looked like an American monopoly (there is a persistent tendency to overlook the situation in Ireland), but developments in Germany and Italy, and later in France, in Spain, Portugal and Greece and in the Scandinavian countries, and recently in countries like Hungary, Poland and Czechoslovakia, illustrate that henceforth constitutional systems based on the rule of law will recognize judicial review of legislation.[18]

There is every appearance that the walls of defence of the inviolability rule are crumbling. The Minister of Justice in the actual Government, who happens to have had an earlier career as a professor of constitutional law, recently promised to send a memorandum to Parliament intended to pave the way for a constitutional amendment on this point. The future of this plan is, however, uncertain, as a parliamentary debate on constitutional problems in early 1991 did not show any definite willingness to accept such a change.

Meanwhile, the debate among the lawyers turned already to the next point: if the Netherlands will finally recognize judicial review of legislation, what form will it take? Two topics are now under discussion. First, if the abolition of the inviolability rule is more or less considered as an extension of the idea of legal protection and of human rights, there seems to be a strong argument for limiting judicial review of legislation to those cases where constitutional

---

[16] *Golder* (Feb. 21, 1975), CEDH series A vol. 17; *Ringeisen* (July 16, 1971), CEDH series A vol. 13; *Benthem* (Oct. 23, 1985), CEDH series A vol. 97.
[17] Case 222/84, *Johnston v Chief Constable of the Royal Ulster Constabulary* [1986] ECR 1663.
[18] See, for a comparative view, AR Brewer-Carias, *Judicial Review in Comparative Law* (Cambridge 1989). Also L Favoreu and JA Jolowicz (eds.), *Le contrôle juridictionnel des lois – légitimité, effectivité et développements récents* (Paris 1986).

provisions on human rights have been violated.[19] Such a limited form of judicial review could have the advantage of excluding legislative choices from judicial supervision which are typically political, such as the exact limits of proportionality in an electoral system based on proportional representation. Secondly, when judicial review is considered as very close to the actual practice of verifying whether statutes are compatible with treaty rules, there would probably be no need to establish a separate constitutional court in the way countries like France and Germany have done. In technical terms, the system of judicial review could be 'diffuse' – as opposed to 'concentrated' – since the examination of the validity of statutes with regard to international law is also done in a 'diffuse' way without giving rise to perceptible difficulties. The fear once expressed that, under a diffuse system, a district court in a remote part of the country might strike down an important piece of legislation in a capricious impulse has not been born out by experience so far. Under the 1953–1956 constitutional amendments, the *Hoge Raad* has given guidance to the development of case law, and there is no reason why it should be otherwise if judges are allowed to look into the constitutionality of statutes. Besides, a diffuse review system has the great advantage that the problem of constitutionality will not be examined in the abstract, but as part of the conflict to be settled, i.e. in connection with the ordinary problems of private, criminal or administrative law the court is dealing with. Thus, the constitutional problem will be reduced to an ordinary legal problem courts have experience with as part of their normal judicial craftsmanship.

If a system of judicial review of legislation will be elaborated along these lines, there seems to be little reason to fear that it will be conducive to a tremendous increase of political power in judicial hands. However, as legal evolution tends to generate its own dynamics, one can not be too sure in one's forecasts. The founding fathers of the United States of America would probably feel uneasy if they could witness the influence courts are having nowadays on such sensitive matters as race relations, abortion or capital punishment.[20]

Even under the present system, Dutch members of Parliament occasionally feel that the process of appointing judges should not completely ignore political views of the highest judges, in particular the members of the *Hoge Raad*. Opinions of this kind are sometimes founded on the idea that there should be a growing political awareness among the judiciary as the social impact of judicial decisions is increasing. However, some politicians also argue that a highest court should more or less reflect political, religious and social opinions living in the country. This unholy idea found some support among Dutch academics, who considered that judges ought to get more roots in society than they presently tend to have. These authors failed to explain, however, why party membership, left wing views or orthodox protestantism can help to give somebody additional roots in society. As judicial appointments in the Netherlands are traditionally made for reasons of professional qualifications, the risk of political appointments is fairly modest. The President of the *Hoge Raad* found it useful, last summer, to state publicly that he had much confidence in the professional capacities of his colleagues on the bench, but that he had no inkling of their political allegiances.

---

[19] Chapter I of the Netherlands Constitution is devoted to fundamental rights.
[20] See Robert H. Bork, *The tempting of America: the political seduction of the law* (New York–London 1990); for a more balanced view: John Hart Ely, *Democracy and distrust* (Cambridge Mass. 1980).

I might perhaps add one personal thought on this matter. It is not unlikely that litigation has increased, and that we witness a growing confidence in the courts, for the very reason that judges are non-political. In a period in which many citizens feel somewhat helpless in the face of a large state system based on a peculiarly 20th century mixture of politics and bureaucracy, they turn to the courts when thinking that their rights and liberties have been disregarded; they do so because courts are actually the only institutions which can effectively assist them without belonging to the politico-bureaucratic system. This may, finally, be the strongest argument in favour of judicial review of legislation.

25 Administrative Law in Scotland: The Public Law/Private Law Distinction Revisited

David Edward

During the late 1970s and early 1980s,[1] the House of Lords under the determined leadership of Lord Diplock developed a distinction, wholly new to those who were brought up on Dicey, between 'public law' and 'private law'. The distinction first appeared in a Scottish case in the speech of Lord Fraser of Tullybelton in *Brown v Hamilton District Council*[2] where judgment was delivered at the same time as two cases in which the distinction was used to explain the nature and scope of judicial review in England: *O'Reilly v Mackman*[3] and *Cocks v Thanet District Council*.[4] Soon afterwards Lord Wilberforce felt it necessary to warn against using 'public law' and private law' as other than 'convenient expressions for descriptive purposes',[5] and the soundness of the distinction has been doubted in Scotland, notably by Professor AW Bradley and Lord Clyde.[6]

Lord Fraser's speech in *Brown* was the catalyst for a new approach to administrative law in Scotland. It led to the setting up of the Dunpark Committee[7] on the procedure for judicial review of administrative action nearly all of whose recommendations were (unusually) implemented without delay. This led in turn to a new growth area in the work of the Court of Session, Scotland's supreme civil court.

---

[1] Beginning with *Town Investments Ltd v Department of Environment* [1978] AC 359, and *Anns v Merton London Borough Council* [1978] AC 728.

[2] (1983) SC (HL) 1.

[3] [1983] 2 AC 237.

[4] [1983] 2 AC 286.

[5] See *Davy v Spelthorne Borough Council* [1984] 1 AC 262 at p. 276.

[6] See Professor Bradley's article, 'Administrative Law', in the *Stair Memorial Encyclopaedia of the Laws of Scotland*, vol. 1, para 205 (p. 63), and Lord Clyde's article, 'The Nature of the Supervisory Jurisdiction and the Public/Private distinction in Scots Administrative Law', in *Edinburgh Essays in Public Law* ed. Finnie, Himsworth & Walker, p. 281.

[7] Set up by the Lord President of the Court of Session under the chairmanship of the late Lord Dunpark 'to devise and recommend for consideration a simple form of procedure, capable of being operated with reasonable expedition, for bringing before the court, for such relief as is appropriate, complaints by aggrieved persons (1) against acts or decisions of inferior courts, tribunals, public bodies, authorities or officers, in respect of which no right of appeal is available, alleging that the acts or decisions are *ultra vires*, or that they have been done or taken without compliance with particular statutory procedural requirements; and (2) of failure of any body or person to perform a statutory duty, which it or he could be compelled to perform in terms of section 91 of the Court of Session Act 1868'. The recommendations of the Working Party were implemented in Rule 260B of the Rules of the Court of Session (SI 1985 No 500, as now amended by SI 1990 No 705).

No tribute to a great Irishman would be complete without a drop of history and a dash of reminiscence, so the editor's suggestion that I should write about Scots administrative law gives me the excuse, as *quondam* senior counsel for the appellants in *Brown*, to explain how the public/private law distinction came to appear in it. The story also serves to illustrate a truth well known to advocates, forgotten by judges and hidden from academic commentators – that the law is created more often by accident of circumstances than by purity of doctrine.

It is difficult now, given the volume of cases going through the courts in England and Scotland, to appreciate the relative novelty in historical terms of administrative law in its new form. A subject called 'administrative law' had, it is true, been taught in the Scottish universities for many years but the content of the course is reflected in the definition given in an encyclopaedia of Scots law published in 1930:

> [Administrative law] is a term used by the Scottish University Commissioners, and borrowed from Continental usage. It may be held to include the great body of statutory law, dealing with police, burgh, county, and local government, poor, public health, education and similar subjects. Perhaps the details of taxation, stamps, excise, and customs fall under this head.[8]

Only those students who struggled to understand Professor JDB Mitchell's enigmatic expositions of constitutional law and, later, Community law were encouraged towards less arid pastures. His concern was both moral and practical, and deserves to be restated:

> We lack a real system of public law, and as a result both individuals (corporate or human) and the state suffer. The individuals are left increasingly to rely on benevolent discretion and the state is impeded, since our reliance on the cumulation of procedural safeguards has slowed the machinery of society to an unacceptable extent. . . . The real issue is . . . one of policing administrative morality.[9]

In the courts, Lord Reid was the first to recognize that the problem was one of substance as well as procedure:

> We do not have a developed system of administrative law – perhaps because until fairly recently we did not need it. So it is not surprising that in dealing with new types of cases the courts have had to grope for solutions, and have found that old powers, rules and procedures are largely inapplicable to cases which they were never designed or intended to deal with.[10]

But there is little opportunity to attack the substance if the procedures are arthritic and Scottish procedure was in need of replacement surgery. The occasion for change proved to be the Housing (Homeless Persons) Act 1977.

By the mid-1970s the problem of homelessness in Britain had become a matter of acute public concern but, for a variety of reasons, government was disinclined to legislate. So the task fell to the Member of Parliament for the Isle of Wight, Stephen Ross, who was successful in the curious lottery by which backbench members are allowed to initiate legislation in the House of

---

[8] *Green's Encyclopaedia of the Laws of Scotland*, 2nd edition, sub nom. 'Law', vol. IX, p. 17.
[9] JDB Mitchell *Constitutional Law* 2nd edition, pp. 320–1 and 300.
[10] *Ridge v Baldwin* [1964] AC 40 at p. 72.

Commons. As luck would have it, the relevant government department already had a draft Bill in a bottom drawer. This was brought out, dusted down and given its second reading in the House of Commons on 18 February 1977 as the Housing (Homeless Persons) Bill.

The terms of the Bill required local housing authorities to make accommodation available to those who fulfilled three conditions: that they were 'homeless', or 'threatened with homelessness'; that they had a 'priority need'; and that they had not become homeless or threatened with homelessness 'intentionally'. Responsibility for determining whether these three criteria were met was placed upon the housing authority. There was no provision for review of, or appeal against, the authority's decision – a classic example of leaving the individual to rely on benevolent discretion.

Introducing his Bill, Mr Ross remarked that:

> There is a lot of feeling that there should perhaps be an appeal procedure against a refusal by a housing authority [to provide accommodation for a homeless person], but to date nobody has come forward with a satisfactory solution to that problem.[11]

A proposal to allow for appeal to a special tribunal was subsequently defeated in Committee.[12]

When the Bill reached the House of Lords later the same year, Lord Gifford, a crusading barrister, moved an amendment to provide, *inter alia*, that:

> A county court in England and Wales, and the sheriff in Scotland, shall have jurisdiction . . . to determine any question
> (*a*) as to whether [the applicant] is homeless or threatened with homelessness
> (*b*) as to whether [he] has a priority need . . .[13]

Introducing his amendment, Lord Gifford warned the House that:

> Your Lordships can, I think, be sure that things are going to go wrong . . . What worries me over this Bill is that we are imposing a duty on authorities to give specific assistance to specific classes of people, but there is no provision at all for enforcing that duty. What is one to say to a person who is wrongly refused accommodation? Should one say: 'Complain to the local Ombudsman'? – surely a useless remedy as far as the individual is concerned; 'Make an application to the High Court for an order of *mandamus*'? which is equally time-consuming and useless in resolving the situation; 'Make a fuss in the public press'? That often happens already to no effect.[14]

Unfortunately for those who were homeless but (as often happens) fortunately for the development of the law, Lord Gifford's predictions were proved right but his amendment was unsuccessful. The Bill reached the statute book in a form which imposed duties on local authorities without saying whether, or if so how, the performance of those duties might be subject to judicial control. Section 3 of the Act did, however, require local authorities to give notice of

[11] *Hansard* vol. HC 926, cols. 902–3.
[12] *Hansard* vol. HC 934, col. 1647.
[13] *Hansard* vol. HL 386, cols. 700–703.
[14] *Ibid.* col. 701.

their decisions and of the reasons for them – a requirement more readily recognizable nowadays than it was then as the hallmark of an act susceptible to judicial review.

Quite soon after the Act came into force disappointed applicants began to take their cases to court. In England they tried both the High Court and the county courts. In the High Court the route to judicial review had been simplified by the reform in 1977 of Order 53 of the Rules of the Supreme Court and subsequently by Section 31 of the Supreme Court Act 1981. But there were those who thought that the High Court was not the most suitable place to determine whether in individual cases up and down the country, local authorities were justified in deciding that applicants were or were not 'homeless', 'threatened with homelessness' or 'intentionally homeless'. Although the county courts did not have jurisdiction to conduct judicial review as such, they could award damages for breach of statutory duty and the Court of Appeal held that a decision on homelessness could be challenged in a common law action of damages in the county court.[15]

In Scotland, where prerogative writs and Chancery orders are unknown, the jurisdictional position ought to have been clearer than it was in England. There was an extensive armoury of suitable forms of action: suspension (broadly equivalent to prohibition), interdict (injunction), declarator (declaration), the petition[16] to require performance of a statutory duty (*mandamus*), a parallel form of action[17] to require performance of other civil obligations and, last but not least, the action of reduction by which an act having legal effect is declared null and deprived of effect. Reduction (recognizable to Community lawyers as the action for annulment) seems to have no precise equivalent in England though it has been said to be 'akin to *certiorari*'.[18] Advocation, the true parallel to *certiorari*, though still available in criminal procedure, was abolished in civil cases in 1868 and replaced by 'appeal' to the Court of Session as part of the process by which a conventional hierarchical relationship was established between the Court of Session and the lower courts, especially the sheriff court.

The sheriff courts had developed from feudal origins to become local courts of general jurisdiction in both civil and criminal matters. The Court of Session was created in 1532 by King James V as a supreme, but functionally unrelated, civil court of general jurisdiction. The Court of Session was not an appellate court but over the years, in rather the same manner as the Court of

---

[15] *Thornton v Kirklees Metropolitan Borough Council* [1979] QB 626; *De Falco v Crawley Borough Council* [1980] QB 460. In *De Falco*, Lord Denning, MR began his judgment in classic style:
   Every day we see signs of the advancing tide. This time it is two young families from Italy. They had heard tell of the European Economic Community. Naturally enough, because it all stemmed from a Treaty made at Rome. They had heard that there was freedom of movement for workers within the Community. They could come to England without let or hindrance. They may have heard, too, that England is a good place for workers. In Italy the word may have got round that in England there are all sorts of benefits to be had whenever you are unemployed. And best of all they will look after you if you have nowhere to live. There is a special new statute there which imposes on the local authority a duty to house you. They must either find you a house or put you up in a guest house. 'So let's go to England,' they say. 'That's the place for us.'
[16] Under section 91 of the Court of Session Act 1868.
[17] For decree *ad factum praestandum* or specific implement.
[18] *R v East Berkshire Health Authority, ex parte Walsh* [1985] QB 152, per Sir John Donaldson MR at p. 162.

King's Bench, it developed a 'supervisory jurisdiction' to fill this gap in the Scottish judicial system.[19] The reform of 1868 was valuable from the point of view of judicial architecture but, as it turned out, it deprived the system of a useful procedural tool.

The Scottish system differed most notably from the English in that the same forms of process could be used in actions against public authorities and against private individuals. Thus the action of reduction was equally available to set aside an unlawful decision of a public body or the contested will of a private individual. Scotland therefore avoided the jurisdictional complications left over from the distinctions between courts of law and courts of equity and between the prerogative writs and other forms of process. Differences in the respective jurisdictions of the Court of Session and the sheriff courts had been eroded by giving the sheriff court concurrent jurisdiction in fields previously reserved to the Court of Session, whose remaining exclusive jurisdiction was largely a ragbag of points of purely historical interest. However, the action of reduction was available only in the Court of Session, although the historical and legal significance of this was not apparent in the early stages of *Brown*.

The defect in Scottish procedure to which the Homeless Persons Act drew attention was that, despite the range of remedies available, there was no quick way of testing the lawfulness of decisions such as those of housing authorities under the Act. Even in cases where special procedures for judicial review had been instituted by statute – compulsory purchase orders, special roads orders and town and country planning decisions[20] – the procedure of review was cumbersome and could take many months.

Onto this infertile ground dropped, in June 1979, the case of the Brown family (father, mother and two small children) who had lived in a council house in Hamilton of which the mother was the registered tenant. The rent was not paid and the family was evicted. The father then applied to the council for accommodation as a 'homeless person' under the Act. This was refused on the grounds that *he* was 'intentionally homeless' – an eminently arguable legal point.

An action was raised in the local sheriff court seeking declarator that Mr Brown was a homeless person with a prior need of accommodation and an order requiring the council to provide him with it. The council challenged the competency of the action on the ground that only the Court of Session could grant such remedies. The sheriff reviewed the authorities cited to him (drawn without distinction from 'public law' and 'private law') and concluded that there was no reason why the action should not proceed in the sheriff court, remarking that it was in everyone's interest that it should do so.[21]

The local authority appealed to the Court of Session and the case came before the Second Division consisting of the Lord Justice-Clerk (Lord Wheatley), Lord Kissen and Lord Dunpark. By this stage a queue of homeless persons cases was pending before the courts and the Lord Justice-Clerk did little to conceal his determination that they should not come to the Court of Session. Hardly, at the best of times, a judge before whom it was easy to plead,

---

[19] Kames, *Historical Law Tracts* no VII. See further Lord Clyde's article, *cit. sup.* at footnote 6.
[20] Acquisition of Land (Authorisation Procedure) (Scotland) Act 1947, first schedule, paras 15 and 16; Special Roads Act 1949, first schedule, paras 14–16; Town and Country Planning (Scotland) Act 1972, sections 232 and 233.
[21] 1980 SLT (Sh.Ct.) 81.

Lord Wheatley was particularly prickly when faced with an argument he did not want to hear. For this and other reasons the appeal turned into a forensic assault course which took more than 18 months to complete. After the first hearing the parties were told to amend their pleadings in order to amplify the facts. This gave the pursuer the opportunity to reformulate his claim as a 'declarator of nullity' – a device (ultimately unsuccessful) intended to reach the same result as reduction but in a form that was competent in the sheriff court. He also added a claim for damages.

There followed a second hearing on the new pleadings. Three weeks later, before judgment was delivered, Lord Kissen died suddenly. All the signs were that the court was split, Lord Kissen tending to agree with the Lord Justice-Clerk on policy but with Lord Dunpark on the law. Only after a third hearing was the case finally decided with Lord Robertson, who replaced Lord Kissen, agreeing with the Lord Justice-Clerk and Lord Dunpark dissenting.

The argument in the Court of Session turned largely on the interpretation of a passage in the opinion of Lord President John Inglis in *Forbes v Underwood*.[22] Inglis was the towering figure of Scots law in the later nineteenth century and his *dicta* have at least the authority of the House of Lords, if not of holy writ. His dominance of the Scottish legal scene can be gauged from the fact that he had already been Dean of Faculty (the elected leader of the Bar) for five years when he defended Madeleine Smith on the charge of poisoning her lover in 1857 and that he held in succession all the great legal offices in Scotland until he died in office in 1891 after 33 years as a judge and 24 as Lord Justice-General and Lord President.[23]

In *Forbes*, the question was whether a sheriff had jurisdiction to compel one of two arbiters (arbitrators) who could not agree, to concur in nominating a 'oversman' to resolve the difference between them. In the course of his opinion, Lord President Inglis said:

> The question whether the sheriff has jurisdiction in such a case is, I think, one of very great importance. The position of an arbiter is very much like that of a judge in many respects, and there is no doubt whatever that whenever an inferior judge, no matter of what kind, fails to perform his duty, or transgresses his duty, either by going beyond his jurisdiction, or by failing to exercise his jurisdiction when called upon to do so by a party entitled to come before him, there is a remedy in this court.
> ... The same rule applies to a variety of other public officers, such as statutory trustees and commissioners, who are under an obligation to exercise their functions for the benefit of the parties for whose benefit those functions are entrusted to them.
> ... Now all this belongs to the Court of Session as the supreme civil court of this country in the exercise of what is called, very properly, its supereminent jurisdiction. It is not of very much consequence to determine whether it is in the exercise of its high equitable jurisdiction, or in the performance of what is sometimes called its *nobile officium*. But of one thing there can be no doubt, that in making such orders

---

[22] (1886) 13 R 465.
[23] Inglis was the last judge to drive to court in a carriage and four. It was he who began his closing speech for Madeleine Smith with words that are often quoted in books on advocacy:
Gentlemen of the jury, the charge against the prisoner is murder, and the punishment of murder is death; and that simple statement is sufficient to suggest to us the awful solemnity of the occasion which brings you and me face to face.
It is rather less well known that, while awaiting the verdict in the advocates' gown room, he was asked what he thought of his client, to which he replied, 'She's a bonny lass, but I wouldn't sup with her'. (This story was told to the present author in 1962 by Sheriff George Wilton, then 100 years old, who had heard it from an advocate who was present at the time.)

against inferior judges, or statutory trustees, or commissioners, or the like, this court is exercising an exclusive jurisdiction – a jurisdiction which cannot possibly belong to any other court in the country.[24]

In *Brown*, the Lord Justice-Clerk dealt brutally with the efforts of counsel to illuminate this *dictum* of Lord President Inglis:

> I find it unnecessary to consider the cases, the institutional writers or the textbooks cited to us in connection with the supereminence of the Court of Session as spoken to by Lord President Inglis. The question is whether the defenders in carrying out their statutory duties here fell within the categories of bodies to whom that doctrine applies. I refer to the purposes of the Act and the duties and responsibilities imposed on the local authorities to effect these purposes. They are the administrators of the policy. They have to carry out certain inquiries, they have to be satisfied on certain matters and they have to do certain things depending on whether they are satisfied or not satisfied about these matters following upon their inquiries. On the face of it there is nothing judicial or quasi-judicial about this exercise. . . . If the local authority transgressed in the execution of their duty . . . so that the complaining applicant has legitimate recourse to the courts of law, then *prima facie* he can go to any court which has the jurisdictional power to grant him the remedy which he seeks. . . . Each type of body has to be examined with reference to its individual powers and duties to see whether or not it falls within or outwith the *dictum* of Lord President Inglis. For present purposes I find it suffices to say that since in my view the local authority here was acting not in a quasi-judicial capacity but in an administrative or executorial capacity, review by the supereminent jurisdiction of the Court of Session alone is not imposed.[25]

Lord Robertson approached the case in the same way, asking first whether the local authority was exercising judicial or quasi-judicial functions and, having decided they were not, holding that their decision could be challenged in the sheriff court by any appropriate form of process competent in that court.[26]

Lord Dunpark followed part of the way down the same road but then diverged. He too held that the decision of the local authority was neither judicial nor quasi-judicial but continued:

> [Assuming] that the decision cannot be so classified, the question remains whether it was a decision which may completely be reviewed and quashed in the sheriff court. . . . Every wrong must have a remedy. Where an applicant for housing accommodation is deprived of his rights under this Act by a decision of a housing authority which is fundamentally null, or so obviously wrong that no reasonable housing authority could have reached it on the facts before it, he is entitled to apply to the courts for enforcement of his rights. As the Act has failed to provide a remedy for him, his only recourse is to the equitable jurisdiction of the courts. . . . I find that the sheriff has no jurisdiction to review and quash decisions of housing authorities, purporting to act in pursuance of this Act, on the ground of fundamental nullity. That is the sole prerogative of the Court of Session in the exercise of its supereminent jurisdiction by providing a remedy where no other exists.[27]

---

[24] (1886) 13 R at pp. 467–8.
[25] 1983 SC (HL) at pp. 10–11.
[26] 1983 SC (HL) at p. 20.
[27] 1983 SC (HL) at pp. 26 and 30–31.

Lord Dunpark's dissent opened the way to an appeal to the House of Lords.[28] A problem that faces the Scottish advocate in the House of Lords is that he knows the judges less well than those at home. Usually, though not always, the two Scots law lords sit in Scottish appeals but the quirks and predilections of the others are frequently known, if at all, from anecdotal evidence only. The safe course is to prepare every possible line of argument and see which of them runs.

Two particular lines of research suggested themselves. The first was to find out more of the background to the *dictum* of Lord President Inglis in order to prove that it did not apply only to judicial or quasi-judicial acts. The other was to read the recent speeches of Lord Diplock since it was a fairly safe bet, given the subject matter, that he would preside.

The first line of research enabled us to date, almost to the day, the beginning of administrative law in Scotland. One of the great judges of the eighteenth century was Patrick Grant, Lord Elchies, who made a Collection of Decisions. His object was admirable: as his editor puts it, it was 'to record with the utmost brevity the principle of law decided by the court, and his great legal powers are shown in the singular ability with which all unnecessary circumstances are rejected, and those alone preserved which entered materially into the decision'. (Oh for an hour of Elchies!) He also made notes for the instruction of his son in which he 'preserved his own view of the case and those of the leading judges who differed from him in opinion; and the votes of the court'. His editor remarks that 'In no instances are the Notes more valuable than in those cases where general questions that had been argued before the court, were either compromised or decided upon other grounds.'[29]

On 8 February 1751, Elchies records that the court heard the case of *Sutherland of Swinzie* concerning the enrolment of landowners with a right to vote in parliamentary elections. The first question was whether those responsible for enrolment, the Commissioners of Supply, had duly taken the oath and were qualified to act. The second was whether their decision not to enrol the pursuer was 'iniquitious'. The defence on the second point was that 'These Commissioners are Commissioners of Parliament, and none of their proceedings can be reviewed by the courts of law'. Elchies says:

> We were very unwilling to determine this last point, because of difficulty, and likewise of manifold inconveniencies on both sides, therefore we determined the first, and found these Commissioners not capable to act, and dismissed the complaint.[30]

Four days later, on 12 February 1751, in the case of *Gordon*, Elchies records that:

> we were forced to determine the question that we so carefully avoided on the 8th in *Sutherland of Swinzie*'s case, viz. the objection to our jurisdiction or powers of revising or altering the proceedings and sentences of the Commissioners of Supply.

---

[28] In Scotland, unlike Engand, an appeal to the House of Lords is available without leave against any final decision of the Court of Session and against a non-final decision where there has been a dissent in the Inner House. It is interesting to speculate whether *Donoghue v Stevenson* would ever have reached the House of Lords if leave to appeal had been required. The case was disposed of very cursorily in the Court of Session – see the procedural history at 1932 SC (HL) p. 33.

[29] Preface to Morison's edition of *Elchies' Decisions* (1813), pp. 1–2.

[30] *Sutherland of Swinzie v Sutherland of Langwell* M. 2436, Elchies no 52.

The court, with Elchies himself in a minority of one, asserted its jurisdiction and struck down the decision of the Commissioners. But the birth of Scots administrative law seems to have been attended with some confusion:

> The President who was of the same opinion with me could not vote having declined himself – and Justice-Clerk was of opinion of the [majority] but did not vote because he did not hear the debate. *Pro* were Minto, Drummore, Haining, Strichen, She-walton – but Murkle was *non liquet* [he declined to vote], and I hardly knew Dun's opinion, who was in the chair.[31]

Study of the old reports showed that, already by the early nineteenth century, the Court of Session had defined the scope of its supervisory jurisdiction in terms which, as summarized in Lord Ivory's notes on Erskine's *Institute*, Lord Diplock described at the hearing as 'remarkably modern':

> The privilege of appeal to the supreme court not being expressly prohibited, an exclusion of its jurisdiction is not to be presumed. ... Even when a final and conclusive jurisdiction is conferred in the broadest terms, still if the inferior court exceed its powers, or refuse to act, or otherwise proceed in a way inconsistent with and not recognized by the Statute, the Court of Session may competently review the proceedings and give redress. ... Upon the same principle, where a particular jurisdiction is appointed under a canal, or road, or other local act, to determine all questions that may arise in carrying such act into execution; if the statutory trustees do not follow the terms of the act, or exceed the powers thereby given, the party aggrieved is not limited to the statutory or local jurisdiction, but may at once apply for his redress in the Court of Session.[32]

Research also showed that the 'statutory trustees or commissioners' to whom Lord President Inglis referred in *Forbes* were none other than the statutory ancestors of the modern local authorities.[33] The acts submitted to judicial review in many of the older cases would certainly be categorized nowadays as 'administrative' or 'executive' rather than 'judicial' or 'quasi-judicial'. Indeed, once the historical context was understood, the cases proved *a fortiori* that such administrative or executive acts could be reviewed only in the Court of Session, being the only Court with power to grant a remedy where no other exists.

(Why then do Ivory's notes, *Forbes* and other authorities persistently refer to the authors of such acts as 'inferior judges', 'inferior courts' and 'inferior jurisdictions'? Initially at any rate, the reason seems to be that many local administrative or executive functions were performed by justices of the peace and sheriffs. The dividing line between the executive and the judicial was not clearly defined, and those who created the Scottish system of local government paid scant regard to Montesquieu. Later, perhaps, the judges of the Court of Session may have thought it prudent to maintain the fiction that in exercising

---

[31] *Sir John Gordon of Invergordon v Sir John Gordon of Embo* (1751) M. 7345, Elchies no 52.

[32] Erskine's *Institute of the Law of Scotland*, Nicholson's edition (1871), I.ii.7, Ivory's footnote 15. (This citation gave rise to the most recondite question ever put to the author as counsel. Lord Fraser asked: 'Mr Edward, can you remind me of the date of Lord Ivory's notes on Erskine?' The answer regrettably was No, so proving that counsel can never do too much homework before appearing in the House of Lords.)

[33] Lord Fraser of Tullybelton in *Brown*, 1983 SC (HL) at p. 43. (An intrusive negative confuses the report of the argument on this point towards the foot of page 38.)

their 'supereminent jurisdiction' they were judges reviewing the acts of judges.)

The hearing in the House of Lords turned out to be another forensic assault course since Parliament was in recess and the hearing was in the Lords' Chamber with counsel appearing in full-bottomed wigs at the Bar of the House. On such occasions a rostrum is erected just inside the gates to the Chamber with just enough space for counsel addressing the House to stand at a small lectern (looking down at the judges) and his opponent to sit perched on a small upright chair with his notebook on his knees. Juniors and instructing solicitors sit immediately behind and below, so the speaker must be careful not to step backwards. In *Brown*, senior counsel for the respondents, a former Olympic sprinter, created an additional hurdle for himself when, on the morning of the second day, he rose to speak and found that he had left his spectacles in his hotel.

As it turned out, the House showed little interest in the results of the research into the origins of Scottish administrative law. For reasons of listing *Brown* was heard before the two English cases, *Cocks* and *O'Reilly*, and it did not need much perspicacity to see that Lord Diplock was impatient to get on, regarding *Brown* as a case of importance only in so far as it might affect the theory of judicial review which he was later to expound in *O'Reilly*. So the second line of research – into Lord Diplock's previous speeches – proved to be more important than the first.

Lord Diplock's most recent pronouncement had been in *Swain v The Law Society*,[34] which concerned the Law Society's compulsory indemnity scheme for solicitors. The question was whether the brokerage commission paid by the insurance brokers to the Society could be applied for the benefit of the profession generally or was to be held by the Society in trust for the contributors to the scheme. The Court of Appeal had held in favour of the contributors.

In the House of Lords, the case was argued for the Law Society on the basis that there was a 'fundamental legal distinction between public law and private law. The remedies for breach of a public duty are public law remedies.' In his speech, Lord Diplock said:

> In dealing with the appeal it is, in my opinion, essential throughout to bear in mind that in performance of its functions the Society acts in two distinct capacities: a private capacity as the successor . . . to the Society of Gentlemen Practisers in the Courts of Law and Equity; and a public capacity as the authority upon whom . . . various statutory duties are imposed and powers conferred by the Solicitors Act 1974.
>
> When acting in its private capacity the Society is subject to private law alone. . . . It is quite otherwise when the Society is acting in its public capacity. . . . [What] they do in that capacity is governed by public law; and although the legal consequences of doing it may result in creating rights enforceable in private law, those rights are not necessarily the same as those that would flow in private law from doing a similar act otherwise than in the exercise of statutory powers.[35]

This passage seemed to offer the solution to a problem that remained in spite of the successful research on the first point. It could not be denied that a person

---

[34] [1983] 1 AC 598.
[35] [1983] 1 AC at p. 600 (argument) and pp. 607–8 (Lord Diplock).

wrongfully refused accommodation by a housing authority would be entitled to damages for breach of the authority's statutory duty. Nor could it be denied that an action of damages for breach of statutory duty could be raised in the sheriff court. Why, then, could the sheriff court not rule on the lawfulness of the authority's decision? To insist that this preliminary question must be determined in the Court of Session seemed pedantic and formalistic. Yet there was a legally qualitative difference between the right to a lawful decision and the right to damages for a breach of statutory duty which, *ex hypothesi*, did not arise until the housing authority's decision had been shown to be unlawful. Lord Diplock's distinction between public and private law and the nature and means of enforcement of the duties they create was, whether doctrinally sound or not, a way of defining that difference.

The argument turned out to be conclusive in *Cocks*, the English case on the same point.[36] Lord Bridge, who recanted the views he had expressed in the Court of Appeal in *De Falco*,[37] adopted the same line of reasoning as Lord Diplock in *Swain*:

[The] functions of housing authorities under the Housing (Homeless Persons) Act 1977 . . . fall into two wholly distinct categories. On the one hand, the housing authority was charged with decision-making functions. . . . These are essentially public law functions. The power of decision being committed by the statute exclusively to the housing authority, their exercise of the power can only be challenged before the courts on . . . strictly limited grounds. . . . On the other hand, the housing authority are charged with executive functions. Once a decision has been reached by the housing authority which gives rise to the . . . housing duty, rights and obligations are immediately created in the field of private law. Each of the duties refered to, once established, is capable of being enforced by injunction and the breach of it will give rise to a liability in damages. But it is inherent in the scheme of the Act that an appropriate public law decision of the housing authority is a condition precedent to the establishment of the private law duty. . . . The fallacy is in the implicit assumption that the court has the power not only to review the housing authority's public law decision but also to substitute its own decision to the contrary effect in order to establish the necessary condition precedent to the housing authority's private law liability.[38]

Lord Fraser, delivering the only speech in *Brown* put his finger on the same point:

The decision on whether the respondent was a homeless person, and if so whether he had become homeless intentionally, is one which in terms of the Act of 1977 is entrusted to the housing authority and to them alone. Their decision effectively determines whether the authority has the duty of making accommodation available for the respondent. . . . A mere declarator that the decision was one which they were not entitled to reach does not get rid of the decision, nor can it open the way for the housing authority to reach a different decision if, on further consideration of the matter in the light of the Court's decision on matters of law, it thinks fit to do so. In a case such as this, where the housing authority is both the decision-making authority and the decision-implementing authority, the proper procedure is for the decision to

---

[36] *Cocks* came on immediately after *Brown*. When counsel for the appellants began to develop the argument, Lord Diplock observed (with truth) 'I think you have had a spy here'.
[37] *Supra*, note 14.
[38] [1983] 2 AC at pp. 292–3 and 294.

be reduced so that a different decision, creating different legal rights for the private party in the position of the respondent, can be made.[39]

Except perhaps for his reference in the last sentence to 'the private party', Lord Fraser (unlike Lord Bridge) did not so much as hint at the public law/ private law distinction until the second last paragraph of his speech, and then only in suggesting that there might be 'advantages in developing special procedure in Scotland for dealing with questions in the public law area, comparable to the English prerogative orders'. Immediately before making this suggestion, he observed that 'the question whether the sheriff court has jurisdiction in this case is entirely separate from the question whether the County Court would have jurisdiction in a similar case in England'.[40] So, although the words 'public law' entered the vocabulary of Scots law in Lord Fraser's speech, they do not seem to have done so as part of his reasoning on the issue in the case.

Lord Fraser had been a lecturer in constitutional law and had written a short textbook on the subject. He was later principal editor, author and co-ordinator of the article on 'Constitutional Law' in the *Stair Memorial Encyclopaedia of the Laws of Scotland*. As a judge he was cautious and he was not at all likely to enunciate new constitutional theories unless necessary. In the case of *Stevenson v Midlothian District Council* two months after*Brown*, he repeated his call for a new procedure without using the words 'public law' at all.[41]

Useful as the public law/private law distinction was for forensic purposes in order to catch the attention of Lord Diplock, Lord Fraser clearly did not regard it as essential to an explanation of why, in Scotland, certain acts can be challenged only by recourse to the supervisory jurisdiction of the Court of Session. If one bears in mind that *Brown, Cocks* and *O'Reilly* were argued successively and that the judgments were delivered in inverse order, his use of the words 'public law' in his plea for speedier and cheaper procedure was surely no more than a shorthand reference to what had, by that time, been said by Lord Diplock in *O'Reilly* and Lord Bridge in *Cocks*. In the words of Lord Wilberforce, 'public law' was 'a convenient expression for descriptive purposes'.

So there is no need to accept, if one does not want to, that the public law/ private law distinction has been made part of the law of Scotland just because of what was said by Lord Fraser in *Brown*. Nevertheless, there *is* an important conceptual distinction between acts, such as delictual acts, which give rise directly to a right to damages or other civil remedies, and acts, such as administrative acts, which must first be deprived of legal effect before such a right can arise. (The distinction is well understood by Community lawyers and underlies Articles 33 and 34 of the ECSC treaty.) If nothing else, Lord Diplock's public law/private law distinction assists in focusing this basic point.

Judges have to find words to express new ideas and it is usually easier to borrow words that are already used in a similar context. New vocabulary helps us to discard formulae that have become stale or fossilized. What is dangerous is not the borrowing as such but the fallacy of supposing that the borrowed vocabulary reflects something that exists independently and immutably in the real world. That is simply to substitute one fossil for another.

[39] 1983 SC (HL) at p. 46.
[40] 1983 SC (HL) at p. 49.
[41] 1983 SC (HL) 50 at p. 59.

Biographical Note

Thomas F. O'Higgins

Born: 23 July 1916
Sunday's Well, Cork City.

Parents: Dr. Thomas F. O'Higgins and
Mrs. Agnes O'Higgins (née McCarthy).

Education: St. Mary's College, Rathmines, Dublin.
Clongowes Wood College, Co. Kildare.
University College Dublin.
Kings' Inns, Dublin.

Married: 3 April 1948 to Thérèse Yvonne Keane,
5 sons, 2 daughters.

Career: (a) Academic
1937 – B.A. Legal and Political Science:
First Class Honours.
Kings' Inns: Junior and Senior Victoria Prizes
First Place Bar Final
Brooke Honour Exam, 2nd Prize.

1937 – Auditor Law Society, U.C.D.
1938 – Auditor Literary and Historical Society, U.C.D.

(b) Professional
1938 – Called to the Bar
Practised Midland and Northern Circuits
Member of Bar Council
1954 – Called to the Inner Bar
1957 – Elected Bencher of Kings' Inns.

(c) Political
1948 – Elected Member of Dáil Éireann for the Constituency
of Leix-Offaly. His brother Michael was also elected as was
his father who became Minister for Defence and later
Industry and Commerce.
Re-elected 1951, 1954, 1957, 1961 and 1965.
Elected Member for South County Dublin 1969.

1949 – Appointed Member of Irish Delegation to the Council of Europe at Strasbourg.

1954 – Appointed Minister for Health in Mr. Costello's 2nd Government. Implemented with general agreement the controversial Health Act 1953. Introduced the Voluntary Health Insurance Scheme. Initiated the replacement of the Dispensary System of General Medical Services with a scheme based on choice of doctor.

1966 and 1973 – Opposition candidate for the office of President of Ireland.
1967 – Chairman and later President of the Irish Council of the European Movement.
1965 to 1972 – Opposition spokesman on Finance.
Deputy-Leader and Vice-President of Fine Gael.

(d) Judicial
1973 – Appointed Judge of the High Court.
1974 – Appointed Chief Justice of Ireland.
1985 – Appointed Judge at the Court of Justice of the European Communities.

(e) Chairman and Founder Member of the Irish Centre for European Law.

Index

Abortion, 162, 236
  right to life of unborn in Irish Constitution, 139, 140, 162
Absolute protection rule, 196
Acquittals, appeals against, 201
Administrative law
  constitutional justice, 149
  judicial review of administrative action
    presumption of constitutionality, 173–174
    unreasonableness test, 189–190, 225
  reasons for decisions, 239
  remedies under Chief Justice O'Higgins, 203–216
    Abenglen Properties case, 207, 208–211, 213, 216
    availability of remedies, 207–208
    Constitution and, 203–207
    scope of judicial discretion, 208–216
  Scotland
    Brown v Hamilton District Council, 283–284, 287–294
    public law/private law distinction, 283–294
Agreements with third countries
  judicial review of constitutionality of, 28
Annulment, actions of, 3, 5, 7, 9
  acts of European Parliament, against, 8
  locus standi of natural and legal persons, 5, 6
Aquinas, Thomas, 147, 148, 149
Aristotle, 19, 142
Arrest and questioning
  Irish criminal law, 194–195

Bacon, Francis, 159
Bail
  Irish criminal law, 195–196
  US Supreme Court, 197
Belgium, 275
Bills
  reference by President to Irish Supreme Court, 151, 169, 170–171
Blasphemous libel, 165

Canon law, 240–241
Certiorari
  availability, 207–208
  ex debito justitiae, 210–211, 212, 216
  judicial discretion, scope of, 208–216
Child of migrant worker
  educational rights, 83, 86–88
  entry and residence rights, 82–83
  grants and scholarships, rights to, 86–88
Church law, 240–241
Churchill, R. R., 54, 62
Citizens of European Community. *See* Community citizens
Clubs
  constitutional law and, 243
Co-operation, principle of, 35
Collective agreements
  indirectly discriminatory provisions, 113–114
Commission of the European Community, 13, 16. *See also* Community institutions
  infringement actions, 34
  inter-institutional proceedings, 27, 28
  proposed democratic control of, 234
  public service employment action plan, 104–105
Common fisheries policy
  conservation regulations, 53
  Hague Resolution of 3 November 1976, 52
  judicial review and, 51–65
  licensing conditions, 57–65
  national quotas, 51–52, 53, 55, 61
  nationality requirements, 55–57, 63
  Pesca Valentia case, 55–57
  quota hopping, 52, 54–60, 222
  residence requirements, 59–62
  total allowable catch, 53, 55
Common good, requirements of
  Irish Constitution, 165, 166, 167
Common market in services, 121–122, 128.
    See further Freedom to provide services
  role of European Court, 125–129
Communicate information, right to
  Irish Constitution, 186–187

297

Community citizens, 105
  entry and residence rights, 83–84
  Maastricht provisions, 105
Community institutions, 4. *See also*
    Commission of the European
    Community
  actions for annulment or inactivity, 3, 5,
    7–9, 10
  cooperation with Member States, 233
  disputes between, 5, 27–28
  fundamental rights, duty to respect, 31
  staff sex discrimination cases, 108–110
Community law. *See also* Community law
    rights; European Community treaties
  annulment or inactivity, actions for, 3, 5,
    7–9, 10
  breach of Treaty obligations, actions for, 5,
    6–7, 9
  co-operation, principle of, 35
  constitutional court, 3–10, 25–32
  constitutional issues, 3–10, 11–12, 25–32.
    See further under Constitutional law
  direct actions, 5, 10, 30
  direct effect. *See* Direct effect doctrine
  directives, direct effect of. *See* Directives
  division of powers, 28
  due process, 239–240
  enforcement
    Community-wide principles, 38–40
    national courts, in, 33–49
  First Company Law Directive, 40, 249
  fisheries. *See* Common fisheries policy
  free movement of persons, 89. *See also* Free
    movement of workers
  fundamental rights. *See under* Community
    law rights
  general principles of law, 31, 242,
    243
  inter-institutional proceedings, 27–28
  judicial review of legislation, 5, 26–29
  jurisdiction of Court of Justice. *See under*
    European Court of Justice
  jurisdiction of national courts, 30, 34–35,
    39–48
  legal integration, process of, 16
  locus standi
    natural or legal persons, 5, 6–8, 127n
  Member States and. *See* Member States;
    National law
  migrant workers. *See* Free movement of
    workers. *See also* Migrant workers
  national law, and. *See under* National law
  non-discrimination rule. *See* Non-
    discrimination on grounds of
    nationality
  pre-emption, principle of, 14, 28
  precedent in, 64
  preliminary rulings, references for. *See*
    Preliminary references to European
    Court
  primacy of. *See* Supremacy of European
    Community law

Community law—*contd*
  principles developed by Court of Justice,
    30–31, 32, 35, 38, 41
  public service exception as concept of,
    91–92
  qualified majority voting, 234
  regulations, 5, 265
  remedies for breaches of, 33, 35–36, 41–49,
    225–226
  rights under. *See* Community law rights
  rule of law, 33n, 41, 203
  sex equality law
    constitutional implications of, 107–120
  subsidiarity. *See* Subsidiarity principle
  treaties, constitutionalisation of, 4, 11–12,
    16
  uniform applicability of, 48
Community law rights. *See also* Equality of
    treatment; Free movement of workers;
    Freedom to provide services; Sex
    equality
  constitutional protection of, 30
  constitutional rights, as, 28, 30
  education rights – migrant students, 79–
    88
  enforcement, 33–49
    Community law remedies, obligation of
      national court to apply, 41–46
    decentralised enforcement, 33–49
    direct effect of directives. *See under*
      Directives
    effectiveness principle, 38–39, 41
    European Court and, 35–48
    Factortame case, 15, 42
    indirect effect of directives, 39–41
    institutional and procedural autonomy,
      38–39
    national diferences, 35
    national time limits, 46–48
    procedural and remedial barriers, 35,
      46–48, 48–49
  fundamental rights
    community institutions bound to
      respect, 31
    equal treatment between sexes, 107,
      108–110
  national law rules impeding access to, 119–
    120
  non-discrimination principle. *See* Non-
    Discrimination on grounds of
    nationality
  protection of, 15
  remedies for breach of, 33, 35–36, 41–49
  services, freedom to provide. *See* Freedom
    to provide services
Community treaties. *See* European
    Community Treaties
Company law
  First Company Law Directive, 40, 249
Comparative constitutional law, 244
Constitution of Ireland. *See* Irish Constitution
    (1937)

Constitution of the United States. *See*
United States Constitution
Constitutional court, 25–26
Court of Justice of the European
Communities as a Constitutional
Court, 25–32
European Communities, for the, 3–10
Constitutional interpretation, 161–167, 169–
178, 179–182. *See also* Constitutional
review
common good, requirements of, 165, 166,
167
conflicting rights, 165
duty of judges, 161
dynamic and evolutionary, 163
historical approach, 163
Irish judge as law-maker, 159–168
judicial creativity, 180
judicial power, primacy of, 150, 157, 181
literal or purposive approach, 164
precedent, 179, 180, 181
presumption of constitutionality, 171, 172,
173–174, 176–177
principles developed by Irish courts, 140–
143
problems of, 169–178
proportionality principle, 202
protection of fundamental rights in Irish
Constitution, 179–182
terminology, 169–170
unenumerated personal rights, 179, 181–
182
Constitutional justice, 146, 148, 149, 238–240
Constitutional law. *See also* Constitutional
interpretation; Constitutional review;
Constitutional rights; Irish
constitutional law
comparative, 244
European Community
approach of Court of Justice, 29–31
constitutional court, 3–10; 25–32
constitutionalisation of the Treaties, 4,
11–12, 16
identification of issues, 26–27, 31
principles developed, 30–31, 32, 35, 38,
41
sex equality law, constitutional
implications of, 107–120
principles developed by Irish judges, 140–
143
Constitutional review of legislation. *See also*
Constitutional interpretation
Acts of the *Oireachtas* – validity, 172–174
applications for judicial review, 206–207
Bills – reference to Irish Supreme Court,
151, 169, 170–171
conformity with Community law, 29–30
French Courts' review, 257–269
jurisdiction of national courts, 34–35
European Community law, 5–6, 26–29
French approach, 258–259
judicial role, 181

Constitutional review of legislation—*contd*
locus standi, 172
Netherlands, in, 273–281
onus of proof, 173, 177
powers of judicial review, 155–157
presumption of constitutionality, 172, 173–
174, 176–177
single judgment rule, 155–156
United States – *Madison v Marbury* case, 14
Constitutional rights. *See further* under Irish
Constitution
enforcement of, 150
European Community law, 28, 30
Constitutionality, presumption of
Irish legislation, 171, 172, 173–174, 176–
177
Contempt of court
freedom of expression and, 184–185
Contract posts
public service exception and, 101–103
Council of Europe, 232
Council of Ministers, 11, 22. *See also*
Community institutions
freedom to provide services, obligations
under, 127–130, 132
inter-institutional proceedings, 27
Court of Justice. *See* European Court of
Justice
Criminal law in Ireland
acquittals, appeals against, 201
arrest and questioning, 194–195
bail, 195–196
constitutionalisation of, 193–202
court of trial, 198–200
criminal procedure, 196
delay – right to trial with reasonable
expedition, 196
double jeopardy, rule against, 200–202
illegally obtained evidence, 197n
legal aid, 196–197
Nulla poena sine lege, 193–194
penalties for offences, 202
presumption of innocence, 195, 200
retroactive legislation, prohibition of, 193–
194
trial of offences, 197–200
unconstitutionally obtained evidence,
admissibility, 153, 195–196, 197n

Damages
actions for, 7
liability in
European Community, 6
Member State, 44–45, 47, 49, 223, 253,
254
Decentralisation. *See also* Subsidiarity
principle
Defamation
fair comment and, 184
Democracy, 181
Democratic control of justice, 153–154
Deportation, 76

Direct actions, 5, 10, 30
  locus standi of individuals, 5, 6–7
Direct effect doctrine, 14, 30, 35, 36
  Community directives. *See under* Directives
  public authority, meaning of, 37–38, 117–
    118, 247–248
Directives
  binding on Member States, 247, 251
  direct effect, 7, 35, 36–38, 107, 116–118
  emanations of the State, meaning of,
    37–38, 117–118, 247–248
  enforcement by national courts, 35, 36,
    38–39
  Foster test, 37–38, 117–118
  individuals, against (horizontal effect),
    39–41, 116, 221, 248, 249, 252
  limited, 36–38
  Marleasing judgment, 39–41, 249–
    254
  national time limits, 46–48
  sex equality case-law and, 116–118
  UK experience, 219–221
  vertical effect, 37–38, 248, 249
  indirect effect, 39–41
  late implementation of, 119–120
  non-implementation by Member State
    Emmott case, 37, 46–48, 253–254
    liability for damages, 44–45, 223, 253
    Marleasing judgment, status after, 247–
      255
    status after prescribed date, 251–252
  obligations of national law, 40–41
Discrimination. *See* Equal Treatment; Sex
  equality
Division of powers. *See* Separation of powers
Double jeopardy, rule against, 200–202
Due process
  Community law, 239–240
  Irish Constitution, 238

Ecclesiastical law, 240–241
Education
  European Community policy, 79–80
  European Convention on Human Rights,
    80n
  grants and scholarships
    rights of non-nationals to, 86–88
  non-discrimination rule, 84–86
  right of access to, 84–86
    child of migrant worker, 83
    migrant students, 79–88
  vocational training courses, access to,
    84–86
EEC Treaty. *See* Treaty of Rome
Effectiveness principle, 38–39, 41
Employment law. *See* Equal pay; Free
  movement of workers; Sex equality
Entry and residence, rights of, 71–72
  Community citizens, 83–84
  families of migrant workers, 71–72, 82–83
  migrant workers, 81–82
  students, 84

Equal pay, 239–240
  Court of Justice case-law, 111–114
    definition of 'pay', 111–112
    indirect discrimination, 112–114
Equality of treatment. *See also* Non-
    Discrimination on grounds of
    nationality
  fundamental rights and, 237–238
  Irish Constitution, 237
  migrant workers, 72–74
  sex discrimination. *See* Sex equality in
    European Community law
  vocational training courses, access to,
    84–86
Euratom Treaty, 4
  education provisions, 79
European Coal and Steel Community, 4, 8,
    79, 275
European Community. *See also* Community
    law; European integration
  agreements with third countries
    judicial review of, 28
  constitutional reform, 11–12
  damages, liability in, 6
  education policy, 79–80
  immigration from Third World and
    Eastern Europe, 67
  influences creating European Union, ,
    11–17
  judicial review of measures of, 30
  law of. *See* Community Law; Community
    law rights
  supranational character, evolution of,
    11–15
European Community law. *See* Community
    law; Community law rights
European Community Patent Convention,
    235
European Community Treaties, 67
  constitutional character, 4–5, 11–12, 16
  education provisions, 79–80
  revision of, 233–235
European Convention on Human Rights, 5,
    162, 194, 196, 201, 234, 235, 236, 237,
    243, 245, 261, 264, 276, 277
  education provisions, 80n
  fair hearing, 279
  freedom of expression, 186
  homosexual activity, 235–236
  legal representation, right to, 197
  privacy, right to, 162
European Court of First Instance, 3, 13,
    228
European Court of Human Rights, 235, 236,
    244, 276, 278
European Court of Justice, 3
  agreements with third countries, review of,
    28
  annulment or inactivity, actions for, 5, 7, 8,
    9
  breach of Treaty obligations, actions for, 5,
    6–7, 9

European Court of Justice—*contd*
  constitutional jurisdiction, 4–9, 26–27
    approach to constitutional issues, 29–31
    constitutional court, as, 3–10, 25–32
    constitutionalisation of Treaties, 11–12
    principles developed, 30–31, 32, 35, 38,
      41, 107–120
  decentralised enforcement of Community
    rights, and, 35–49
  direct actions, 5, 10, 30
  direct effect of directives. *See further*
    Directives
    Marleasing judgment, 39–41, 249–254
  due process, 239–240
  equal pay cases, 111–114
  European integration, role in, 14–16, 17
  fisheries litigation, 51–65
  free movement of workers
    case-law on, 67–78
    concept of 'worker', 81–82
    public service exception, 89–106
  freedom to provide services – *Gouda* and
    Van Binsbergen judgments, 121–133
  fundamental rights, 8
  influence of, 14–16
  inter-institutional proceedings, 5, 27–28
  judicial activism, 9, 11–12, 14–15, 67, 132
  judicial review
    common fisheries policy, 51–65
    Community measures, 30
    legislation, 5, 6, 7–8
    Member State action and legislation, 27,
      29–30
  jurisdiction of, 26–29
  locus standi
    individuals, 5, 6–7
    privileged applicants, 8, 127n
  migrant students' rights, 80–88
  negative integration, 127, 129, 130, 133
  political court, seen as, 32
  preliminary rulings, references for. *See*
    Preliminary references to European
    Court
  primacy of Community law, principle of.
    See Supremacy of Community law
  procedural justice, 48
  public service employment, concept of,
    93–103
  public service exception
    interpretation of, 89–106
  reinforcement of authority of, 16
  remedial powers, 30, 33–34
  sex equality law, constitutional
    implications, 107–120
  subsidiarity disputes, 22–23
European Defence Community, 275
European Institute of Public Administration,
  20
European integration, 11. *See also*
  Subsidiarity principle
  citizenship of European union, 105
  Court of Justice, role of, 14–16, 17

European integration—*contd*
  federalist approach, 12–13, 14, 16–17
  functionalist approach, 13–14, 16
  influences creating a European Union,
    11–17
  intergovernmental conferences, 3, 4, 19, 21,
    235
  Irish constitutional law and, 233–235
  Maastricht summit (1991), 11, 21, 23, 33,
    105
  public service exception and, 105–106
  Single European Act, 77
  uniform applicability of Community law,
    barriers to, 35, 48
European Parliament
  actions of annulment against, 8
  Community constitutional reform, 13
  Institutional Affairs Committee, 13
  inter-institutional proceedings, 27
European Social Charter, 108
European union. *See under* European
  integration
Evidence
  unconstitutionally obtained evidence,
    admissibility, 153, 165–166, 196,
    197n
Extradition, 241

Fair procedures, right to
  Irish Constitution, 141, 151, 154, 201,
    207n, 238, 238n–239n
Family of migrant worker
  entry and residence rights, 71–72, 82–
    83
Federalism, 236
  federalist approach to European union,
    12–13, 14, 16–17
Fisheries. *See* Common fisheries policy
Foreign workers. *See* Migrant workers
Foster test, 37–38, 117–118, 248
France
  administrative courts, 262–264
  Civil Code, 148
  Conseil Constitutionnel, 3, 27, 194, 202n, 259,
    260–261, 267
  Conseil d'Etat, 14, 16, 259, 260, 262–264,
    268, 269
  Constitution of 1958, 258, 259, 260, 261,
    264–267
  Court of Cassation, 261–262, 266
  national provisions and Community law,
    257
    French courts' review of conformity,
      257–269
  separation of powers, 259
Free movement of goods, 29, 243
Free movement of persons, 81n, 89. *See further*
    Free movement of workers; Public
    service exception
  migrant students' rights, 79–88
  non-discrimination on grounds of
    nationality, 89

Free movement of workers, 29, 67–68, 79,
    81n, 81–82, 89
  entry and residence rights, 71–72, 81–84
    families, 71–72, 82–83
  equality of treatment, 72–74, 84–88
    promotion and other conditions of
      employment, 104
  European Court case-law on, 67–78
  national language requirements – *Groener*
    case, 73
  procedural guarantees, 76
  public order exception, 76
  restrictions on, 74–77, 89. *See also* Public
    service exception
  scope of rules, 68–71
  substance of guarantee, 71–74
  Treaty provisions, 89–90
  worker, definition of, 68–70, 81–82
Freedom of expression, 276
  blasphemous libel and, 165
  European Convention on Human Rights,
    186
  Irish Constitution and, 183–191
    limitations on right – *State (Lynch) v
      Cooney*, 187–190
    scope of guarantee, 185–187
  US Constitution, 185–186
Freedom to provide services, 243
  Court of Justice and *Gouda* judgment, 121–
    133
  discrimination on grounds of nationality,
    124, 125–126
  non-discriminatory restrictions, 122–124,
    125, 126, 128–129, 132
  Treaty provisions, 121–122
French Revolution, 14, 257
Functionalist approach to European
  integration, 13–14, 16
Fundamental rights, 232–233. *See also*
  Constitutional rights
  Community institutions bound to respect,
    8, 31
  equal treatment as between sexes, 107,
    108–110
  equality, and, 237–238
  Irish Constitution. *See also* Irish
    Constitution (1937): rights and
    freedoms
    Observations on the Protection of
      Fundamental Rights in, 179–182
  moral principles and legislative
    intervention, 235–237

Gouda judgment, 121–133
Grants and scholarships
  migrant students' rights, 86–88

Hague Resolution of 3 November 1976, 52
Homosexual activity, restrictions on, 235–236
Horizontal direct effect, 223, 248, 249, 252
House of Lords Select Committee on Political
  Union subsidiarity principle, 23

Human rights, 234. *See also* European
    Convention on Human Rights;
    Fundamental rights
  equal treatment as between sexes, 107,
    108–110

Immigration, 67
Implied powers, doctrine of, 14
Inactivity, actions for, 5, 7
Indirect discrimination, 112–114
Individuals
  direct effect of directives against, 116, 223,
    248, 252–253
  locus standi
    direct actions in European Court, 5, 6, 7
Injustice, 153–154
Innocence, right to presumption of, 200
Institute of Economic Affairs, 20
Inter-institutional proceedings, 27–28
Intergovernmental Conferences (1991), 3, 4,
    235
  subsidiarity principle, 19, 21
Internal market. *See further* European
  integration public service exception
    and, 105–106
International agreements, 28, 233
International Covenant on Civil and Political
  Rights (1966), 194, 196, 200, 264
International Labour Convention (No. 111,
  1968), 108
Ireland. *See also* Criminal law in Ireland;
    Irish Constitution; Irish constitutional
    law
  fisheries, 51–52, 53, 55–57, 65
  freedom of expression
    broadcasting ban on *Sinn Fein*, 187–190
  Special Criminal Court, 199
  statutes, constitutional validity. *See under*
    Constitutional review of legislation
Irish Constitution (1937)
  administrative law remedies, and, 203–207
  administrative misunderstandings of, 240
  Christian basis of, 162
  common good, requirements of, 165, 166,
    167
  interpretation. *See* Constitutional
    interpretation
  judicial independence, 146
  justice, concept of, 146, 147
  legislative powers, 161
  Preamble, 142, 162, 164
  prudence, justice and charity, founded on,
    142
  reference of Bills under Art. 26, 151, 169,
    170–171
  retroactive legislation prohibited, 193
  rights and freedoms, 149, 151
    access to solicitor, 197n
    bodily integrity, 140
    communicate information, right to, 186–
      187
    conflicting rights, 150–151, 165

Irish Constitution (1937)—*contd*
  rights and freedoms—*contd*
    due process, 238
    enforcement of, 150
    equality before the law, 237
    fair procedures, 141, 151, 154, 201, 207n,
      238, 238n–239n
    freedom of expression, 183–191
    interpretative principles, 140–143
    judicial protection, 179–182
    justice, 141
    liberty, 164
    limitations on, 164
    litigate, right to, 141
    livelihood, right to earn, 141, 202n
    marital privacy, 141, 162, 163
    natural rights, 148, 149, 164
    non-citizens, 164
    personal rights, 140–141
    presumption of innocence, right to, 200
    privacy, 141, 162, 163, 165
    property, 141, 148, 202n
    travel outside the State, 141
    trial in due course of law, 196, 198, 199,
      201
    trial with reasonable expedition, 196
    unborn, right to life of, 139, 140, 162
    unenumerated personal rights, 140–141,
      149, 150, 160, 179, 181–182, 186
    work, right to, 141
  separation of powers, 145, 149, 161, 201
  supremacy of, 146
Irish constitutional law
  Church law, and, 240–241
  comparative constitutional law, 244
  constitutional justice, 238–240
  Constitutions comprised in, 229, 244–245
  European Community law included in,
    229–233
  European integration, and, 233–235
  exclusive EC powers, 230–231
  fundamental rights. *See also* Constitutional
    rights
    equality, and, 237–238
    moral principles and permissible scope
      of legislation, 235–237
    protection of, 179–182
  international agreements, 233
  judicial review of legislation. *See*
    Constitutional review of legislation
  misunderstandings of the 1937
    Constitution, 240
  Northern Ireland, and, 237
  private clubs, 241
  proportionality, principle of, 229
  public international law, 241
  State prerogatives, 243–244
  unconditionally obtained evidence –
    exclusionary rule, 153, 165–166, 197n
  widening scope of, 229–245
Irish Free State Constitution (1922), 137,
  145–146

Irish Supreme Court, 26
  criminal procedure, constitutionalisation
    of, 196–197
  judicial review of legislation. *See*
    Constitutional review of legislation
  single judgment rule, 155–156

Judicial activism, 9, 11–12, 14–15, 67, 132
Judicial creativity, 180
Judicial power
  abuse of, 181
  constitutional interpretation, 181
  criticisms of decisions, 157, 184
  democratic control of justice, 153–154
  independence of judiciary, 146
  interpreter of the Constitution, 150, 157,
    181
  judge-made law, 181
  judicial review of legislation, 155–157. *See
    further* Constitutional review of
    legislation
  limitations on freedom of judiciary, 146–
    147
  reasons for decisions, requirement to give,
    149–150
  separation of powers, function to preserve,
    149
  social and political questions,
    determination of, 151–154
Judicial restraint, doctrine of, 174
Judicial review, 181. *See also* Administrative
    law
  common fisheries policy, and, 51–65
  Court of Justice. *See under* European Court
    of Justice
  legislation. *See* Constitutional review of
    legislation
Justice
  concept of, 147, 204
  democratic control of, 153–154
  infringements of, 153–154

Labour law. *See* Equal pay; Free movement
    of workers; Sex equality
Law Reform Commission, 165
Legal aid, 196–197
Legal persons. *See* Natural or legal persons
Legal profession, 154
  freedom to provide services, 122n–123n
Legal representation, right to, 197
Legislation. *See also* Constitutional review of
    legislation; National law; Statutory
    interpretation; Subsidiarity principle
  fundamental rights, moral principles and
    permissible scope of legislation, 235–
    237
  judge-made law, 159–168, 181
  retroactive legislation, constitutional ban
    on, 193–194
Liberty, right to, 164
Liberty of expression. *See* Freedom of
    expression

Litigate, right to, 141
Livelihood, right to earn, 141, 202n

Maastricht Conference (1991), 11, 21, 33
  citizenship of European Union, 105
  subsidiarity principle, 23
Marital privacy, right to, 141, 162, 163
Marleasing judgment, 39–41, 249–254
Member States. *See also* National courts;
    National law
  direct actions against, 5, 6, 10, 30
  division of powers between Community
      and, 28
  fisheries. *See* Common fisheries policy
  fundamental interests, 28–29
  judicial review of measures by European
      Court, 27, 29–30, 34
  late implementaiton of directives, 119–120
  national measures governed by
      Community principles, 244–246
  non-compliance with Community law, 33,
      37
  non-implementation of directives. *See
      further* under Directives
    liability for damages, 44–45, 47, 49, 223,
        253
    Marleasing judgment, 39–41, 247–255
  power-sharing. *See* Subsidiarity principle
  specific legal duties under Community law,
      233
Migrant students
  rights under Community law, 79–88
    entry and residence, 84
    grants and scholarships, 86–88
  sickness insurance requirement, 84n
  vocational training, equality of access to,
      84–86
Migrant workers, 67–68. *See also* Free
    movement of workers
  deportation procedure, 76
  educational rights, 81–88
  entry and residence rights, 71–72, 81–83
  equality of treatment, 72–74, 101
  exclusion from public service posts. *See*
      Public service exception
  guarantee of free movement, 71–74
  meaning of 'worker', 68–70, 81–82
  restrictions on free movement, 74–77, 89
  vocational training, right of access to, 81,
      84–86
Morality
  legislative restrictions on grounds of, 162,
      235–237

National courts
  Community law jurisdiction, 30, 34–35,
      39–48
    enforcement of Community law rights,
        30, 33–49
    French Courts' review, 259–271
    interpretation of national law, 40, 117,
        118–119, 209, 251–256

National courts—*contd*
  Community law jurisdiction—*contd*
    Marleasing judgment, 251–256
    national rules, power to set aside, 7, 42,
        43, 267–268
    remedies, 41–46
National law
  Community law and, 34–35
    direct effect of directives. *See* Directives
    freedom to provide services, restrictions
        on – *Gouda* judgment, 122–132
    impact of Community law, 229–269
    judicial control, 7
    non-implemented directives, status after
        Marleasing, 247–255
    precedence over conflicting national law,
        7
    rules impeding access to Community
        Law rights, 119–120
    sphere of Community law, 242–244
    supremacy of Community law. *See*
        Supremacy of Community law
  Community validity of, 222–223, 250–251
    disputes over conformity, 29–30
    French experience, 257, 258–264
    jurisdiction of national court, 34–35
National security
  public service exception justified on
      grounds of, 95–96
National sovereignty, 11, 21
Nationality
  discrimination on grounds of. *See* Non-
      discrimination on grounds of
      nationality
Natural law, 147
Natural or legal persons
  right of action before European Court, 5,
      6–8, 127n
Natural rights, 148, 149, 164
Negative integration, 127, 129, 130, 133
Netherlands
  Constitution, 273–275
  Hoge Raad, 274, 275, 276, 277, 278, 280
  human rights protection, 276–280
  judicial appointments, 280
  judicial review of legislation, 273–281
Non bis in idem principle, 200–201
Non-discrimination on grounds of
      nationality, 31, 38, 243
  educational establishments, access to, 84–
      86
  educational grants and scholarships, 86–
      88
  free movement of persons, 89
  freedom to provide services – *Gouda*
      judgment, 124–125
  migrant workers, 72–74, 104
    exceptions to right of free movement, 89.
      See also Public service exception
  national fishing quotas and, 63–64
Non-nationals. *See* Migrant students;
    Migrant workers

Northern Ireland
Bill of Rights proposal, 237
Nulla poena sine lege, 193–194
Nursing posts
nationality requirements, 99–100, 101

O'Higgins, Thomas F., 20, 193, 201, 229, 253
administrative law remedies under, 203–216
constitutional interpretation, 141, 142, 179
freedom of expression, 184, 185, 188, 189, 191
justice, concept of, 204
unconstitutionally obtained evidence, 194, 195

Papalism, 181
Part-time workers
indirect discrimination, 112–114
Pensionable ages, 115–116
Pluralist education, 80
Populism, 180–181
Portugal, 51, 54
accession of, 67
Constitution of 1976, 196
Pre-Constitution statutes, consistency of, 174–178
Pre-emption, doctrine of, 14, 28
Precedent, 179, 180, 181, 208
in Community law, 64
Pregnancy and maternity, 115
Preliminary references to European Court, 5–6, 10, 16
discretionary, 226–227
mandatory, 227–228
UK experience, 226–228
Prerogative rights of the State, 241–242
President of Ireland
power to refer Bills to Supreme Court, 151, 169, 170–171
Primacy of Community law. *See* Supremacy of European Community law
Privacy, right to, 162, 163, 236
limitations on, 162, 165
Procedural justice, 48
Procedural rules
power of national court to set aside, 42, 43, 267–268
Property rights
Irish Constitution, 141, 148–149
Proportionality, principle of, 31, 103, 114, 243
Irish Constitutional law, 202, 231
Public bodies
direct enforceability of directives against, 247–249
Foster test, 37–38, 117–118, 248
exception from free movement of workers guarantee. *See* Public service exception
Public international law
Irish constitutional law and, 241
Public order or morality
freedom of expression limited by, 188

Public policy exception
free movement of workers, 74–75
Public service exception, 77, 89–106
characteristics of the public service, 98–100
Commission programme to eliminate restrictions, 104–105
Community law, as concept of, 91–92
concept of public service employment, 89–90, 93–100
conditions for application of, 93–97
contract workers, 101–103
Court of Justice guidelines, 93–97
exercise of powers conferred by public law, 94
functional test, 97
general interests of the State, 94–96
institutional approach, 97
internal market implications, 105–106
judicial interpretation of, 89–106
national legal designations, 92–93
nursing and teaching posts, nationality requirements for, 99–100, 101
promotion and other conditions of employment, 103–104
purpose of, 90–91

Quadragesimo Anno (Papal Encyclical, 1931), 19
Quota hopping
common fisheries policy, 52, 54–60, 224

References for preliminary ruling. *See* Preliminary references
Regulations of European Community
direct applicability of, 265
Remedies. *See also* Administrative law remedies
breaches of Community law, 33. *See also* Damages
national courts, 33–49
sex equality law, 118
UK experience, 223–224
Residence rights. *See* Entry and residence, rights of
Rights and freedoms. *See* Fundamental rights; *See also* under Irish Constitution (1937)
Roman Catholic Church
canon law, 242–243
Royal Institute of International Affairs, 20
Rule of law, 12, 30, 33, 41
access to effective remedy, 203

Sanctions in European Community law. *See* Remedies
Scotland
administrative law, 283–294
Brown v Hamilton District Council, 283–294, 287–294
Court of Session, 286

Separation of powers
    Community and Member States, between,
        28
    French approach, 261
    Irish Constitution, 145, 149, 161, 201
Services. *See also* Freedom to provide
        services
    education excluded from definition of
        (EEC Treaty), 84n
Sex equality in Community law
    Community institutions – sex
        discrimination cases, 108–110
    direct effect aspects, 116–118
    effective remedies, need for, 118
    exceptions provided in directives, Court's
        approach to, 114–116
    fundamental right to equal treatment, 108–
        110
        national context, 110
    indirect discrimination, 112–114
    national law rules impeding access to
        Community Law right of, 119–120
    nightwork exception, 115
    pensionable ages, 115–116
    pregnancy and maternity exceptions, 115
    social security matters, 119
Sickness insurance requirement
    migrant students, 84n
Single European Act, 15, 77
Social and political matters, judicial
        determination of, 151–154
Social security
    sex discrimination prohibited, 119
Spain, 67
    Civil Code, 40, 251
    common fisheries policy and, 51–65
    Constitution of 1978, 196, 201
    Constitutional Court, 194
Spouse of migrant workers, rights of, 71–72,
        82–83
Stare decisis, 179
State bodies
    direct enforceability of directives
        against
        concept of State, 37–38, 117–118, 247–
            249
    public service exception to free movement
        of workers, 90–91. *See further* Public
        service exception
State prerogatives, 241–242
Statutory interpretation. *See also*
        Constitutional review of legislation;
        National law
    Community law rules, 250, 250–251
    conformity with EC directives, 222–223,
        226, 250–251
    constitutional justice, requirements of,
        238–239
    intention of parliament, 162–163
    presumption of constitutionality, 171, 172,
        173–174, 176–177
Students. *See* Migrant students

Subsidiarity principle, 3, 228
    adjudication of disputes, 22–23
    constitutional principle, as, 20
    effectiveness test, 21–22
    House of Lords Select Committee on, 23
    justiciable, whether, 22–23
    Luxembourg text of 20 June 1991, 19, 22
    Masstricht text, 23
    necessity test, 21–22
    Treaty of Rome, 22
Supremacy of European Community law,
        7,14, 30, 35, 40, 224, 251, 252, 266
    all provisions of national law, over, 40, 267
    legal basis of, 264–267
    non-implemented directives and, 251, 252
Supreme Courts. *See* Irish Supreme Court;
        See also under Netherlands; United
        States Supreme Court
Swiss Civil Code, 166

Teachers
    nationality requirements for posts, 99, 100
    trainee included in definition of 'worker',
        82, 100n
Third country nationals
    common fisheries policy and quota
        hopping, 55–57
Time limits, 46–48
Training. *See* Vocational training
Travel, right to, 141
Treaty of Rome, 67. *See also* European
        Community Treaties
    actions for breach of, 5, 6–7, 9
    annulment or inactivity, actions for, 3, 5,
        7–8
    co-operation principle, 35
    constitutional character, 5–7, 26, 30, 35
    damages, actions for, 5, 6
    free movement of persons, 89
    freedom to provide services, 121–127
    judicial remedies, 30
    jurisdiction of Court of Justice, 26
    new legal order created by, 268
    references for preliminary ruling, 5–6, 10,
        16
    subsidiarity principle, 22
Trial
    in due course of law, 196, 198, 199, 201
    with reasonable expedition, 196

Unborn, right to life of
    Irish Constitution, 139, 140, 162
Unenumerated rights
    Irish Constitution, 140–141, 149, 151, 160,
        179, 181–182, 186
United Kingdom, 21. *See also* Scotland
    common fisheries policy and, 57–60, 63, 64
    Community law and national law,
        interface between, 219–228
        procedural law, 224–225
        substantive law, 223–224
    Community law remedies, 225–226

United Kingdom—*contd*
  direct effect of directives, 221–223
  European Communities Act 1972, 219–221
  incorporation of Community law into national legal order, 219
  judicial review of administrative action, 288
  preliminary references to European Court of Justice, 226–228
United Nations Universal Declaration of Human Rights (1948), 194
United States Constitution
  First Amendment, 185–186
  Fourteenth Amendment, 162
  judicial review of legislation, 14, 25, 155
  privacy, right to, 162
  subsidiarity principle, 19–20

United States Supreme Court, 11, 162, 278
  bail, entitlement to, 197
  influence in shaping federal state, 14
  jurisdiction, 25
  unconstitutionally obtained evidence, admissibility, 196
Unspecified rights. *See* Unenumerated rights

Ventotene Manifesto, 13, 14
Vocational training, right of access to, 79, 85–86
  equality of treatment, 84–86
  families of migrant workers, 83
  migrant workers, 81

Workers' rights. *See* Equal pay; Free movement of workers; Sex equality in Community law